Encyclopedia of the
American Indian Movement

Recent Titles in the
Movements of the American Mosaic Series

Encyclopedia of Cesar Chavez: The Farm Workers' Fight for Rights and Justice
Roger Bruns

Encyclopedia of the American Indian Movement

Bruce E. Johansen

Movements of the American Mosaic

 GREENWOOD

AN IMPRINT OF ABC-CLIO, LLC
Santa Barbara, California • Denver, Colorado • Oxford, England

Library of Congress Cataloging-in-Publication Data

Johansen, Bruce E. (Bruce Elliott), 1950–
  Encyclopedia of the American Indian Movement / Bruce E. Johansen.
      p. cm. — (Movements of the American mosaic)
  Includes bibliographical references and index.
  ISBN 978-1-4408-0317-8 (hardcopy : alk. paper) — ISBN 978-1-4408-0318-5 (ebook)
1. American Indian Movement—History—Encyclopedias.   2. Indians of
North America—Politics and government—Encyclopedias.   3. Indian activists—
United States—Encyclopedias.   4. Indians of North America—Civil rights—
Encyclopedias.   5. Indians of North America—Government relations—
Encyclopedias.   I. Title.
  E98.T77J63   2013
  323.1197—dc23   2012041178

ISBN: 978-1-4408-0317-8
EISBN: 978-1-4408-0318-5

17   16   15   14   13   1   2   3   4   5

This book is also available on the World Wide Web as an eBook.
Visit www.abc-clio.com for details.

Greenwood
An Imprint of ABC-CLIO, LLC

ABC-CLIO, LLC
130 Cremona Drive, P.O. Box 1911
Santa Barbara, California 93116-1911

This book is printed on acid-free paper ∞

Manufactured in the United States of America

Contents

Introduction

Alvin M. Josephy Jr. conveyed the shock that many mainstream Americans experienced as they watched the American Indian Movement (AIM) rise up in rebellion on the evening news, as described in the *New York Times Sunday Magazine,* March 18, 1973. Josephy, vice president and senior editor at American Heritage Publishing, was a consultant on Indian issues for Richard M. Nixon's White House and author of several books. Josephy also was widely respected by Native Americans across the country. He wrote:

> The Indian occupation and destruction of the Bureau of Indian Affairs Building in Washington, D.C. last November, and the succeeding dramatic events at Wounded Knee, South Dakota, the burning of the courthouse at Custer, S.D. . . and the scattered—but spreading—rash of similar violent confrontations between Indians and whites in different parts of the country have been shockers. (Josephy, 1973, 18)

Another observer at the time said that "The world woke to news that seemed as incredible as a landing from outer space" (Burnette and Koster, 1974, ix). "Indians *that* militant?" asked Josephy.

Rising out of more than a century of poverty and pervasive repression, stoked by the example of the movement against the Vietnam War and the upheaval among black and Chicano civil-rights activists, the AIM was moving the debate over "the Indian problem" to a new level. And not just AIM—many Native peoples were standing up for long-ignored rights in old treaties under other organizational banners—fishing rights in Western Washington under the aegis of the Survival of American Indians Association, Iroquois land rights, resistance to coal and uranium mining via the Coalition for Navajo Liberation.

This is the story of that movement.

History comes alive in two ways: One employs description of important events involving large numbers of people. In this case, American Indians were taking part in a paradigm shift of historic proportions, involving reaction to shared suffering that collided with political awareness that expressed itself to an explosion of activism. These events deserve description and analysis. A second view of history is personal and anecdotal, involving the telling of stories illustrative of larger trends, like sparks off a larger flint. One sees Oren Lyons defusing a Molotov cocktail at the Bureau of Indian Affairs (BIA) occupation during November of 1972, for example. Some wanted to blow up the building with their stack of Molotov cocktails, but others snuffed the fuses. In another flash of memory, Yakama fisherman Sid Mills challenging a state fisheries agent to a fistfight, *mano a mano*—as the agent takes him up on it.

Suzan Shown Harjo, was on the scene as AIM members barricaded themselves inside the BIA headquarters in Washington, D.C.:

> With a theatrical flourish, [Russell] Means lit a long fuse to the Molotov cocktails and yelled, "It's a good day to die." A chorus of voices exclaimed, "Bulls**t." [several] stamped on the glowing fuse until it was not only extinguished, but also shredded.
>
> "You can't do that," Onondaga faith keeper Oren Lyons said sternly to Means. "You can't kill the people and destroy all those records. This is only a battle, not the war." (Harjo, 1992)

During July 1975 (a year after the Boldt ruling) Mills (whose age was listed as 28 in a newspaper account) and Sandy Miller, 48, a Washington State Fisheries patrolman, decided to vent their differences in an old-fashioned fistfight. Mills was listed as executive director of SAIA at the time. The newspaper account (Fish Agent, 1975, n.p.) said the fisticuffs took place as the state was seizing 18 fishing nets that its agents alleged the Indians had strung illegally across the Nisqually River. Mills confronted Miller and challenged him to put down his nightstick and fight man-to-man. Miller accepted the challenge, and found himself on the ground with a bloody nose before several other fisheries agents intervened and handcuffed Mills.

Every American Indian of the time shared searing memories of abuse. As AIM was protesting the murders of Oglala Lakotas in South Dakota (and the Coalition for Navajo Liberation was doing the same thing in the Southwest), wanton murder also was afflicting American Indians in cities of the U.S. Northeast. Leroy Shenandoah, an Onondaga and a Green Beret in Vietnam, was beaten brutally in Philadelphia and shot to death by police. The act was fobbed off as "justifiable homicide" (Josephy, 1973, 74).

As AIM was organizing and Alcatraz Island was being occupied, Vine Deloria Jr.'s *Custer Died for your Sins* became a bestseller in 1969, skewering government officials, anthropologists, missionaries, and others with his trademark sardonic wit, giving white America some "tough love," reflective of the anger that propelled the Red Power movement:

> Some years back Richard Nixon warned the American people that Russia was bad because she had not kept any treaty or agreement signed with her. You

can trust communists, the saying went, to be communists. Indian people laugh themselves sick when they hear these statements. America has yet to keep one Indian treaty or agreement despite the fact that the United States government signed over hundred such agreements and treaties with Indian tribes. It would take Russia another century to make and break as many treaties as the United States has already violated. (Deloria, 1969, 28)

The scope of Native American political revival included a large number of people and groups who were not members of AIM per se, but who were important to the assertion of Native American human and civil rights at the same time. There were no "card-carrying" members of AIM. People flowed in and out of various groups. Thus, this becomes an encyclopedia of "the American Indian movement "(lower case) at some points. Other organizations carried on similar work at the same time, including the Coalition for Navajo Liberation, the Survival of American Indians Association, the National Indian Youth Council. United Native Americans (in California), and the United Indians of all Tribes (in Seattle).

Vine Deloria Jr., for example, was never officially "of" AIM, but he did write the books that inspired many of its members. Different groups shared the same goals and others. Covering AIM and ignoring the many others would provide a very limited record. Such a limitation also would be profoundly unfair, and everyone in the movement knows it. To quote one authority, in the Native American scholarly journal *American Indian Quarterly:*

> AIM members consider themselves to be part of a two-fold American Indian movement—first, part of an organization known as AIM, and second, as part of a nationwide movement in which the revival of Indian strength and pride are exemplified in the struggle for sovereignty and rights. Whether undertaken by AIM, the National Congress of American Indians, the National Indian Youth Council, or other organizations, tribes, or individuals. (Bonney, 1977, 222)

What does the Native American wave of activism have to show two generations hence? Some things have changed, and some have not. Overall, however, much of Native America is taking part in a revival due on no small part to the fact that demands of people some took to be rabble-rousing renegades have become policy. Sometimes I wish I had a time machine I could take back to 1970. I want to tell people back then what has happened since, and watch their jaws drop. Society-wide, I would have stories to tell: the Berlin Wall has fallen; the Soviet Union has dissolved; Nelson Mandela has retired after two terms as the president of South Africa. Homosexuals give the rest of us fashion advice on mass-market television. We carry around little boxes in our pockets that give us instant access to other people worldwide, as well as more information than anyone back then might have imagined. Salsa out-sells catsup.

Among outside observers of Indian country, the popular trope is that the various American Indian movements dissolved into internecine squabbles. That has been a factor. Many commentators fail to observe, however, how deeply the goals of Native American activism in the 1960s and 1970s have become enmeshed in governance today.

In Western Washington, fishing rights sought by members of Survival of American Indians Association are legally established, and the fishing tribes comanage the resource with the state that snipped their nets and seized their boats 40 years ago. Across North America, Native American languages are being revived. Elsewhere, parts of the Coalition for Navajo Liberation's program are Navajo Nation policy now. The mining and milling of uranium are illegal in Navajo Country, after two generations of Navajo pain and suffering stemming from the radioactive rock. Native graves and remains are legally protected, and human remains are being returned to their owners.

Forty years ago, AIM protested beer sales to drunken Oglala Sioux at Whiteclay, Nebraska. Today, the Oglala Lakota tribal council at Pine Ridge has filed suit against the major beer companies that distribute their wares in that tiny border town, seeking $500 million in damages for ruined Native lives. (The companies have sought to have the suit dismissed on grounds of discrimination, that they have a right to profit, and Indians have a right to get drunk. Thomas Jefferson rolls in his grave.) However, just as in 1970, Indians are still buying the beer and falling down drunk. Some Oglalas are still being murdered for sport by young white toughs.

I want to take a time machine back to 1970 and tell people that—I choose my words carefully because the tribe doesn't like to brag—the Muckleshoots, one of these fishing tribes, is doing very well. A small Western Washington indigenous nation of about 2,400 people, the Muckleshoots, within two decades has developed from grinding impoverishment, down to its last half-acre of common land, to a financial powerhouse that provides scholarships for its young people and new houses for its elders. Energized by legal recognition of its treaty fishing rights during the 1970s and gaming (first bingo, then a casino) during the 1980s and the 1990s, the Muckleshoots, with business acumen and generosity (but without the sometimes deadly factional violence that has afflicted some other Indian peoples in similar situations) have become the second-largest employer in southern King County (behind the Boeing Company), meanwhile providing services and employment to a growing population.

My coauthor Roberto Maestas, whose political orientation usually did not lead him to religious figures of speech, referred to all of this as "the miracle at Muckleshoot." The situation at Muckleshoot is a singularly powerful example of a renaissance that has been taking place throughout Indian Country.

I was with Roberto during October 2009, beginning a history of El Centro de la Raza, when he asked me: "Have you been to Muckleshoot recently?" "No,

I hadn't," I replied, "not since my days as a young reporter for the *Seattle Times* during the early 1970s." Driving southeast along State Highway 164, through thick woods, I recalled shacks needing paint, and rusting cars needing windshields. "You have got to see what *los Indios* have done," he said. And so we went, to witness a 40-year revival Roberto, who became an ally of the Muckleshoots during the fish-war days, when he led Latinos lending aid to fishing-rights protesters against state raids. His elder daughter, Amalia, an attorney with the tribe, is married to Muckleshoot John Daniels Jr., with four children. On that November afternoon, as I watched a skirt of snow descended over majestic Mount Rainier, Roberto squired me around, making introductions.

Taking my imaginary time machine back to 1970, how would I explain to people living at that time what has happened since? In the case of the Muckleshoots, who would have guessed that the path out of poverty would involve a judge appointed by a Republican president, a bingo hall, a casino, and a lot of spirit, mixed with a great deal of business sagacity? This is where the energy of the decades-old rights battles has gone.

Further Reading

Bonney, Rachel A. "The Role of AIM Leaders in Indian Nationalism." *American Indian Quarterly* 3, no. 3 (Autumn, 1977): 209–24.

Burnette, Robert and John Koster. 1974. *The Road to Wounded Knee.* New York: Bantam, 1974.

Deloria, Vine, Jr. *Custer Died for Your Sins: An Indian Manifesto.* [1969] Norman: University of Oklahoma Press, 1988.

"Fish Agent, Indian Fight it Out." *Tri-City Herald,* November 21, 1975, n.p.

Josephy, Alvin M, Jr. "Wounded Knee and all That: What the Indians Want. *New York Times Sunday Magazine*, March 18, 1973, 18–19, 66–83.

Chronology

1959	Tuscaroras, led by Wallace (Mad Bear) Anderson attempt citizens' arrest of Indian Commissioner Glenn L. Emmons.
1961	Chicago Indian Conference.
1961–1962	National Indian Youth Council organized.
1964	Survival of American Indians Association organized; large-scale "fish ins" begin on rivers near Puget Sound. Fish-ins provide a model used in occupation of Alcatraz.
1964	On March 4, in the first attempt to occupy Alcatraz Island, five American Indians claim it for four hours, asserting jurisdiction under the 1868 Fort Laramie Treaty. First proposal to establish a cultural center and university there.
1968	On December 18, Cornwall Bridge occupied on the Akwesasne Mohawk reservation, on the United States and Canada, in protest of restrictions on free movement of Iroquois people and goods across the U.S.-Canada border. A lawsuit follows that forces both countries to respect such rights under the Jay Treaty (1794).
1968	United Native Americans (UNA) formed in the San Francisco Bay Area by Lehman Brightman.
1968	Minneapolis AIM organizes with community meeting and street patrol, because of extensive police brutality.
1969	On November 9, Richard Oakes leads a second brief occupation of Alcatraz Island as 14 people camp overnight, then depart.
1969	On November 20, the 19-month occupation of Alcatraz begins, as about 100 American Indians land on the island. United Indians of All Tribes reclaims federal land in the name of Native Nations. First Indian radio broadcasts—Radio Free Alcatraz—heard in the Bay Area of San Francisco.

1969	AIM plays a role in starting Minneapolis Indian Health Board, the first Native American Native health care provider in the nation to provide services in a city.
1969	During December, Dennis Banks and other members of AIM visit Alcatraz for about two weeks to study confrontational politics and land seizures as political tactics.
1970	AIM creates a legal rights center; by 1994, more than 19,000 clients had been represented by this agency.
1970	AIM seizes abandoned property at a former naval air station near Minneapolis as a base for Indian education.
1970	First sit-in at Bureau of Indian Affairs' Washington, D.C., head office; 24 arrested for trespassing. They are released after BIA Commissioner Louis Bruce intercedes.
1970	AIM works with Wisconsin Lac Court Orieles Ojibwa, seizing a dam controlled by Northern States Power that had flooded large areas of their reservation. More than 25,000 acres eventually returned that provide a base for business development.
1970	On August 29, members of United Native Americans, who have been active in the occupation of Alcatraz Island, stage symbolic takeover at Mount Rushmore National Monument.
1970	On Thanksgiving Day, AIM seizes replica of Mayflower on 350th anniversary of Pilgrims' landing at Plymouth Rock.
1970	Occupation of Ft. Lawton in Seattle, with a multiethnic alliance. While the tactic is similar to on-going occupation of Alcatraz Island, this occupation results in establishment of a Native American cultural center, Daybreak Star.
1970	In a speech on July 8, President Richard M. Nixon ends termination policies meant to destroy reservations begun during the Eisenhower administration. Nixon also announces that federal policies regarding American Indians will henceforth encourage self-determination, which he defines mainly as economic development by corporations.
1971	After 11 years of negotiations, Alaska natives negotiate land claims providing 44 million acres and $962.5 million.
1971	During May, Russell, Ted Means, Clyde Bellecourt, Mitchell Zephier, and Sylvester Smells scale Mount Rushmore and hold a prayer ceremony before National Park Service rangers arrest them.

1971	On June 11, about 15 people still on Alcatraz Island are removed by FBI agents, U.S. marshals, and FBI agents, ending the occupation after 19 months and nine days.
1971	On July 4, AIM stages a protest on Mount Rushmore to publicize the Oglala Lakota legal claim to the Black Hills.
1971	During the fall and winter, Onondagas and supporters block expansion of Route 81 through their reservation south of Syracuse.
1972	AIM establishes the Red School House in St. Paul, offering culturally relevant education. Heart of the Earth Survival School also begun to combat high dropout rates of Native students in other schools
1972	During February, more than 1,000 AIM members and supporters lay siege to Gordon, Nebraska, enraged over the murder of Raymond Yellow Thunder.
1972	Trail of Broken Treaties, October–November; three caravans begin in Seattle, San Francisco, and Los Angeles, merging in Minneapolis. The caravan arrives in Washington, D.C., the week before national elections and seizes BIA headquarters, AIM also presents its "Twenty Points" to President Nixon. The federal government, in retaliation, cuts funds to survival schools. Funding later is restored after AIM challenges the legality of cancellation.
1972	On September 21, Richard Oakes, a leader at Alcatraz, dies after being shot. The shooter, Michael Morgan, asserts that Oakes ambushed him, but no evidence exists of a physical struggle. A charge of murder is reduced to involuntary manslaughter, as Morgan walks free on grounds of self-defense.
1972	On October 10, a multiethnic alliance led by Chicanos occupies the empty Beacon Hill School in Seattle to establish El Centro de la Raza, on the model of Alcatraz and Fort Lawton. El Centro, "the center of all races" becomes instrumental in Native American activism under principal founder Roberto Maestas.
1973	On February 6, several hundred AIM demonstrators damage two police cars and raze the Chamber of Commerce in Custer, South Dakota as they protest the murder of Wesley Bad Heart Bull.
1973	Between February 27 and May 8, the hamlet of Wounded Knee on the Pine Ridge reservation, South Dakota, is occupied. Several police forces and U.S. Army troops pump more than 500,000 rounds of ammunition into the hamlet; two Native men (Buddy Lamont and

Frank Clearwater) and one FBI agent are killed as more than 1,200 people are arrested.

1973–1976   Following the siege of Wounded Knee, on Pine Ridge, a "Reign of Terror" commences as a paramilitary force called the Guardians of the Oglala Nation (GOONs) and vigilantes kill at least 66 AIM members and supporters. The GOONs are loyal to Tribal Chairman Richard Wilson, an adamant opponent of AIM. William Janklow, governor of South Dakota, pledges to eradicate AIM. The FBI, in charge of investigating major crimes on Indian reservations, declines to investigate most of the murders.

1974   On February 12, United States District Court Judge George Boldt rules that Indians are entitled to an opportunity to catch as many as half the fish returning to off-reservation sites which had been the "usual and accustomed places" when the treaties were signed.

1974   In Geneva, Switzerland, AIM starts the International Indian Treaty Council, to represent Western Hemisphere Native peoples at the United Nations. The IITC achieves nongovernmental observer status at the UN in 1977.

1974–1976   Wounded Knee trials: The U.S. government files almost 200 charges against AIM members and others who took part in the Wounded Knee occupation. A large majority of the charges are dismissed or result in not-guilty verdicts. U.S. District Judge Fred Nichol dismisses charges in a major trial due to government misconduct which "formed a pattern throughout the course of the trial" so that "the waters of justice have been polluted."

1975   On June 26, a shootout between AIM and police results in the deaths of two FBI agents (Jack Coler and Ronald Williams) on the Pine Ridge Reservation. Ronald Williams and one Indian man, Joe Stuntz-Killsright, an AIM member from Coeur d'Alene, Idaho. Leonard Peltier later is convicted of the FBI agents' killings after two other defendants (Bob Robideau and Dino Butler) are found not guilty. Peltier serves two life terms on the conviction, and is denied clemency despite a declaration by Amnesty International that he is a political prisoner.

1975   Little Earth of United Tribes: AIM establishes its first housing project, operated with federal funding.

1976   Trail of Self Determination: Four years after the AIM's Trail of Broken Treaties lit up the United States' political landscape on election eve, the Trail of Self-Determination attempted another publicity coup, arriving July 4, the bicentennial Independence Day, and was mainly ignored by Washington, D.C.'s political establishment.

1977   AIM begins MIGIZI Communications in Minneapolis, to share Indian news and other information.

1977   In Geneva, Switzerland, AIM sponsors an International Treaty Conference under the aegis of the United Nations, the U.N.

1978   AIM begins education programs for Native American inmates at Minnesota's Stillwater Prison. Other programs later are modeled after these.

1978   Circle of Life Survival School begins on Minnesota's White Earth Indian Reservation.

1978   Between February 11 and July, American Indian trek across the United States from Alcatraz Island to Washington, D.C., in the "Longest Walk" to dramatize forced removals of Native peoples and to publicize attempts to abrogate treaties.

1978   Women of All Red Nations (WARN) established on Native women's issues, especially government-sponsored sterilization.

1979   AIM begins the American Indian Opportunities Industrialization Center (AIOIC) for job training, to reduce unemployment in Native American communities.

1979   *United States v. Washington* (Boldt Decision) upheld by U.S. Supreme Court.

1980   The U.S. Supreme Court rules that the United States owes the Lakota Sioux compensation and interest from the seizure of the Black Hills in 1877, under the Ft. Laramie Treaty of 1868. The Oglala Lakota reject the payment, which by 2011 grew to more than $1 billion.

1981–1983   AIM splits into factions over support for indigenous peoples in Nicaragua issue, and other issues.

1987   AIM Patrol restarted in Minneapolis after serial killings of American Indian women.

1989   A federal law enabling construction of the National Museum of the American Indian also orders the Smithsonian Institution to repatriate Native American remains and funerary objects.

1990   Native American Grave Protection and Repatriation Act signed into law at the federal level, to protect Indian gravesites on federal public lands against looting.

1991	National Coalition on Racism in Sports and Media started with AIM leadership to address sports-mascot issues; AIM leads a walk in Minneapolis to the 1992 Superbowl; Minneapolis *Star-Tribune* in 1994 stops using Indian mascot names in its reporting.
1992	Native Americans and non-Indian supporters criticize celebrations related to the 500th anniversary of Christopher Columbus' first landing. Some of the largest demonstrations under AIM aegis stop Columbus Day celebrations in Denver, Colorado.
1993	20th anniversary of Wounded Knee occupation observed on site.
1994	Between February 11 and July 15, AIM members and supporters walked across the United States west to east in a "Walk for Justice" that began on Alcatraz Island to publicize unjust treatment in prison of Leonard Peltier.
1998	AIM provides security for Native American protest at Ward Valley, in Southern California. The 113-day occupation produces a victory for several Colorado River tribes against disposal of nuclear wastes.
1999	During October, about 2,000 Native peoples from the United States and Canada gather at Alcatraz Island to remember the 1969 occupation on its 30th anniversary.
2008	"Longest Walk 2" recalls the first Longest Walk 30 years earlier. Longest Walk 2 arrives in Washington, D.C., from San Francisco during July of 2008, exactly three decades after the first one. It was even longer (8,200 miles), with participants from more than a hundred tribes and nations, as well as Maoris (from New Zealand), and a number of non-Indians.

A

Adams, Henry L.

(Born 1943)
Fort Assiniboine-Sioux

While activists such as Russell Means and Dennis Banks became very well known during the Native American revival of the 1960s and 1970s, Henry ("Hank") Adams provided much of the movement's intellectual energy, but remained relatively unknown to the general public. Adams was notable for his humility and his ability to keep a cool head in a volatile situation. "Part of leadership is not the person who holds the office," he said, "but they are the leaders who act through the agency of others" (Trahant, 2006). Vine Deloria Jr. described Adams as one of the most intelligent people he had ever met (Shreve, 2011, 116). During the early 1970s, Deloria (1974, 26) wrote an article about Adams titled "The Most Important Indian."

Adams was described as "tireless, fiery, chain-smoking, lights-out brilliant, and soul-deep loyal to a sacred undertaking" (Wilkinson, 2000, 44). Adams's life illustrated the interconnected nature of Native American activist groups during the years that national attention often seemed fixated on the American Indian Movement (AIM). In addition to his pivotal role in that group, Adams also shaped the National Indian Youth Council and the Survival of American Indians Association, which focused on fishing rights in Western Washington.

Billy Frank Jr., who has known Adams for more than 50 years, remembers him as "the skinny Indian kid with black-rimmed glasses . . . getting beaten up, arrested, and jailed. Those were the hard times, but we laughed a lot. I started calling Hank 'Fearless Fos'—from the character in the *Li'l Abner* cartoon strip—after he got shot while tending a net on the river. I still call him fearless today, because that's what Hank is. He's fearless" (Wilkins, 2011, vii).

"Famously self-effacing, Adams was a crucial behind-the-scenes figure in practically every scene of the militant Indian revival of the last four decades," wrote *Indian Country Today*, continuing:

> He is best known in the history books for his negotiations with the White House to resolve the takeover of the BIA [Bureau of Indian Affairs] building in Washington in 1972 during the Trail of Broken Treaties protest and to wind down the 10-week siege of Wounded Knee in 1973. Both incidents could have caused untold casualties, but his ability to gain the confidence of both sides is credited with keeping bloodshed to a minimum. (*Indian Country Today*, 2006)

Hank Adams presents a letter from the White House to traditional Sioux Chief Frank Fools Crow, left, at border of Pine Ridge Reservation on May 5, 1973 in Scenic, South Dakota. (AP/Wide World Photo)

Adams's Early Life

Henry L. Adams was born May 16, 1943, in Wolf Point (also known as Poverty Flats), on Montana's Fort Peck Reservation. While growing up, Adams worked as a fruit and vegetable picker to help support himself.

Adams's mother married a Quinault and moved to coastal Washington State, where Hank graduated from Moclips High School in 1961. At that school, he was a starting football and basketball player, editor of the school newspaper and annual, as well as student-body president. During high school, Adams worked in a sawmill on the reservation. After dropping out of college at the University of Washington, Adams became involved in fishing-rights protests. Adams also became special projects director of the National Indian Youth Council (NIYC), whereupon the NIYC's most notable special project became fishing rights in Western Washington State. The Indians were fishing under century-old treaties that allowed them to take fish in their "usual and accustomed places." The state refused to recognize the treaties until they were enforced by federal judge George H. Boldt in 1974.

Adams also developed a passion for politics that was expressed in campaign work for John F. Kennedy and his brother Robert. At the same time, Adams also played an important but largely unrecognized role publicizing fishing rights in

Western Washington by inviting notable people, such as actor Marlon Brando and comedian Dick Gregory, to hoist nets alongside Indians on the Nisqually River and to face arrest by state game and fish officials.

Adams became notorious for rousing members of the press corps in the very early hours of the morning to make sure they would be on the scene to witness state raids on fishing Indians, especially when Brando put his notable body on the line. Newspaper reports described "a new kind of Indian warfare in which Hollywood showmanship and Madison Avenue promotion methods are used for defense" (Chrisman, 2006). Adams produced and directed a documentary *As Long as the Rivers Run* in 1970 on the fishing-rights issue.

In 1964, Adams made news by refusing induction into the U.S. Army (under the draft) until and unless treaty rights were respected by the U.S. government. The government did not see his case, so Adams was forced to serve. Released from the Army after the typical two-year draftee enlistment, Adams was more determined than ever to fight for treaty rights. Adams was arrested for fishing deemed illegal by the state several times between 1968 and 1971. During January, 1971, Adams was shot in the stomach and seriously wounded while fishing near Tacoma, Washington, along the banks of the Puyallup River. The State of Washington failed to arrest anyone in association with the shooting. Adams also played a major role in 1968 in a protest march by more than 1,000 Indians and supporters in the state capital of Olympia.

The Fishing Battle Continues

Everywhere in the fishing controversy, activists found the fingerprints of Hank Adams. He enticed Charles Kuralt, then a renowned correspondent for CBS News, to cover the "fish-ins" at Frank's Landing. He also played a major role in writing, and raising funds to publish, the American Friends Service Committee's report *Uncommon Controversy*, which provided a sober, scholarly analysis of treaty fishing rights. Adams also was at the head of a column of Native students who, in 1966, visited University of Washington Law Professor Ralph Johnson in his office and asked him to teach an undergraduate course in Native American law. Johnson had no experience in the area at the time, but he acquired it. Along the way, in 1972, Johnson published a seminal law-journal article that influenced the course of fishing rights litigation before the U.S. Supreme Court (Johnson, 1972). Johnson taught the course until he died, in 1999 (Wilkinson, 2000, 46).

The fishing-rights case also was evolving in the federal courts. Before the Boldt Decision (1974) paved the way for full federal affirmation of treaty fishing rights, two other cases, known to the public as Puyallup I (1968) and Puyallup II (1973), illustrated how the law was changing. The majority opinion in both cases was written by William O. Douglas, who had been raised in Eastern Washington.

In 1968, he found that the state could legally regulate off-reservation fishing if such regulation was "reasonable and necessary" to achieve "conservation" of the species. The state argued that it had been doing just that. In 1973, however, in a case regarding the state's ability to close the fishery for steelhead (which it defined as a game fish that Indians were not allowed to harvest), Douglas ruled that the state's system was not necessary for conservation.

What had happened? Douglas and other justices had read Professor Johnson's article, which analyzed the U.S. Supreme Court's errors in rulings on fishing rights (Johnson, 1972). Adams had put him on the case six years earlier. In addition, Douglas' wife, Cathy, also a lawyer, had visited Frank's Landing at the behest of Hank Adams. She studied the case and became convinced that the Indians were correct.

The Twenty Points

Adams in 1971 authored a 15-point national program "to remove the human needs and aspirations of Indian tribes and Indian people from the workings of the general American political system and . . . reinstate a system of bilateral relationships between Indian tribes and the federal government" (Josephy, 1973, 74). This document became the basis for Adams's "Twenty Points," which laid the intellectual basis for the Trail of Broken Treaties that crossed the United States in 1972, ending with an occupation of the Bureau of Indian Affairs headquarters building in Washington, D.C., a few days before that year's presidential elections.

Caravans had assembled in Seattle, a center of fishing-rights activism, and in San Francisco, the site of the 1969 American Indian occupation of Alcatraz Island, a former federal prison. The two groups merged in Minneapolis, the birthplace of the AIM. A smaller caravan from Los Angeles also joined the two others in Minneapolis. There, the group issued the Twenty Points, a document that advocated revival of American Indian sovereignty. Among other things, the Twenty Points demanded repeal of the federal law that had ended treaty-making in 1871, restoration of the ability to negotiate and sign treaties; a commission that would review past violations of treaties, new consideration of treaties that had never been ratified by the U.S. Senate, and elimination of all state jurisdiction over American Indian affairs.

The Trail of Broken Treaties caravan moved on to Washington, D.C. Upon its arrival on November 3, 1972, the protesters learned that too little lodging was available. The marchers had not planned to take over the Bureau of Indian Affairs headquarters building at the conclusion of the Trail of Broken Treaties. However, the decision was made after the participants learned that the only lodging available to them in Washington, D.C., was a rat-infested church basement.

The protesters decided to stay in the Bureau of Indian Affairs building for several hours until security guards sought to remove them forcibly. At that point, events turned violent. The protesters seized the building for six days as they asserted their demands that native sovereignty be restored and immunity be granted to all protesters. Files were seized and damage was done to the BIA building (AIM leaders asserted that federal agents had infiltrated the movement and had done most of the damage). On November 8, 1972, federal officials offered immunity and transportation home to the protesters. The offer was accepted and the crisis was resolved for the moment. A few months later, however, many of the same themes were sounded as AIM occupied the hamlet of Wounded Knee, South Dakota.

Adams also worked with actors and actresses, as well as other entertainers he had met in the course of the fishing-rights struggle (including Marlon Brando, Jane Fonda, and Dick Gregory) to find movie treatments and scripts that accurately portrayed contemporary American Indian life (Wilkins, 2011, 182–90, 196–97). As he explained in his recommendation to Brando for Sandra (Johnson) Osawa's script titled *Dakah* in 1982:

> This project could be a real breakthrough for Indian script writers, but more importantly for Indian storylines or contemporary dramas about Indian life— which do not focus centrally upon Indian–white conflicts, or find the hackneyed "conflict of cultures" as the only drama assignable to Indians. . . . Indians do live and exist even without the presence of white people there to affirm it. (Wilkins, 2011, 197)

Following the Indian movement's most visible struggles during the 1970s, Adams continued to be active in national and international issues. He was active in shaping the post-Boldt era of fishing rights in Washington State (and elsewhere in the United States) and in presenting the grievances of the Miskito and other Native peoples of Nicaragua's Atlantic Coast to that country's government. He negotiated Native water rights in the Pacific Northwest and fought successfully to get U.S. government funding and recognition for the Little Bighorn Battlefield National Monument Indian Memorial. David Wilkins (2011, 14), who edited a collection of Adams' writings published in 2011, said that "Adams' brilliance is evident in the bevy of writings, speeches, and testimonies on topics that also include civil rights, media and literature, trust and land issues . . . and taxation and economic concerns."

Honoring Adams

Adams continued to advise Native American peoples as a speaker well after AIM's heyday. Like Billy Frank Jr., he became part of the Washington State official infrastructure that maintains fishery resources through the Northwest Indian Fisheries Commission. He also sometimes lectured at the college level, especially at the University of Washington Law School. The newspaper *Indian Country Today* honored Adams with its American Indian Visionary Award in 2006. At the National Press

Club in Washington, D.C., the award was presented to Adams as attorney Susan Hvalsoe Komori said: "Hank's a genius. He knows things we don't know. He sees things we don't see." "Adams was always the guy under the radar, working on all kinds of things," said Billy Frank Jr., a Nisqually who chaired the Northwest Indian Fisheries Commission (Trahant, 2006).

"Hank Adams is the activist's activist who engaged the intellectual and practical efforts required to achieve proper recognition of Indian people. Starting in the 1960s and sustaining to the present, Hank Adams is recognized for his qualities of vision, courage, commitment, discipline—and particularly—the quiet modesty and natural humility of his example," *Indian Country Today's* award citation said (Trahant, 2006).

Writing in *Indian Country Today*, the journalist Les Whitten (2006) said that "Hank Adams is one of the bravest and finest men I have ever known. His bravery is not foolhardy or mad, but that of one who totally recognizes the dangers he faces and goes ahead anyway—not once, but year after year. When I say 'finest,' I think of his kindness, intelligence, humor, and his persistence in good causes."

Further Reading

"Biography: Hank Adams." Answers.com. 2006, http://www.answers.com/topic/hank-adams.

Chrisman, Gabriel. "The Fish-in Protests at Franks Landing." Seattle Civil Rights and Labor History Project. 2006, http://depts.washington.edu/civilr/fish-ins.htm.

Deloria, Vine, Jr. *Behind the Trail of Broken Treaties: An Indian Declaration of Independence.* Austin: University of Texas Press, 1985.

Deloria, Vine, Jr. "The Most Important Indian." *Race Relations Reporter* 5, no. 21 (November, 1974): 26–28.

"Hank Adams Papers, 1958–1978." Seeley G. Mudd Manuscript Library, Princeton University. Archived 20078, http://www.princeton.edu/~mudd.

Harjo, Suzan Shown. "Harjo: Why Native Identity Matters: A Cautionary Tale (Ward Churchill Smacked by Indian Columnist)." *Indian Country Today*, February 10, 2008, http://www.indiancountry.com/content.cfm?id=1096410335.

"Indian Country Today: Hank Adams, the Lifelong Activist." Northwest Indian Fisheries Commission. March 1, 2006, http://www.nwifc.org/2006/01/hank-adams-wins-indian-country-todays-american-indian-visionary-award/.

Johnson, Ralph W. "The States Versus Indian Off-reservation Fishing: A United States Supreme Court Error." *Washington Law Review* 47, no. 2 (1972): 207–36.

Josephy, Alvin M, Jr. "Wounded Knee and all That: What the Indians Want." *New York Times Sunday Magazine,* March 18, 1973, 18–19, 66–83.

Shreve, Bradley. *Red Power Rising: The National Indian Youth Council and the Origins of Native Activism.* Norman: University of Oklahoma Press, 2011.

Trahant, Mark. "Honoring an American Indian Visionary." *Seattle Post-Intelligencer,* March 5, 2006, http://www.seattlepi.com/opinion/261658_trahant05.html.

Whitten, Les. "Tribute to Hank Adams." *Indian Country Today*, January 12, 2006, http://www.highbeam.com/doc/1P1–118940793.html.

Wilkins, David E., ed. *The Hank Adams Reader: An Exemplary Native American Activist and the Unleashing of Indigenous Sovereignty*. Golden, CO: Fulcrum, 2011.

Wilkinson, Charles F. *Blood Struggle: The Rise of Modern Indian Nations*. New York: W.W. Norton, 2005.

Wilkinson, Charles F., and Hank Adams. *Messages from Frank's Landing: A Story of Salmon, Treaties, and the Indian Way*. Seattle: University of Washington Press, 2000.

Akwesasne Mohawk Counselor Organization

During the last half of the 20th century, Ray Fadden (who, having been born in 1910, lived to be almost 100 years of age) was a principal figure in the revitalization of Mohawk language and culture. First as founder of the Mohawk Counselor Organization during the 1940s, then the Six Nations Indian Museum in the 1950s, Fadden and his family have taught many hundreds of Mohawks and other Iroquois the value of their heritage. Fadden's activism presaged that of the AIM and other organizations during the 1960s.

Fadden also has been very active in environmental and wildlife preservation in the Adirondacks. "If you kill the forest, you kill your own grandchildren," he has said (Barreiro, 1984, 5). Fadden became a living legend to many who knew him. Ron LaFrance, an Akwesasne Mohawk who was one of Fadden's students, said: "He has been father, grandfather, teacher, and friend to three generations of Mohawks" (Barreiro, 1984, 3).

An Eagle Scout, Fadden during the early 1940s began the first Boy Scout troop at Akwesasne. When he sensed anti-Indian prejudice in the larger organization, Fadden founded his own youth group, which awarded dressed feathers instead of merit badges and visited historic Iroquois sites. The Akwesasne Mohawk Counselor Organization sought to educate Mohawk children in respect to woodcraft technologies, Native American history, Mohawk traditions, and in so doing to enhance their self-image. Fadden took the group's members to various locations throughout the Northeastern United States to view actual sites that were historically significant in Iroquois history.

"Under Ray's tutelage," said Doug George-Kanentiio, one of his students, "A Native boy or girl was never the same. They went from his classroom holding their heads high and well-prepared to become leaders in their own right" (George-Kanentiio, 1997, n.p.). Fadden also instructed his students in the ways of other cultures, taking special note of Africa, from the days of slavery to persistent media stereotypes of recent years.

With Fadden's guidance, the students sought out elders to learn Haudenosaunee oral tradition. With elders' help Fadden's students learned "the significance of wampum belts while making facsimile belts. They learned how to build different structures because elders taught them to build these structures, mostly in miniature. They learned to make clothes and headdresses by being taught to make them. These were all skills that were on the verge of dying out in the communities" (Jennings, 1998, 166).

Fadden infused members of the Akwesasne Mohawk Counselor Organization with a knowledge base that would allow them to be employable as cultural "ambassadors," primarily as Adirondack region summer-camp counselors, to correct negative stereotypes of Native American people. He also was concerned with enabling Native young people to draw on their own culture for economic self-sufficiency. Some did become self-sufficient this way, especially in jewelry making, as multimedia artists, and in education as museum and film consultants (Jennings, 1998, 166).

The counselors collected and shared information with each other. With Fadden's help, they then wrote their findings and collections in narrative form, producing illustrations where necessary. Some information was published in pamphlets, some in charts and drawings. These publications were then sold to produce revenue for the organization. By 1948, the Six Nations Cultural Historical Series included 26 pamphlets and 37 charts (Jennings, 1998, 167).

According to one observer, "Multicultural education [today uses] . . . teaching methods Fadden was prevented from using in the public school system in the 1930s and 1940s. Even in today's political climate, however, his use of multiple learning style approaches, his observation and subsequent application of Native instructional methods, his ability to actively involve his students in research and publication, the multiple field trips, and the establishment of a museum collection would be remarkable. The passage of more than fifty years has proven Fadden right: the people will continue" (Jennings, 1998, 171–72).

Further Reading

Barreiro, Jose. "View From The Forest: An Elder's Concern," *Indian Studies: American Indian Program at Cornell* 1, no. 3 (Fall, 1984): 4–7.

George-Kanentiio, Doug. "Ray Fadden-Tehanentorens is the Teacher behind Six Nations Museum," Syracuse *Herald-American*, 1997, n.p.

Jennings, Nadine Nelson. "In The Spirit Of The Kaswentha: Cultural Literacy In Akwesasne Mohawk Culture." Ph.D. dissertation, 1998, Indiana University of Pennsylvania.

Akwesasne Notes

Created by Native people, the news journal *Akwesasne Notes* provided a Native American point of view during the creation and early years of the revival movement during the late 1960s onward.

Pollution of the Akwesasne community air, land, and water provoked Mohawks to leave home and seek work across the United States and Canada, mainly after World War II. Many worked in the military and urban construction trades, among the legendary "Mohawks in High Steel." The traditional farming and hunting economy no longer supported a growing population. In so doing, people at Akwesasne became acquainted with the rising clamor for recognition of civil and human rights by Native and other disenfranchised peoples. They became leaders in national forums, of which the newspaper *Akwesasne Notes* was one. The North American Indian Traveling College and White Roots of Peace also spring from the same origins.

The Haudenosaunee (Iroquois) confederate model also produced traveling diplomats who were adept at bringing diverse peoples together. Many of these people were well-educated, avid readers who sensed the value of a national news journal during the rising "Red Power" era. Thus *Akwesasne Notes* was born as a project of Akwesasne's traditional Mohawk governing council, the Mohawk Nation Council of Chiefs.

Started in the late 1960s, with American Indian activism's modern reassertion, *Akwesasne Notes* has since been one of the foremost Native-owned editorial voices for Native American rights in the United States and Canada. In a trade where advertising pays most of the bills, it carried nearly none. At a time when newspapers have come to resemble poor cousins of television, it rarely published color (until its last years), relying instead on pages dense with text. In a media world of mega-corporations, *Akwesasne Notes* operated on a shoestring budget, rarely paying contributors or editors and fiercely maintained its editorial independence.

In December, 1968, the idea for such a journal was born around the kitchen table of Ernie (Kaientaronkwen) Benedict at Akwesasne. Benedict was a graduate of Canton, New York's St. Lawrence University who had edited two small newspapers on the reservation during the 1940s and early 1950s. John Fadden, Tom Porter, Mose David, Mike Boots, Iran Benedict, Alec Gray, Mary Tebo, Anne Jock, and others cut and pasted reports from newspapers across the continent into the first issues of *Akwesasne Notes*.

The first editor of the newspaper was Jerry Gambill, a non-Native Canadian, who was given the Mohawk name Rarihokwats. Gambill was employed as a community-assistance worker in the Canadian Department of Indian Affairs when he first traveled to Akwesasne. He was fired from his government job in 1967, but remained at Akwesasne, living on Cornwall Island. Gambill edited *Akwesasne Notes* until 1977, followed John Mohawk, a Seneca scholar (1977–1984). Peter Blue Cloud and George-Kanentiio, both Mohawks, edited the newspaper between the mid-1980s and early 1990s.

Begun mainly as a news service that reprinted reports on the burgeoning Native-rights movement, a cheap newsprint edition that ran on little or no money reached a circulation of 50,000 copies across the United States. George-Kanentiio traced its growth:

[*Akwesasne Notes*] quickly expanded its scope to include reports about Native events from across North America. . . . Within months of its inception,

Akwesasne Notes exploded across the nation and was soon found in every aboriginal community. It found fertile ground on college campuses also. The newspaper was carried in alternative bookstores, hawked on street corners, and sold at Native powwows. Initially only a few hundred copies were printed, but the circulation grew to over 10,000 within a year and it would reach 150,000 within eight years. Throughout its history, which lasted until 1998, it was printed up to eight times a year, but six was the norm. It was tabloid in size with up to 64 pages of hard news, social activities, and profiles, which was a break from the larger page sizes and made mailing the editions much cheaper. (George-Kanentiio, 2011)

Akwesasne Notes covered the occupation of Alcatraz in its second year of publication with uncommon acuity. Other coverage included reports on a heated intellectual debate over whether the Iroquois Great Law helped inspire the U.S. Constitution, a report from indigenous peoples in Australia contributed by a Mohawk family who visited there, the latest plans for coal mining on the Hopi reservation, and an account of negotiations between Nicaraguan native peoples and the government. Other articles reported on repression of Tibetan natives by the Chinese and the organization of U.S. chapters of the Green Party. *Akwesasne Notes* also described Native resistance to destruction of Brazil's rain forests, detailed accounts of human-rights violations in Guatemala, reported trade agreements between American Indian tribes and third-world nations, discussed a proposed world constitution, and editorially supported Greenpeace.

As publicity about the AIM's activities waned, so did *Notes'* circulation, from 1977's peak of more than 125,000 in 1977 to about 10,000 during the 1980s. The paper still accepted no paid advertising, so its budget, dependant on subscriptions, was always tight. The Mohawk Nation Council subsidized publication as well. Most subscribers received the paper by mail. The publication had a geographic reach that few newspapers could match, with copies being mailed to indigenous people and their supporters around the world. As a voice of Akwesasne's traditional government, the newspaper's content reflected its global approach to issues involving indigenous rights, but the focus of its coverage remained the Haudenosaunee. *Akwesasne Notes* demolished any notion of the "noble savage" as its pages carried detailed accounts not only of internal dissension, but also of occasional murder and fraud, along with graphic descriptions of the abysmal living conditions on many reservations.

However, wrote George-Kanentiio,

The politics of *Notes* remained the same, although longer analytical essays became standard. Its writers covered a new era of activism. Rather than confrontation on the local front, Native leaders took their concerns to international forums in Europe and Asia, the United Nations, and innumerable tribunals.

The 1978 Native conference in Geneva, Switzerland, and the 1982 Russell Tribunal on the abuse of human rights on Indian territory by the United States were the best examples of extended *Notes* coverage. *Notes* was often the only source for comprehensive coverage of these momentous events.

John Mohawk left *Notes* in 1984 to initiate Buffalo State University's Native Studies department. Peter Blue Cloud, a poet from Kahnawake, a Mohawk territory near Montreal, then edited the paper for two years, during which he gave it a more artistic focus, including high-definition photography and etchings. George-Kanentiio then assumed the editorship, holding the post until 1992, a time of acute conflict over gambling at Akwesasne.

The editors and writers of *Akwesasne Notes* had to be on guard against arsonists (the paper was strongly opposed to gambling), but also maintained an international focus, the Mapuchis of Chile to the Saamis of Scandinavia. The paper's offices were torched in December, 1986, burning a substantial archive. No one was arrested for the crime. With aid from Salli Benedict (one of Ernie's children, 1954–2011) and others, the paper was installed in a new communications center with a local radio station.

On January 9, 1988, another firebomb razed the newspaper's offices during gambling-related violence at Akwesasne. Installed in a new office with mostly donated equipment gathered from a worldwide network of supporters, *Akwesasne Notes* didn't miss a bimonthly issue after it sustained $200,000 in uninsured losses from the midwinter fire. The fire gutted the Nation House that had been the newspaper's home for much of the previous two decades. In its first editorial after the fire during spring 1988 *Akwesasne Notes* wrote:

> Our offices were torched by those amongst us here at Akwesasne who oppose our reporting on the conflicts that are plaguing the Haudenosaunee [Iroquois] nations. . . . With the gambling, the cigarette smuggling, the violence . . . it is understandable why those criminal elements amongst us are opposed to a free press disseminating information about the illegal and immoral activities around us. . . . They almost succeeded in putting us out of business . . . but we will survive. (Johansen, 1993, 26–27)

Following gambling-related turmoil at Akwesasne, the newspaper stopped publishing. George-Kanentiio resigned as editor in 1992 to move to Oneida to join the family of his new wife, the noted singer Joanne Shenandoah. Darren Bonaparte, an assistant editor of *Indian Time*, the local reservation paper and Salli Benedict took over. It resumed in early 1995 in a glossy magazine format. For almost two years, the magazine provided a showcase for Native American issues and artwork. Unable to support the expenses of such a format, the publication reverted to tabloid newspaper format in 1997, then ceased publication again.

Looking back in 2011, George-Kanentiio commented: "The spirit of activism and confrontation, of protest and occupation, gave way to a raw form of capitalism and profit in which hard-fought-for rights and independence were converted into casino gambling, tobacco sales, and drug dealing. Street gangs copied from the Bloods and Crips replaced AIM warriors, while Native governments elected to turn away from unity as they sought to protect their respective economic fiefdoms. Striving for money replaced striving to build the movement" (George-Kanentiio, 2011).

Further Reading

George-Kanentiio, Doug. "*Akwesasne Notes*: How the Mohawk Nation Created a Newspaper and Shaped Contemporary Native America." Manuscript copy provided by author, September 15, 2011.

Johansen, Bruce E. *Life and Death in Mohawk Country*. Golden, CO: North American Press/Fulcrum, 1993.

Alcatraz Occupation

(1969–1971)

American Indian activism and nationalism was transformed by the occupation of the former Federal Penitentiary at Alcatraz Island by about 300 Native Americans and supporters that began on November 20, 1969. The activists said they were requesting title to the island under a federal law that gave Indians first refusal on federal "surplus" property. A number of regional groups, including the newly formed AIM, came together at Alcatraz, even though the occupation itself ended without achieving its stated goal of establishing a cultural center there.

The group that seized the abandoned federal prison at Alcatraz in San Francisco Bay called itself Indians of All Tribes (IAT). It combined the efforts of the AIM with many other local and West Coast organizations, and provided a fertile ground for organizing. National networks were formed on Alcatraz Island that later were crucial as activists organized a march across the United States during 1972 to protest broken treaties, followed, during the last week of the 1972 election campaign, by an the occupation of the Bureau of Indian Affairs headquarters in Washington, D.C., followed by the occupation of Wounded Knee (1973). Occupants came and went from Alcatraz to take part in other Native American rights events—most notably fishing-rights protests in Western Washington State that were peaking at about the time Indians had seized Alcatraz.

The week before the initial occupation of Alcatraz in November, 1964, for example, Bob Satiacum, a Puyallup, was arrested for exercising treaty fishing rights near Tacoma. Marlon Brando was arrested at the same time, along with John J. Yargan, a staff assistant to San Francisco's archbishop. People shuttled back and

Indian leaders Max Bear of South Dakota, left, Chief Eagle Feather of Rosebud, South Dakota, center, and Dennis Banks, American Indian Movement leader, right, discuss anti-Indian legislation on Alcatraz Island in the middle of the San Francisco Bay, February 11, 1978. (AP Photo/Paul Sakuma)

forth between the major Alcatraz occupation and fishing-rights protests in Western Washington during 1969, 1970, and 1971, as well.

In an action that had been contemplated before the Alcatraz occupation, about 80 Indians occupied an abandoned Strategic Air Command (SAC) base near Davis, California November 3, 1970, with the intention of starting an Indian university. Jack Forbes, a Lenape and Powhatan who was a professor at the University of California at Davis, led this occupation, and said at the time that the 640-acre SAC base was much more suitable to long-term development than cold, isolated Alcatraz (Smith, 2012, 157). In addition, the SAC site contained usable buildings, something Alcatraz did not offer. A college, Deganawida-Quetzalcoatl University, was founded and operated for more than 35 years, until lack of funding closed it. The federal government deeded the land to U.C.-Davis instead of the Indian-led university.

People who would become prominent later took part at Alcatraz. For example, Wilma Mankiller, who would become the first female grand chief of the Oklahoma Cherokees, was among the occupants. "Alcatraz . . . changed my life forever," said Mankiller, who was 23 years of age during the Alcatraz occupation

(Hightower-Langston, 2006). Mankiller credited the occupation as a catalyst for her early political development: "It gave me the sense that anything was possible. Who I am and how I governed was influenced by Alcatraz" (Winton 1999, 10).

Leaders of the Alcatraz occupation included Walter Means, Russell Means' father; George Mitchell and Dennis Banks, both founders of the AIM; and Richard Oakes, who, as founder of Indians of All Tribes, became the occupation's major leader during its first few months, until his daughter died on the island. These leaders and others were purposively forging bonds that wove together many different Native American tribes and nations. Stephen Cornell wrote in *The Return of the Native*: *American Indian Political Resurgence*, "Their politics was often confrontational and explicitly supratribal" (Cornell, 1988, 198).

At Alcatraz, Dennis Banks, for example, met and brought into AIM John Trudell, a Santee Sioux, who became one of the group's main strategists during the 1970s. At about the same time, Banks also met and made common cause with Russell Means, an Oglala Lakota, who became AIM's most inventive publicist. It was Means who thought up the ideas of occupying Mount Rushmore (in 1970) and taking over a replica of The Mayflower at Plymouth, Massachusetts, during Thanksgiving of 1971.

The Alcatraz Occupation Emulated

The occupation of Alcatraz Island was emulated across the United States. Troy Johnson's *The American Indian Occupation of Alcatraz Island: Red Power and Self-determination* (1996, 2008) contains an appendix that describes several occupations of varying length across the United States between 1970 and 1975 that were carried out on the same model.

Deep into the winter of 1970–1971, Bruce Oakes, a cousin of Richard Oakes, was fired up by a fundraising visit to New York State by Alcatraz veterans David Leach and LaNada Means. Plans were hatched to seize another piece of isolated land that had been declared surplus by the federal government: Ellis Island, the former point of entry for millions of immigrants from Europe. Organizers acquired boats, fuel, and supplies, and set out to cross the harbor on a bitterly cold night, only to find that their motorboats' fuel lines had frozen. In the meantime, another organizer had called the media to announce the invasion.

The would-be occupiers heard the news on the radio and watched as police swarmed over the site in boats and helicopters. Located by police, the Indians were escorted to station house in Brooklyn, but not charged with anything, because all they had done was gather some boats on the shoreline. Later, they tried to convince the television talk show host Merv Griffin to help them occupy the island. He declined, but gave them $100 to get something to eat (Smith and Warrior, 1996, 92–93).

Troy R. Johnson traced the spread of land occupations as a tactic across the United States:

> The occupation of Alcatraz Island was followed by a number of attempted and successful takeovers and occupations by supra-tribal urban groups: Fort Lewis and Fort Lawton in Washington; Ellis Island in New York; federal land in Santa Rosa and Shasta, California; abandoned missile sites and military installations in Davis and Richmond, California, Minneapolis, Milwaukee, and Chicago; and Mount Rushmore and the Badlands National Monuments. (Johnson, 2008, 292)

San Francisco Bay as Center of Activism

The San Francisco Bay area was a major relocation site for the Bureau of Indian Affairs during the 1960s, so when Indian political activism began, the area became a major center. Native peoples organized through self-help organizations that provided social contacts and services that the BIA had ignored. The Bay Area had about 30 "social clubs" serving Native families who had immigrated to the area by the time the call went out to occupy "the island" (Johnson, 2008, 294). A new generation of young Native people was growing up in the cities, going to college, and sharing experiences that led to a sense of betterment, according to Troy R. Johnson, who has written incisively about the subject:

> The Alcatraz occupation came out of the Bay Area colleges and universities and other California college campuses where young, educated Indian students joined with other minority groups during the 1969 Third World Liberation Front strike and began demanding that colleges offer courses relevant to Indian students. Indian history written and taught by non-Indian instructors was no longer acceptable to these young students, awakened as they were to the possibility of social protest to bring attention to the shameful treatment of Indian people. (Johnson, 2008, 294)

Early Attempts at Occupation

The major occupation of Alcatraz Island that began November 20, 1969, was preceded by two very short attempts. The first, in March 9, 1964, lasted only four hours, and involved only five Native residents of the Bay Area. At the time, the federal government was about to transfer ownership of the island (which had been closed as a prison in 1963) to the city of San Francisco. The Indians had heard of a clause in the 1868 Treaty of Fort Laramie that reserved for the Sioux all abandoned federal land in areas that had once belonged to the Sioux. (Defining Alcatraz as Sioux land, even if this clause had existed, was something of a stretch).

Roughly 20 young Indians and supporters as well as media took part in the 1964 occupation. The *New York Times* described the Indian rationale for the occupation: "Wearing their tribal regalia, the five men conducted a victory dance and then planted a large American flag. Each then proceeded to physically stake his claim to a portion of the island. Talking with reporters, the Indians then offered to purchase Alcatraz at the price of 47 cents per acre, the price per acre equivalent to that of a settlement being debated for the taking of Indian land from the California Indians" (Johnson, 2008a, 289).

The second brief occupation was undertaken by Richard Oakes and several Native American friends, all students at San Francisco State University. In late October, 1969, the San Francisco Indian Center was destroyed by fire. Oakes and the other were looking for a new meeting place. Several Native Americans chartered a boat and circled Alcatraz, but did not land.

They returned in greater numbers on November 9, 1969, calling themselves The Indians of All Tribes, landed, and read a Proclamation. They had planned a symbolic claim of the Island in the name of all Native peoples, but not an actual occupation. Overcome, perhaps, by the gravity of the moment, however, Oakes led his four friends in a plunge off the boat, into San Francisco Bay, swimming to the island. They staked a claim, but the caretaker asked them all to leave, and they did. Later the same night, 14 Indians returned with sleeping bags and food and spent the night camping. The next morning they departed on request of the caretaker.

The Final Occupation

The final and most substantial occupation began 10 days later, after more American Indian students had been recruited from the University of California at Los Angeles (UCLA) with the aid of Ray Spang and Edward Castillo. The group met in Campbell Hall, future home of the American Indian Studies Center and the journal *American Indian Culture and Research Journal*, as well as in private homes and Los Angeles Indian bars. On November 20, 89 Native people landed on the Island (Johnson et al., 1997, 26–27).

On November 20, after nightfall, Indians on several boats out-maneuvered U.S. Coast Guard boats and helicopters. The Coast Guard blockade continued for two more days in an attempt to impede the arrival of more Indians and supplies. According to Oakes, it was "completely ineffective . . . we needed food and supplies . . . we couldn't have survived without all the people who ran that blockade" (Johnson, 2008a, 291).

After the start of the major occupation, Native people streamed in from across the United States and Canada, as well as Mexico, and parts of South America. The number living there long-term grew quickly to about 250. Many more came and went for brief periods—13,000 in November, 1969, alone, according to Historian Troy R. Johnson (Johnson, 2008, 289). For many of them, it was their first long-term exposure to other Native peoples from across the hemisphere.

Troy R. Johnson described widespread support for the occupiers from the San Francisco Bay area:

> The non-Indian private sector responded to calls for assistance from the Indians on the island. Non-Indian citizens, particularly the Asian-American community of San Francisco, responded to the needs of the occupiers. They provided clothing, food, water, medical supplies, and school supplies for the children, despite a U.S. Coast Guard blockade of the island. Celebrities such as Jane Fonda, Robert Redford, and Marlon Brando visited the island and encouraged private parties to support the effort not only by donating usable items but by contacting politicians as well. (Johnson, 2008a, 289)

On November 21, Oakes and an attorney, speaking for Indians of All Tribes, presented demands to the Department of Interior's regional coordinator: full title to the island, with money for a university and cultural center administered by Native people.

Dennis Hastings, a young Omaha who later would become his tribe's historian, told Earl Caldwell of the *New York Times* a few days after the final occupation had begun: "My folks back home on the reservation are so proud of us and what we're doing." Hastings, a second-year student at Sacramento State College, "sat on a ledge high on the rim of Alcatraz and looked across through the hedge at San Francisco," wrote Caldwell, and continued: "If we have to, we'll fight for this island. They can kill us but they can't kill our spirit" (Caldwell, 1969, 43).

Copious media attention provided a national platform for discussion of American Indian issues relating to self-determination during this wave of activism. On December 16, 1969, the occupants of Alcatraz said:

> We are issuing this call in an attempt to unify our Indian brothers behind a common cause. . . . We are not getting anywhere fast by working alone as individual tribes. If we can get together as brothers and come to a common agreement, we feel that we can be much more effective, doing things for ourselves, instead of having someone else doing it, telling us what is good for us. So we must start somewhere. We feel that we are going to succeed, we must hold on to the old ways. This is the first and most important reason we went to Alcatraz Island. (Johansen, 2005, 342)

Unique Challenges

The occupation of an abandoned prison on a remote island presented some unique problems for its roughly 100 steady inhabitants. Many were basic things, such as the needs, after days and weeks, to bathe with something other than a pail of cold water (with no wash cloth or towel) in a place that was usually chilly, and often swept by gale-force winds. Not everyone was an Indian activist. Mission Street drunks took up residence in some of the cells. The place became a destination for young people looking for a party. The old prison offered thousands of places to hole up and carry on private business. "The island became a truly wild place, a strange combination of a constant pow-wow and a street fight," wrote Paul Chaat Smith and Robert Allen Warrior (1996, 34).

Governing a group of people who were innately distrustful of authority was a constant challenge. Oakes, a Mohawk from Upstate New York, became the occupation's best-known spokesman, a job that often took him off the island to raise funds and speak to members of the media. Among the occupiers, rumors spread, with no substance, that he was embezzling money.

The AIM tried to police the island, but the occupants called them "The Bureau of Caucasian Affairs." A group of young toughs organized, called itself "The Thunderbirds," and roamed the island, threatening and beating some of the residents (Smith and Warrior, 1996, 66). Others vandalized the prison grounds. While Smith and Warrior described the Thunderbirds as a gang that beat people on the island, others said they were more of a San Francisco Indian social group. Others asserted that they bootlegged liquor.

Troy Johnson wrote that "The more militant and vocal Indians began to seize control of the Indian occupation force. Daily life on Alcatraz began to deteriorate sharply. Hygiene on the island was extremely poor, from sewage disposal to the preparation of food. Reports also began to surface that the sale and use of drugs was very much in evidence" (Johnson, 2008, 291).

Very quickly, walls and doorways of the old prison were covered with graffiti establishing a sense of place—This was Native land, owned (and, just as importantly, managed) by Native people: "You are on INDIAN Land;" "WARNING: Keep off INDIAN Property" (painted atop a sign that had read "WARNING: Keep off U.S. Government Property"); "This Land is My Land" (atop a major doorway, attached to the seal of the U.S. penal system) (Johnson, 1996, 150). Other signs read: "Indian Land, Indians Welcome;" "United Indian Property;" "Home of the Free—Indian Land" (Johnson et al., 1997, 189–90).

Mattel, the large toy company, donated hundreds of new toys, but food was sometimes scarce on the island. A few generators provided little more than power for a few light bulbs. Native people from reservations clashed with urban Indians that they thought looked and acted more like hippies in their buckskins and beads. Hank Adams said that Alcatraz, for many of them, was an exploration of figuring out "what being Indian was all about" (Smith and Warrior, 1996, 61).

Visits, Fires, Schools, and Deaths

By the second week of December, 1969, occupiers of Alcatraz had started the Big Rock School for their children in the auditorium of what had been the prison's main cell block. In addition to the usual curricular materials (reading, writing, arithmetic, English, social and natural sciences, and health) students were taught Native American history, arts, crafts, and cultural heritage. Crafts included bead-work, leatherwork, creation of regalia, and others. Teachers were drawn from the occupants: some had experience in off-island schools, and others who had little formal schooling but did know craftwork. The school included grades one through six, and became a model for an American Indian Charter School in Oakland, California, across San Francisco Bay, which outlasted the occupation by many years (Josephy et al., 1999, 192–93).

Several people were injured in the concrete and steel maze. The Coast Guard, having once been scorned as "the man," ended up providing ambulance service from the island to the mainland. On January 3, 1970, Yvonne Oakes, a 12-year-old child of Richard and Anne Oakes, fell three stories down a stairwell, and died five days later in an Oakland Public Health Service hospital of massive head injuries. Oakes left the island.

During April, 1970, Vine Deloria Jr. visited Alcatraz, having recently published *Custer Died for Your Sins: An Indian Manifesto*. It was his second visit; Deloria had observed the occupation during its first few days. He was impressed by the oc-cupiers' boldness and energy, but believed they were inexperienced. Deloria told a press conference that "only ten Indians in the country are qualified to negotiate with the federal government," implying that none of the ten were present at Alcatraz (Smith and Warrior, 1996, 82). The occupiers' governing council took notice of press reports quoting Deloria on April 3, and sent him a letter, asking for help ("our dire need for consultation") (Smith and Warrior, 1996, 82). The government, in the meantime, was waiting for the occupation to fizzle, "acting as if they didn't exist" (Smith and Warrior, 1996, 83).

On June 1, 1970, a large fire raged through parts of Alcatraz. Four historical buildings were razed. Trudell told the press that someone had set the fires to make the occupants look bad. This was one of several fires on the island during the occu-pation. LaNada Means was badly burned in one of them, but survived and returned. Later, *Ramparts* magazine put her on its cover under the headline "Better Red than Dead." Jane Fonda read the magazine, arranged to visit, and became close friends with LaNada. She even joined her on a visit to LaNada's family in Idaho (Smith and Warriors, 1996, 93–94).

After a year, the initial 200 to 300 occupiers were down to about 80 regulars, as donations continued to arrive from all over the world. The Washington Redskins football team donated a $600 television set (this would have been about $3,000 in 2012 dollars). The set didn't run on the generator (another donation) that supplied electricity after the federal government cut the power. Phone lines had been cut, and firewood was scarce. Water was being hauled in from the mainland in jugs after the government stopped the faucets. Trudell told the press that conditions were not unlike those on many reservations—except, perhaps, for the donations of high-heeled shoes and formal gowns (Johnson, 1996, 2008, 85, 144–46).

During late 1969 and 1970, LaNada Boyer and others worked with the San Francisco architectural firm McDonald and Associates to create a plan for Thunderbird University and Cultural Center. This proposal was named after them. The plan was presented to the public on November 20, 1970, the first anniversary of the main occupation. The Thunderbird University plan, projected to cost $6 million ($25–$30 million in 2012 dollars) was to provide 300 Indian students with free tuition for classes in Native arts and crafts, law, ecology, and languages. The plan envisaged a round ceremonial lodge encircled by 96 apartment-sized residences of glass and steel, in the design of tipis.

The occupation continued for another year, until mid-June, 1971, as the number of people on the island slowly declined. Shelving and furniture were being broken apart for firewood; salt water was being used to flush the toilets. The people living on the island without electricity, heat, or running water came down with the flu. The federal government fretted about the darkening of a lighthouse on the island; two oil tankers collided during January, 1971 at night, shrouded in darkness.

The Government Decides to End the Occupation

While the government could have charged many of the occupants with several variants of trespassing and destruction of government policy, the standoff continued for several months after Yvonne Oakes died, and her father left the island. A new seven-member governing council was elected (including Stella Leach, John Trudell, LaNada Means, and others). Meanwhile, some rich people had floated by on yachts and flashed power-fist salutes.

On May 26, 1970, the federal government cut off remaining phone and electrical service. The occupation continued. San Francisco's Unitarian Church donated a 30-kilowatt generator. By November 20, 1970, the annual anniversary of the occupation, only two of the original landing crew remained, LaNada Boyer and John Whitefox (John Trudell had arrived on November 30, 1969).

The U.S. government repeatedly gave the occupiers a few days to vacate the island under threat of eviction by force, but U.S. Marshalls demurred, in part because President Richard Nixon, a Quaker, was in favor of improving policies toward Native Americans. In public, however, Nixon regarded the occupiers as renegades. On June 7, 1971, however, with 15 people left on Alcatraz, the government decided to end the standoff after 19 months. Four days later, in the afternoon, Coast Guard boats surrounded it. Roughly 30 armed federal agents debarked from three boats and a helicopter, taking less than an hour to arrest the last occupiers, without resistance.

So ended one of the cardinal events in the Native American movement. The occupants departed Alcatraz during 1971 without achieving their expressed goals of gaining title to the island and building an American Indian culture center. The island was too remote to support a lasting cultural center. The occupation did focus attention, as no one had done before, on the issues of American Indian identity, self-determination, and tribal lands. As an attempt to forge an organization the Alcatraz occupation failed miserably, but as a marquee for the state of Native society generally it was a media bonanza. It also forged friendships among many Native activists that would shape the course of the movement. Beginning with Alcatraz occupation, the focus of Native American activism switched from issues affecting one tribe at a time, to "supra-tribal" issues that were interconnected. Peoples affected by common issues, such as fishing rights, found common cause more easily. Actions including the Trail of Broken Treaties, in 1972, ending with the occupation of BIA head offices in Washington, D.C., as well as the occupation of Wounded Knee the next year were related directly to the occupation of Alcatraz Island.

Alcatraz was, and remained, a symbol.

Further Reading

Blue Cloud, Peter. *Alcatraz is Not an Island.* Berkeley, CA: Wingbow, 1972.

Caldwell, Earl. "Determined Indians Watch and Wait on 'the Rock." *New York Times*, December 10, 1969, 37, 43.

Cornell, Stephen. *The Return of the Native*: *American Indian Political Resurgence*. New York: Oxford University Press, 1988.

Deloria, Vine, Jr. "Alcatraz, Activism, and Accommodation," *American Indian Culture & Research Journal* 18 (1994): 25–32.

Forbes, Jack D. *Native Americans and Nixon: Presidential Politics and Minority Self-determination*. Los Angeles: American Indian Cultural Center, 1984.

Fortunate Eagle, Adam. *Alcatraz! Alcatraz! The Indian Occupation of 1969–71*. San Francisco: Heyday, 1992.

Hightower-Langston, Donna. "American Indian Women's Activism in the 1960s and 1970s." Indymedia March 21st, 2006. http://www.indybay.org/news/2006/03/1809545.php.

Johansen, Bruce E. *The Native Peoples of North America: A History*. Westport, CT: Praeger, 2005.

Johnson, Troy R. *Alcatraz Is Not An Island*. Documentary. San Francisco: Diamond Island Productions, 1999.

Johnson, Troy R. *The American Indian Occupation of Alcatraz Island: Red Power and Self-Determination*. Lincoln: University of Nebraska Press, 1996, 2008.

Johnson, Troy R. *The Occupation of Alcatraz Island: Indian Self-Determination and the Rise of Indian Activism.* Urbana: University of Illinois Press, 1996.

Johnson, Troy R. "Red Power," in Bruce E. Johansen and Barry Pritzker, eds. *Encyclopedia of American Indian History.* Santa Barbara, CA: ABC-CLIO, 2008, 287–97.

Johnson, Troy R. "The Roots of Contemporary Native American Activism," in Albert Hurtado and Peter Iverson, eds. *Major Problems in American Indian History.* Boston: Houghton-Mifflin, 2001.

Johnson, Troy R. and Joane Nagel, eds. "Alcatraz Revisited: The 25th Anniversary of the Occupation," *American Indian Culture & Research Journal* 18, no. 4 (special edition, 1994). Los Angeles: American Indian Studies Center.

Johnson, Troy, Joane Nagel, and Duane Champagne, eds. *American Indian Activism: Alcatraz to the Longest Walk.* Urbana: University of Illinois Press, 1997.

Josephy, Alvin M., Jr., Joane Nagel, and Troy Johnson, eds. *Red Power: The American Indians' Fight for Freedom.* Lincoln: University of Nebraska Press, 1999.

Kemnitzer, Luis. 1994. "Personal Memories of Alcatraz, 1969," *American Indian Culture and Research Journal* 18, no. 4(1994): 103–109.

Smith, Paul Chaat and Robert Allen Warrior. *Like a Hurricane: The Indian Movement from Alcatraz to Wounded Knee.* New York: The New Press, 1996.

Smith, Sherry L. *Hippies, Indians, & the Fight for Red Power.* New York: Oxford University Press, 2012.

Talbot, Steve. "Free Alcatraz: The Culture of Native American Liberation," *Journal of Ethnic Studies* 6, no. 3 (Fall, 1978): 80–89.

Winfrey, Robert Hill. "Civil Rights and the American Indian: Through the 1960s." PhD diss., Department of History, University of Oklahoma, Norman, 1986.

American Indian Movement, Early History

During the summer of 1968, several hundred people from the Minneapolis-St. Paul Native American community, most of whom were Anishinabe (also known as Chippewa and Ojibway), met with several activists, including Herb Powless, Dennis Banks, Russell Means, George Mitchell, Clyde Bellecourt, Harold Goodsky, Eddie Benton-Banai, Mary Jane Wilson, Pat Ballanger, and several others. They demanded relief from police harassment in the community, as well as from federal Indian policies that prevented Native people from controlling their own lives.

The AIM was created at these meetings. High unemployment, substandard housing, illness, poverty, and racist treatment by police compelled the new group to reexamine treaty rights and create a program that sought reclamation of Native lands and rights. At its founding meetings in 1968, "American Indian Movement" was not the consensus first choice for a name. It was "Concerned Indians of

America," until everyone realized that the name would be abbreviated "CIA"—as in "Central Intelligence Agency."

An "Indian patrol" started to follow police in Native American neighborhoods, modeled on Black Panther patrols in Minneapolis and Oakland, California (Cohen, 1973). Arrests of Native Americans declined within a few months to citywide averages. Charles Deegan Sr. was the best-known organizer of this patrol. Legal assistance also was provided to people after arrest.

Whereas the National Indian Youth Council (NIYC, organized in 1964) was formed mainly by Native American young people with rural, reservation roots, AIM at the beginning was comprised mainly of young Indians who had grown up in cities. More than half of Native American people in the United States lived in cities by the 1960s. It was not unusual, therefore, that major movements for social justice, such as AIM, should emerge in cities, and then work their way back to reservations. AIM activists rediscovered their tribal identities by returning to the reservations and consulting with elders during the 1970s. In this way, AIM was a product of a half-century of federal-government programs that had relocated many Native American people from reservations to cities. The rationale of these programs was to provide employment. Urbanization also destroyed languages and other manifestations of Native American culture, and hasten assimilation on a "melting pot" model, meanwhile making reservation land available to non-Indian farmers, ranchers, and corporations.

Urbanization degraded people as Native Americans became alienated in the cities, prone to unemployment, poverty, alcoholism, and abuse of illegal drugs. The creation of AIM was a cry for unity and self-affirmation to address all of these problems. Thus the emphasis on community patrols, employment programs, and education, as well as a powerful thrust to define life, culture, and history from a newly appreciated Native perspective.

In 1977, Rachel Bonney wrote in the *American Indian Quarterly*, a journal written and edited largely by American Indian intellectuals:

> Urban Indians face problems not shared with other urban minorities. . . . Difficulties in adjusting to the urban milieu are compounded by assimilation pressures while at the same time Indians face discrimination pressures in areas of employment, housing, welfare services, and ordinary daily life. A value system which stresses brotherhood, sharing and generosity, lack of aggression and competition in interpersonal relationships, and a tendency to withdraw from conflict situations makes acceptance of the values of the dominant society difficult. (Bonney, 1977, 211)

Thus AIM became a cultural hybrid—rediscovering Native traditions, but doing so in a very assertive way that demanded attention from the dominant society. The members of AIM found that they were remaking themselves as well as changing a cultural milieu. Addressing alcoholism became a prominent example because it was so pervasive. One study (Graves, 1970, 37) found that American Indians in Denver were arrested 20 times the rate of Anglos, and eight times that of in-migrating Latinos. The vast majority of arrests (93 percent among Navajos) were for abuse of alcohol.

Members of AIM then sought to

re-establish a sense of awareness in Indian identity and pride in the Indian heritage. . . . Initially they concentrated on problems of discrimination against Indian people, manifested in police harassment and high arrest rates of Indian people, particularly for drunkenness . . . eradication of negative stereotypic images of Indians, the revitalization of Indian sovereignty [with attention to] treaty violations, and the development of Indian nationalism. (Bonney, 1977, 212)

AIM Broadens Its Reach

Once it became established in Minneapolis, AIM began to extend its reach to national treaty and land-ownership issues, as its membership increased and many chapters formed in other cities and on reservations. By late 1972, by one unofficial count, 43 AIM chapters had been started in the United States and another half-dozen in Canada (Churchill, 2008, 639). After two years of developing locally, AIM soon expanded activities beyond Minneapolis. Elsewhere in Minnesota, in 1972, AIM criticized Chippewa leaders when they allowed non-Indians to exploit reservation resources (including fishing rights). Also in Minnesota, AIM blocked traffic at the Cass Lake Convention Center in defense of treaty fishing rights. AIM subsequently expanded its focus to include cultural renewal, employment programs both in cities and in reservation communities across the United States. In addition, AIM also often supported indigenous interests and issues outside the United States.

Opposition to sports-mascot caricatures of indigenous peoples (such as the Washington Redskins, Cleveland Indians, and Atlanta Braves) also became a staple of AIM activity, which sometimes involved organized protests at the Super Bowl and World Series. As early as 1969, AIM advocated a change of mascot for the University of Nebraska at Omaha (UNO) Indians, and won. The UNO Indians became the Mavericks.

While AIM's leadership developed a special talent for headline-grabbling protests, it was more than a media facade. The organization also founded housing programs, an American Indian Opportunities and Industrialization Center (for job training), and AIM Street Medics, as well as a legal-aid center. The organization also developed its own schools, such as the K-12 Heart of the Earth Survival School (started in 1971) and the Little Red Schoolhouse. Taking the Black Panther Party's programs as a model, AIM concentrated on improving the lives of community members, including a news service that brought people reports not available in other media.

At the same time, AIM was expanding its base to reservations, most notably the homeland of the Oglala Sioux at Pine Ridge, South Dakota, where an acute political struggle developed with Tribal Chairman Richard (Dick) Wilson. The struggle between AIM and Wilson also took place within the realm of tribal politics. Russell Means, an Oglala who had helped found AIM, challenged Wilson's bid for reelection in 1974. In the primary, Wilson trailed Means, 667 votes to 511. Wilson won the final election over Means by fewer than 200 votes in balloting that the U.S. Commission on Civil Rights later found to be permeated with fraud. The Civil Rights Commission recommended a new election, which was not held. The General Accounting Office (an arm of Congress) at the same time found that the Wilson regime could not account for $300,000 worth of federal highway funds, but did not levy any penalties. By 1972, AIM also was forming alliances with traditional Native spiritual people, such as Leonard Crow Dog, of the Rosebud reservation (east of Pine Ridge), a Brûlé Lakota, who hosted AIM at an annual sun dance.

From its earliest days, AIM linked its political agenda to those of other minority peoples, finding common cause with the civil-rights movement on issues such as high levels of unemployment, poor housing, and racism. In addition to the Black Panthers, AIM allied with the All African Peoples Revolutionary Party, led by Stokely Carmichael (Kwame Turé). Links also developed with the Chicano-rights group Crusade for Justice, in Denver and with El Centro de la Raza, a Latino-led multicultural organization in Seattle. Activists in AIM also allied with the Brown Berets and Chicano Moratorium, as well as Operation Push, led by Jesse Jackson, with a head office in Chicago, and the Puerto Rican Young Lords Party in New York City. European American activists joined AIM via the Venceremos Brigade and Vietnam Veterans against the War.

The American Indian Movement and black activists made common cause consciously, and often during the late 1960s and early 1970s. Stokely Carmichael, a leader in the Black Panthers as well as the Student Non-violent Coordinating Committee (SNCC), which spearheaded many black sit-ins in the South, was invited to speak with AIM leaders in Rapid City (Smith, 2012, 191). Ralph Abernathy, Martin Luther King's principal assistant in the Southern Christian Leadership Conference (SCLC) visited Wounded Knee during the AIM occupation and told the press:

> I have made a pilgrimage from the tomb of Martin Luther King, Jr. to Wounded Knee. This is a great symbol, I believe. It ought to express to the American people that two great peoples who have suffered greatly in the past are committed to seeking justice together in the future. (Smith, 2012, 199)

Roughly fifteen members of the Wounded Knee Legal Offense/Defense Committee traveled to Omaha in 1973 to hear Angela Davis address a meeting to form a "National Defense Organization Against Racist and Political Repression." Davis' remarks explicitly included American Indians and Latinos as well as blacks (Smith, 2012, 213).

Some of AIM's early strategy was pure media theater. On Thanksgiving weekend, 1970, on the 350th anniversary of the Pilgrim landing at Plymouth Rock, AIM seized a replica of the Mayflower at Plymouth, Massachusetts. AIM argued that Thanksgiving should be regarded as a National Day of Mourning; it used the day to protest continuing taking of Indigenous peoples' resources and lands. A year later, for a few days, AIM members took possession of Mount Rushmore for a few days to point out traditional Lakota Sioux title to South Dakota's Black Hills, in which the sculpture is located. The Lakota consider the Black Hills sacred, and the giant stone portraits of four U.S. presidents a desecration. The Black Hills (*Paha Sapa*, "Hills that are Black" to the Lakota) were designated as theirs in Treaty of Fort Laramie (1868), but were seized in abrogation of the treaty after discovery of rich gold deposits there by a U.S. Army unit led by Col. George Armstrong Custer during 1874.

1972: Nationwide Marching and Seizure of the BIA Headquarters

Playing a leading role on the national stage by late 1972, AIM organized the Trail of Broken Treaties caravan across the United States, from Seattle and San Francisco to Washington, D.C., where it occupied and ransacked the Bureau of Indian Affairs (BIA) headquarters, in protest of its policies, demanding enforcement of treaties and fundamental change days before a U.S. national election. (A year before AIM's seizure of the BIA headquarters in 1972, a delegation had marched into the same building and occupied it for a few hours before meeting with Louis Bruce, a Mohawk and Lakota who was BIA Commissioner. They talked and then departed.)

Having arrived in Washington a week before national elections in 1972, AIM put a list of "Twenty Points" before President Richard Nixon and Congress, which demanded:

1. Restoration of treaty making (ended by Congress in 1871).

2. Establishment of a treaty commission to make new treaties (with sovereign Native Nations).

3. An address by Indian leaders to Congress.

4. Review of treaty commitments and violations.

5. Consideration by the Senate of Unratified treaties.

6. A pledge by the United States to govern all Indians according to treaty terms.

7. Relief for Native Nations for treaty rights violations.

8. Recognition of the right of Indians to interpret treaties.

9. A joint Congressional committee on reconstruction of Indian relations.

10. Restoration of 110 million acres of land taken from Native Nations by the United States.

11. Restoration of terminated rights.

12. Repeal of state jurisdiction of Native tribes and nations.

13. Federal protection for offenses against Indians.

14. Abolishment of the Bureau of Indian Affairs.

15. Creation of a new office of Federal Indian Relations.

16. Creation of a new office to remedy breakdown in the constitutionally pre-scribed relationships between the United States and Native Nations.

17. Laws making Native nations immune to commerce regulation, taxes, and trade restrictions by states.

18. Protection of American Indian religious freedom and cultural integrity.

19. Establishment of national Indian voting with local options; free national Indian organizations from governmental controls.

20. Affirm[ation] of health, housing, employment, economic development, and education for all Indian people. (Wittstock and Salinas, n.d.)

"Unlike the American civil-rights movement, with which it has been compared, AIM has seen self-determination and racism differently," wrote Laura Waterman Wittstock, and Elaine J. Salinas. "Desegregation was not a goal. Individual rights were not placed ahead of the preservation of Native Nation sovereignty" (Wittstock and Salinas, n.d.).

Reacting Strongly to Murders of Indians

AIM reacted quickly and viscerally against cases in which whites who killed American Indians were let off easily by local police, prosecutors, and courts. Raymond Yellow Thunder, age 51, was murdered in Gordon, Nebraska, by Leslie and Melvin Hare, two young white brothers. At trial, they were sentenced for manslaughter, not murder, which inflamed Native people in the area. AIM called a rally at Gordon, Nebraska, in protest.

In Gordon, AIMsters streamed, about 1,400 strong, into the town, doubling its population, to protest Yellow Thunder's death. A county prosecutor dismissed the assault that killed Yellow Thunder as "a cruel practical joke . . . by pranksters" (Hendricks, 2006, 28). It was a context in which a one-time Rapid City chief of police had suggested lodging drunken Indians in garbage cans. With his usual media-snaring flair for the dramatic, Russell Means told the rally that Hares would be charged with murder within 72 hours, or AIM would wipe the town of Gordon off the map. The Hare brothers soon became two rare whites to be prosecuted, convicted, and then imprisoned for homicide of a Native American.

During January 1973, AIM gathered in Rapid City to plan its new year when reports arrived that a young Oglala, Wesley Bad Heart Bull, had been lethally stabbed in Buffalo Gap, nearby Bad Heart Bull, a Lakota, was stabbed to death at a bar off the reservation by Darrell Schmidt, a white male, who was arrested but released on $5,000 bail, and charged only with assault.

Local police and prosecutors showed no inclination to seek justice, so Bad Heart Bull's mother asked AIM for assistance. Arriving in Custer, according to one account,

> The Indians were then met by a combined force of local, county, and state police tactical units, overseen by FBI observers. In the ensuing struggle, the Custer County Courthouse and the local chamber of commerce building were set ablaze and most of the Indians, including Russell Means, Dennis Banks, and Bad Heart Bull's mother Sarah were subsequently arrested on charges of riot and arson. The trials dragged on for years and resulted in convictions of most of the defendants. Sarah Bad Heart Bull was sentenced to serve a year in jail, while her son's killer never spent a day behind bars. (Churchill, 2008, 641)

Shortly after the riot in Custer, Richard Wilson convinced the BIA that he should supervise the vote that might impeach him. Wilson was retained by a 14 to 0 vote of the Tribal Council, after which he celebrated by declaring any political meeting on the reservation illegal. At this point, traditional elders at Pine Ridge asked AIM to intervene, setting the stage for the 71-day siege at Wounded Knee.

Seizure of Wounded Knee (1973)

In February, 1973, following its occupation of the BIA headquarters, AIM seized the small community of Wounded Knee, South Dakota, site of a major massacre in 1890, to protest corruption in the U.S.-sanctioned government of the Pine Ridge reservation led by Wilson. At Wounded Knee, AIM seized the Sacred Heart Church and the Gildersleeve Trading Post. This occupation provoked an armed stand-off that lasted 71 days, into May. Two people were shot to death, at least 12 were injured, and about 1,200 arrested (Minnesota Historical Society, n.d.). The confrontation also became a worldwide media event that focused attention on problems afflicting American Indians.

AIM had planned a press conference at Wounded Knee February 27, 1973, about the lack of civil rights at Pine Ridge. The site was chosen because as many as 350 Native people had been slaughtered there late in December 1890 in what the U.S. Army still calls the last "battle" of the Plains Indian wars. About 150 opponents of the Wilson regime gathered at a small hamlet near the grave site (a trading post and a church comprised most of it). Media were called.

The activists soon learned that the Guardians of the Oglala Nation (GOONs), a tactical squad established by Wilson with BIA money, had ringed the area with roadblocks, sealing the press out, and preventing their escape. What had been planned as a single afternoon of protest was turning into a 71-day siege, as dozens of FBI agents arrived, followed soon thereafter, by the first week of March, by at least 300 armed federal marshals and BIA police SWAT teams. The people inside took some old guns from the trading post and began to live off food in a freezer until they arranged smuggling routes through the local rolling hills between roadblocks. The police ringing the hamlet stopped and arrested anyone who approached in a motor vehicle, a total of several hundred people.

Within days, the area had the look of a battle site, roamed by armored personnel carriers, surveyed from the air by reconnaissance aircraft from the Strategic Air Command in Omaha. At night, military flares lit up the sky. Grass was burned in a half-mile radius around the encampment to impede smuggling. An estimated half-million rounds of ammunition were fired into the hamlet as Buddy Lamont, an Oglala, and Frank Clearwater, an Apache, were killed, and many others were wounded. The occupiers gave up after officials agreed to an investigation of Wilson's behavior, and a meeting with elders about violations of the Fort Laramie Treaty, neither of which took place. In the meantime, media from all over the world arrived in droves to witness the modern "Indian war," and received a full dose of life at Pine Ridge.

At the Academy Awards, which took place during the Wounded Knee occupation, Marlon Brando turned down an award for his role in "The Godfather" to support Native American efforts. Brando had long been involved in Northwest fishing rights, and after Wounded Knee provided aid to some AIM members while the FBI pursued them.

AIM's International Profile

Following the Wounded Knee occupation, AIM acquired a true international profile, and used it through the International Indian Treaty Council (IITC), headed by Jimmie Durham, who used the United Nations as a forum for indigenous rights.

In 1977, the IITC achieved consultative status at the UN, the first Native American group with it. Durham organized an "Indian Summer in Geneva," and played an important role in the initiation of the UN Working Group on Indigenous Populations during 1982. This group provided a channel to report abuses of Native rights to the UN; it also played a key role for drafting a Universal Declaration of Rights of Indigenous Peoples for debate and affirmation by the UN General Assembly. This measure moved ponderously, however, and may have outlived the IITC; a draft was completed in 1993, and was still under review by the UN Commission on Human Rights as of this writing.

The "Reign of Terror"

Following the Trail of Broken Treaties and occupation of Wounded Knee, Russell Means returned home to the Pine Ridge Reservation, where he was an enrolled member of the Oglala Lakota and a property owner, to find himself banned by President Dick Wilson, a vehement opponent of AIM. Wilson began making use of his GOONs to trail and in some cases to assassinate members of AIM at Pine Ridge. Quickly, Pedro Bissonette organized the Oglala Sioux Civil Rights Organization (OSCRO) to impeach Wilson.

The Denver Civil Rights Division conducted an investigation during the summer of 1975 that supported Wilson opponents' allegations that they had been targets of a "reign of terror" during the previous two years on the part of Wilson's regime with the complicity of the federal government. At least 66 AIM members or supporters were killed between the end of the Wounded Knee occupation in May, 1973 and the end of 1976.

The Denver Civil Rights Division called for a Congressional investigation of the FBI's behavior at Pine Ridge, but nothing happened. In the meantime, AIM called the GOONs a death squad that operated on a model used against dissidents by military governments in Latin America with support and funding by the Central Intelligence Agency. The supporters of AIM described counterintelligence operations (COINTELPRO in the FBI's jargon) that also had been used to destroy large parts of the Black Panther Party.

Shootout at the Jumping Bull Ranch, 1975

In the midst of the "reign of terror," a shootout at the Jumping Bull Ranch at Pine Ridge June 26, 1975, took the lives of two FBI agents: Ronald Williams and Jack Coler, and one Indian man, Joe Stuntz Killsright, an AIM member from Coeur d'Alene, Idaho. The FBI blocked the area, not allowing media access, claiming that AIM guerillas had drawn the agents into the area (they had appeared on their own accord with a warrant for a pair of stolen cowboy boots). The reservation soon was being roamed by 400 FBI agents in combat clothing, carrying M-16s, looking for suspects, raiding homes of suspected AIM members. All of this was part of the Reservation Murders (RESMURS) investigation. In the meantime, the FBI still was complaining that it lacked manpower to investigate many other reservation murders.

Leonard Peltier later was convicted of the FBI agents' killings after two other defendants (Bob Robideau and Dino Butler) were found not guilty. Butler and Robideau were tried in Cedar Rapids, Iowa, during June 1976. The government's case was damaged by false witnesses; both were found not guilty on all counts by an all-white jury. The jury, in its verdict, said that Butler and Robideau had acted in self-defense, doing "only what any reasonable person would do, under the circumstances" that had been created on Pine Ridge (Churchill, 2003, 280).

The FBI never investigated the death of Stuntz Killsright, who had been killed by a sniper. The scene immediately was besieged by 150 BIA police in riot gear and a number of vigilantes, along with William Janklow.

National Marches in 1976 and 1978

AIM also organized other caravans, one of which was the Trail of Self-Determination (1976) and two Longest Walks (1978 and 1988), with a focus on spiritual issues, native sovereignty and, anti-Indian legislation in Congress that sought to terminate treaty rights and limit water rights.

The first of two Longest Walks began on February 11, 1978, on Alcatraz Island, and concluded 3,200 miles later July 15, 1978, at the Washington Monument in Washington, D.C., with several thousand people of all races rallying behind a sacred pipe that had been carried the entire distance. Traditional elders then smoked tobacco that had been loaded into the pipe on Alcatraz Island. Boxer Muhammad Ali, actor Marlon Brando, Senator Ted Kennedy, and other celebrities joined the rally. A week later, the U.S. Congress passed the American Indian Religious Freedom Act.

According to Troy R. Johnson, "The event was . . . intended to expose and challenge the backlash movement against Indian treaty rights that was gaining strength around the country and in Congress. This backlash could be seen in a growing number of bills before Congress to abrogate Indian treaties and restrict Indian rights" (Johnson, 2008, 297).

Ten years later, during July of 1988, a second Longest Walk arrived in Washington, D.C., having trekked 8,200 miles on a circuitous walk through 26 states (on a northern and a southern route) that had started from the San Francisco Bay area, with more than 100 Native nations and tribes represented. Non-Native people also took part, as did international peoples from as far away as New Zealand's Maoris. The political agenda of this walk, detailed in a 30-page "Manifesto of Change," focused on protection for Native American sovereignty, including sacred sites, as well as environmental problems on Native lands, including global warming.

Disruption by the FBI

AIM's media-savvy approach to issues that made headlines also provoked the FBI, which regarded AIM as a terrorist group, to develop programs that would corrode AIM members' trust in each other. These tactics also were used against other minority organizations that President Richard Nixon deemed extremist, such as the Black Panther Party through programs such as COINTELPRO (Counter-Intelligence Program), which applied the "snitch jacket," as some members of these groups became convinced that others were spying on them for the government. While some informers (such as Douglass Frank Durham) were real, others probably were not. Some leaders (the best known was Anna Mae Aquash) may have been murdered on suspicion of FBI involvement.

The Wounded Knee occupation resulted in a large number of FBI investigations and federal trials (Wounded Knee Trials), most of which ended with not-guilty verdicts. On the reservation, a shooting war developed between AIM, its supporters, and police supported by the federal government and Wilson's regime. At least 66 people died, many as a result of political murders. During this period two FBI agents were shot to death, and an international dragnet resulted in a conviction of Leonard Peltier.

The effects of the FBI's campaign were devastating. During the 1970s, AIM broke into factions that have persisted since. The group was never nationally cohesive, and never maintained a national membership list. The FBI's tactics accelerated AIM's disintegration.

A Factional Split

Following the 1970s, when the AIM helped to transform the activist landscape in the United States, differences in personalities and political orientations caused the organization to break into antagonistic factions during the 1980s, a pattern that has continued to the present.

By the late1980s, AIM had one nucleus in Minneapolis, with a number of loose allies in other cities. Major dissent centered in Colorado. The factions even investigated and compiled reports criticizing each other in so-called "Tribunals." The AIM Grand Governing Council (GGC) in Minneapolis asserted a right of ownership to the name "American Indian Movement" and associated trademarks. Many other chapters did not accept the GGC's control or direction.

The Minneapolis office asserted control of a national network, but AIM had never had a national membership list. Dennis Banks and the Bellecourt brothers usually spoke for this group and its AIM Grand Governing Council. Vernon Bellecourt died in 2007.

At the same time, a network of dissident chapters formed a loose coalition with Colorado AIM. Ward Churchill and Russell Means, as well as Glen Morris led the

AIM-International Confederation of Autonomous Chapters, based in Denver and Boulder. The divide became so deep that each faction accused the other of betraying the movement.

Further Reading

Bonney, Rachel A. "The Role of AIM Leaders in Indian Nationalism," *American Indian Quarterly* 3, no. 3 (Autumn, 1977): 209–24.

Churchill, Ward. "American Indian Movement," in Bruce E. Johansen and Barry Pritzker, eds. *Encyclopedia of American Indian History*. Santa Barbara, CA: ABC-CLIO, 2008, 638–46.

Cohen, Fay G. "The Indian Patrol in Minneapolis: Social Control and Social Changes in an Urban Context." PhD dissertation, University of Minnesota, 1973.

Graves, Theodore D. "The Personal Adjustment of Navajo Indian Migrants to Denver, Colorado," *American Anthropologist* 72, no. 1 (1970): 35–54.

Hendricks, Steve. *The Unquiet Grave: The FBI and the Struggle for the Soul of Indian Country*. New York: Thunder's Mouth Press, 2006.

Johnson, Troy R. "Red Power," in Bruce E. Johansen and Barry Pritzker, eds. *Encyclopedia of American Indian History*. Santa Barbara, CA: ABC-CLIO, 2008, 292–97.

Minnesota Historical Society. "American Indian Movement (AIM)." History Topics. No date. http://www.mnhs.org/library/tips/history_topics/93aim.html

Smith, Sherry L. *Hippies, Indians, & the Fight for Red Power*. New York: Oxford University Press, 2012.

Wittstock, Laura Waterman and Elaine J. Salinas. "A Brief History of the American Indian Movement." No date. http://www.aimovement.org/ggc/history.html

Americans Before Columbus

Americans Before Columbus (ABC), a newspaper published by the National Indian Youth Council (NIYC) beginning in October, 1963, became the first activist organ of the "Red Power" era, "articulating a new ideology that was at once traditional, new, and even militant . . . forcefully expressing the organization's core values of tribal sovereignty, self-determination, treaty rights, and cultural preservation" (Shreve, 2011, 13, 94). Very quickly, more than 180 Native tribal councils subscribed to it. Bruce Wilkie (Makah) and Hank Adams (Assiniboine-Sioux) played a major role in *ABC*'s early editions as it spread word of "fish-ins" among Native peoples in Western Washington after 1964. The membership of NIYC soon grew to more than 3,000 people, as fishing rights became NIYC's first major focus.

Tillie Walker, a Mandan who worked at United Scholarship Service (USS), which helped supply Native students with academic financial support out of an office in Denver, was *ABC's* first editorial coordinator. The first edition took issue with the National Congress of American Indians (NCAI), whose members were characterized as wasting "time, energy, and money on petty tattle-tailing and personal vengeance" (Shreve, 2011, 115). The second edition turned the focus to fishing rights in Washington State, most notably to the state's crackdown against the Muckleshoots, Puyallups, and Quinaults. The paper compared the "war" against the Indian fishing rights in the Pacific Northwest to the extermination of the buffalo on the Great Plains. By 1969, *ABC* was circulating 8,000 copies per issue (Shreve, 2011, 185).

The newsletter contained many notable names, such as Native American poet Joy Harjo and author, scholar, and activist Vine Deloria Jr. It also published a special edition on Native American religious freedom. It also inquired into reasons for Indians' high rates of alcohol abuse, the implications of language loss, and surveys of issues affecting indigenous peoples throughout the Western hemisphere. To establish an international context, the editors of *ABC* pointed out that Native peoples within the United States comprised less than one-tenth of those in the western hemisphere.

Some issues of *ABC* are archived on microfilm at the Center for Southwest Research in the Zimmerman Library at the University of New Mexico Library (ZIM CSWR Mfilm E51 A26 1961–1965), along with the NIYC magazine *Aborigine* (ZIM CSWR Mfilm E51 A26 1961–1965). Some editions of *ABC*, singularly or in small groups, are sometimes also sold by rare book dealers for as much as $50, despite their acidifying newsprint.

Further Reading

"ABC: Americans Before Columbus." *OCLC On-line Union Catalogue.* Dublin, OH: OCLC, 1998.

Bloom, Alexander and Wini Brienes. *Takin' it to the Streets.* New York: Oxford University Press, 1995.

National Indian Youth Council. Web page. http://www.niyc-alb.org/history.htm.

Shreve, Bradley. *Red Power Rising: The National Indian Youth Council and the Origins of Native Activism.* Norman: University of Oklahoma Press, 2011.

Anderson, Wallace (Mad Bear)

(1927–1985)
Tuscarora. Treaty-Rights Activist

Wallace "Mad Bear" Anderson was a noted Native American rights activist during the 1950s, before a general upsurge in Native self-determination efforts a decade later that gave birth to the AIM. Anderson, working among the Haudenosaunee (Iroquois) used direct-confrontations strategies that AIM later utilized. Like many

AIM activists, Anderson late in his brief life became a spokesman for Native American sovereignty in several international forums.

Edmund Wilson recalled Anderson as "a young man in a lumberjack shirt and cap, broad of build, with a round face and lively black eyes" was born in Buffalo, New York, and raised on the Tuscarora reservation near Niagara Falls (Wilson, 1960, 67). The name "Mad Bear" was first used by Anderson's grandmother in reference to his hot-headedness. He adopted the name from her. Anderson served in the U.S. Navy during World War II at Okinawa. He later also served in Korea. Anderson became an activist after his request for a GI Bill loan to build a house on the Tuscarora reservation was rejected.

Anderson led protests against Iroquois payment of New York State income taxes as early as 1957. At the height of the protest, several hundred Akwesasne (St. Regis) Mohawks marched to the Massena, New York state courthouse, where they burned summonses issued for unpaid taxes. In 1958, Anderson played a leading role in protests of a 1,383-acre seizure of Tuscarora land by the New York Power Authority for construction of a dam and reservoir. Anderson and other Iroquois deflated workers' tires and blocked surveyors' transits. When the Tuscaroras refused to sell the land, a force of about 100 state troopers and police invaded their reservation. Anderson met the troopers and police with 150 nonviolent demonstrators who blocked their trucks by lying on the road.

During March 1959, Anderson helped compose a declaration of sovereignty at the Iroquois Six Nations Reserve in Brantford, Ontario, the settlement established by Joseph Brant and his followers after the American Revolution. The declaration prompted an occupation of the reserve's Council House by Royal Canadian Mounted Police. During July 1959, Anderson traveled to Cuba with a delegation of Iroquois and other Native Americans to exchange recognitions of sovereignty with Fidel Castro, whose revolutionary army recently had seized power in Havana.

At about the same time, Anderson coordinated opposition to condemnation of Tuscarora land involving New York State construction of a dam to increase the power-generation capacity of Niagara Falls. "The case was appealed," wrote Vine Deloria Jr. in *Behind the Trail of Broken Treaties* (1974), "and the federal court had to do mental gymnastics in order to find in favor of the state. Twisting language in an unprecedented manner, the federal courts characterized the New York Power Authority as a federal instrumentality with powers of condemnation, and denied the Tuscarora the right to protect their lands" (Deloria, 1974, 20–21).

The Tuscaroras assembled a demonstration in front of Dwight Eisenhower's White House, but no one granted their request for a meeting. With Anderson in the lead, the group invaded the Department of the Interior and attempted to make a citizens' arrest of Indian Commissioner Glenn L. Emmons. "War whoops echoed down the staid halls of the building, and startled bureaucrats watched as the Iroquois stalked the halls of Interior" wrote Deloria (1974:21). "He was spirited out a side door as the Indian contingent, blood in their eyes, came into his office. Indians watched and laughed as the Interior Department tried to pass the incident off as the actions of a few communist-inspired radicals. But they never forgot that the Tuscaroras had stood up for Indian treaty rights and the international status of the tribes at a time when few men were willing to stand for any principles at all" (Deloria, 1974, 21).

During 1967, Anderson formed the North American Indian Unity Caravan, which traveled the United States for six years as the types of activism that he had pioneered spread nationwide. Anderson also gathered opposition to termination legislation and carried it to Washington, D.C., from 133 Native American tribes and nations, effectively killing the last attempt to buy out reservations in the United States. In 1969, Anderson helped initiate the takeover of Alcatraz Island.

Anderson died during December, 1985 after a long illness at age 58 on the Tuscarora Reservation in New York State.

Further Reading

Anderson, Wallace (Mad Bear). "The Lost Brother: An Iroquois Prophecy of Serpents," in Shirley Hill Witt and Stan Steiner, eds. *The Way: An Anthology of American Indian Literature.* New York: Vintage, 1972, 243–47.

Deloria, Vine, Jr. *Behind the Trail of Broken Treaties.* New York: Delacorte Press, 1974; Austin: University of Texas Press, 1985.

Wilson, Edmund. *Apologies to the Iroquois.* New York: Farrar, Straus & Cudahy, 1960.

Aquash, Anna Mae Pictou

(1945–1976)
MicMac. American Indian Movement Activist

On February 24, 1976, Roger Amiott, a rancher, found the body of Anna Mae Aquash, one of the AIM's leading activists, near Wanblee, in the northeastern section of the Pine Ridge Indian Reservation. "At a quarter to three in the afternoon, a rancher on that part of the South Dakota steppe that crumbles in to the badlands was looking for a place to run a fence when he turned a bend in a gully and found, curled on its left side, clothed in a maroon jacket and blue jeans, and looking for all the world like someone sleeping in perfect peace, a corpse," wrote Steve Hendricks (2006, 3). This discovery initiated a decades-long debate over who had killed her, which shed much light on the tense relationship between AIM and the FBI during the 1970s.

Aquash was one of at least 66 people, many of them AIM activists, who were killed for political reasons on the Pine Ridge reservation during that period. Most of these murders were never investigated by the FBI, which is responsible for fact-finding related to major crimes on most Indian reservations.

Rebecca Julian, left, Anna Mae Pictou Aquash's eldest sister, and Aquash's eldest daughter, Denise Maloney, hold a portrait of Aquash Sunday, June 20, 2003, at Shubenacadie, Nova Scotia. (AP Photo/Carson Walker)

Early Life

Aquash was born of MicMac (or Mi'kmaq) heritage March 27, 1945, near Shubenacadie, Nova Scotia. Her family (she had two older sisters and an older brother) spent much of their youth in Pictou Landing, a MicMac reserve. Her father earned a small income creating beadwork, and exercised a traditional influence on his children. He died when Anna Mae was only 11 years of age, however. Her mother had left the family. Anna Mae, whom many people would later say was a brilliant woman, dropped out of Milford High School after the ninth grade.

By the early 1960s, Anna Mae was picking potatoes and berries in Maine; later she moved to Boston with Jake Maloney, also a MicMac. She worked at a sewing factory while he opened a karate school. They had two children, then moved back to New Brunswick, and married. Their marriage ended in 1969, after which Anna Mae moved back to Boston, went back to work sewing, and volunteered at the Boston Indian Council. Having heard AIM cofounder Russell Means speak, she was inspired to become active in the organization.

She also came to know Nogeeshik Aquash, an Ojibwa artist from Walpole Island in Ontario, Canada and, with him, took part in AIM's Trail of Broken Treaties in 1972, as well as the occupation of Wounded Knee a few months later. Anna Mae and Nogeeshik married in a traditional Lakota ceremony during the Wounded Knee occupation. For the next three years, Anna Mae became closely allied with AIM leadership in various activities across the United States.

Aquash was a close friend of Leonard Peltier, Dennis Banks, Russell Means, and others who were arrested and charged in connection with the Wounded Knee occupation in 1973, and other events. Following the shooting deaths of FBI agents Jack Coler and Ronald Williams at the Jumping Bull Compound on the Pine Ridge Indian Reservation in June, 1975, Aquash was pursued and arrested by the FBI as a possible material witness to the crime.

Controversy Following Aquash's Death

W. O. Brown, a pathologist who performed autopsies under contract with the Bureau of Indian Affairs, arrived at Pine Ridge a day after discovery of Aquash's body. After examining the body, Brown announced that the woman, who still had not been officially identified, had died of exposure to the brutal South Dakota winter.

The FBI decided that the only way to identify the woman was to sever her hands and send them to the FBI's crime laboratories near Washington, D.C. Agents on the scene thought that the body was too badly decomposed to take fingerprints at Pine Ridge. Ken Sayres, BIA police chief at Pine Ridge, would say later that no one had been called to the morgue to attempt identification of the body before the hands were severed.

A week after the body was found, Aquash—now missing her hands as well as her identity—was buried at Holy Rosary Catholic Cemetery, Pine Ridge. On March 3 the FBI announced Aquash's identity. Her family was notified of the death on March 5. The family refused to believe that she had died of natural causes. At 32 years of age, Aquash had been in good health and knew how to survive cold weather. She did not drink alcohol or smoke tobacco. Her friends remembered that she had smuggled food past federal government roadblocks into Wounded Knee during another brutal South Dakota winter, almost three years to the day before her body was found. A new autopsy was demanded.

In the midst of the controversy, Aquash's body was exhumed. Her family retained an independent pathologist, Gary Peterson, of St. Paul, Minnesota. Peterson reopened Aquash's skull and found a .32-caliber bullet, that he said had been fired from a gun placed at the base of her neck. The bullet was easy to find and Peterson thought it should have been found during the first autopsy. Asked about the bullet he had not found, W. O. Brown, the BIA coroner, replied, according to an account in the *Washington Star,* May 24, 1976, "A little bullet isn't hard to overlook" (Johansen and Maestas, 1979, 106).

Following identification of Aquash, the Canadian government and the U.S. Commission on Civil Rights demanded an investigation. The U.S. Justice Department announced that it would look into the case, but the "investigation" languished in bureaucratic limbo. Aquash's friends refused to let her spirit pass away. On March 14, Aquash's body was wrapped in a traditional star quilt, as several women from Oglala Village mourned her passing for two days and two nights.

The Conviction of Arlo Looking Cloud

Twenty-seven years after Aquash's murder, federal agents on April 2, 2003, arrested a man and charged him with the death. Arlo Looking Cloud, 49, was arrested in Denver and pleaded innocent to a charge of first-degree murder. Looking Cloud had worked as a security guard for AIM, checking people at the gates of events and patrolling the grounds, said Paul DeMain, editor of the bimonthly newspaper *News from Indian Country*. At the time, AIM was beset by internal disputes (and was infiltrated by FBI informers), DeMain said (Walker, 2003).

On February 6, 2004, Looking Cloud was convicted of the murder. In *The Unquiet Grave* (2006), Steve Hendricks built a case that members of AIM had assassinated Aquash after FBI infiltrators, using disinformation techniques (applying a "snitch jacket") convinced some AIM leaders that she was a government informer. In an Interview in *News from Indian Country* by Shelly Davis (Mid-January, 1994), Bob Robideau claimed that the Bellecourt brothers had provocateured (or bad jacketed) Aquash as an FBI agent.

In *The Unquiet Grave*, Hendricks asked whether Looking Cloud acted alone. If not, who else was involved? Hendricks asserted that is that a number of AIM leaders—no one knows precisely who—ordered Aquash shot on suspicion that she was acting as an FBI informant. But was she? "Only the FBI could separate the snitches from the snitch-jacketed," Hendricks (2006, 61) wrote, recalling that the FBI had seeded AIM with informants purposefully to create the paranoia that made such an assassination likely. Thus, Aquash's grave (and a number of others) remains "unquiet" to this day.

Further Reading

Banks, Dennis and Richard Erdoes. *Ojibwa Warrior: Dennis Banks and the Rise of the American Indian Movement*. Norman: University of Oklahoma Press, 2004.

Brand, Johanna. *The Life and Death of Anna Mae Aquash*. Toronto: Lorimer, 1978.

Churchill, Ward and Jim Vander Wall. *Agents of Repression: The FBI's Secret War Against the Black Panther Party and the American Indian Movement*. Boston: South End Press, 1990.

DeMain, Paul. "AIM Supporters Convene in Minneapolis for Ceremony." 1994, http://www.coloradoaim.org/history/1994PaulDemainsupportstheBellecourts.htm.

Downs. Alan C. "Aquash, Anna Mae Pictou," in Bruce E. Johansen and Barry M. Pritzker eds. *Encyclopedia of American Indian History*, Santa Barbara, CA: ABC-CLIO, 2007, 651–53.

Hendricks, Steve. *The Unquiet Grave: The FBI and the Struggle for the Soul of Indian Country*. New York: Thunder's Mouth Press, 2006.

Johansen, Bruce. "Peltier and the Posse." *The Nation*, October 1, 1977, 304–307.

Johansen, Bruce E. and Roberto F. Maestas. *Wasi'chu: The Continuing Indian Wars*. New York: Monthly Review Press, 1979.

Matthiessen, Peter. *In the Spirit of Crazy Horse*. New York: Viking, 1991.

Walker, Carson. "Man is Arrested in Activist's Death." Associated Press in Indigenous-NewsNetwork@topica.com, April 2, 2003.

Weir, David and Lowell Bergman. "The Killing of Anna Mae Aquash." *Rolling Stone*, April 7, 1977, 51–55.

Arizona American Indian Movement Chapter

During the 1990s, the Arizona chapter of the AIM was active in naming issues, most notably sports mascots and geographical names involving the "S-word"—squaw. The chapter, with members in Phoenix, Flagstaff, Tempe, and other locales, also took a stand against exploitation of Naive ceremonies by non-Indians, as well as in favor of compassion with regard to immigration issues involving Arizona's border with Mexico. The AIM Chapter in Arizona, once also active in several national issues (in opposition to grave desecration, and in favor of a presidential pardon for Leonard Peltier) appeared from lack of Web site traffic to have gone defunct by roughly 2009.

While it was active, the Arizona chapter targeted "plastic medicine men," usually whites, who started "pay to pray" Sacred Inipi Ceremonies, commonly called sweat lodges. "We have been notified, by several sources, that many of these 'sweats' are being run either by non-Indian people, Indian people with no authorization to do so, or for profit," the chapter said in 1998. The chapter said it was taking a "zero-tolerance" policy toward "corrupt or bastardized ceremonies of this type, and the individuals who conduct them. To the charlatans that corrupt our ancient, sacred ceremonies, we say, "you are being watched."

Arizona AIM cautioned participants in these ceremonies to be skeptical, "Be careful who your teachers are. . . . Do not pay to pray" (American Indian, 1998).

"Know your teachers and spiritual leaders. Learn how they live their lives away from these lodges, and ask yourselves if their lives can be held up to scrutiny, and if their lives are an example for others to follow. If not, then find a traditional person, speak with them, and ask if you can join the ceremony conducted by them. Your lives will be better by distancing yourselves from frauds, charlatans and profit-seekers."

Arizona AIM's Youth Council in 1997 became active opposing the exploitation of American Indian names, both in sports mascots and geographical locations. A local focus became the use of "squaw" in several Arizona locations. "The term 'redskins' is one of the most degrading and racist terms used in the common vernacular today," the chapter said. Its members continued: "It is akin to calling your sports teams and mascot the 'niggers,' 'spics,' 'hebs,' or 'chinks.' Imagine, if you will a team called the 'niggers' whose mascot was a Caucasian wearing blackface, a grass skirt, and bone through his nose. Not a very pleasant image, is it? Well neither is the one of a Caucasian dressing up in some . . . store bought regalia, painting his face with his mother's make-up, donning painted chicken feathers and slapping himself in the mouth" (American Indian, 1998).

Arizona AIM pointed out that "The Thesaurus of *Slang lists* the term "squaw" as a synonym for *prostitute*, *harlot*, *hussy*, and *floozy*. In the Algonquin languages the word "squaw" means vagina. In the Mohawk language the word "otsikwaw" means female genitalia. Mohawk women and men found that early European fur traders shortened the word to "squaw" because that represented what they wanted from Mohawk women" (S-Peak, n.d.). The dehumanizing of people has been an integral part of justifying seizure of land, AIM Arizona said.

"Europeans and European Americans spread the use of the word as they moved westward across the continent. Through communication and education American Indian people have come to understand the derogatory meaning of the word. American Indian women claim the right to define ourselves as women and we reject the offensive term 'squaw'" (S-Peak, n.d.).

On immigration issues, Arizona AIM came to the defense of the 24,000-member Tohono O'ohdam Nation (also called Papagos), which has a homeland that spans the U.S.-Mexican border. Several hundred of Tohono O'ohdam live on one side of the, and must use services on the other side. At a time of heightened concern regarding border security, they find themselves at risk of deportation just to visit a doctor at the tribal hospital. They live in Mexico, but the hospital is in the United States. Many lack documents required to cross the border. This problem originated with the Gadsden Purchase (1853), at which time the United States bought land from Mexico, south of the Gila River. For many years, the problem was largely ignored, but as immigration enforcement tightened, a visa required approval of several government agencies on both sides.

Further Reading

"American Indian Movement Arizona Chapter Addresses the Desecration of Sacred Ceremonies." Statement of American Indian Movement, Arizona Chapter, February 2, 1998. http://www.dickshovel.com/dese.html.

"Some Border Compassion, Please. Local Issues: American Indian Movement Arizona Chapter. No date. http://www.oocities.org/aim_arizona_chapter/localissues.html.

"'S-Peak:' American Indian Movement Arizona Chapter. SQUAW: Facts on the Eradication of the "S" Word. No date. http://www.oocities.org/aim_arizona_chapter/S-Peak.html.

"Welcome to the American Indian Movement, Arizona Chapter. What is the American Indian Movement?" No date. http://www.oocities.org/aim_arizona_chapter/.

B

Bad Heart Bull, Wesley

(Died 1973)

During January 1973, the American Indian Movement (AIM) gathered in Rapid City to plan its new year when reports arrived that a young Oglala, Wesley Bad Heart Bull, had been lethally stabbed outside the one bar, which along with a liquor store, a bank, and a post office on a dirt road, comprised the town of Buffalo Gap, 50 miles south of Rapid City. Darrell Schmidt, a white male, was arrested, charged initially with manslaughter, but released on $5,000 bail, after the charge was reduced to assault.

The town of Custer is close enough to Rapid City to be regarded nearly as a suburb. To the Lakota Sioux, both towns are freighted with historical significance. Both are located within the borders of the Great Sioux Nation as defined by the 1868 Treaty of Fort Laramie, and both benefited from the discovery of gold by a U.S. Army unit led by George Armstrong Custer in 1874, two years before a combined force of Lakota and Cheyennes lifted Custer's scalp at the Little Big Horn. The expedition of 1874 was outfitted to explore for gold, and found it, igniting a rush of white prospectors into the Lakotas' sacred *Paha Sapa*, "Hills that are Black."

In late 1972, Rapid City was still recovering from a huge flash flood during June that had killed 231 people in a small city of 40,000 who found themselves swept away by the rampaging waters of Rapid Creek. As large numbers of AIM veterans of the 1972 BIA takeover in Washington, D.C., assembled in the area looking for a spark, one was provided by the murder of Bad Heart Bull. Whites in "Rapid," as it is commonly called there, had cast a nervous eye on the AIM march in the Nebraska border town of Gordon the previous year. The BIA occupation was a major subject of news coverage after that. Now, "Rapid" found itself in the sights of what AIM's leaders called "sensitivity training" (Smith and Warrior, 1996, 178).

Bad Heart Bull's family and the members of AIM took the charge (so common after murders of Indians in South Dakota and Western Nebraska when anyone was charged at all) as an insult. Local police and prosecutors showed no inclination to seek justice, so Bad Heart Bull's mother asked AIM for assistance. Protesting Native people, organized by AIM, then converged on the county courthouse in Custer, S.D., and were met by police in riot gear. Russell Means, David Hill, and Dennis Banks met with the prosecutor, who did not satisfy them, an outcome that instigated a riot during which several hundred people attacked the Custer County

Courthouse and the nearby tiny Custer Chamber of Commerce building. The weather, which was bitterly cold with snow squalls, made setting fires difficult, but after much effort, AIMsters torched two police cars and Custer's small Chamber of Commerce in a very small building.

While Raymond Yellow Thunder had been a family man and career cowboy, Bad Heart Bull had 19 arrests on his rap sheet; he was being sought at time for an assault that had left the victim with facial fractures and a torn windpipe (Smith and Warrior, 1996, 183). The riot in Custer February 6 had more to do with the state of Native civil rights than with Bad Heart Bull's character, however. In death, Bad Heart Bull found himself cast as a hero, a role he had never filled in life. The caravan of AIMsters arrived in cars with trunks loaded with Molotov cocktails.

Members and supporters massed in Custer, the size of the march soon exceeding the population of the town. At the protest, "The Indians were then met by a combined force of local, county, and state police tactical units, overseen by FBI observers. More than 30 people were arrested that afternoon in Custer, most on charges of riot and arson, including Russell Means, Dennis Banks, and Sarah Bad, Heart Bull's Wesley's mother, who was beaten by a nightstick-wielding State Trooper.

By late afternoon, the riot ended and those who hadn't been arrested left town in cars with bumper stickers that had long been a popular AIM reference to another incident that at the time was 96 years in the past: "Custer Had It Coming" (Smith and Warrior, 1996, 185).

Following the riot, something happened that few people had expected: the firebrand leaders of AIM and city officials in Rapid City and nearby towns called an unofficial truce and began to talk seriously what had been afflicting Native people in Western South Dakota. The whites saw another side of the Lakota: elders and children making a case for justice, peace, and economic opportunity on Pine Ridge, a destitute reservation east of Rapid City. The whites were realizing that the riot had reasons: racism exists, requiring remedies. Wallace Black Elk met with Rapid City's superintendent of schools, sharing the scared pipe with an audience, as he said: "A dream comes true as we sit and talk . . . and not turn on each other with guns" (Smith and Warrior, 1996, 188).

Bad Heart Bull's mother, Sarah, was sentenced to one to five years in prison for assaulting a police officer, while the white man who had killed her son received two months' probation (Josephy, 1982, 245). The judge in the case gave her only 24 hours to find a home for her children (Smith and Warrior, 1996, 271).

Further Reading

Johnson, Troy R. "Occupation of Wounded Knee," in Bruce E. Johansen and Barry Pritzker, eds. *Encyclopedia of American Indian History*. Santa Barbara, CA: ABC-CLIO, 2008, 303–305.

Josephy, Alvin M., Jr. *Now That the Buffalo's Gone: A Study of Today's American Indians.* New York: Knopf, 1982.

Smith, Paul Chaat and Robert Allen Warrior. *Like a Hurricane: The American Indian Movement from Alcatraz to Wounded Knee.* New York: New Press, 1996.

Banks, Dennis

(Born 1937)
Anishinabe (Ojibwa)

Beginning during the late 1960s, Dennis Banks became nationally and internationally notable as a prominent Native American activist, primarily as cofounder of the AIM. In that role, he was a leader in the standoff between the FBI and U.S. Army with AIM at Wounded Knee, South Dakota during 1973. Banks played a role in gathering several hundred Indians to protest anti-Native violence, such as the murder of Raymond Yellow Thunder, in Gordon, Nebraska. Banks and other AIM leaders led about 1,400 AIM members and supporters into Gordon, Nebraska, more than doubling the town's population to protest Yellow Thunder's death.

American Indian Movement leader Dennis Banks, holding his daughter Tashina, talked to reporters outside the California State Supreme Court in Sacramento, California, on November 11, 1977. (AP/Wide World Photo)

Early Life

Banks was born April 12, 1937 at Federal Dam on the Leach Lake Objibway (Anishinabe) reservation in Minnesota. He was raised with siblings by his grandparents, and learned traditional life ways from them. At one point, Banks killed a porcupine, and proud of his first kill as a hunter, told his grandparents. Alarmed that he had killed an animal for no good reason, they told him to return to the forest, find the animal's body, and pray over it, then clean and cook it, all the while asking its forgiveness. Banks never forgot this experience.

At the age of 5, in 1942, Banks was forced into the Pipestone boarding school when, as he later recalled, "An agent from the Bureau of Indian Affairs—a large-bellied man smelling of cheap cigars and beer—came into our house waving a bunch of papers and yelling 'Where are those kids who will be going?'" (Banks and Erdoes, 2004, 24). Banks, strong-willed from the beginning, deeply resented the coercion of the boarding schools. He ran away, was caught and beaten, then ran away again.

After finishing his education in a public high school, Banks, in 1954, joined the U.S. Air Force and was stationed in Japan. Returning to poverty in Minnesota a few years later, Banks was arrested and convicted for stealing groceries to feed a family of ten. He was married at the time to "Jeanette, a beautiful Indian woman," who had brought four children into the relationship. They had four more together. "I had a miserable, minimum-wage job that could not support us," Banks said, "So I stole food to put on our table" (Banks and Erdoes, 2004, 60).

After several scrapes with the law, Banks landed a successful job at Honeywell Corp. before he took up AIM as a career. He was put in charge of Native American recruitment, and connected roughly 400 Native people with jobs at the company (Smith and Warrior, 1996, 130).

The Birth of AIM

In prison, Banks was determined to educate himself. At the same time, he was impressed by the civil-rights struggle. Banks studied the history of U.S. government treaty-making with American Indians, the status of treaties in the Constitution's Article VI as "the supreme law of the land." Following his release, Banks was among the original founders of AIM in Minneapolis during 1968, with Russell Means and Vernon and Clyde Bellecourt. The first purpose of AIM was to bring Native Americans together to resist police brutality. With Means, another prominent cofounder of AIM, Banks developed a talent for attracting media attention.

During 1972, Banks was a leading organizer of the Trail of Broken Treaties, which began in San Francisco and Seattle as two converging caravans that arrived in Washington, D.C., a few days before the 1972 national elections. The members of the caravan seized and ransacked the BIA's headquarters.

AIM members and supporters rallied again early in 1973, beginning on February 27 to occupy the Village of Wounded Knee, in South Dakota for 71 days, at a time when, by Banks' account, Indians in South Dakota were treated no better than Blacks in Apartheid-ruled South Africa. Wounded Knee soon was surrounded by several hundred well-armed federal agents and troops, and became a battle site, with fire-fights most nights, and several casualties. Two Indian men died from government gunfire during the siege.

Raw Racism at Wounded Knee

Raw racism was palatable when the hamlet of Wounded Knee was seized. Means found, at a small museum, a 19th-century ledger of receipts for beef. The cavalry captain in charge had invented names for the Indians who were provided with beef, such as "Shits in His Food, She Comes Nine Times, F—ks His Daughter, and Maggott Dick, to recall a few" (Hendricks, 2006, 63).

In his memoir, *Ojibwa Warrior* (2004), Banks recalled dealing with the practical problems of a besieged group under fire. At first, they lived off the stocks of the village grocery store, but these didn't last long. They tried rationing, as well as smuggling food from the outside. The occupants also "liberated" cattle from nearby ranches. Steve Hendricks, author of *The Unquiet Grave: The FBI and the Struggle for the Soul of Indian Country*, described Banks, who used wry humor as he justified killing and eating whites' cattle that he called illegal immigrants in the Independent Oglala Lakota Nation. Joking, Banks and his compatriots called their prey "slow elk." Banks wrote:

> Some of our young warriors who hunted the slow elk were from the city. They didn't quite know how to go about it. Once they led in a cow that none of them knew how to kill or butcher. A white reporter shot and skinned it for them. Another time they came in with an ancient stringy bull whose meat was likely to break our teeth. I put up a poster showing the rear end of a bull with big balls and a cow with an udder. I jokingly wrote underneath: "This is a bull. This is a cow." (Banks and Erdoes, 2004, 189)

Soon to face several federal criminal charges, Banks and compatriots slipped out of Wounded Knee near the end of the siege. While many political murders on Pine Ridge went without investigation by the FBI, the government poured its resources into prosecuting AIMsters who had occupied the hamlet. After 562 arrests and 185 federal indictments related to the occupation, the government obtained only 15 convictions. At a rate of 7.7 percent, that conviction rate was one-tenth the average for criminal trials in the Eighth Circuit, in which the cases were tried, according to Steve Hendricks (2006, 141). The legal campaign was not meant to obtain convictions as much as it was pursued to dismember AIM by tying activists into legal knots.

Following the occupation of Wounded Knee, the Pine Ridge reservation was plunged into more than three years of near-warfare between AIM and its adversaries in the tribal government, during which at least 66 people, most of them affiliated with AIM, were killed violently.

Sanctuary in California and Onondaga

Banks evaded prosecution by taking sanctuary for a time in California under protection of an executive order from Gov. Jerry Brown. California officials refused to extradite him to South Dakota, in part because Attorney General William Janklow, who was given to bombastic overstatement, had pledged to kill AIM members. While in California, Banks earned an associate of arts degree at Davis University, and also served as chancellor of Deganawidah-Quetzalcoatl (D-Q) University, developing educational programs while organizing in 1978 a march from Alcatraz Island to Washington, D.C, called the Longest Walk, protesting legislation in Congress to abrogate treaties.

Later, Banks took shelter on the Onondaga Nation in New York State, where FBI jurisdiction was not accepted by the Haudenosaunee (Iroquois) Confederacy. Banks met with Tadadaho (Speaker) Leon Shenandoah, who placed his request for sanctuary before the confederacy's council. The council debated the issue, and accepted Banks' residency. "You are safe under the wings of the Onondaga Nation," Shenandoah told Banks (Banks and Erdoes, 2004, 332).

Banks's Return to South Dakota

During the late 1980s, Banks's energies were concentrated on measures to protect Native American graves and human remains. He organized a campaign in Kentucky that resulted in statewide legal protections after robbers desecrated Native graves in Uniontown. Banks also organized several more ceremonial runs in the United States and Japan. His first autobiography, *Sacred Soul*, was published in Japan during 1988.

Weary of life in exile, Banks returned to South Dakota in 1984 to face criminal charges stemming from confrontations there. William Janklow, who was governor at the time, told Banks he could return to South Dakota safely. Banks served 13 months in prison on a conviction related to the Custer riot. Afterwards, he taught Native American traditions and organized sacred runs around the world. Later, Banks worked at Pine Ridge as a substance-abuse counselor. He also continued to spent considerable time working on legislation to prevent desecration of Indian graves. Banks also worked on unsuccessful efforts to free Leonard Peltier. Returning to his homeland at Federal Dam in 2002, Banks maintained a natural-foods business.

Banks remained active in Native American politics throughout the 1990s, although he was not as often in the national spotlight. He took acting roles in several films, including War Party, *The Last of the Mohicans*, and *Thunderheart*. During the first half of 1994, Banks helped organize a five-month "Walk for Justice" across the United States on behalf of Peltier. About 400 people took part in the march, and 28 completed the entire 3,000-mile walk. The Walk for Justice ended in Washington, D.C., on July 15, at a rally calling on President Bill Clinton to pardon Peltier. Clinton refused repeated parson appeals throughout his presidency.

Further Reading

Banks, Dennis and Richard Erdoes. *Ojibwa Warrior: Dennis Banks and the Rise of the American Indian Movement.* Norman: University of Oklahoma Press, 2004.

Deloria, Vine, Jr. [1974]. *Behind the Trail of Broken Treaties.* Austin: University of Texas Press, 1985.

Hendricks, Steve. *The Unquiet Grave: The FBI and the Struggle for the Soul of Indian Country.* New York: Thunder's Mouth Press, 2006.

Schaaf, Gregory. "Banks, Dennis," in Bruce E. Johansen and Barry M. Pritzker, eds. *Encyclopedia of American Indian History.* Santa Barbara: ABC-CLIO, 2007, 656–57.

Bellecourt, Clyde

(Born 1936)
(*Nee-Gon-We-Way-We-Dun*, "Thunder before the Storm")

With his brother Vernon Bellecourt, Clyde Bellecourt has been a major figure in the history of the AIM from its founding in Minneapolis during the late 1960s. Both Bellecourts later became leaders of the AIM Grand Governing Council after AIM broke into factions during the late 1970s and early 1980s.

Clyde Bellecourt was a leader of AIM's patrol that trailed police and monitored their abuse in the Minneapolis Native American community. He was a major planner of the Wounded Knee occupation in 1973, as well as several marches and protests. He also was a major figure in the initiation of Native-controlled schools under AIM aegis, as well as an AIM center that provided assistance with Legal matters and the International Indian Treaty Council. While AIM was organizing, Bellecourt met Dennis Banks. At AIM's first organizing meeting in 1968, Clyde gave a passionate speech and, on the basis of it, was elected the group's first chairman.

Clyde Bellecourt has been one of AIM's most active leaders as principal organizer of the National Coalition on Racism in Sports and the Media, as well as board chair of American Indian OIC (Opportunities Industrialization Center, an employment-training program) that has provided ways for American Indians to escape dependence on welfare.

Born May 8, 1936, Clyde Howard Bellecourt, was one of 12 children (seventh eldest) of Charles and Angeline Bellecourt on Minnesota's White Earth Anishinabi (also known as Ojibwa and Chippewa) reservation in and near Leech Lake. From his childhood, Bellecourt asked why Native languages and culture were not respected. He chaffed at having to attend a mission school under strict supervision of Benedictine nuns. Bellecourt's parents spoke the Anishinabi language at home, but he lost it in boarding schools. Later, following the family's move to the Minneapolis urban area, he continued to make trouble in school. Following many detentions, Bellecourt ended up in a prison in St. Cloud, convicted of burglary and armed robbery. He was later transferred to Minnesota's Stillwater State Prison.

Reviving Culture in Prison

At Stillwater, during 1962, Bellecourt was serving time in solitary when Eddie Benton-Banai, also an Ojibwa, contacted him through a peephole, organizing a Native cultural group. Bellecourt soon worked his way out of solitary into an honors dormitory. With Benson, Bellecourt also organized more than two-thirds of more than 100 Native inmates at Stillwater in the Indian American Folklore Group. With William Whipple Warren's *History of the Ojibwe Nation* as a text and a donated drum, Benton and Bellecourt began to revive Native culture in the prison, as inmates in other lockups took notice and organized their own clubs.

Both men were convinced that Native Americans had to take control of their own destinies instead of depending on government. They sought to offer "education about being Indians, instead of just rotting in prison making license plates. I guess we had the first real Indian Studies program in the country" (Matthiessen, 1991, 34). Prisons in the Midwest and Great Plains proved to be an excellent place to educate Indians; less than 1 percent of Minnesota's population was Native, compared to 8 percent of its prison inmates. In neighboring South Dakota, 6 to 7 percent of the people were Indian, but they made up at least 25 percent (sometimes more than 30%) of prisoners.

The club grew as it staged pow-wows and brought some families to Stillwater to take part, using the events as educational experiences. Two years later, in 1964, Bellecourt was freed from prison and he returned to Minneapolis ready to replicate his experiences. He tried to work with churches and government agencies, but found that "they weren't interested in any programs that might have led toward real economic independence for Indians" (Matthiessen, 1991, 34). That frustration, which was experienced by many Native people in Minneapolis and elsewhere, contributed to the birth of AIM.

Following the Wounded Knee occupation, Bellecourt was arrested by the United States, along with Russell Means, Dennis Banks, and others. However, according to Peter Matthiessen's account (1991, 99), "the evidence against Clyde

Bellecourt was so paltry that, as in the case of the 12 indictments filed against him after the Trail of Broken Treaties, the charges were finally dismissed." By the mid-1970s, Bellecourt was devoting much of his time to development of Indian survival schools modeled on AIM's Heart of the Earth Survival School, begun in 1972. By 2010, after almost 40 years, more than 10,000 students had attended this school.

After the year 2000, Bellecourt continued to live in Minneapolis directing the Grand Council of AIM and some other chapters, even as dissident chapters in Colorado and other places rejected his authority. Members of dissident AIM chapters "banned" both Clyde and his brother Vernon during the 1990s, alleging that they had been involved in drug-related activities and had worked covertly for the U.S. government. Both Bellecourts denied all charges.

Bellecourt has continued an active campaign against Indian-themed sports mascots through the National Coalition on Racism in Sports and the Media. He also heads Heart of the Earth, Inc., an AIM interpretive in Minneapolis. Bellecourt also founded a scholarship program that awarded $222,687 between 2005 and 2010. Bellecourt and others in AIM continue to be active in Minneapolis. In 2001, he called upon the Minneapolis public schools to improve Native students' chances of graduating. A study had indicated that only about 15 percent of Native American students who began high school during 1996 had graduated after four years.

Further Reading

Matthiessen, Peter. *In the Spirit of Crazy Horse*. New York: Viking, 1991.

Mosedale, Mike. "Bury My Heart." City Pages (Minneapolis), February 16, 2000. http://www.citypages.com/2000–02–16/news/bury-my-heart/

Nabakov, Peter. *Native American Testimony: A Chronicle of Indian-White Relations from Prophecy to the Present, 1492–1992*. New York: Viking Press, 1991.

Smith, Paul C. and Robert A. Warrior. *Like a Hurricane*. New York: The New Press, 1996, 128–32.

Bellecourt, Vernon

(1931–2007)
(*Wa-Bun-Inini*, "Man of Dawn"), Ojibway. Political Activist

Vernon Bellecourt, one of the AIM's founders during the late 1960s and early 1970s, later gained considerable notoriety for his energetic opposition to the use of Native American images as sports mascots. Through the National Coalition on Racism in Sports and Media, Bellecourt organized many protests against the Washington Redskins, Cleveland Indians, Atlanta Braves, and Kansas City Chiefs, among many

American Indian Movement (AIM) leader Vernon Bellecourt tells reporters AIM leaders will discuss how to get the federal government to honor broken treaties, July 24, 1973. (AP Photo/Ted Powers)

others, as he asserted that the mascots perpetuated negative stereotypes. He once was arrested for burning the Cleveland Indian, Chief Wahoo, in effigy.

Bellecourt was born with the Ojibway name *Wa-Bun-Inini* (Man of Dawn), on October 17, 1931 on the White Earth reservation, Minnesota, to a father who had been disabled during a German mustard gas attack in World War I. His mother raised at least a dozen children in a house without electric power or running water. Vernon left school after eight years. He was sent to prison at age 19 for robbing a bar. In prison, Bellecourt learned how to cut hair as both a barber and a beautician; he started a business along those lines after his release. Moving to Denver, Vernon and his brother Clyde started an AIM chapter to reclaim Native American heritage.

Having been an amateur boxer and an unsuccessful burglar, Bellecourt ended up at Stillwater Prison in Oklahoma for a time, where he staged a short hunger strike, then studied for his GED degree. He also earned a license in steam engineering at the prison's heating plant. Once out of prison, he worked for some time at Northern States Power.

Vernon Bellecourt first gained international recognition during 1972 as a lead organizer of a cross-country AIM caravan, the Trail of Broken Treaties, which embarked in two groups from San Francisco and Seattle, converging before arriving in Washington, D.C., where they occupied the Bureau of Indian Affairs headquarters building a few days before national elections. During the Trail of Broken Treaties, Vernon Bellecourt took part in some very aggressive fund-raising among a Mormon congregation in Salt Lake City. He was physically evicted from the church, but came away with $1,000 that was spent on gas and food (Smith and Warrior, 1996, 143).

Later, Bellecourt became a focus of considerable press coverage after he met with international political leaders such as Col. Muammar el-Quaddafi of Libya, whom he described as a "very warm, sensitive human being" (Martin, 2007, C-12) and Yasir Arafat, leader of the Palestinian Liberation Organization (PLO). He also helped organize conferences on Native American rights sponsored by the United Nations and played a major role in unsuccessful efforts to gain release from prison for Leonard Peltier, who had been convicted of killing two FBI agents on the Pine Ridge reservation. Bellecourt also met with Venezuelan President Hugo Chavez to request discount heating oil for residents of Indian reservations.

After roughly 1990, AIM split into bitterly contemptuous factions. Bellecourt, his brother Clyde, and others maintained a national office of AIM, with a Grand Governing Council, in Minneapolis, but many local-level chapters refused to recognize it. One was Colorado AIM, in which a leading role was played by Ward Churchill, who later was fired from his professorial position in Ethnic Studies by the University of Colorado.

Bellecourt died October 13, 2007 of pneumonia, in Minneapolis.

Further Reading

Martin, Douglas. "Vernon Bellecourt, Mascot Foe, Dies at 75." *New York Times*, October 17, 2007, C-12.

"Penthouse Interview: Vernon Bellecourt. He is the Symbol of the Most Militant Indian Group since Geronimo." *Penthouse International Magazine for Men*, July, 1973, 59–64, 122, 131–32.

Smith, Paul Chaat and Robert Allen Warrior. *Like a Hurricane: The American Indian Movement from Alcatraz to Wounded Knee.* New York: New Press, 1996.

Bissonette, Pedro

(1944–1973)

Pedro Bissonette, the main leader of the Oglala Sioux Civil Rights Organization (OSCRO) was the first to suggest a caravan to Wounded Knee as a "symbolic confrontation," with an *en masse* presence at the massacre site for a press conference to demand a congressional investigation into present-day violations of the 1868 Fort Laramie Treaty, "with special emphasis on the Wilson regime" (Churchill and Vander Wall, 1988, 141). The primary aim was a short-term event, not the prolonged armed confrontation with Wilson's regime and the U.S. government that would involve the first call-out of the U.S. Army on domestic soil since the Civil War.

Bissonette was "a small, scrappy boxer who became a the main spokesman for the traditionals," according to author Peter Matthiessen, who quoted Dennis Banks: "He was a truly spiritual man, I think—one of the few men of that quality I have ever met—and he was also very fair, very generous, trying to take care of his people, with a lot of humor even in hard times" (Matthiessen, 1991, 66).

Pedro Bissonette was born in 1944, a son of Joseph Bissonette Jr. and Susan Lone Elk. Little is known of his early life. As the Wounded Knee siege was ending, on April 27, 1973, Bissonette was arrested by the FBI and charged with "interfering with a federal officer in performance of his duties" (Churchill and Vander Wall, 1988, 200). The FBI then used the arrest as a pretext to pressure Bissonette to testify against AIM members who had been prominent at Wounded Knee, telling him that otherwise he would face up to 90 years in prison. He flatly refused.

On October 17, 1973, Bissonette was confronted on a street in Whiteclay, Nebraska, south of Pine Ridge, by a man that OSCRO later said was GOON Cliff Richards. They engaged in a fistfight, during which Richards was knocked to the sidewalk. Bissonette walked away. Whiteclay was off the reservation and out of the BIA police's and GOONs' jurisdiction, but a dragnet soon developed. Twenty police cars and several aircraft swept the area in search of him. An OSCRO statement said that "They hunted Pedro down like an animal and murdered him in cold blood" (Churchill and Vander Wall, 1988, 201). He died the same day.

Pine Ridge BIA Superintendent Kendall Cunningham told a different story to the Associated Press, that Bissonette had fired shot at two Pine Ridge BIA police who were attempting to arrest him on a warrant, after which he was stopped at a roadblock and again attempted to shoot at an officer. He was then, Cunningham told the AP reporter, "shot fatally at close range" (Churchill and Vander Wall, 1988, 201). The BIA police never produced the weapon that they said Bissonette had used. Wounded Knee Legal Defense/Offense Committee attorney Mark Lane viewed the body shortly after Bissonette was shot and determined that what Cunningham had defined as "shot fatally at close range" consisted of at least seven bullet holes, evidence of a beating, and tear gas burns. The FBI closed the case as "open and shut justifiable homicide" (Churchill and Vander Wall, 1988, 203).

Further Reading

Churchill, Ward and Jim Vander Wall. *Agents of Repression: The FBI's Secret Wars Against the Black Panther Party and the American Indian Movement.* Boston: South End Press, 1988.

Matthiessen, Peter. *In the Spirit of Crazy Horse.* New York: Viking, 1991.

Blatchford, Herbert

(ca. 1936–1996)

Herbert Blatchford, a Navajo, was among a core of Native American students who founded the National Indian Youth Council (NIYC) during the early 1960s, and turned it into a major force in the "Red Power" Movement. The founders of the AIM turned to the NIYC for advice when they formed AIM in 1968.

Blatchford was descended from a family of shepherds who traced their history to the Navajo (Diné) leader Manuelito. Young Herbert was an excellent student at a Methodist mission school on the Navajo reservation; he was described by a fellow student as "the strong, silent type of Navajo who was extremely intelligent" (Shreve, 2011, 47). After a tour of duty in the U.S. Air Force, Blatchford during the early 1950s attended and earned an undergraduate degree at the University of New Mexico, where he formed the Kiva Club with several other Native American students; he was elected its president in 1954. While he was an excellent student, Blatchford from the beginning questioned the usefulness of Anglo-American higher education. He regarded this model as excluding Native American culture and hiding the dominant culture's history of aggression against Native peoples.

Blatchford was among activist students who formed the Regional Indian Youth Council from several Native collegiate groups in the late 1950s, which included several hundred students throughout the Southwestern United States. This group then expanded its scope, especially to the fishing-rights battles of the Pacific Northwest, and became the NIYC in the early 1960s. Blatchford worked at the New Mexico State Department of Education before he became executive director of NIYC. After the Chicago Indian Conference in 1961, he said that "This unity would not be allowed to dissipate" (Shreve, 2011, 98). Blatchford often shared leadership duties of the NIYC with Mel Thom.

With Shirley Hill Witt, Blatchford edited *Aborigine*, an NIYC newsletter, which was used to recruit about 200 new members during the 1960s, as Blatchford and others distributed the newsletters to several college Indian clubs, as well as regional meetings. As NIYC grew, however, it was plagued with factions, and Blatchford was ousted from his leadership role in 1965. He split with Thom, who alleged that Blatchford had not been able to keep NIYC's finances in order (Shreve, 2011,

151–52). Blatchford then worked as president of the Northwest New Mexico Economic Opportunity Council, and as director of the Gallup [New Mexico] Indian Community Center. Witt later said that Blatchford's loss hurt NIYC, because "It was he who kept rationality functioning amongst us" (Shreve, 2011, 152).

Blatchford was fired as leader of the Gallup center in 1972 by its owner, Frankie Garcia, who also owned a bar, because Blatchford was trying to get Indians to stop drinking. Blatchford then rejoined NIYC in Albuquerque and was involved in its campaign to stop coal gasification on the Navajo reservation. His broader attempts to give NIYC an environmentalist focus failed, however, so he left it again. On December 1, 1996, he was killed in a fire at his home near Gallup (Shreve, 2011, 207).

Further Reading

Shreve, Bradley G. *Red Power Rising: The National Indian Youth Council and the Origins of Native Activism.* Norman: University of Oklahoma Press, 2011.

"Boldt Decision" (*United States v. Washington*, 1974)

The "Boldt Decision" [*United States v. Washington:* 384 F. Supp. 312 (1974)], which defined fishing rights of 14 Native American tribes in Western Washington State, produced major changers in federal law, as well as the economic livelihood of Native people who were subject to the ruling. Until Boldt's ruling, the U.S. Supreme Court consistently had sided with the state. The ruling occurred during a time of intense Native American political activity, including civil disobedience, which played a major role in the U.S. Justice Department's decision to pursue the case.

Boldt invested more than three years in the case; he used 200 pages to interpret the wording of the treaties in an opinion which some legal scholars believe is the most carefully researched, thoroughly analyzed ever handed down in a Native fishing-rights case. During the next three years the Ninth Circuit Court of Appeals upheld Boldt's ruling, and the U.S. Supreme Court twice let it stand by refusing to hear an appeal by the State of Washington. In 1979, as the state of Washington refused to abide by the ruling (Judge Boldt's court had taken control of enforcement), the U.S. Supreme Court affirmed it.

The revolution that began with activist Indians' "fish-ins" arrived in the chambers of the law via an important law-journal article, published in the *Washington Law Review* during 1972, by University of Washington law professor Ralph W. Johnson, who had become the most influential legal scholar on the issue. Hank Adams and other activists had convinced Professor Johnson to take up the subject.

Indians had been asserting their rights to fish according to the treaties ever since the treaties were signed. In 1896 (*Ward v. Race Horse*), 1905 (*United States v. Winans*), 1942 (*Tulee v. Washington*), and 1968 (*Puyallup Tribe v. Department of Game*), as the U.S. Supreme Court fundamentally accepted the state's position that the law allowed its regulation of Native American fishing for conservation of the resource. Johnson's analysis revealed that the Court had been recycling its own original legal error: "No valid basis for the existence for such state power can be found," he wrote (Johnson, 1972, 208).

The Supreme Court's Error

Treaties, as the "supreme law of the land" under the U.S. Constitution, wrote Johnson (1972, 208), cannot allow unilateral regulation "unless the treaty so provides or unless Congress so legislates." Neither had occurred. "Therefore," Johnson wrote, "the Supreme Court should clearly hold that the states have no power to regulate Indian off-reservation fishing unless and until Congress expressly delegates the power to do so" (Johnson, 1972, 208). Boldt's decision corrected this issue, and it was upheld by the Supreme Court.

The Boldt ruling affirmed the treaty fishing peoples' decades-long assertions of their rights, fundamentally and explicitly. Boldt used an 1828 edition of *Webster's American Dictionary* for his contemporary definition of "in common with," a phrase in the treaties, as entitling Native people to half the salmon catch running through their *traditional* waters, *before* the treaties were signed. Legally, "stations" were defined as fixed, specific locations such as weirs or platforms. "Grounds" were defined as larger areas that could contain several "stations." The ruling also contained several other endorsements of sovereignty that were not specific to fishing, holding that the state could not discriminate against Native peoples, and that the intent of Congress was to enhance Native self-government.

The Boldt decision challenged the allocation of legal power in an ambit much broader than fishing alone. The treaties could no longer be dismissed by the state or subject solely to its own definition by police power. Native peoples became equal in the eyes of the law. In 1972, the Muckleshoots, for example, stopped a city of Tacoma proposal to build a pipeline along the Green River, part of their traditional fishing grounds. The project was allowed only after Tacoma agreed in court to pay $20 million, provide a fish hatchery to the Muckleshoots, and add 100 acres to their holdings. As the fishing-rights case was being adjudicated during the early 1970s, the Muckleshoots began to issue their own license plates for government's vehicles, and were challenged by the state of Washington, which took them to court. Their right to issue the plates was upheld during July, 1985 by the United States Court of Appeals for the Ninth Circuit.

The Limits of the Boldt Decision

United States v. Washington was limited to the 14 named Native peoples, to Western Washington, and to salmon (anadromous fish) that are born in fresh water, migrate to the ocean, then return to their birthplaces to spawn. Numerous other, smaller fishing peoples (many of whom have no federal recognition), as well as fishing activity east of the Cascades and in other states (such as Oregon) were not included. Allocation of shellfish was left for later adjudication. The Boldt decision defined its applicable territory as the watersheds of Puget Sound and the Olympic Peninsula north of Grays Harbor, and adjacent offshore waters. The case includes hatchery-bred fish.

Barbara Lane, an anthropologist from British Columbia, conducted research for the tribes represented in the case. She had the exceedingly difficult task of establishing which areas constituted the "usual and accustomed" fishing grounds used by the Native peoples before reservation boundaries were established. As a researcher on the federal case, Lane also addressed the use of nets as a traditional form of fishing and the definition of fishing "in common" for distribution of harvestable salmon and steelhead.

Judge Boldt's ruling found that:

1. Treaties reserved to Indian tribes fishing rights that are distinct from those of other citizens;

2. Off-reservation Indian fishing rights extended to every place each tribe customarily fished;

3. Indians had reserved rights to a fair share—50 percent—of the harvestable fish exclusive of on-reservation catches and of fish taken for subsistence and ceremonial purposes;

4. The state may regulate Indian off-reservation fishing only to the extent necessary for conservation, but not in ways limiting treaty rights to state-preferred times and fishing methods;

5. The state classification of steelhead as a "game" fish restricted Indian fishing rights and violated the treaties; and

6. Fourteen treaty tribes, plus three more upon federal approval, were entitled to share in the decision. (U.S. Commission, 1981)

The Washington State Department of Game had argued that no special right existed for Indian fishing but that Indians needed a special allocation, which it would determine according to the state's definition of conservation requirements and the demands of sports and non-Native commercial fishers. The State of Washington also asserted that Native fishing people were obliged to abide by state laws, which restricted fishing to reservation boundaries contained in treaties. Judge

Boldt denied all of this. As of 1974, the court estimated that within the jurisdiction of the case 794 Native fishing people were active, compared to 6,600 non-Indian commercial fishers and 283,650 sports fishers.

Seizure of fishing gear and other property was held to be illegal under Boldt, as the state also was prohibited from limiting the types of technology that Native fishing people may use. Some opponents of Native fishing rights had argued that they should be limited to the technologies that were in use when the treaties were signed. They applied no such technological limits to non-Indian sports or commercial fishing activities.

Judge Boldt placed Native fishing rights in a broader social, economic, and legal context:

> The treaty-secured rights to resort to the usual and accustomed places to fish were a part of larger rights possessed by the treating Indians, upon the exercise of which there was not a shadow of impediment, and which were not much less necessary to their existence than the atmosphere they breathed. The treaty was not a grant of rights to the treating Indians, but a grant of rights from them, and a reservation of those not granted. In the Stevens treaties, such reservations were not of particular parcels of land, and could not be expressed in deeds, as dealings between private individuals. The reservations were in large areas of territory, and the negotiations were with the tribes. The treaties reserved rights, however, to every individual Indian, as though described therein. There was an exclusive right of fishing reserved within certain boundaries. There was a right outside of those boundaries reserved for exercise "in common with citizens of the Territory." (*U.S. v. Washington*, 1974, 80)

Further Reading

Annual Report for 1995: Muckleshoot Tribal Council. Auburn, WA: Muckleshoot Indian Tribe, 1995.

Johnson, Ralph W. "The States Versus Indian Off-reservation Fishing: A United States Supreme Court Error," *Washington Law Review* 47, no. 2 (1972): 207–36.

Tizon, Alex. "The Boldt Decision: 25 Years—The Fish Tale That Changed History." *Seattle Times*, February 7, 1999. http://community.seattletimes.nwsource.com/archive/?date=19990207&slug=2943039

Tulee v. Washington 315 U.S. 681 (1942).

U.S. Commission on Civil Rights. "Fishing in Western Washington—a Treaty Right, a Clash of Cultures," in *Indian Tribes, a Continuing Quest for Survival: A Report of the United States Commission on Civil Rights*, 61–100. Washington, D.C.: U.S. Government Printing Office, 1981.

United States v. Washington: 384 F. Supp. 312 (1974).

United States v. Winans 198 U.S. 371 (1905).

Ward v. Race Horse 163 U.S. 504(1896).

Brando, Marlon

(1924–2004)

From fishing-rights protests in the Pacific Northwest to aiding AIM leaders on the ramparts of Wounded Knee, the actor Marlon Brando was frequently involved in activism on behalf of American Indians from the 1960s through the 1970s. He became the only actor in history to decline an Academy Award (an Oscar)—and he did it as a protest of how the majority society was treating indigenous peoples. Brando's decision to decline the Oscar was broadcast world-wide on television as the AIM faced off with U.S. Army troops and other federal law-enforcement agents at Wounded Knee. Brando also provided AIM activists with aid—including the keys to his own car—as they fled the FBI's dragnet after the occupation.

Brando, Zionism, and Civil Rights

Brando was politically involved on many fronts, including the campaign for a Jewish homeland, which he highlighted as early as 1946 by performing in Ben Hecht's play "A Flag is Born," about the Zionist cause. He also donated large amounts of money to the *Irgun*, a political and paramilitary organization supporting the Zionist cause. Brando also became involved in the civil-rights movement, as he played a role in Martin Luther King's March on Washington during 1963. After King was assassinated on April 4, 1968, Brando canceled his lead role in "The Arrangement," a feature film, to work in civil rights full time. "I felt I'd better go find out where it is; what it is to be black in this country; what this rage is all about," Brando said on the late night ABC-TV Joey Bishop Show (Vintage, n.d.).

At about the same time, Brando also contributed several thousand dollars to scholarship funds provided in the name of Medgar Evers, a civil-rights worker who was assassinated in Mississippi. He also was a major donor to Dr. King's Southern Christian Leadership Conference (SCLC), as well as the Black Panther Party, but he withdrew his support from the Panthers after some of its members advocated violence. Brando's film *Sayonara* engaged the theme of interracial romance.

Brando Goes Fishing

Brando took part in some of the earliest Native American "fish ins," in 1964, climbing into boats blatantly illegally (he, of course, had no treaty rights), tempting state game and fishing agents to arrest him, which they did. Brando also became a friend of the fiery orator Clyde Warrior, a founder of the National Indian Youth Council (NIYC), which made fishing rights in Western Washington state its major focus during the early 1960s.

Brando, who had been invited to the fish-ins by Hank Adams, drew in Dick Gregory and Peter and Jane Fonda to lend support to Puget Sound Indian fishing rights. Brando also gave money to Native groups and needy individuals, and returned 40 acres of land he owned in California to Indians (he deeded it to the Survival of American Indians Association), apologizing for being 400 years late with the gift. He added in *Newsweek*: "Christ Almighty, look at what we did in the name of 'democracy' to the American Indian. We just excised them from the human race. We had four hundred treaties with the Indians and we broke every one of them" (Reyes, 200–6, 76).

Brando was arrested on March 2, 1964 while fishing with the Puyallups along with John Yaryan, a clergyman, an event that put the fishing-rights struggle in headlines around the world. Brando was released on a technicality, however, and not tried. The comedian Dick Gregory fished several times during the spring of 1966, was arrested, convicted, and he served 40 days of a 90-day sentence in the Thurston County Jail (American Friends, 1970, 108–111).

On March 3, 1964, during a large fishing-rights demonstration at the Washington State Capitol in Olympia, Native leaders and Brando met with Washington Governor Albert Rosellini for several hours, after which the governor spoke to the demonstrators. While Rosellini congratulated them for exercising their rights, he refused to back off of the state's insistence that it would set the rules restricting Indian fishing. Siding with white sports-fishing groups, Rosellini characterized Indian fishing as a threat to conservation of the species, at a time when Native catch amounted to no more than 6 percent of the total (Shreve, 2011, 130–32, 136).

The fish-ins continued for years, attracting multiethnic support from many places. The confrontations by this time had become quite physical, especially on the Nisqually River adjacent to Frank's Landing, a few miles from Olympia, the state capital, and on Puyallup fishing grounds near Tacoma. On October 15, 1965, "an emotion-charged battle of paddles, sticks, and stones ensued" (American Friends, 1970, 110). At the same time, Brando also supported the Alcatraz Island occupation with money, as well as a visit to show solidarity.

Declining an Oscar for "Best Actor"

During the occupation of Wounded Knee, Sacheen Littlefeather, a movie actress and activist, refused to accept the Academy Award as best actor in *The Godfather* on behalf of Brando at the 1973 Academy Awards on March 27. At the awards ceremony, Littlefeather said: "Marlon Brando . . . has asked me to tell you, in a very long speech which I cannot share with you presently—because of time [the producer had given her only 45 seconds]—that he . . . very regretfully cannot accept this very generous award . . . I beg at this time that I have not intruded upon this evening and that we will, in the future . . . our hearts and our understanding will meet with love and generosity. Thank you on behalf of Marlon Brando" (News, 1973). Brando said of American Indians: "We murdered them. We lied to them. We cheated them out of their lands. We starved them into signing fraudulent agreements that we called treaties which we never kept. We turned them into beggars on a continent that gave life for as long as life can remember" (Brando, 1973).

A few people in the audience applauded, but many more jeered until Littlefeather walked off the stage. Later in the evening, Clint Eastwood wondered aloud whether he should present the award for Best Picture "on behalf of all the cowboys shot in John Ford westerns over the years," and Raquel Welch said, "I hope the winner doesn't have a cause," before announcing the winner of the Best Actress Oscar. Co-host Michael Caine criticized Brando for "Letting some poor little Indian girl take the boos," instead of "[standing] up and [doing] it himself" (News, 1973).

After the ceremony, Littlefeather shared the text of Brando's statement with the press. Brando said that while he did not wish to "offend or diminish this occasion, I do not feel that I can, as a citizen of the United States, accept this or any award. . . .The motion picture community as much as anyone has been responsible for degrading the Indian" (News of the Odd, 1973). Brando said of American Indians: "We murdered them. We lied to them. We cheated them out of their lands. We starved them into signing fraudulent agreements that we called treaties which we never kept. We turned them into beggars on a continent that gave life for as long as life can remember" (Brando, 1973).

Aiding AIM Fugitives

Brando provided AIM activists with vehicles, money, and access to legal assistance while they were on the run from the FBI after the occupation of Wounded Knee. In *Ojibwa Warrior*, Dennis Banks describes visiting Brando's home with Leonard Peltier while they were fugitives from the FBI late in 1975. According to Banks, "Brando gave them the keys to his motor home and handed Dennis a roll of money to help them on their way" (Brando, 2004). The cash added up to about $10,000—more than $40,000 in 2012 dollars.

On November 14, 1975, 11 days before indictments were handed down in the deaths of two FBI agents at Pine Ridge (for which Leonard Peltier later was convicted) Oregon state police stopped a van registered to Brando near Ontario, in eastern Oregon. Anna Mae Aquash was in the van, along with Russell Redner, Kenny Loudhawk, and KaMook Banks (Dennis Banks' wife) Peltier and Banks also were in the van, but they escaped a hastily erected FBI blockade (Johansen and Maestas, 1979, 89–90).

Brando also was among several thousand people who took part in "The Longest Walk," which traversed the United States during the late spring and summer of 1978, arriving in Washington, D.C., July 15, led by traditional elders to the Washington

Monument. The march sought to address several political issues, including the incarceration of American Indian political prisoners, forced relocation at Big Mountain, and others. Other non-Indian supporters included Senator Ted Kennedy and the boxer Muhammad Ali. President Jimmy Carter refused to meet with representatives of the marchers, but Congress did pass the American Indian Religious Freedom Act, one of the issues raised by the marchers.

Further Reading

American Friends Service Committee. *Uncommon Controversy: Fishing Rights of the Muckleshoot, Puyallup, and Nisqually Indians.* Seattle: University of Washington Press, 1970.

Banks, Dennis and Richard Erdoes. *Ojibwa Warrior: Dennis Banks and the Rise of the American Indian Movement.* Norman: University of Oklahoma Press, 2004.

Brando, Marlon. "The Godfather: That Unfinished Oscar Speech." *New York Times*, March 30, 1973. http://www.nytimes.com/packages/html/movies/bestpictures/godfather-ar3.html.

Johansen, Bruce E. and Roberto F. Maestas. *Wasi'chu: The Continuing Indian Wars.* New York: Monthly Review Press, 1979.

"Marlon Brando—Blood brother to the Redman." American Indian Movement of Colorado. July 2, 2004. http://www.coloradoaim.org/blog/2004/07/marlon-brando-blood-brother-to-redman.html.

News of the Odd. March 27, 1973. http://www.newsoftheodd.com/article1027.html

Reyes, Lawney L. *Bernie Whitebear: An Urban Indian's Quest for Justice.* Tucson: University of Arizona Press, 2006.

Shreve, Bradley. *Red Power Rising: The National Indian Youth Council and the Origins of Native Activism.* Norman: University of Oklahoma Press, 2011.

Vintage Classics. Marlon Brando Tribute: Civil Rights. No date. http://levitchcrocetti.proboards.com/index.cgi?board=marlonbrando&action=display&thread=1050.

Brightman, Lehman

(Born 1930)

In 1969, as Alcatraz was occupied, Lehman Brightman initiated and then supervised the United States' first program in Native American Studies at the University of California—Berkeley. He also taught in the field at D-Q University, the University of California in San Diego, Sacramento State University, and Contra Costa College in San Pablo, California. At the same time, he wrote prolifically on Indian education.

Brightman, of Lakota and Creek heritage, who had been raised in Oklahoma, also cofounded United Native Americans in 1968, with LaNada Boyer, who said that his "intelligence, wit, and concern led him to become a strong Native American advocate" (Johnson, et al., 1997, 89). The UNA was an early activist organization that had an important role in supporting the occupation of Alcatraz Island between 1969 and 1971. Brightman led an occupation of Mt. Rushmore at the same time. Later, he also played a role in the takeover of Wounded Knee in 1973. Brightman also helped to coordinate the Longest Walk (1978), as well as the Long Walk for Survival (1980).

Brightman was a talented football player while a student at the University of Oklahoma, where he also ran track. After earning a BA degree there, Brightman earned an MA at the University of California/Berkeley. He also served in the Korean war for a year as a U.S. Marine, where he was wounded in combat. Brightman said later that he viewed high school and college mainly as places to play football. The Marines gave him a sense of purpose, however. "When I came back from the Marine Corps, I had straightened up," he said. "It taught me to be responsible. Most people who served in the Marines are proud of it. Before the Marines, my life wasn't structured. I've lived my whole life since structured, and I learned that from the Corps" (Professor, n.d.).

Brightman did not take part directly in the Alcatraz occupation, but handled liaison onshore. Even before he became director of the University of California at Berkeley Native American Studies program in the fall of 1969 (when Alcatraz was first occupied), Brightman organized Native Americans to picket the San Francisco Federal Building and other locations in support of treaty rights and other issues. He would assemble people with signs and a bullhorn and then call the media. He also edited and published a militant newsletter titled *The Warpath*.

Brightman also was a master of parody, and inventor of the "Bureau of Caucasian Affairs" and "reservations for white people," concepts that originated during the Alcatraz occupation of 1969–70. (Complete text is available in "Primary Sources.") It began:

> Lehman L. Brightman, the Commissioner of Caucasian Affairs, has announced the following new policies: The Indians hereby give the whites four reservations of ten acres each at the following locations: Death Valley, The Utah Salt Flats, The Badlands of South Dakota, and the Yukon in Alaska. These reservations shall belong to the whites "for as long as the sun shines or the grass grows" (or until the Indians want it back). All land on the reservations, of course, will be held in trust for the whites by the Bureau of Caucasian Affairs, and any white who wants to use his land in any way must secure permission from Commissioner Brightman. Of course, whites will be allowed to sell handicrafts at stands by the highway. (The Bureau of Caucasian Affairs)

Brightman led the UNA in testimony before the U.S. Senate about abuse of Native peoples in boarding schools and in Indian Health Service hospitals. He was perhaps the most active person in the United States in opposing IHS involuntary sterilization of Native American women, and suffering a libel suit by doctors in the process. Roughly 3,400 Native women were sterilized each year between 1973 and 1976, according to Brightman. Even after lawsuits and protests, sterilizations continued into the late 1970s at some hospitals. No one will ever really know how many women were really sterilized during the seventies. His educated guess (without exact calculations to back it up) was that 40 percent of Native women and 10 percent of Native men were sterilized during the decade. Brightman estimated that the total number of Indian women sterilized during the decade was somewhere between 60,000 and 70,000 (Johansen 1998).

Brightman fathered three children: Lehman Jr., Gall, and Quanah, with a family home in Pinole, California. During his later years, Brightman also worked on a Native American civil-rights movement history. On July 22, 2011, Brightman came near death when he suffered a stroke, but he partly recovered. At that time, Brightman's friends issued an appeal for financial aid to help pay medical expenses, mortgage, and overdue taxes.

Further Reading

"The Bureau of Caucasian Affairs." The Bureau of Caucasian Affairs. http://www.pantherslodge.com/una.html

Johansen, Bruce E. "Sterilization of Native American Women Reviewed by Omaha Master's Student." For: José Barreiro (editor-in-chief of *Native Americas,* September, 1998. http://www.ratical.org/ratville/sterilize.html

Johnson, Troy, Joane Nagel and Duane Champagne, eds. *American Indian Activism: Alcatraz to the Longest Walk.* Urbana and Chicago: University of Illinois Press, 1997.

"Professor Lehman L. Brightman—President of United Native Americans on KAOS." March 4, 2011. http://ravenredbone.wordpress.com/2011/03/04/professor-lehman-l-brightman-president-of-united-native-americans-on-kaos/

Smith, Paul Chaat and Robert Allen Warrior. *Like a Hurricane: The Indian Movement from Alcatraz to Wounded Knee.* New York: The New Press, 1996.

Brown, Norman

(Born 1959)

Norman Brown, a Navajo who was between 15 and 17 years of age at the time of the Jumping Bull shootout in which two FBI agents were killed in June, 1975, was coerced into false testimony which he repudiated at the trial of Leonard Peltier, who was convicted of murdering the agents.

Brown, who was slight (5-foot-2, about 120 pounds), had known Peltier for two years at the time of the shootout. They had met at a sun dance. The Jumping Bull compound had turned into a convivial camp. Brown and other boys helped move water into the house owned by the elderly Jumping Bulls, whom they called "grandma and grandpa" (Matthiessen, 1991, 148). Brown also helped with a security detail at the camp.

On June 26, 1975, when shooting broke out between AIM occupants of the camp, FBI agents, U.S. marshals, Bureau of Indian Affairs police, and Richard Wilson's GOON squad, Brown found himself with Joe Stuntz Killsright, who was shot to death in the confrontation. Later, with Peltier and others, Brown escaped the firefight by following an eagle (which they took to be a good omen) through prairies and forests.

Within two days of the shootout, the FBI had assembled Operation RESMURS (Reservation Murders), and Brown was on their short list, mentioned in FBI memos as one AIM member who had fired at the dead agents. On September 5, 1975, the FBI arrested Brown, among others, at Crow Dog's Paradise. He was briefly interrogated about the murders, released, and then, a few days later, arrested again.

Brown provided testimony at the Cedar Rapids, Iowa trial of Dino Butler and Bob Robideau that aided the defense, even though he had been called to the stand by the prosecution. Having implicated Robideau and Butler under the secret shroud of a grand jury (and under FBI pressure), in open court Brown said that while several AIM members had fired shots, he couldn't place any of them in the vicinity of the agents. While the prosecution alleged that AIM members had drawn the agents into an ambush, the defense argued that the incident had been chaotic, and the people in the compound were acting in self-defense. Brown's testimony tended to support that view, and the jury agreed, finding Robideau and Butler not guilty.

Brown was interviewed in the Peltier case by FBI special agents J. Gary Adams and O. Victor Harvey on September 27, 1975. Brown was told that if he didn't tell them what they wanted to hear, he might never walk the earth again, and might never see his family. The implication was that the FBI would find a way to put Brown in prison for life. The FBI's tactics put Brown into severe cognitive dissonance, since he regarded Peltier as his mentor, as well as his friend. He responded by acting compliant in private, and then subverting the prosecution's case in open court. "If I could take the place of Leonard Peltier [in prison], I would do so without hesitation," Brown said in 1989 (Matthiessen, 1991, 577).

Brown was frightened into false testimony that he had seen Peltier carrying an AR-15 rifle near the scene where the agents had been shot. He repudiated this statement on the stand at Peltier's trial, saying only that he had seen Peltier carrying the gun. When the prosecutor [Evan Hultman] tried to get Brown to return to the coerced version, he said: "Are you trying to *tell* me *I* saw them down there [during the firefight in which the two agents were killed]"? (Churchill and Vander Wall, 1998, 301). Brown told Hultman: "It was the agents who said I saw them. It seems like you are calling me a liar" (Matthieseen, 1991, 331).

Further Reading

Churchill, Ward and Jim Vander Wall. *Agents of Repression: The FBI's Secret Wars Against the Black Panther Party and the American Indian Movement*. Boston: South End Press, 1988.

Matthiessen, Peter. *In the Spirit of Crazy Horse*. New York: Viking, 1991.

Bruce, Louis Rooks

(1906–1989)
Dakota Sioux and Mohawk

Louis R. Bruce served as commissioner of the Bureau of Indian Affairs (BIA) during President Richard M. Nixon's first term, from 1969 through most of 1972. Bruce's tenure coincided with activist Native American political movements during the late 1960s and 1970s. Bruce was the third person of Native American descent to serve as commissioner of the BIA. The first was the Seneca Ely Parker, appointed after the Civil War by President Ulysses S. Grant. The second was Robert F. Bennett, who led the agency under President Lyndon Johnson, from 1966 to 1969.

Bruce joined the AIM occupation for a time in an "act of solidarity," an action that later cost him his job. Following AIM's occupation of the BIA's headquarters building, President Richard Nixon fired Bruce, most probably because he had sympathized with the occupiers (Bruce at one point was said to have flashed an AIM membership card, although AIM had no such cards).

Bruce was raised on the Onondaga reservation south of Syracuse in New York State. His father, Louis Bruce, a Mohawk, worked as a dentist, a major-league baseball player, and a Methodist missionary. He was a stern and highly religious person who taught his son to value education. Bruce's mother, Nellie Rooks, was Dakota (Sioux). Bruce attended Cazenovia Seminary, at his father's behest, the only Native American student there, where he excelled in several sports and graduated in 1929.

Bruce then worked his way through Syracuse University as a construction worker, farmhand, waiter, and employee of a saw mill and became a star pole-vaulter. After his graduation from college, Bruce worked as a clothing-store manager, as an official in the Works Progress Administration, and as a dairy farmer. He married Anna Wikoff, a former classmate at the Cazenovia Seminary, in 1930. In 1935, Bruce went to work in New York State as director for Indians for the National Youth Administration of the Works Progress Administration. The agency, a Great Depression employment program, put Native young people to work teaching Indian culture and history at summer camps.

He was a founder and executive secretary of the National Congress of American Indians (NCAI). Bruce also was an unofficial advisor to New York Governor

Thomas Dewey and a friend of First Lady Eleanor Roosevelt. He worked on many New Deal programs during the 1930s to preserve Native American art, dance, music, and other oral traditions. In 1957, Bruce played a major role in organizing the first Native American Youth Conference. In the late 1950s, he chaired the President's Advisory Committee on Indian Affairs during the Eisenhower administration.

In September of 1969, President Nixon appointed Bruce, who was dairy farmer at the time, as well as a registered Republican, as commissioner of Indian Affairs. Bruce's tenure at the BIA was introduced by Nixon as a sweeping change, making "progress through participation" the new Indian policy: "[The] voice of the Indian will be heard on all questions affecting the life of the Indian. It is not this administration's policy to tell the Indian what to do, but rather to help the Indian to do what needs to be done" (Forbes, 1984, 34). Bruce set out to "Indianize" the bureau by appointing a number of Native Americans to influential positions. His aim was to create a true service agency.

Bruce's policies at the BIA ran up against a considerable amount of opposition from interests that had benefited by keeping Native Americans in a subordinate position. In this respect, his ouster recalled that of the first BIA commissioner of Native American descent, Ely Parker, who had been drummed out of the office almost exactly a century earlier.

Bruce moved to reorganize the BIA to allow more Native control of programs. During November of 1972, he tried to reconcile the positions of AIM and the Nixon administration while the militants occupied the BIA headquarters building. This attempt at negotiation was characterized as coddling the militants by Bruce's superiors in the Interior Department. Interior Secretary Rogers Morton said "Right now he [Bruce] couldn't even sell a hot dog in that building." Interior Department Assistant Secretary for Public Land Management Harrison Loesch said Bruce had "blown it. He is over there in bed with them [AIM], and we don't like it from Air Force One [e.g. Nixon] on down" (Forbes, 1984, 96). Bruce was then forced to resign; he was replaced by John O. Crow, who called Bruce an "incompetent" who had "given aid to the unruly mob" (LaCourse, 1972, 5).

Even during Bruce's term, very little progress was made in removing corporate control over natural resources on reservations that resulted in below-market returns and overexploitation of timber, mining, grazing land, oil, and other resources. The companies were still using the Interior Department's "trust" relationship with Indian tribes to make them "the last frontier of industrial exploitation" (Forbes, 1984, 39). Leon Cook, an Ojibwa who had been placed in charge of economic development by Bruce resigned in frustration, telling Bruce that "You talk advocacy, but neither you nor the secretary [Rogers Morton] nor the administration has proven to me nor to Indian country that the Bureau or the federal government are in fact advocating the protection of these resources. . . . You . . . further condon [*sic*] the continued theft of Indian land, water, and natural resources" (*NICO News*, 1971, 2).

After his dismissal as BIA commissioner, Bruce started and directed Native American Consultants Inc., to provide advice to Native American organizations. On May 24, 1989, Bruce died of cancer and heart disease in Arlington, Virginia. He was survived by his wife, as well as three children, a sister, and eight grandchildren.

Further Reading

Ballentine, Betty and Ian. *The Native Americans Today.* Atlanta, GA: Turner Publishing, 1993.

Cook, Joan. "Louis R. Bruce, Ex-Commissioner Of Indian Affairs, Is Dead at 83." *New York Times*, May 24, 1989. http://www.nytimes.com/1989/05/24/obituaries/louis-r-bruce-ex-commissioner-of-indian-affairs-is-dead-at-83.html.

Forbes, Jack D. *Native Americans and Nixon: Presidential Politics and Minority Self-determination.* Los Angeles: American Indian Cultural Center, 1984.

NICO News, 1, no. 2 (January, 1971): 2.

Burnette, Robert

(Born 1926)
Rosebud Sioux

Robert Burnette, a former chairman of National Congress of American Indians (NCAI) between 1961 and 1963 as well as tribal chairman at Rosebud (adjacent to the Pine Ridge reservation, to the east) was active in the AIM by 1972, and first advanced the idea of a caravan across the United States to Washington, D.C., to raise the salience of Indian-policy issues. Burnette also was a chronicler of the movement in mass-market venues, including *The Tortured Americans* (1971) and *The Road to Wounded Knee* (1974).

Burnette's suggestion for the caravan that became the Trail of Broken Treaties was made during August, 1972 at a sun dance attended by several AIM members at Crow Dog's Paradise on the Pine Ridge reservation. "This shall be our finest hour if we are successful at maintaining discipline that shall bring fruit to our hungry people" he said (Smith and Warrior, 1996, 139). Burnette's idea was to forbid alcohol; and drugs, and to act with utmost dignity.

In many ways, Burnette stood between the young firebrands of AIM and the suit-and-tie Indians of NCAI. Nevertheless, his idea was taken up at a planning meeting September 30, 1972 at a meeting in Denver. Burnette eventually became co-chair of a planning committee for the march with Winnebago Reuben Snake. The committee planned three caravans leaving from Los Angeles, San Francisco, and Seattle, converging in St. Paul on October 23.

During his leadership of NCAI, Burnette had worked in Washington, D.C., and so younger members of AIM assumed he would be an effective front man for the caravan. Closing in on the national capital days before a presidential election, Burnette saw the caravan as a way to educate the Congress, the general public, and the president. Lost in excitement over the idea was political reality: the president and Congress would be out of town on the campaign trail. Burnette saw the caravan as a spiritual exercise, without drugs or alcohol, Indians on the best behavior: "This shall be our finest hour if we are successful in maintaining discipline that shall bring fruit to our hungry people" (Smith and Warrior, 1996, 139).

Burnette had pledged to deliver coordination and resources (such as housing) to the more than 700 people who arrived in Washington, D.C., after the caravan. He told the press that several churches already had made commitments. He even said that many people in the District had offered their own homes. For the most part, he was unable to deliver, and was severely criticized by other AIM leaders. In the meantime, Burnette's agenda, with its symbolic tipis and ceremonies at Arlington National Cemetery and the Iwo Jima memorial, fell apart as federal authorities refused to cooperate. The result was an unplanned ransacking of the Bureau of Indian Affairs head office. Burnette himself found lodging in a private home, but the rest were faced with spending their first night in a cramped, rat-infested church basement.

This was the end of Burnette's active role in AIM.

Further Reading

Burnette, Robert and Richard Erdoes. *The Tortured Americans.* Englewood Cliffs, NJ: Prentice-Hall, 1971.

Burnette, Robert and John Koster. *The Road to Wounded Knee.* New York: Bantam, 1974.

Smith, Paul Chaat and Robert Allen Warrior. *Like a Hurricane: The American Indian Movement from Alcatraz to Wounded Knee.* New York: New Press, 1996.

Butler, Darrell Dean (Dino)

(Born 1942)

Darrell Dean (Dino) Butler was a major figure in the AIM from 1974 through confrontations with the FBI and Pine Ridge reservation police after the occupation of Wounded Knee. He was one of two AIM members who were found not guilty of murdering two FBI agents at Pine Ridge on June 26, 1975. Leonard Peltier later was convicted of the murders.

Having been removed by force during mid-1800s from the Rogue River region in northern California and southern Oregon, Butler's ancestors were marched to the Government Hill Agency, the present-day Siletz reservation. Butler was born on April 8, 1942 in Portland, Oregon; his youth was spent in logging camps near Siletz. Butler was sent to MacLaren Boys School at the age of 13 after he had wandered more than 100 miles from his parents' home. The system classified him as "incorrigible."

In 1959, Butler was serving time, standing next to another Native man who hit a guard. Butler was convicted of his first felony and sentenced two more years in the Oregon State Penitentiary for assault. By the time he was released, said Butler, he had lost whatever spiritual traditions his grandmother had taught him, and "I couldn't really relate to anything except drinking and drugs" (Matthiessen, 1991, 137).

A Fiery, Angry Young Man

Butler was a fiery, angry young man who was arrested several times for assault and other charges that landed him in lockup. Having joined the AIM in 1974, he began to attend traditional ceremonies, as his energies were channeled into work for Native treaty rights and sovereignty.

Butler saw his "rebirth" in AIM as a spiritual reawakening: "Some people say that AIM has always been here. Some say it's a reawakening of our spiritual being. AIM to me is a spiritual reawakening within myself. Our people had to learn them from the beginning, so this evolution has always been going on among natural people of the natural world" (Relinquishing, 1995). Butler stressed that many Native people came to AIM from prisons and other oppressive institutions: "When we started becoming acquainted with AIM and the teachings, a lot of us had come out of prisons, institutions, the orphanages, the bars, and years of being oppressed. We brought that hate with us into the Movement. That's why we were so quick to pick up the guns and the arms to fight our enemy" (Relinquishing, 1995).

After he joined AIM, in his early thirties, Butler became a bodyguard for Russell Means. He also became a close friend of Leonard Peltier. He also married a young Inuit, Nilak Butler, who also became active in AIM. "A small, quiet man of thirty-two with a soft voice and a round, dark, unblinking gaze [and] a sad-eyed smile" as described by Peter Matthiessen (1991, 137), Butler regretted the fact that his remnant Tututni band, from the mouth of the Rogue River had been nearly wiped out during the 19th century. Only a few elders spoke the band's language, which Butler attempted to learn.

A Fire-Fight and a Trial

On the morning of June 26, 1975, the Butlers were camped in a tipi a half-mile south of the Jumping Bulls' house east of Pine Ridge village with several other AIM members. It was a spiritual camp, with a sweat lodge, but given recent violence that had killed several AIM members at Pine Ridge, many people had rifles. Two FBI agents, Jack R. Coler and Ronald A. Willliams, drove into the compound seeking a pair of stolen cowboy boots. The members of AIM were not prepared for a shootout; the compound was filled with women and children. Harry and Cecelia Jumping Bull recently had celebrated their 50th wedding anniversary (Matthiessen, 1991, 157).

Shooting broke out, however, as more FBI agents, as well as Bureau of Indian Affairs and Pine Ridge reservation police (GOONs) arrived. When the firefight was over, Coler, Williams and one Indian man, Joe Stuntz Killsright, lay dead. While the FBI mounted an international manhunt to find suspects in the agents' killings, Killsright's death was never seriously investigated. Following the shootout, most of the AIM members fled the compound, where the Jumping Bull's house had been filled with holes by incoming fire. Leonard Peltier fled to Canada and was extradited; later he was convicted of the FBI agents' killings after three other defendants—Bob Robideau, Dino Butler, and Jimmy Eagle—had been indicted as well, but not convicted.

Butler and Robideau were arrested and placed under $250,000 bond each, assuring that they would remain in jail until their trial. On July 13, 1975, both were found not guilty by a federal court jury in Cedar Rapids. The trial had been transferred out of Rapid City, South Dakota, after the defense argued that obtaining an unbiased jury there would have been impossible. Robideau and Butler discussed making a false confession to the crime to help Peltier (who was in Canada at the time), but decided against it (Matthiessen, 1991, 580–81).

The government's case was weak, damaged by weak ballistic evidence, lack of eyewitnesses, and false witnesses. At one point, during testimony of government witness Wish Draper, Butler shouted "Liar!" (Matthiessen, 1991, 297). Defense Attorney William Kunstler even led another government witness James Harper, into confessing that he had lied many times to get what he wanted (Matthiessen, 1991, 297). The trial also featured testimony by FBI director Clarence Kelly about FBI counterintelligence (COINTELPRO) activities.

Kunstler provoked Kelly into losing his temper when he raised the subject of the many AIM members and supporters who had been killed at Pine Ridge with scanty attention from the FBI, which is responsible for investigating major crimes on Indian reservations. Kelly then defended the FBI's massive response to the shooting of its agents: "If they are threatened they have a right to defend themselves" (Matthiessen, 1991, 308). Having drawn Kelly into making the defense's main point about self-defense, Kunstler excused the witness with his outburst ringing in the jury's ears.

Robideau and Butler were found not guilty on all counts by an all-white jury. Butler and Robideau admitted having been present at Jumping Bull's the day of the shootout, and having exchanged fire with the agents—in the course of "defending our women and children" (Matthiessen, 1991, 286). The jury, in its verdict, said that

Butler and Robideau had acted in self-defense, doing "only what any reasonable person would do, under the circumstances" that had been created on Pine Ridge (Churchill, 2003, 280).

An Arrest and a Fast in Canada

While traveling to a Native ceremony in Canada during 1981, Butler was arrested and charged with killing two Canadian police officers. He refused to mount a defense after a sacred pipe was refused entry into the courtroom, but evidence was so scanty that the jury found Butler not guilty anyway. In the meantime, between 1981 and 1984, Butler served time in the Canadian prison system and established precedents for indigenous religious ceremonies there (Relinquishing, 1995). Butler and other Native men fasted for their rights to religious expression.

In Parliament, Canada's attorney general was asked "why Indian people were having to fast to death for religious freedom in the prison system?" He was asked, "Don't you think that's kind of embarrassing the Canadian people?" (Relinquishing, 1995). "I remember the first time I was allowed to 'officially' pray within the walls of that institution," Butler said later.

> They came to my cell and handcuffed and shackled me and marched me out to the Protestant minister's office. I was allowed to hold an abalone shell with some sage and cedar in it and I prayed that way. That was the beginning. In the end we had a sweat lodge and I had my pipe and could keep it inside my cell and brothers were fasting inside the prisons. Things that were never allowed before and never thought of before in their system. (Relinquishing, 1995)

Life in a Spiritual Camp

After his return to the United States, Butler spent much of the late 1980s at a spiritual camp in Redwood, California; during 1992, Butler returned home to Siletz where, with companion Juanita Whitebear and family, he took an active part in the Oregon Native Youth Council, "a grassroots organization dedicated to helping native Youth and their families establish identity as indigenous people that is not steeped in confusion and violence" (Relinquishing, 1995).

The Oregon Native Youth Council has been concerned with restoring Native language and other attributes of culture, combating alcoholism, drug abuse, and gang activity. "I grew up and saw a lot of adults drink themselves to death, knowing they were dying and yet they kept drinking. To me, that's always been so sad that someone would just give up on life so much. To know that they're dying and do it anyway. And that's what we're concerned about—not giving that kind of life to our children," said Butler (Relinquishing, 1995).

Butler's critique of majority society has remained largely unchanged: "You Christians, you are a lost people with no identity in this land. The only God you have is your technology, which will destroy you because of the greed it demands" (Matthieseen, 1991, 279).

Further Reading

Churchill, Ward. "The Bloody Wake of Alcatraz: Repression of the American Indian Movement During the 1970s," in Ward Churchill, ed. *Perversions of Justice: Indigenous Peoples and Angloamerican Law.* San Francisco: City Lights, 2003, 263–302.

Matthiessen, Peter. *In the Spirit of Crazy Horse.* New York: Viking, 1991.

"Relinquishing a Legacy of Hatred; Embracing Respect For All Life Conversations with Dino Butler." Interview Conducted by E. K. Caldwell (Cherokee/Shawnee, poet, lead interviewer for *News from Indian Country.* 1995. http://www.dickshovel.com/dino.html.

C

Camp, Carter

(Birth Date Not Known)

Carter Camp, a Ponca, was a leader in the Oklahoma AIM who became a confidante of the leadership, including Dennis Banks and Clyde Bellecourt. Later, he left AIM over allegations that he was a government informant—rumors that may have been planted by the FBI in an attempt to create distrust within AIM's leadership.

Camp was one of AIM's spokesmen during the Trail of Broken Treaties in 1972, and one who watched a symbolic protest turn into a sometimes-violent occupation of the Bureau of Indian Affairs' headquarters in Washington, D.C. According to Camp, AIM had not planned on occupying the building until BIA leadership sneered at them that the agency was "not in the housing business" (Matthiessen, 1991, 54). A polite reception would have avoided the confrontation, Camp said later. Instead, the BIA called police and provoked the marchers. Only after that did AIM barricade the building and vow to stay, and to pledge that they would not be removed without a fight.

Camp also took part in the occupation of Wounded Knee during 1973, and became one of several advocates of declaring a sovereign Native American nation there on the basis of the 1968 Fort Laramie Treaty. He was an advocate of discipline who inveighed against the use of alcohol and other drugs as well. Within days, the occupiers' declaration of sovereignty was met with a siege by several police agencies. Camp was one of several AIM members indicted by the federal government for their roles in the occupation, but served only a short sentence in jail for skipping a sentencing hearing. He said later that sadness over the deaths of Buddy Lamont and Frank Clearwater played a large part in convincing the occupiers to leave Wounded Knee on May 7, 1973, after 71 days (Matthiessen, 1991, 80).

The use of the snitch-jacket technique ravaged AIM, when used along with the planting of real informants, such as Douglass Durham. After a while, people who had known each other for years began to cast suspicions. At one point, for example, Clyde Bellecourt suspected Carter Camp of being paid off by the FBI. One evening Camp's younger brother Craig beat up on a buddy of Russell Means and Clyde Bellecourt. Craig brought Carter into the argument, which devolved into accusations of his complicity with the FBI. Banks said that while

American Indian Movement (AIM) leader Dennis Banks holds an envelope addressed to the Justice Department containing the ashes of a federal proposal for Indians to evacuate Wounded Knee, March 5, 1973, after AIM leaders burned the document. Russell Means, center, and Carter Camp look on. (AP/Wide World Photo)

Camp could give an eloquent speech, he was too immature for a leadership role in AIM.

This story has several versions. In one, Camp called Bellecourt a coward because he had refused to carry a gun at Wounded Knee (Matthiessen, 1991, 85). A violent argument ensued, after which Camp borrowed a handgun and shot Bellecourt in the stomach. Bellecourt later tried to salvage Camp's ruined reputation within AIM, but Means insisted that Camp be tossed out of AIM. Camp left, taking much of AIM's Oklahoma chapter with him (Churchill and Vander Wall, 1988, 214–15).

Further Reading

Churchill, Ward and Jim Vander Wall. *Agents of Repression: The FBI's Secret Wars Against the Black Panther Party and the American Indian Movement*. Boston: South End Press, 1988.

Matthiessen, Peter. *In the Spirit of Crazy Horse*. New York: Knopf, 1991.

Central Indiana AIM Support Group

The Central Indiana AIM Support Group formed during the late 1990s as an affiliate of the AIM Grand Governing Council in Minneapolis, in its own words, "First and foremost to support and endorse the National American Indian Movement in all directives . . . sovereignty issues, burial desecration issues, sports and other mascot issues, and obtaining the freedom of political prisoner, Leonard Peltier" (Central, n.d.).

In addition, the group pledged to "On a local level, our goal is to protect the welfare, both spiritual and physical of all Indian people, and help to educate the non-Indian population on the conditions of the American Indian today, as well as to promote understanding of the past histories that have led to these conditions" (Central. n.d.). Pat Adams, founding chairperson, expressed a desire to bring Native and non-Native people together on common issues, and to favor policies that would aid future generations.

Kylo Prince, an Ojibwa from the Long Plain First Nation in Manitoba, Canada, was a leader of the group. Prince's own past was indicative of Indiana Native peoples' diverse origins, as well as the pasts of many AIM members. He was born of Lakota as well as Ojibwa blood and spent his early years in Winnipeg, but was adopted by a family at age 8 in Seymour, Indiana. Having graduated from Brownstown Central High School, in 1988 Prince joined the U.S. Marine Corps. Mustering out of the military, Prince returned to his home near Winnipeg, and was drawn to revival of his Native roots, including the sweat lodge and other ceremonies with his extended family.

Having escaped alcohol and drugs in his youth, and having served prison time in Manitoba for robbery, Prince changed after he fathered two children. Prince's "true walk on our Red Road" began during 1995 on a vision quest that he undertook during a brutally cold Manitoba winter. He also took part in a Sun Dance. He also provided counseling for Native Americans, like him, who were adopted by non-Indians. Returning to Indiana again, Prince served as a Native American Community Center of Bloomington board member and provided counseling to penitentiary inmates.

Marking Peltier's birthday became a centerpiece of Central Indiana AIM's program. On September 12, 2011, members held a celebration of his 67th birthday near the entrance of the downtown Indianapolis Birch Bayh Federal Courthouse. Like Prince, Peltier shares Anishinaabe, Dakota and Lakota blood. A smiling Kylo Prince, was depicted in "NUVO, "Indy's Alternative Voice," a Web site, presenting a white cake with red lettering ("Happy Birthday, Leonard"), spiked with metal files, perhaps illustrative of a desire to see Peltier released from prison (Lovely, n.d.).

In addition to a birthday cake, members of AIM, hoisted banners and signs in support of Peltier, as they collected signatures on a petition for clemency to be delivered to President Barack Obama. Local news report said that the group was "drawing attention through the display of a large dream catcher, singing traditional songs around a drum and wearing the regalia of their various tribes" (Lovely, September 16, 2011).

In 2011, Peltier, at 67 years of age, remained in prison, in U.S. Penitentiary in Lewisburg, Penn. Still he is a target of law enforcement who is frequently moved within the penitentiary system. He was held in solitary confinement June 27 through September 12, 2011, for minor infractions of prison regulations. September 12 he was moved to the high-security U.S. Penitentiary at Coleman, Florida, far from his home among the Turtle Mountain Band of Chippewa Indians, making visits by family very difficult.

Central Indiana AIM operates in a rather tense political context locally. In 2008, the entire membership of the Indiana's Native American Indian Affairs Commission walked out at once to protest disrespect by Republican Gov. Mitch Daniels. One of the issues was use of more than $157,000 (as of August, 2011) deposited in trust to address Native American issues from sale of "Indiana: Land of Indians" vehicle license plates (Lovely, September 21, 2011).

Further Reading

Central Indiana AIM Support Group. Mission Statement. No date. http://www.oocities.org/capitolhill/7153/

Lovely, Lori. "Effort to Start a New Indiana AIM Chapter." *NUVO: Indy's Alternative Voice*. No date. http://www.nuvo.net/indianapolis/effort-to-start-a-new-indiana-aim-hapter/Content?oid=2351505

Lovely, Lori. "Birthday Rally Seeks Freedom for Leonard Peltier." *NUVO: Indy's Alternative Voice*, September 16, 2011. http://www.nuvo.net/NewsBlog/archives/2011/09/16/slideshow-leonard-peltier-birthday-rally

Lovely, Lori. "Land of the (disrespected) Indians." *NUVO: Indy's Alternative Voice*, September 21, 2011. http://www.nuvo.net/indianapolis/land-of-the-disrespected-indians/Content?oid=2351498

Chicago Conference

(1961)

In 1961, Native American voices of protest were raised at the American Indian Chicago Conference. This conference was the opening salvo for a decade-plus wave of Native activism that would change the legal, social, and economic face of Native America. It was organized at the behest of President John F. Kennedy by Sol Tax, professor of anthropology at the University of Chicago as a forum to enable Native

American peoples to express their views regarding their own futures. This gathering helped to ignite a social and political movement among many Native Americans that had an influence on later, better-known events. Also during 1961, a group of young, college-educated American Indians formed the National Indian Youth Council (NIYC). This organization had deep roots in impoverished, traditional Indian communities.

More than 400 Indians from 67 tribes and nations gathered at the Chicago Conference, a wide spectrum of student activists, tribal leaders, and professionals who had made their way in the majority society. They produced a Declaration of Indian Purpose, which, among other things, "called for the government's recognition of the right of tribes to participate in the decision-making process for all policies and programs that would affect them" (Josephy, 1982, 224).

Professor Tax, editor of *Current Anthropology* and founder of the University of Chicago, School of Anthropology also stirred some resentment among Native Americans by, according to Steve Talbot, by trying to control what they were doing. At Alcatraz, for example,

> He began to take over—sending telegrams, contacting the press, speaking for unilaterally; that is, he bypassed the authority of the Indians of All Tribes council and did not consult with other members of the committee. A powerhouse of energy and accustomed to being in command, he just could not let the Indians run their own occupation" (Johnson et al., 1997, 110).

Further Reading

Johnson, Troy, Joane Nagel, and Duane Champagne, eds. *American Indian Activism: Alcatraz to the Longest Walk.* Urbana: University of Illinois Press, 1997.

Josephy, Alvin M., Jr. *Now That the Buffalo's Gone: A Study of Today's American Indians.* New York: Knopf, 1982.

Churchill, Ward

(Born 1947)
Cherokee (Disputed)

Ward Churchill has been a leading figure in the Colorado chapter of the AIM that has spearheaded dissent from the "Grand Council" in Minneapolis. As a professor of Native American Studies at the University of Colorado until 2007, Churchill authored many provocative books with titles like *Fantasies of the Master Race* and *A Little Matter of Genocide*. He was no stranger to controversy, but beginning early in 2005 he became the target of a nation-wide campaign by right-wing opponents of his stated belief that the victims of the September 11, 2001, attacks on the World Trade Center had acted like "Little Eichmanns," cogs in an imperial machine.

Until that time, Churchill had built a reputation as a prolific, often incendiary, and widely cited author and activist. Churchill said that the university had dragged up years-old accusations to retaliate for his political beliefs, allowing opponents with political motives to cherry-pick his writings for assertions of factual errors and scholarly misconduct. Churchill was relieved of his university post for plagiarism and scholarly misconduct after a lengthy investigation, the first University of Colorado tenured professor to be fired for cause. At the same time, a number of Churchill's opponents accused him of ethnic-identity fraud in claiming Cherokee heritage, but these charges did not play a part in the university's investigation.

A Controversial Life

Ward Churchill, who was named after his grandfather, was born to Jack LeRoy Churchill and Maralyn Lucretia Allen in Urbana, Illinois, in 1947. Churchill's parents divorced before his second birthday. Churchill's high-school classmates recalled him as "a friendly teen who liked to debate politics" (Curtin et al., 2005, A-1). He graduated from Elmwood Community High School during 1965, and was drafted a year later to serve a tour of duty in Vietnam as the war there escalated.

Churchill has variously described his service in Vietnam as editor of an Army newspaper and as a member of an elite reconnaissance patrol (Curtin et al., 2005, A-1). Service in Vietnam formed Churchill's politics hard left. After discharge, he burned a U.S. flag on the steps of the Peoria County Courthouse. He attended meetings of Students for a Democratic Society and became friends with Mark Clark, a Black Panther leader who later was killed in a shootout with police in Peoria. Churchill also became friends with Russell Means about the time of the 1973 siege at Wounded Knee, and wrote some speeches for him.

Churchill, who is 6-foot-5, and smokes two to four packs of Pall Malls a day, took his first teaching job was as an art instructor at Black Hills State College, Spearfish, South Dakota, during 1975 and 1976. Churchill became a lecturer at the University of Colorado in 1978 and was granted tenure in the university's Communications Department in 1991. After that, he transferred to Ethnic Studies.

Churchill's "Little Eichmanns" statement first reached the attentive ears of various right-wing media gatekeepers during January, 2005, after he had been invited to Hamilton College, with a student body of about 1,750, which is housed in century-and-a-half old stone buildings near Utica New York. Churchill had been invited as part of a panel discussion on the limits of free speech titled "Limits of Dissent." Very quickly, the real world intruded with an academic debate over how far an individual could take free speech. The debate was canceled because of the uproar.

On February 3, 2005, CU-Boulder Interim Chancellor Phil DiStefano (with Arts and Sciences Dean Todd Gleeson and Law School Dean David Getches) initiated a 30-day review of Churchill's speeches and writings to determine whether he had overstepped the boundaries of academic conduct, and whether his "Little Eichmanns" statement and others might be grounds for dismissal. The University of Colorado Ethnic Studies Department, the chancellor's office, and Churchill himself received about 1,000 e-mails and dozens of phone calls *each day* at the height of the controversy during February, 2005, many of which were explicitly racist.

Churchill has been arrested by Denver police while protesting Denver's Columbus Day parade, having described it as a "celebration of genocide that caused millions of Indians' deaths with the advent European colonization" (Johnson, 2005). Denver has experienced the largest protests of Columbus Day in the world. In 2004, about 240 protesters, including Churchill, were arrested for blocking the parade. Churchill and several other leaders of the protest later were acquitted in Denver County Court on charges of failure to obey a police order to disperse.

A Dispute Over Churchill's "Indianness"

The controversy over Churchill quickly spread from his right to engage in unpopular political commentary to other matters, including the nature of his ethnic identity. Questions about Churchill's ethnicity had dogged him for many years. During May 1994, he was granted an "associate membership," or honorary status, with the Keetoowah Cherokee. He would have had to show proof of one-quarter blood quantum to be granted full membership; he said that he has 3/16. In July that year, the Keetoowah Cherokee stopped issuing associate memberships. Late in May, a revised statement from the United Keetoowah Band of Cherokee Indians asserted, according to a report in the *Rocky Mountain News*, that it had found no legal records to indicate that Churchill is a federally recognized American Indian (Brennan, 2005, 16-A). The statement also clarified the group's reasoning behind its award to Churchill of an associate membership by the Tahlequah, Oklahoma-based tribe in 1994.

Official certification of Native American status has long been a debatable credential. Many Native people resent having to prove their ethnicity (like a dog's breed, some complain) at the behest of a government agency created under United States law. Some assert that the whole idea of classifying people by degree of blood is an Anglo-American notion born in the 19th century of a desire to divide people racially, and to determine who was eligible for treaty annuities. Others have blood in Native groups that no longer have organized governments or government recognition.

The university decided not to pursue the identity question on the rationale that declarations of race for affirmative-action purposes are self-identified (as are U.S. Census classifications). If the university had pursued this question regarding Churchill, it would have opened the cases of everyone else who had declared a minority identity on a university employment form.

On September 9, 2005, the University of Colorado, having found that Churchill's comments about the World Trade Center bombings were free speech, initiated a formal inquiry into earlier charges of research misconduct against him, including allegations that he had published work mischaracterizing blood-quantum requirements in the Indian Arts and Crafts Act of 1990 and the General Allotment Act of 1887; that he had repeatedly advanced a theory charging the U.S. Army with an act of genocide against the Mandans in 1837 by intentionally spreading smallpox; that he plagiarized the work of Professor Fay Cohen of Dalhousie University in Nova Scotia, Canada, and that he had plagiarized a defunct Canadian environmental group's pamphlet on a water-diversion project that was never undertaken.

In his defense, Churchill said the allegations were trivial. Natsu Saito, C.U. associate professor of Ethnic Studies and Churchill's wife, stated that "Out of dozens of accusations . . . ranging from treason to advocacy of violence to personal threats to misrepresenting his identity to plagiarism, all that remain are a handful of questions regarding historical interpretation and the conventions of citation or attribution" (Saito, 2005). "On the whole," argued Churchill, "I submit that no scholar with a comparably extensive publication record would have fared better. Certainly, my accusers would not. The real question, then, is not the integrity of my scholarship. Rather, it is whether the University of Colorado is going to subject the writings of all its faculty to a degree of scrutiny similar in 'rigor' to that visited upon mine" (Churchill, September 9, 2006).

Investigative Report and Subsequent Events

The university assembled a five-member committee of scholars, which investigated the charges for several months, researching historical events and calling witnesses. The committee then released a 125-page report on May 9, 2006, which found Churchill culpable on six of seven instances of plagiarism, falsification, and violation of academic research norms, and called for suspension or termination of his employment.

Churchill asserted that the committee, acting as prosecutor and judge, had done "exactly what it accuses me of doing: it tailored its report to fit its conclusions" (Churchill, May 20, 2006). Churchill's books contain roughly 12,000 references by his count. He said that not even "any even marginally prolific scholar's publications could withstand the type of scrutiny to which mine has been subjected." The work under examination was "years, sometimes decades, old," Churchill argued (Churchill, May 20, 2006, 2).

On June 13, casting secret ballots, Colorado University's Standing Committee on Research Misconduct accepted the special committee's report. Six of nine members who cast ballots (two were ex-officio, without voting authority) said he should be fired, saying he "has committed serious, repeated and deliberate research misconduct," including plagiarism and fabrication of material (Burnett, 2006).

The Research Misconduct committee's 20-page report and recommendations were forwarded to Provost Susan Avery and Arts and Sciences Dean Todd Gleeson, who then sent them to Interim Chancellor Phil DiStefano, who made the final decision to terminate Churchill's employment contract, subject to approval by the CU Board of Regents. After DiStefano recommended on July 26 that Churchill be fired, he was entitled to one more review: an appeal to the university's Committee on Privilege and Tenure, which upheld the original findings.

David Lane, Churchill's attorney, retorted that the committees' findings were a pretext for firing on freedom-of-speech grounds. "It's window dressing," Lane said. "They want to make it look legitimate so then they can fire him and say, 'Look, it had nothing to do with free speech'" (Johnson, June 27, 2006).

Lane filed a lawsuit based partially on those grounds seeking reinstatement of Churchill at the university. A Denver District Court jury found that Churchill's political views had played a substantial role in the firing, but awarded him only $1 in damages. On July 7, 2009, Judge Larry J. Naves refused to reinstate Churchill at the University of Colorado, saying that the Board of Regents had acted in a judicial capacity when Churchill was dismissed. The board thus was legally protected from the lawsuit, the judge ruled. Lane said he would appeal.

An appeals court and the Colorado Supreme Court let the local ruling that fired Churchill stand. After the Supreme Court ruling September 10, 2012, Lane said that it "spends 55 pages saying the regents are above the law" (Frosch, 2012, A-12). Lane said he would appeal the case to the U.S. Supreme Court.

Further Reading

Brennan, Charlie. "Tribe Clarifies Stance on Prof. Milder Statement Explains Churchill's 'Associate' Label." *Rocky Mountain News,* May 21, 2005, 16-A.

Burnett, Sara. "C.U. Panel: Fire Prof. Churchill Should be Cut Loose, Say Six of Nine Who Cast Secret Ballots." *Rocky Mountain News*, June 14, 2006. http://www.rockymountainnews.com/drmn/education/article/0,1299,DRMN_957_4773332,00.html.

Churchill, Ward. "Some People Push Back: On the Justice of Roosting Chickens." 2001. http://www.kersplebedeb.com/mystuff/s11/churchill.html

Churchill, Ward. "Statement of Ward Churchill." September 20, 2006.

Curtin, Dave, Howard Pankratz, and Arthur Kane. "Questions Stoke Ward Churchill's Firebrand Past." *Denver Post,* February 13, 2005, A-1.

Frosch, Dan. "Professor's Dismissal Upheld by Colorado Supreme Court." *New York Times,* September 11, 2012.

Johansen, Bruce E. *Silenced! Academic Freedom, Scientific Inquiry, and the First Amendment Under Siege in America.* Westport, CT: Praeger, 2007.

Johnson, Kirk. "University of Colorado Chancellor Advises Firing Author of Sept. 11 Essay." *New York Times,* June 27, 2006. http://www.nytimes.com/2006/06/27/education/27churchill.html

Saito, Natsu Taylor. "Update on University of Colorado's Investigation of Ward Churchill." September 10, 2005. [Personal e-mail message]

Wesson, Marianne. *Report of the Investigative Committee of the Standing Committee on Research Misconduct at the University of Colorado at Boulder concerning Allegations of Research Misconduct against Professor Ward Churchill.* May 9, 2006. www.colorado.edu/news/reports/churchill/churchillreport051606.html

Clearwater, Frank

(1925–1973)

Frank Clearwater was killed during a firefight during the occupation of Wounded Knee in which the AIM was badly out-matched: old rifles, for the most part, against 4,000 rounds of .50-caliber ammunition that was capable of piercing armor. Clearwater had arrived the day before he was shot with his wife Morning Star, age 37, who was three months pregnant, from North Carolina. They were not AIM members. He was sleeping in the hamlet's Catholic Church when a bullet came through the wall and "tore off the back of his head" (Churchill and Vander Wall, 1988, 161). Five other AIM people were injured during the same assault, but their bullets were removed by medicine men or medical people in a clinic on the grounds.

When they realized that Clearwater was near death, a call went out for an evacuation helicopter, but the federal command post denied permission. Instead, AIM was told to bring him out in a vehicle under a white flag. Despite two white flags, the vehicle endured a gauntlet of gunfire as if carried Clearwater between Wounded Knee and federal lines. Clearwater's wife asked to accompany him, and was granted a safe-conduct pass by word-of-mouth. Despite this, she was arrested by FBI agents, dragged away, and imprisoned at Pine Ridge. Clearwater died on April 25, never having regained consciousness (Churchill and Vander Wall, 1988, 162).

After Clearwater was shot, the FBI issued a press release that erroneously asserted he was a "white man" (he was Cherokee) who had been dishonorably discharged by the U.S. Army, and then reenlisted under false pretenses. The FBI statement's own credibility was reduced by its botching of his name as "Frank Clear" (Matthiessen, 1991, 77). The people of AIM later dedicated a Sun Dance to Clearwater, along with other people who had been killed on or near Pine Ridge: Buddy Lamont, Raymond Yellow Thunder, and Pedro Bissionnette.

Further Reading

Churchill, Ward and Jim Vander Wall. *Agents of Repression: The FBI's Secret Wars Against the Black Panther Party and the American Indian Movement.* Boston: South End Press, 1988.

Matthiessen, Peter. *In the Spirit of Crazy Horse.* New York: Knopf, 1991.

Cleveland, Ohio, American Indian Movement

Founded in 1972, the American Indian Movement Cleveland Autonomous Chapter (Cleveland AIM) has been best known for its long-time opposition to the Cleveland Indians' baseball team's "Chief Wahoo" mascot. Cleveland AIM was initiated in 1972 by Russell Means. Beginning that year, then again in 1995 and 1999, Cleveland AIM filed suit against Cleveland Baseball to change the "Cleveland Indians" team name and "abolish its shameful, racist Indian-head logo and mascot. "Chief Wahoo. . . will continue to pursue all avenues of disruption until 'Chief Wahoo' has gone the way of 'Little Black Sambo' and the 'Frito Bandito'" (Cleveland, n.d.). The chapter's lawsuits against Indian-themed mascots have not succeeded, as members of Cleveland AIM protested the mascot every opening day. The group did, however, convince the Oberlin School Board to change its "Oberlin Indians" name and mascot.

Cleveland entered professional baseball more than a century ago with a team named the Spiders; in the team's first year, the Spiders lost 134 games. Later, the team was called the "Naps." The Cleveland Indian name was adopted by a vote of the fans during 1914. Chief Wahoo was first mentioned in print by a Cleveland *Plain Dealer* columnist during the 1940s and first sewn onto Cleveland Indian uniforms in 1947.

Until the year 2000, the Cleveland Indians' official media guide maintained that the name was adopted in honor of Louis Sockalexis, a Penobscot who played for the Spiders between 1897 and 1899. Therefore, many Indian fans boasted that the name was an honor, not an insult. The media guide first mentioned the Sockalexis story in 1968 (just as early protests began to roll in from the new AIM).

Sockalexis was said to have been the first Native American to play in baseball's major leagues. It is unknown whether this is true, or spin-control meant to turn a slur into a belated act of affirmative action. In 1999, the media guide devoted an entire page to the Sockalexis "story" which was coyly declared bogus a year later. In January, 2000, the wording of the guide was changed, with the reference to Sockalexis taken as "legend." The old version was proved factually inaccurate by Ellen Staurowsky, a professor at Ithaca College, New York, who maintained that the team should drop its Indian moniker. Any change could cost the baseball club dearly, because Chief Wahoo is among the best-selling sports images on clothing, caps, and other merchandise.

Sockalexis began playing baseball at Holy Cross College, Worcester, Massachusetts, less than five years after the massacre at Wounded Knee. He was raised on the Indian Island reservation in Old Town, Maine. By 1897, he was playing baseball at Notre Dame, a school from where he was expelled after only a month because of public drunkenness. The Cleveland Spiders then signed him to a professional contract for $1,500. At first, Sockalexis experienced something of a hitting streak. By the middle of his first season with the Spiders, he was hitting .335. It has been said that some fans "took to wearing Indian headdresses and screaming war whoops every time Sockalexis came to bat" (Nevard, n.d.). During July of 1897, Sockalexis got drunk and injured himself. He spent most of the rest of his baseball career on the bench, before being released in 1899. For a decade after that, Sockalexis performed manual labor in Cleveland as he continued to suffer from alcoholism. He died in 1913. A novel based on his life (*The Cleveland Indian: The Legend of King Saturday*) was written by Luke Salisbury.

Cleveland AIM's web page says that it "welcomes diversity; any person who embraces and actively supports self-determination, spirituality, solidarity, and sobriety for indigenous peoples and indigenous nations are welcome to join our ranks" (Cleveland, n.d.).

Further Reading

"Cleveland [Ohio] American Indian Movement." No date. http://www.clevelandaim.us/

Nevard, David. "Wahooism in the USA." *A Red Socks Journal.* No date. http://www.ultranet.com/~kuras/bhxi3d.htm

Coalition for Navajo Liberation

The Coalition for Navajo Liberation (CNL) organized in the U.S. Southwest at about the same time the AIM organized in Minneapolis. The CNL organized around several issues, including mutilation murders of Navajos and federal energy policy that was defining Navajo country as a "national sacrifice area" for the mining of coal and uranium.

Protesting Murders of Navajos

The bodies of ten Navajo, most of them middle-aged men, were found with their sex organs gouged out during 1973 and 1974. Willie Harrison's body had its ears cut off and had been burned from the waist down. Andrew Acquie, 47, Arnold Cellion, 44, and Alfred Yazzie, about 24, had been stabbed more than 30 times each. A broom handle was shoved up one 70-year-old Navajo man's anus. Another man died after a firecracker was exploded in his anus. This provoked demonstrations by as many as 10,000 Navajo in Farmington, New Mexico, a reservation border town, of which CNL was a key organizer.

Arrests were made in three of the murders. Three white teenagers—Delray Ballinger, 17, Howard Bender, 17, Matthew Clark, 16, were sent to a juvenile reformatory in Springer, NM, for two years, then, in May, 1976, paroled to states outside New Mexico. These murders were similar to the deaths of Indians such as Raymond Yellow Thunder, among many, who had become the focus of mass protests by AIM in South Dakota and Nebraska. The CNL, however, did not possess Russell Means' national media savvy, so the Navajo murders went largely unreported outside that area.

John Redhouse, associate director of the National Indian Youth Council, himself a Navajo, said:

> We didn't see the murders as the acts of . . . crazy kids. We see them as part of a whole racist picture. For years it has been almost a sport, a sort of sick, perverted tradition among Anglo youth of Farmington High School to go into an Indian section of town and physically assault and rob elderly and sometimes intoxicated Navajo men and women . . . for no apparent reason, other than that they are Indians. (Johansen and Maestas, 1979, 62)

The CNL also campaigned against sale of alcoholic beverages to Navajos in border towns, with little success. Fred Johnson, an early CNL leader, said that one of CNL's first priorities was to "remove the scourge of the white man's alcohol that is destroying the physical and spiritual strength of our people" (Johansen and Maestas, 1979, 67). Johnson filed suit to have six Farmington-area bars closed as public nuisances because they were patronized almost exclusively by Navajos. The suit went nowhere.

Johnson later was killed in the crash and explosion of a small airplane under circumstances that had many CNL members contending that he had been assassinated.

Growing Opposition to Coal and Uranium Mining

The CNL also fought against coal and uranium mining on the Navajo reservation. Enlisting the aid of Navajo sheepherders such as Emma Yazzie, who was 70 years of age at the time, who had seen their herds devastated by mining pollution (Johansen and Maestas, 1979, 143–44).

Yazzie took visitors to the bottom of coal strip mines near hogan to watch draglines at work, telling them: "Don't go alone. They'll turn you away. They're afraid of me!" (Johansen and Maestas, 1979, 145). Yazzie had been known to show her disgust at the mining by unearthing surveyors' sticks and dumping them on supervisors' desks.

Yazzie found herself between coal strip mines and the Four Corners coal-fired electrical plant, which puts out a polluting plume so large that NASA astronauts observed it from Earth orbit. Her sheep had, by 1976, become small, skinny, and sickly, with gray wool. The Four Corners plant exports power to Los Angeles, Phoenix, Las Vegas, Nevada, and other cities in the region. Yazzie's Hogan has no electricity.

The Navajo Nation contains the largest uranium deposits in the United States. The CNL's position on uranium was considered radical when it was first advanced in the 1970s, but it priced to be a harbinger. In 2005, with increasing numbers of former miners dying from lung cancer, the Navajo Nation became the first Native American nation to outlaw uranium exploration and mining on its lands. In 2006 and 2007, Representative Henry Waxman, Democrat of California, chair of the Budget and Government Oversight Committee, demanded a plan from five federal agencies to clean up the contamination caused by more than 500 abandoned uranium mines on the Navajo Nation, in what he called "A 40-year history of bipartisan failure and a modern American tragedy" (Press Release, 2011). In 2008, Congress authorized a plan to clean up contaminated soil, water, and structures.

The most deadly threat in Navajoland, however, was uranium mining. Opposition to uranium mining was considered a radical political position in the 1970s, when CNL pressed the case that it would bring death and environmental damage. Three decades later the Navajos' government made such mining illegal after many of the miners died from radiation poisoning.

Further Reading

Brugge, Doug and Timothy Benally. *The Navajo People and Uranium Mining*. Albuquerque: University of New Mexico Press, 2006.

Eichstaedt, Peter. *If You Poison Us: Uranium and American Indians*. Santa Fe, New Mexico: Red Crane Books, 1995.

Johansen, Bruce E. and Roberto F. Maestas. *Wasi'chu: The Continuing Indian Wars*. New York: Monthly Review Press, 1979.

Pasternak, Judy. *Yellow Dirt: An American Story of a Poisoned Lands and a People Betrayed*. New York: Free Press, 2010.

"Press Release: Navajo Film & Media Campaign Win Clean Up of Uranium." The Return of Navajo Boy. August 22, 2011. http://navajoboy.com/29661/press-release-navajo-film-media-campaign-win-clean-up-of-uranium/.

Colorado, American Indian Movement of

The Colorado AIM has long been a thorn in the side of the AIM Grand Governing Council in Minneapolis, home base of Glenn Morris, Ward Churchill, and allies. Colorado AIM has been (as a national leader of the "Autonomous Chapters of AIM") an ideological mirror-image of the national organization, to the point of indicting it for crimes against Native American traditions.

The acerbic nature of the split within AIM was indicated on November 4, 1994, in Rapid City, South Dakota, when Colorado AIM announced "final verdicts" of a tribunal that found Grand Council leaders Vernon and Clyde Bellecourt guilty on eight charges. The tribunal had been held on March 26 and 27, 1994, in San Rafael, California. The Bellecourts earlier had expelled Colorado AIM, a declaration that its members defied.

After taking part in a street theatre event to stop the Columbus Day Parade, an unidentified protester leads a chant against parade participants on October 8, 2005, in Denver, Colorado. (AP Photo/David Zalubowski)

Colorado AIM declares that it "has rooted its political, social, cultural and economic program in four basic, essential, and non-negotiable principles: Spirituality, Sovereignty/Self-determination, Support and Sobriety" (Colorado, n.d.). Colorado AIM relishes street agitprop. Its range of activities has been very broad— from picketing liquor stores that sold of Crazy Horse Malt Liquor. Denver has many occasions when political opposites face off.

On January 18, 1992, Colorado AIM members taking part in a Martin Luther King Day parade and rally confronted Ku Klux Klan members on the steps of the Colorado State Capitol, provoking a small riot. The previous year, Colorado AIM led an anti-Klan rally in Aurora, a suburb of Denver; on April 20, also in 1991, they had led another anti-Klan rally at the State Capitol. An AIM history noted that "Colorado AIM security is outstanding; Klan gets pummeled and are escorted away under a heavy police presence" (Colorado, n.d.).

On May 10, 1988, the City of Denver locked the Tall Bull Memorial Grounds south of the city. Colorado AIM demanded that the site reopen to allow spiritual ceremonies. After the city refused, AIM organized a march to the gate, after which the city relented at the last moment. Glenn Morris, speaking for Colorado AIM "negotiated with city for cooperative agreement to allow the Indian community exclusive use of Tall Bull Grounds. . . . This agreement remains in effect" (Colorado, n.d.).

In January 1991, AIM demanded that the City of Denver monitor the site of a new airport there for Indian remains. The city hired an Indian monitor. On September 28, 1988, Colorado AIM published a column in the *Rocky Mountain News* on Indian contributions to the U.S. Constitution. The chapter also participates in many other activities, such as sacred runs, sun dances, and pow-wows.

Colorado AIM long carried out a spirited debate on the op-ed pages of the *Rocky Mountain News* and *Denver Post* replying to the many times that editorials criticized their conduct, especially with regard to Columbus Day parades.

Marching Against Columbus Day

Colorado AIM has organized the largest protests of Columbus Day anywhere, some of which have ended in small riots with numerous arrests. On October 8, 1994, Colorado AIM bought an advertisement in the *Rocky Mountain News* headlined "Goodbye Columbus." On October 10, 1993, Colorado AIM shut down the Denver Columbus Day parade with aid from more than 2,000 supporters in 50 allied groups.

On April 19, 1990, *The Rocky Mountain News* published a column, submitted by Glenn Morris, criticizing veneration of Columbus as a hero. The column was called "The Big Lie." A statue of Columbus in Civic Center Park became a center of conflict. On January 19, 1990, Colorado AIM sent a letter to Denver Mayor

Federico Peña, suggesting that statue be removed. Peña declined. Russell Means on Columbus Day 1990 splattered blood on the statue and was arrested. He made a case that the blood spattering was an expression of freedom of speech, and a judge agreed, dismissing the charges on February 7, 1990. The *Rocky Mountain News* and *Denver Post* condemned the decision.

Following the court ruling that Denver's city government had violated international law by granting a permit for the city's Columbus Day parade, a large celebration that had been planned for 1992 (the 500-year anniversary of Columbus' first landing in the Americas) was canceled. By 2000, however, the parades were being held again, and Denver AIM was out in force with a network of non-Native supporters. Columbus Day again had become a very big deal in Denver, as, in 2002, more than 240 protesters were arrested after they disrupted the parade. Later, all charges were dropped.

Colorado AIM also extended its reach against Columbus Day, in 1991 traveling to Corpus Christi, TX, at invitation of a local AIM chapter, to protest Columbus events there. On June 26, 1992, members of Colorado AIM were acquitted of charges from four arrests after they blocked a 1991Columbus Day Parade

Further Reading

"Colorado American Indian Movement." No date. http://www.coloradoaim.org/

Cornwall Bridge (Ontario) Occupation

(1968)

As the AIM was becoming organized in Minneapolis during 1968, activism in defense of treaty rights was being expressed among members of the Haudenosaunee (Iroquois) Confederacy on the border of the United States and Canada, in defense of free movement of people and goods, a necessary right for people living on a reservation (St. Regis Mohawk, called Akwesasne by people who live there) that spans the border.

The Iroquois, who pre-date European Americans in the area by many centuries, have often regarded the U.S.-Canadian border as an artificial inhibition. Their right to cross this border (and transport goods without tolls or customs duties) is recognized in the United States by the Jay Treaty (1794) and in Canada by the Treaty of Ghent (1814). Until the late 1960s, however, authorities in both the United States and Canada ignored the treaty rights (Johnson, 1996, 2008, 39–40).

On December 18, 1968, Iroquois on both sides of the border occupied an international bridge at Cornwall, near Akwesasne, stopping traffic on a vital transport link to demonstrate their rights. Mike Mitchell, who later became a leading political figure at Akwesasne, transported a number of common household goods over the border and submitted to arrest to provide a test case in the Canadian court system. The Canadian authorities had been more aggressive in restricting border-crossing rights, which had been argued since the 1920s by the Indian Defense League. Canadian courts dismissed the charges during 1969 and opened a new era with respect to border-crossing rights.

The Conflict over Border-Crossing Rights

Akwesasne Mohawk activist Ernie Benedict became a major organizer of the International Bridge blockade of 1968 at Akwesasne. At the time, Canadian policies curtailed Mohawks' freedom of movement across the international border that are guaranteed under the Jay Treaty of 1794. Benedict began his long-time support of border-crossing rights with the Indian Defense League of America, when he attended the annual border-crossing events at Niagara Falls, with Chief Clinton Rickard, the "Fighting Tuscarora." Benedict, with others, helped collect money to fight Akwesasne's first battle for border crossing litigation in 1956.

From Benedict's home on Cornwall Island, the Mohawks of Akwesasne prepared to blockade the nearby International Bridge and force the issue of policies that required them to pay customs duties on anything worth more than $5, including food and other necessities of daily life. Benedict acted as lead media spokesman for the Akwesasne community as the blockade unfolded.

The Iroquois' right to cross the U.S.-Canada border freely has been acknowledged legally (in treaties) by both countries, but practical day-to-day matters (such as the right to buy goods for personal use on one side and transport them to the other) was not being respected. Michael Kanentakeron Mitchell, who later would serve as the Mohawk Council of Akwesasne's Grand Chief, with the support of at least 400 Akwesasne community members and visitors from the Assembly of First Nations, transported a number of basic goods across the border to force a test case. Mitchell was arrested and assessed a duty of $361.64. To create a legal challenge, Mitchell refused to pay the duty. The goods were given away as gifts (and a demonstration of traditional trading relationships) at the Tyendinaga Mohawk territory in Canada.

Canada's National Film Board recorded the blockade in a 1969 documentary titled *You are on Indian Land*. More than 100 Mohawks, mostly women, children and young men, imposed a wall of bodies that stopped traffic between the United States and Canada. Police arrested 41 Mohawks, who later were released; charges were dropped. After a second blockade in February, 1969 and a long series of negotiations and court cases, Canadian officials agreed to abide by the terms of the treaties.

Mitchell was sued in the Canadian federal court system, with Canada's Minister of National Revenue as defendant. Mitchell's brief stated that he, as a Mohawk resident at Akwesasne, had a right (under the Canadian Constitution Act of 1982) to transport "usual goods" into Canadian territory for the use of community members without duty. Mitchell's items were all legal goods (drugs and firearms, alcohol, and plants face special legal limitations). Hon. Justice William P. McKeown affirmed Mitchell's rights, and ordered the defendant to pay legal costs, a bill of $293,991.92 (Grace-Kobas, 1997, n.p.). Realizing here the rule of law was headed, long before the courts upheld the Mohawks' rights officially, customs officials began to allow greater tolerance of the Mohawks' right to transport the necessities of life across the border duty-free.

"The ruling was very complicated, and we did not win on all points," said Robert W. Venables, a professor at Cornell University, who testified on Mitchell's behalf. "Essentially the judge ruled that the Mohawks do have the right to trade regardless of contemporary political boundaries drawn by non-Indians, and they have the right to trade in 'usual goods.' He ruled that their treaty rights were still intact under the new [Canadian] Constitution. This was an important precedent" (Grace-Kobas, 1997, n.p.).

"I was particularly pleased with the court decision because the judge was very sensitive to the social structure of the Haudenosaunee," Venables added. "McKeown cites respectfully the testimony of the Mohawks and refers respectfully to those aspects of Mohawk society that were clearly distinct from Canadian and U.S. society and doesn't judge them inferior. It was a joy for me to see that. It was an amazingly sensitive decision that respected Mohawk points of view" (Grace-Kobas, 1997, n.p.).

The bridge occupation had a galvanizing effect on Native peoples across the United States as it was widely covered in mainstream print and electronic media, as well as in *Akwesasne Notes*. According to Vine Deloris Jr. in *Behind the Trail of Broken Treaties* (1974), "News of the Cornwall Bridge became a prominent discussion topic of Indians across the continent, and the success of the Mohawks was noted carefully by the Indians who wanted action" (Deloria, 1974, 35).

Further Reading

Grace-Kobas, Linda. "Lecturer Will Describe Recent American Indian Rights Case in His Class." *Cornell Chronicle*, August 21, 1997. http://www.news.cornell.edu/Chronicle/97/8.21.97/Venables.html

Johansen, Bruce E. *Life & Death in Mohawk Country*. Golden, CO: North American Press/Fulcrum, 1993.

Johnson, Troy. *The Occupation of Alcatraz Island: Red Power and Self Determination*. Urbana: University of Illinois Press, 1996.

"Custer Battlefield," AIM Protests at

Almost immediately after George Armstrong Custer lost his life (with the rest of the men he commanded) along the Little Bighorn River in 1876, the site was given the name "Custer Battlefield" by the United States government's Park Service, "a name offensive to many Indians, particularly descendants of those who won the battle" (War, 2011). The site was turned in to a shrine by Custerphiles, with locales such as "Last Stand Hill." The AIM started protesting the name in 1976 (the centenary of the battle) and continued until the name was changed to the Little Bighorn Battlefield National Monument.

On June 25, 1988, the anniversary of the Custer battle, Dakota, Montana and Colorado AIM marched on the site and pressed their case for a change of its name. In 1991, Congress changed the name. The Custerphiles were not pleased. At the same time, Congress authorized a Native American memorial to honor Indians who fought there.

"After some hesitation, due mainly to the amazing persistence of the Custer mystique," according to *National Parks Traveler,* a publication of the National Park Service, the Park Service actively supported the changes. It also began promoting Indian participation in ceremonies at the battlefield, including them in park management and staffing; three have served as superintendent since 1989, the year after AIM's last protest there (War, 2011).

Further Reading

"Colorado American Indian Movement." No date. http://www.coloradoaim.org/

"War and Consequences: The American Indian Movement vs. the National Park Service at Fort Laramie, Part II." *National Parks Traveler*. April, 2011. http://www.nationalpark straveler.com/2011/04/war-and-consequences-american-indian-movement-vs-national-park-service-fort-laramie-part-ii7992

D

Deloria, Vine, Jr.

(1933–2005)
Standing Rock Sioux

Vine Deloria Jr., a Standing Rock Sioux, first became nationally known during the late 1960s, following publication of his book *Custer Died for Your Sins.* His role in the national and international conversation regarding Native American issues rose with the organization of the AIM and other activist groups during the late 1960s and 1970s. Deloria also rose to national prominence as a spokesman for Native American self-determination movements, becoming a widely respected professor, author, and social critic in several fields, including law, religion, and political science, as well as Native American Studies. He was the best-known founder of Native American studies as a field of scholarly inquiry in the late 20th century.

By the late 1990s, Deloria was described as:

[T]he most significant voice in this generation regarding the presentation and analysis of contemporary Indian affairs, their history, present shape, and meaning. . . . No other voice, Indian or white, has as full a command of the overall data of Indian history or affairs, and no other voice has the moral force, the honesty, to admit mistakes and to redress them, or the edge to bite through the layers of soft tissue, through the stereotypes, myths, and outright lies, to the bone . . . marrow of Indian affairs. (Dunsmore, 1996, 411)

A Renowned Family

Deloria was part of a renowned Sioux family that has exercised a significant impact on American life and letters. As a member of the faculty at Columbia University beginning in 1929, his aunt Ella Cara Deloria (1889–1971) gained notice as an outstanding anthropologist and linguist. She wrote *Dakota Texts* (1932), which is bilingual in Dakota and English, and *Speaking of Indians* (1944), a description of Native life before the arrival of Europeans.

Ella Cara Deloria was born in Wakpala, South Dakota. Her Dakota name, *Anbpetu Wastewin,* meant "Good Woman of the Day." She attended Oberlin College and Columbia University, from where she graduated in 1915 with a bachelor's degree. After working as a school teacher and an employee of the YMCA (in Indian education), she returned to Columbia as a professor of

Vine Deloria Jr., right, talks with Vernon Bellecourt on the steps of Cedar Rapids, Iowa's Federal District Court Building, July 8, 1976. (AP/Wide World Photo)

anthropology, where she worked with Franz Boas on two major studies of Dakota language. She also authored a novel, *Waterlily*, during the 1940s. It was published in 1988, 17 years after her death. In her later years, she continued to write, speak, and work with reservation mission schools as she added to her Dakota grammar, fearing that it might join other Native languages in historical oblivion before she could finish.

One of the first American Indians to become an Episcopal minister, Philip Deloria (Yankton Sioux, 1854–1931) is one of about 90 historical figures whose statues surround "Christ in Majesty" at the Washington, D.C., National Episcopal Cathedral. As the long-time rector of St. Elizabeth Mission on the Standing Rock reservation, Philip Deloria was said to have converted thousands of Sioux to Christianity. He was the father of Ella Cara Deloria and grandfather of Vine Deloria Jr. Vine Deloria's son, Philip, is a professor of history at the University of Michigan and a renowned author and scholar.

Vine Deloria's Early Life

Vine Deloria Jr. was born in Martin, South Dakota, on the Pine Ridge Indian reservation on March 26, 1933. Educated in reservation schools during his early years, Deloria served in the Marine Corps between 1954 and 1956. He earned a Bachelor of Science degree at Iowa State University in 1958, and a Bachelor of Divinity at the Lutheran School of Theology in 1963. After that, Deloria served as executive director of the National Congress of American Indians (NCAI). At the same time, Deloria was a member of the U.S. Board of Inquiry on Hunger and Malnutrition. Serving on this board, he found black children in the Mississippi Delta eating red clay to deal with hunger.

Early in his life as an activist, Deloria channeled his intellectual efforts into legal studies, entering the University of Colorado Law School during 1967. He took up legal studies expressly in order to advance Native rights. Deloria completed study for his law degree in 1970, and later, in 1990, joined the University of Colorado's faculty, teaching until his retirement in 2000. Deloria's home department was history, but he also was affiliated with ethnic studies, religious studies, political science and the law school, one indication of academic respect he commanded across many disciplines.

Deloria on Red Power

During April, 1970, Deloria, had recently published *Custer Died for Your Sins: An Indian Manifesto*, when he twice visited Alcatraz during the Indian occupation of the island. He was impressed by the occupiers' boldness and energy, but believed they were inexperienced. Deloria told a press conference that "only ten Indians in the country are qualified to negotiate with the federal government," implying that none of the 10 were present at Alcatraz (Smith and Warrior, 1996, 82). The occupiers' governing council took notice of press reports quoting Deloria on April 3, and sent him a letter, asking for help, citing "our dire need for consultation" (Smith and Warrior, 1996, 82).

Deloria described the seizure of Alcatraz as a "masterstroke of Indian activism," even as he faulted its organizers' inexperience (Johnson, et al., 1997, 30). About 10 years after the occupation of Alcatraz ended, Deloria visited the island "and heard a surprisingly mild and pro-Indian explanation of the occupation from a Park Service guide." Deloria's own assessment was more pointed: "The Indians were well-represented in the media from the Alcatraz occupation through the Wounded Knee trials, but, unfortunately, each event dealt primarily with the symbols of oppression and did not project possible courses of action that might be taken to solve problems" (Johnson et al., 1997, 50).

Deloria saw potential in the younger movements, but also a danger of factionalism between them and older groups. Deloria wrote that "urban Indians have become the cutting edge of the new nationalism . . . . [even as] the tribal leaders were cringing in fear that the activists would totally control Indian affairs" (Smith and Warrior, 1996, 122). He wrote as the younger activists captivated national attention via the seizure of Alcatraz and other initiatives.

In an essay titled "Toward a Common Indian Front," distributed by the National Indian Press Association News Service in December, 1970 (during the Alcatraz occupation), Deloria proposed that older, established Native American groups (the NCAI and the National Tribal Chairmen's Association) work together with two newer, younger, and more militant groups, the National Indian Youth Council and the AIM. Deloria, who had served as president of NCAI between 1964 and 1968, also proposed, in Resolution 26, that the NCAI make common cause.

As a best-selling author whose work heralded the explosion in Native American civil-rights activity (*Custer Died for Your Sins* was published in 1969, just as AIM was organizing), Deloria was the best-known Native intellectual of his time, perhaps of all time. As the "father" of Native American studies, he had ties with students who formed the backbone of both NIYC and AIM. He also had ties with both reservation and urban peoples, and so formed a unique bridge between rural and urban, older and younger.

Common Themes of Deloria's Writings

Deloria's written works (including more than 20 books and more than a hundred major articles) often stress a common theme: that sin is a major element in American history, and that "the sinners are those who have stolen and desecrated the land" (Dunsmore, 1996, 413). On this subject, Deloria quoted Curley, a Crow chief, who is best known in history as one of the scouts for George Armstrong Custer at the Battle of Little Bighorn in 1876. Curley is not known as a great Native American philosopher, but his words, spoken in 1912, evoke memories of Tecumseh, Sea'th'l ("Seattle" is Anglicized), and Black Elk:

> The soil you see is not ordinary soil—it is the dust of the blood, the flesh and the bones of our ancestors. We fought and bled and died to keep other Indians from taking it, and we fought and bled and died helping the whites. You will have to dig down through the surface before you find nature's earth, as the upper portion is Crow. . . . [T]he land is my blood and my dead; it is consecrated; and I do not want to give up any portion of it. (Dunsmore, 1996, 415)

As early as the 1950s, Deloria was engaging in acute criticism of the Indian Claims Commission, arguing that it was a device to avoid treaty issues (such as the nature of Native American sovereignty), not to address them. He pointed out that laws and regulations announced as "help" to Indians often perpetuated colonialism. Historically, Deloria argued, the rights of Native Americans have trailed those of other ethnic groups in the United States. For example, slavery of Alaska natives was not outlawed until 1886, two decades after the United States Civil War.

Deloria has won a broad audience among a wide variety of people for asserting, with a sharp wit, contradictions in the general cant of contemporary American life. For example, in *We Talk, You Listen* (1970), Deloria recalled a conversation with a non-Indian who asked him: "What did you [Native Americans] *do* with the land when you had it?" Deloria said he didn't understand the ecological irony of such a question until he learned that the Cuyahoga River, which runs through Cleveland, was catching fire because of pollution. "After reviewing the argument of my non-Indian friend," wrote Deloria, "I decided that he was probably correct. Whites had made better use of the land. How many Indians could have thought of creating a flammable river?" (Deloria, 1970, 9).

Deloria defined the differences between European and Native American views of the land this way:

> The tribal-communal way of life, devoid of economic competition, views land as the most vital part of man's existence. It is THEIRS. It supports them, tells them where they live, and defines HOW they live. Land does not have the simple sentimentality of purple mountains majesty . . . . Rather it provides a center of the universe for the group that lives on it. As such, the people who hold land in this way always have a home to go to. Their identity is secure. They live with it and do not abstract themselves from it and live off it. (Deloria, 1970, 175)

"It will take a continuing protest from an increasingly large chorus," wrote Deloria (1992, 2), "to reprogram the psychology of American society so that we will not irreversibly destroy the land we live on." His sense of urgency at the speed of environmental deterioration during the last years of the 20th century is palatable: "Only a radical reversal of our attitudes toward nature can help us," he said (1992, 2). "Nor do I look forward to paying the penalties that Mother Earth must now levy against us in order for Her to survive." He continued:

> It remains for us now to learn once again that we are part of nature, not a transcendent species with no responsibilities to the natural world. As we face the twenty-first century, the next decade will be the testing ground for this proposition. We may well become one of the few species in this vast universe that has permanently ruined our home. (Deloria, 1992, 3)

Commenting on the missionaries to the Indians, Deloria sometimes condensed half a millennium of history in North America into one sentence: when the missionaries came, they had the Book [*The Bible*], and Indians had the land. Now, Deloria said, they have the land and Indians have the Book. Deloria called for adaptation of Native American land ethics to a general non-Indian society that finds itself faced with the environmental damage pursuant to two thousand years' experience exercising the biblical commandment to multiply and subdue the earth.

Deloria was known for his sharp wit on stage. Addressing 500 students at Boise State University February 28, 1998, he jested about 19th-century pseudo-scientific assumptions that Europeans were the most intelligent race because they had the largest skulls. That was before "the discovery that Apaches had something like 100 cc's more cranial capacity than Harvard professors," Deloria joked (Etlinger, 1998, 1-B).

Throughout his life, Deloria wrote a number of books and articles that took issue with Euro-centric interpretations of reality. His early books, such as *Custer Died for Your Sins* (1969), *We Talk, You Listen* (1970), and *Of Utmost Good Faith* (1971) continued to spread to new, younger audiences. In all of his works, Deloria has asserted Native American rights of occupancy to the land. Under international law, according to Deloria, Native American nations possess an equitable title of occupancy over lands upon which they live, "and this occupancy was not to be disturbed except by voluntary and lawful sales of lands to the European country claiming the legal title to the area in question" (Lyons, 1992, 283).

Deloria's writings also compare the metaphysics of Native American and European points of view, especially in legal and religious matters. In *God is Red* (1973), Deloria argued that American Indian spiritual traditions, far from being out-of-date, are more congruent with the needs of the modern world than Christianity, which he said fosters imperialism and disregard for Earth's ecological future (Johnson, 2005). In *God is Red*, Deloria also contrasts Native American religion's melding of life with a concept of sacred place to the artificial character of Old World doctrines.

Entering his late sixties by the year 2000, Deloria often walked with a cane. When people asked him about it, he was prone to joking that he had "been bitten by a rabid Republican and got a staph infection" (Wilitz, 1997, 1). Complaining about the left-leaning nature of the professoriate, Vincent Carroll, editorial-page editor of Denver's *Rocky Mountain News* (and a perennial critic of Deloria), pointed out that Deloria was the only registered Republican among faculty of the History Department at the University of Colorado at Boulder. Carroll, unlike those who knew Deloria, did not seem to realize that Deloria was joking when he had registered as a Republican.

Deloria had a talent for setting direction on important issues in Native America in just so many well-chosen words. For example, sounding a note similar to Oren Lyons' (sovereignty is as sovereignty does), Deloria said:

> There are hundreds of conferences on sovereignty where people just get up
> and talk and talk and talk, but very few will do the hard work to go out and

exercise the sovereignty that already exists. They spend all of their time trying to define sovereignty more clearly, and that's absurd if 'sovereignty' means that any political entity can negotiate on an equal basis with any other. . . . So sit down and work out a deal!" (Chapman, 2001, 286)

Deloria Passes Over

Deloria died November 13, 2005, in Wheat Ridge, Colorado, following complications of surgery for a ruptured abdominal aortic aneurysm. Before the surgery complications, Deloria had struggled with recovery problems from colon cancer surgery.

"The great indigenous visionary, philosopher, author and activist Vine Deloria, Jr. passed over to join his ancestors today, November 13, 2005," said a statement from the Colorado AIM (In Honor, 2005). "The passing of Vine creates a huge intellectual and analytical void in the native and non-native worlds" (In Honor, 2005). "It is safe to say that without the example provided by the writing and the thinking of Vine Deloria, Jr., there likely would have been no American Indian Movement, [and] there would be no international indigenous peoples' movement as it exists today" (In Honor, 2005).

"He had the courage and the vision," the statement continued, "to challenge the dominating society at its core. He was unapologetic in confronting the racism of United States law and policy, and he was prophetic in challenging young indigenous activists to hone their strategies. He was our elder statesman and mentor. . . . For many of us, Vine was a contemporary Crazy Horse" (In Honor, 2005). A public memorial for Deloria was held in Golden, Colorado, and a scholarship fund was initiated in his name.

For many days and weeks after his passing, the news rippled through Deloria's vast network in the United States and around the world, by email and personal contact, hand-to-hand, ear-to-ear, to "all our relations," in a Native American sense. Many who knew Deloria drew comfort from the belief that he will be in the other world when they pass over.

Remembering Deloria

University of Minnesota American Indian Studies Professor David Wilkins, who is Lumbee, wrote in *Indian Country Today* that Deloria "was never quite comfortable with the notion that he was, in fact, the principal champion of tribal nations since he wanted—no, demanded—that each Native nation express confidence in its own national identity, develop its own unique talents and together wield their collective sovereignty, that is, their dignity and integrity, in a way that enriches them and the nations around them as well." Reacting to his own influence, Deloria tried as best he could to spread his intellectual wealth around.

"Above all," wrote Wilkins, Deloria "fought tirelessly for human, not just indigenous, freedom and for ecological respect and common-sense approaches to heal the environment's many wounds. Deloria believed that America's national soul would never be cleansed until justice had been fully achieved by indigenous nations, blacks, Latinos, Asian-Americans, women, impoverished whites, any disempowered groups, and especially young people" (Wilkins, 2005).

University of Colorado professor Charles Wilkinson, an expert in American Indian law, called Deloria "probably the most influential American Indian of the past century" and stated that "he was also a wonderful human being, brilliant, bitingly funny and profoundly warm and compassionate, always willing to lend a hand or lift a spirit" (Dahl, 2005).

Disrespect from the Rocky Mountain News

The same day that Deloria was remembered and put to rest in a suburb of Denver, Vincent Carroll, still seemed to be seething over Deloria's playful response to his relentless effort to portray the University of Colorado faculty as a hotbed of political liberalism. In a column on the newspaper's editorial page, Carroll recalled Deloria as "wacky" (Carroll, 2005). Carroll condemned Deloria as anti-scientific, and for maintaining, in *Red Earth, White Lies* (1996), that American Indians "existed here 'at the beginning,' probably as contemporaries of dinosaurs, and this bizarre claim only hints at his contempt for much science" (Carroll, 2005).

Beating Indian drums, and demanding a meeting with editors (which was not forthcoming), the Colorado AIM picketed the *Rocky Mountain News* the Monday after Deloria was buried. AIM's spokesman Glenn Morris said that Carroll had slurred a man who was "the equivalent of Thurgood Marshall, Frederick Douglass and Martin Luther King rolled into one in the eyes of the Indian world" (AIM Fire, 2005, n.p.).

While editors at the *Rocky Mountain News* recalled Vine Deloria Jr. as a "crank" and a "wacko," *Indian Country Today's* editors described the affection for him that poured from Native America at the same time:

We remember the beloved teacher for his generosity of spirit. As a professor, Deloria mentored and touched many people across all ethnic and religious persuasions while always managing to teach and guide the work of scores of Native graduate students and young activists, many of whom went on to gain success and prominence on their own. He wrote prefaces and introductions and recommendations by the dozens in careful assessments of the work at hand, but was always ready to add his considerable gravity to the work of newer hands. He would not tolerate fuzzy thinking, however, and could and would hold his students to task. . . . In every generation, to paraphrase the late Creek Medicine Man Phillip Deere, there is one who hits the click-stone just right, and sparks the fire. In his generation, Vine Deloria Jr. sparked the intellectual fire of political, legal, historical and spiritual illumination. He lighted the path to the fountainhead of knowledge, which points the way ahead. (In Memoriam, 2005)

An obituary in the *New York Times* recalled that "While his *Custer* book, with its incendiary title, was categorized at the time as an angry young man's anthem, Mr. Deloria's real weapon, critics and admirers said, was his scathing, sardonic humor, which he was able to use on both sides of the Indian-white divide. He once called the Battle of the Little Bighorn, where Lt. Col. George Armstrong Custer and the Seventh Cavalry were defeated by a combined force of Sioux and Northern Cheyenne in 1876 in the Montana territory, "a sensitivity-training session" (Johnson, 2005). "We have brought the white man a long way in 500 years," he wrote in a *New York Times* op-ed article during 1976. "From a childish search for mythical cities of gold and fountains of youth to the simple recognition that lands are essential for human existence" (Johnson, 2005).

Further Reading

"AIM Fire: The American Indian Movement Targets the Rocky." *Denver Westword*, December 15, 2005, n.p.

Carroll, Vincent. "On Point: Vine Deloria's Other Side." *Rocky Mountain News*, November 18, 2005. http://www.rockymountainnews.com/drmn/columnist/0,1299,DRMN_23972_106,00.html#bio

Cassirer, Ernest. *An Essay on Man*. New Haven, CT: Yale University Press, 1944.

Chapman, Serle L. *We, the People: Of Earth and Elders, Vol. II*. Missoula, MT: Mountain Press Publishing Co., 2001.

Dahl, Corey. "Indian Activist and Popular Author Dies; Vine Deloria Jr. was a Retired C.U. [Colorado University] Professor." *Boulder (Colorado) Daily Camera*, November 15, 2005. http://www.dailycamera.com/bdc/obituaries/article/0,1713,BDC_2437_4239604,00.html

Deloria, Vine, Jr. "Commentary: Research, Redskins, and Reality," *American Indian Quarterly* 15, no. 4 (Fall, 1991): 457–68.

Deloria, Vine, Jr. *God is Red: A Native View of Religion*. Second ed. Golden, CO: North American Press/Fulcrum, 1992.

Deloria, Vine, Jr. *The Metaphysics of Modern Existence*. San Francisco: Harper & Row, 1979.

Deloria, Vine, Jr. *Red Earth, White Lies: Native Americans and the Myth of Scientific Fact*. New York: Scribner, 1995.

Deloria, Vine, Jr. *We Talk, You Listen: New Tribes, New Turf*. New York: Macmillan, 1970.

Dunsmore, Roger. "Vine Deloria, Jr.," in Andrew Wiget, ed. *Handbook of Native American Literature*. New York: Garland Publishing, 1996, 411–15.

Etlinger, Charles. "Indian Scholar Blows Holes in Theories: Deloria Says Lazy Scientists Adjust Facts to Fit Ideas." *Idaho Statesman*, February 28, 1998, p. 1-B.

George-Kanentiio, Doug. "Deloria as I Knew Him." *Indian Time* 23, no. 46 (November 17, 2005): 2–3.

Hughes, J. Donald. *American Indian Ecology*. El Paso: University of Texas Press, 1983.

"In Honor of Vine Deloria, Jr. (1933–2005)." Statement by Colorado American Indian Movement, November 14, 2005.

"In Memoriam: Vine Deloria Jr." *Indian Country Today*, November 17, 2005. http://www.indiancountry.com/content.cfm?id=1096411939

Johnson, Kirk. "Vine Deloria Jr., Champion of Indian Rights, Dies at 72." *New York Times*, November 15, 2005. http://www.nytimes.com/2005/11/15/national/15deloria.html.

Johnson, Troy, Joane Nagel, and Duane Champagne, eds. *American Indian Activism: Alcatraz to the Longest Walk*. Urbana: University of Illinois Press, 1997.

Lyons, Oren, John Mohawk, Vine Deloria, Jr., Laurence Hauptman, Howard Berman, Donald A. Grinde, Jr., Curtis Berkey, and Robert Venables. *Exiled in the Land of the Free: Democracy, Indian Nations, and the Constitution*. Santa Fe, New Mexico: Clear Light Publishers, 1992.

Smith, Paul Chaat and Robert Allen Warrior. *Like a Hurricane: The Indian Movement from Alcatraz to Wounded Knee*. New York: The New Press, 1996.

Wilitz, Teresa. "An Anniversary Celebration: Native American Author Exults in Gadfly Role at Newberry Conference." *Chicago Tribune*, September 15, 1997, 1 (Tempo).

Wilkins, David. "Native Visionary Spoke for All Disadvantaged Americans." *Indian Country Today*, December 1, 2005. http://www.indiancountry.com/content.cfm?id=1096412026

Williams, Matt. "Renowned Native American Scholar Dies." *Colorado Daily*, November 14, 2005. http://www.coloradodaily.com/articles/2005/11/14/news/c_u_and_boulder/news2.txt.

DeSersa, Byron

Died 1976

Byron DeSersa, a grandson of Black Elk (who was prominent in John Neihardt's *Black Elk Speaks*) was very outspoken in criticism of Richard Wilson and his regime on the Pine Ridge reservation before he was killed following a car chase by several GOONs (Guardians of the Oglala Nation, Wilson's tactical squad). As an attorney (and one who had held a post with the Oglala Sioux tribe) DeSersa was dangerous to Wilson. He had often written for a newspaper edited by his uncle (which had been firebombed by the GOONs in 1973) and was a major organizer for the campaign of Al Trimble, who unseated Wilson as tribal chairman in 1975 (for a term that began in 1976), by a three-to-one margin.

Early on the morning of January 30, 1976, the GOONs gave chase behind a car occupied by DeSersa and three companions, near Wanblee, on the Pine

Ridge reservation. After a four-mile chase they overtook DeSersa's car and riddled it with bullets. The car rolled into a ditch, after which the GOONs came after DeSersa as he told his companions to flee for their lives. One of DeSersa's legs was nearly cut off by a hail of bullets. He might have survived with medical attention, but the GOONs were too busy chasing the passengers through nearby woods to call an ambulance. He bled to death (Churchill and Vander Wall, 1988, 204).

The FBI was summoned to the scene by residents of Wanblee. The FBI agents said that they lacked "probable cause" to arrest anyone, despite the fact that the residents had supplied names of several suspects. An outraged group of Wanblee residents gave the GOONs until sunset to get out of town, and the FBI agents on the scene gave them a lift to Pine Ridge Village. The U.S. Commission on Civil Rights later confirmed the account of the murder, and Charles David Winters was charged with it; three other GOONs also eventually went to trial: Billy Wilson (a son of Dick Wilson) and Chuck Richards were acquitted on grounds of self-defense (although no one in DeSersa's car had been armed). Winters and Dale Janis plea-bargained to second-degree manslaughter. Each served two years in prison.

The arrests and trials were an anomaly during the GOON's time at Pine Ridge. Most murders were not investigated.

Further Reading

Churchill, Ward and Jim Vander Wall. *Agents of Repression: The FBI's Secret Wars Against the Black Panther Party and the American Indian Movement*. Boston: South End Press, 1988.

Johansen, Bruce E. and Roberto F. Maestas. *Wasi'chu: The Continuing Indian Wars*. New York: Monthly Review Press, 1979.

Disenrollment

The AIM chapter in Central California has taken a position in opposition to "disenrollment," by which Native tribes remove people from membership rolls, usually on grounds of insufficient "blood quantum," or degree of Indian blood. Disenrollment has become an issue most notably within tribes that have revenue-producing casinos and other businesses that provide members with per capita payments and other benefits, such as health care, scholarships, housing, and more.

Each tribe sets its own membership standards, and personal issues and politics sometimes pay a role in enrollment decisions. In some cases, such as that of the New York Oneidas, large numbers of people have been disenrolled for stating their opposition to political leadership. In this case, the disenrolled members have been

Some of more than a hundred ousted members of tribes from California and five other states who gathered on May 21, 2005, to denounce being disenrolled from their tribes. (AP Photo/Francis Specker)

denied considerable amounts of money generated by the Turning Stone Casino and other business ventures supervised by Ray Halbritrter and his hand-pickled "Men's Council" (Johansen, 2002).

In California, several small Native tribes with lucrative gambling operations have disenrolled several thousand members after questioning their bloodlines. The wave of disenrollments began in the 1990s after the rise of gambling brought many people onto tribal rolls. In California, more than 60 tribes brought in $7 billion in gaming revenue during 2010 (Dao, 2011, A-1). In a few cases, tribal members receive "per caps" of as much as $15,000 a month, after many years of grinding poverty. In 10 years, roughly 2,500 people have been disenrolled in California. The state has an American Indian population of 362,000 (Dao, 2011, A-1). "Sometimes, it is political vendettas or family feuds that have gotten out of hand," said David Wilkins (a Lumbee), who teaches at the University of Minnesota as a professor of American Indian Studies I (Dao, 2011, A-1). Disenrollment "destroys their connection to their ancestors, their cultural heritage, their tradition," said Laura Wass, Central California director for AIM "You have to go to iron gates and beg for entrance to your own land" (Dao, 2011, A-22).

Under present legal provisions, disenrollment decisions may not be appealed.

Further Reading

Dao, James. "In California, Indian Tribes with Casino Money Cast Off Members." *New York Times*, December 13, 2011, A-1, A-22.

Johansen, Bruce E. "The New York Oneidas: A Case Study in the Mismatch of Cultural Tradition and Economic Development." *American Indian Culture & Research Journal* 26, no. 3 (2002): 25–46.

"Dog Soldiers"

Douglass Durham, an informer within the AIM for the FBI, created, on paper, a fake band of 2,000 AIM "Dog Soldiers," renegades that he said were trained in "The Northwest Territory," hell-bent on blowing up the Charles Mix County Courthouse in South Dakota by rigging the valves on its boiler. Durham also told the FBI that an unspecified "action" was planned by the "Dog Soldiers" against the South Dakota state capitol in Pierre, as well as a bombing that would damage the Ft. Randall Dam near Pickstown, South Dakota. Durham went on to say that AIM's "Dog Soldiers" were planning the assassination of the state's governor, a plan to snipe at tourists on interstate highways, and assault the state prison, among other things (Johansen and Maestas, 1979, 43–56).

In memos furnished by Durham to the FBI (and later released amidst much media coverage) Charles Abourezk, son of U.S. Senator James Abourezk, was said to have been part of an arms-smuggling ring in Omaha, Nebraska, involving entirely fake locations such as "Red Man Street" and "Isla Vista," which, said the memos, "believed to be a suburb of Omaha." "Believed to be" was not very credible. Anyone with access to a map could have determined that no "Isla Vista" exists near Omaha.

Rene Howell of 20 North Street, Rapid City, was very surprised to find that her living room had been fingered by the FBI's "Dog Soldier" memos as the meeting place for AIM members whom the memos said would coverage there to pick up their marching orders and weapons to terrorize South Dakota. Her living room was good-sized, but nowhere nearly large enough to hold 2,000 "Dog Soldiers" with their M-16s, carbines, and rocket launchers on June 25, 1976.

Someone must be pulling someone's leg, Howell told a staff member from Senator Abourezk's office who delivered the memos to her. Someone was taking this business seriously, Howell learned, when Rapid City police disguised as construction workers flooded a vacant lot next to her house and began digging— looking, she supposed, for that cache of M-16s, carbines, and rocket launchers that the memos said was waiting for the "Dog Soldiers." Wasn't all of this uncomfortably close to the 100th anniversary of Custer's Last Stand? (Johansen and Maestas,

1979, 45–47). And what did Howell think of it all? "A waste of taxpayers' money," she said (Johansen and Maestas, 1979, 49).

Further Reading

Johansen, Bruce E. and Roberto F. Maestas. *Wasi'chu: The Continuing Indian Wars.* New York: Monthly Review Press, 1979.

Durham, Douglass Frank

(1937–2004)

The most spectacular role of a FBI informant inside the AIM belonged to Douglass Frank Durham, a non-Indian who became AIM's chief of security, and a bodyguard for Dennis Banks.

After high school, Durham was trained in "special tactics" by the Central Intelligence Agency, including demolitions, sabotage and burglary, both useful in secret "black ops." He was stationed for a time at a secret CIA base in Guatemala. He also worked with Cuban exiles in gunrunning, sabotage, and air support for the abortive Bay of Pigs invasion of Cuba in 1961.

Later, he worked with the police in Des Moines, Iowa, where he also ran a prostitution ring out of a cafe called The Why Not. This led to arguments with his wife, during which Durham beat her to death. She died July 5, 1964. He was charged with second-degree manslaughter, and was examined by a police psychiatrist, who said he was a violent schizophrenic, "unfit for office involving public trust" (Churchill and Vander Wall, 1988, 220). He later was involved in the heroin trade and other smuggling under Mafia aegis.

By 1973, Durham was being paid $1,000 a month (about $4,000 in 2011 dollars) to infiltrate AIM for the FBI. He made contacts inside Wounded Knee, where he called himself a photographer for a purported radical Midwest magazine, *Pax Today*. He then joined AIM through its Des Moines chapter, and worked his way into the national leadership in Minneapolis, where Banks made Durham his bodyguard and appointed him as AIM's first director of security. He also directed the Wounded Knee Legal Defense/Offense Committee for a while, and thus maintained an inside track on its legal defense in the Wounded Knee trials. On meeting Durham, and taking a long look into his eyes, Leonard Peltier told a friend, Leroy Six Toes, "That guy's a rat." Six Toes agreed, "Yeah, he's a rat." Peltier then told Banks, "Hey, there' something wrong with this guy. How well do you know him?" Banks became irritated at Peltier (Chapman, 2001, 242).

Durham's reports to the FBI during the Wounded Knee occupation contained a mixture of fact and fiction. At one point, he told the U.S. Senate Subcommittee on Internal Security that on Easter Sunday, April 22, 1973, "AIM members hung a man from a cross in full view of marshals and some members of the press. For approximately six hours [the man's] body was pummeled" (Johansen and Maestas, 1979, 52). He also asserted that AIM had planned to blow up a church in Des Moines, Iowa, and kidnap the state's governor, Robert Ray. Neither occurred. Durham also was acting as an agent provocateur inside AIM, issuing directives that leaders should be armed at all times, and prepared to engage the police and FBI in guerilla warfare, even as other members of AIM disavowed such tactics.

Durham was confronted with evidence of his role with the FBI in March, 1975, and ousted from AIM. John Trudell, national chairman of AIM while Durham was penning his fiction (and as the FBI distributed it), said that rumors of AIM's supposed terrorism were being used to justify its repression—payback for the occupation of the BIA headquarters in 1972 and Wounded Knee a year later. "They've been doing it for hundreds of years. Each time we want our resources and lands, they paint us up as savages," Trudell said (Johansen and Maestas, 1979, 53).

After he was discovered and dismissed from AIM, Durham developed an extensive anti-AIM campaign. He went on the road with a lecture tour sponsored by the arch-conservative John Birch Society, branding AIM members as gun-toting communist terrorists. He also testified in similar character before the U.S. Congress. In 1976, Durham created wholly fictional memos describing a fake band of AIM revolutionaries called the "Dog Soldiers." The FBI distributed these "teletypes" nationally, and watched as they were broadcast on the CBS, NBC, and ABC evening news. Later, FBI director Clarence Kelly admitted that the tale of the "Dog Soldiers" was entirely fictitious (Churchill and Vander Wall, 1988, 185).

Durham also cooked up a similarly fake memo involving a United front between the Crusade for Justice (a Latino group in Denver), the Students for a Democratic Society, and AIM that was said to be stockpiling hand grenades, M-16 rifles, and rockets to "kill a cop a day" by luring police into ambushes (Churchill and Vander Wall, 1988, 281). As with the Dog Soldier memos, the FBI, heedless of its credibility, released this bogus piece of intelligence to the public.

Further Reading

Chapman, Serle L. *We, the People: Of Earth and Elders, Vol. II.* Missoula, MT: Mountain Press Publishing Co., 2001.

Churchill, Ward and Jim Vander Wall. *Agents of Repression: The FBI's Secret Wars Against the Black Panther Party and the American Indian Movement.* Boston: South End Press, 1988.

Johansen, Bruce and Roberto Maestas. *Wasi'chu: The Continuing Indian Wars.* New York: Monthly Review Press, 1979.

Durham, Jimmie

(Born 1940)
Cherokee

Jimmie Durham, an internationally known essayist, sculptor, and poet, also was a major organizer in the AIM during the 1970s. He played a major role in organizing AIM's diplomatic arm, the International Indian Treaty Council (IITC), which achieved access to various forums in the United Nations, as the first indigenous American "Type II" (consultative) non-governmental organization (NGO).

Born in Washington, Arkansas during 1940, Durham first displayed his talents in dramatic arts performance and literature to the civil-rights movement during the 1960s. His first show as a visual artist was mounted in Austin, Texas, during 1965. Three years later, he moved to Geneva, Switzerland to study at L'École des Beaux-Arts. While at the Ecole des Beaux-Arts, Durham formed a group that he and his associates called Draga, which sought to bring the arts into contact with the public. He already was working on indigenous issues in an international venue. With a Mapuche from Chile and a Quechua from Bolivia, Durham formed a group called Incomindios to support Native peoples of the Western Hemisphere.

Durham returned to the United States during 1973 to become a leader in AIM. He led the IITC from 1974 until 1980. The main purpose of the IITC was to publicize the need to decolonize indigenous peoples; toward this end, it played a major role in a major United Nations conference on indigenous issues in 1977 that drew delegations from 98 native peoples around the world.

When AIM broke into factions, Durham returned to his life as an artist. He continued political work as a leader of artists, as his sculptures challenged conventional notions of Native American art. Between 1981 and 1983 he directed the Foundation for the Community of Artists in New York. During 1983, Durham published a book of poems, *Columbus Day*, with West End Press.

Four years later, he moved to Cuernavaca, Mexico. He then returned to Europe in 1994, where he staged a number of exhibits in London, Antwerp, Brussels, and other cities. He also published widely in a number of artists' journals. A book of essays, *A Certain Lack of Coherence*, was brought out by Kala Press in 1993. In his artwork and writing, Durham returns occasionally to themes of the American West. In 2005, for example, he cocurated *The American West*, an attack on cowboy and Indian mythology, at Compton Verney, in the United Kingdom.

Durham has published extensively, as his artwork continued to challenge conventions in Europe and the United States. A large number of interviews of him also have been published in artistic journals. According to Durham, the underlying cause of conflict between nontraditional and traditional Native American people is:

The traditional vision of American Indians with the [sacred] Pipe centers around a harmony of a circle, harmony of every part of life with our animal brothers and sisters and with our human brothers and sisters and a reverence for the sacredness of life. And this seems to come in conflict with white people's mentality . . . .on Pine Ridge . . . [the] the non-traditionals, the mixed-bloods, have accepted the white man's money, the white man's way of life and that is the difference. (Messerschmidt, 1983, 8)

Durham has been critical of many non-Native "progressives:"

Racism often takes the subtle forms of assuming Indian people to be just like white people, or *totally* different from white people, or other unspoken generalities, which further blind the people to the realities of Indian culture. It is also the primary cause of the most hateful piece of miscommunication now going on between Indians and white progressives: "political missionary-ism". . .

The second block is the colonial tool that I call "romanticism." The United States has used romanticism more effectively to keep Indians oppressed than it has ever been used on any other people. The basis of that romanticism is of course the concept of the "Noble Savage," but the refinements over the years have worked their way into how *every* non-Indian thinks about us, and how we think about ourselves. In the United States there is a special vocabulary of English *deliberately* developed to maintain oppression of Indians. This vocabulary has connotations of "primitiveness," backwardness, savagery, etc., and affects the ways every Indian and non-Indian in the United States thinks about Indians, whether or not people are conscious of them. (Durham, 1993)

He continued:

Some people get the idea that "traditional" Indians want to go back to the "good old days." Especially, they imagine that because of our grave concern over the environment we are escapists who want to reject technology and progress. That is another part of the romantic stereotype. We have, and have always had, technology. We accept all technology that contributes to the well-being of our people, which *must* include the well-being of the Earth itself and all the life upon it; that acceptance is neither a new thing nor an "accommodation": *it is one of our traditions.* (Durham, 1993)

Further Reading

Appleford, Rob. "Jimmie Durham and the Carpentry of Ambivalence," *Social Text* 28, no. 4 (2010): 91–111.

Canning, Susan. "Jimmie Durham." *The New Art Examiner* 23, no. 2 (1995): 31–35.

Durham, Jimmie. "American Indian Culture: Traditionalism and Spiritualism in a Revolutionary Struggle," in Jean Fisher, ed. *A Certain Lack of Coherence: Writings on Art and Cultural Politics*. London: Kala Press, 1993. http://historymatters.gmu.edu/d/6904

Durham, Jimmie. "Attending to Words and Bones: An Interview with Jean Fisher." *Art and Design* 10, no. 7–8(1995): 47–55.

Durham, Jimmie. *Columbus Day*. Albuquerque, New Mexico: West End Press, 1983.

Durham, Jimmie. "Geronimo!" in Lucy R. Lippard, ed. *Partial Recall: Photos of Native North Americans*. New York: The New Press, 1992, 55–58.

Durham, Jimmie. In Jean Fisher, ed. *A Certain Lack of Coherence: Writings on Art and Cultural Politics*. London: Kala Press, 1993.

Durham, Jimmie. "Jimmie Durham: Interviewed by Mark Gisbourne." *Art Monthly* 173 (February, 1994): 7–11.

Durham, Jimmie. *Jimmie Durham: My Book, the East London Coelacanth*. London: ICA Book Works, 1993.

Durham, Jimmie. *The Second Particle Wave Theory*. Sunderland, UK: University of Sunderland, 2005.

Durham, Jimmie. "'Various Element of Cowboy Life' & 'Cherokee-US Relations.'" *The American West*. Compton Verney, Warwickshire: Compton Verney, 2005, 9–22, 51–59.

Lippard, Lucy. "Jimmie Durham: Postmodernist Savage," *Art in America* 81, no. 2 (February, 1993): 62–69.

Messerschmidt, James W. *The Trial of Leonard Peltier*. Boston: South End Press, 1983.

Mulvey, Laura et al. *Jimmie Durham*. London: Phaidon, 1995.

Shiff, Richard. "The Necessity of Jimmie Durham's Jokes," *Art Journal* 51, no. 3 (1992): 74–80.

Taussig, Michael. "Jimmie Durham," in Isabel Carlos, ed. *On Reason and Emotion: Biennale of Sydney 2004*. Sydney: Biennale of Sydney Ltd., 2004, 82–85.

E

Eagle, James Theodore (Jimmy)

(Born 1957)

Jimmy Eagle, a young AIM activist (and a grandson of Gladys Bissonette), was charged with the murders of two FBI agents (Jack Coler and Ronald Williams) at the Jumping Bull ranch on the Pine Ridge reservation on June 26, 1975, during a shootout between AIM and several police agencies.

Leonard Peltier later was convicted of the FBI agents' killings after two other defendants (Bob Robideau and Dino Butler) were found not guilty. Charges were dropped against Eagle.

The day before the agents were fatally shot, on June 25, Williams and Coler had been searching for Eagle and two other AIM members, on charges of theft and assault with a deadly weapon, following the theft of a pair of cowboy boots at a party. The two agents visited the traditional reservation village of Oglala, known as an AIM redoubt, but had been unable to locate Eagle. The two agents were looking for Eagle on June 25 when they entered the Jumping Bull property. No one in the area would admit to having seen Eagle for several days, however (Matthiessen, 1991, 172). Residents there told the agents to leave when they could produce no search warrant.

Within two days of the shootout at Jumping Bull's, FBI agents had visited Gladys Bissonnette at her home, looking for Eagle, telling her he was under investigation for murder (Matthiessen, 1991, 206). Gladys still was recovering from the violent death of her cousin's son Pedro Bissonnette, who had lost his own parents, lived in Gladys' home, and called her "mother" (Matthiessen, 1991, 206).

On July 9, Eagle turned himself in at the U.S. Marshals' office in Rapid City on a charge of shooting James Catches on May 17, 1975. He was promptly arrested for stealing the cowboy boots and held on $25,000 bond (Matthiessen, 1991, 212). On July 28, he was arraigned in federal court in Rapid City, now charged with murdering Coler and Williams. The charge was based solely on remarks made by his cellmates in Rapid City a few days before the arraignment. The FBI said that Eagle had bragged to the cellmates about his role in the murders. His bond was raised to $250,000.

Following his conviction on felonious assault in the shooting of Catches October 12, 1975, Eagle was ordered held on the two agents' murders, as Andrew Bogues, a federal judge, noted that he had, in one year, Eagle, at age 19, had been involved in enough criminal activity that, if convicted, could send him to prison for the rest of his life (Matthiessen, 1991, 240). November 25, he was one of our AIM members formally indicted by a grand jury for the agents' murders, despite a sworn statement given to the FBI by Hazel Little Hawk November 12 that he had spent June 26, 1975, indoors with Gladys Bissonnette (Matthiessen, 1991, 242). The other four indicted by the Grand Jury were Robert Robideau, Darrell Butler, Jimmy Eagle, and Leonard Peltier. By that time, all but Peltier were being held in prison or jail. Peltier, who had escaped to Canada, was later apprehended and extradited to the United States.

On August 9, 1976, after Butler and Robideau had been acquitted at Cedar Rapids, Iowa, the FBI announced that charges against Eagle would be dropped, so that the prosecution could concentrate on Peltier. The FBI confessed that its case was weak, although Eagle had told people other than his cellmates in Rapid City that he had killed special agents Coler and Williams (Matthiessen, 1991, 578–79).

Eagle was paroled in 1977, having served part of a six-year term for the shooting of Catches. In October, 1977, Eagle, who was drunk, shot his uncle (who nearly died) during an argument over car keys. He was jailed at Pine Ridge, but freed a year later by his girlfriend, Wilma Blacksmith, who came to the jail with a .22 rifle. Gladys Bissonnette later was arraigned for aiding the escape and harboring him. Eagle, who never seemed far from the business end of smoking gun, was rearrested, imprisoned, and released several times in subsequent years (Matthiessen, 1991, 430).

Further Reading

Matthiessen, Peter. *In the Spirit of Crazy Horse*. New York: Viking, 1991.

El Centro de la Raza (Seattle)

El Centro de la Raza took root in the deep soil of multiethnic Seattle, perhaps the only city in the United States (maybe in the world) where a community led by Chicanos could rebuild an old school in what was becoming a mainly Asian community, drawing support from them, as well as blacks, whites, and Native Americans—a wok, soul food, meat and potatoes, tacos, and smoked salmon, side-by-side. What other organization would receive an award from President George H. W. Bush *and* Sandinista Nicaragua.

In a multiethnic city, Chicanos often found themselves in the middle of the action—a bridge ethnicity with ties to nearly everyone.

The AIM had close ties with El Centro de la Raza. The Trail of Broken Treaties Northwest caravan departed Seattle from El Centro. The Leonard Peltier Defense Committee's central office was located there. Peltier himself maintained a car-repair business out of El Centro before the 1975 shootout at the Jumping Bull ranch at Pine Ridge turned him into a fugitive. In early 1973, Roberto F. Maestas, El Centro's principal founder, was married to Estela Ortega in an Indian ceremony at El Centro. They spent their honeymoon at Wounded Knee during the winter of 1973, joining the AIM in the 71-day occupation on the site of the 1890 massacre.

El Centro de la Raza nurtured Native American ties from its beginnings in 1972. It grew up with the fishing-rights battles. The occupants of the old school on Beacon Hill were fortified during the initial occupation in October of 1972 by roughly 300 hundred pounds of salmon from Native people in the Nisqually delta, taken in danger of life and limb from assault by state game and fish agents. After the Nisquallys brought the cache of salmon, a ceremony was performed to bless it. Then the Indians said: "You're going to need this fish. It's going to be long haul. Count on us for whatever we can do" (Martinez, 2004, Tape 7).

The occupation that created El Centro during the fall of 1972 was modeled in part after the earlier, similar, take-over of Alcatraz Island in San Francisco Bay by a coalition of American Indians. Closer to home, but less well-known nationally, the take-over of the Beacon Hill School was patterned on an occupation of another piece of abandoned public property, Seattle's Fort Lawton, by Native peoples and their allies during 1970. While the Alcatraz occupation netted little in the long-range except media attention (the site later was abandoned), the similar takeover at Fort Lawton resulted in the creation of the Daybreak Star Center, a world-renowned Native American cultural center and meeting place.

The takeover of the Beacon Hill School also was aimed at tangible, enduring results. El Centro de la Raza's scope of community activism was shaped fundamentally during its early years by farm worker struggles and fishing-rights controversies the length of Puget Sound. One of the most notable recent Native-rights issues beginning during the 1960s was the right to fish in Pacific Northwest waters in accordance with treaties signed during the 1850s—a right that had been routinely denied by state authorities to that time.

Further Reading

Johansen, Bruce E. and Roberto F. Maestas. *Nuestra Familia, Nuestra Casa, Con Amor: Seattle's El Centro de la Raza.* Manuscript copy, El Centro de la Raza History Project, 2011.

Martinez, Regino. Transcript, Interviews with Roberto F. Maestas, Seattle, 2004. Tape 7 of 9.

F

Factions, American Indian Movement

Following the 1970s, when the AIM helped to transform the activist landscape in the United States, differences in personalities and political orientations caused the organization to break into antagonistic factions during the 1980s, a pattern that has continued to the present. By the late 1980s, AIM had one nucleus in Minneapolis, with a number of loose allies in other cities. Major dissent centered in Colorado. The factions even investigated and compiled reports criticizing each other in so-called "Tribunals." The AIM Grand Governing Council (GGC) in Minneapolis asserted a right to ownership of the name and AIM trademarks. Many other chapters did not accept the GGC's control or direction.

The Minneapolis office asserted control of a national network, but AIM had never had a national membership list. Dennis Banks and the Bellecourt brothers usually spoke for this group and its AIM Grand Governing Council. Vernon Bellecourt died in 2007.

At the same time, a network of dissident chapters formed a loose coalition with Colorado AIM. Ward Churchill and Russell Means, as well as Glen Morris led the AIM-International Confederation of Autonomous Chapters, based in Denver and Boulder.

The divide became so deep that each faction accused the other of betraying the movement.

A number of issues provoked the factional split, but policy toward the Sandinista government of Nicaragua and its treatment of Native minorities on the country's Atlantic Coast emerged as a catalyst during the mid-1980s.

A chronology from Colorado AIM recounted:

November 10, 1985: Russell Means, Glenn Morris, Hank Adams, World Council of Indigenous People, National Indian Youth Council and Survival of American Indian Association are invited to visit Indians in Nicaragua and determine their status. Upon their return, they hold a press conference in support of Indian self-determination and criticize the Sandinista Indian policy. Colorado AIM follows with a position in support of the Indigenous Peoples of Nicaragua. Minneapolis AIM continues to support the Government of Nicaragua and AIM splits over the issue. (Colorado, n.d.)

During subsequent years, the factions tried and failed to arrive at a "truce" over the Nicaragua issue. By February 27, 1986, an "AIM Summit" was held at Oglala, on the Pine Ridge Reservation, with Colorado AIM hosting. Vernon Bellecourt refused to attend. A month later, on March 27, 1988, Colorado AIM called a meeting in Denver "for the purpose of reconstituting the movement." Many leaders were invited: Russell Means, Dennis Banks, SlowTurtle (Wampanoag), Lenny Foster, Robert Cruz, Madonna Thunderhawk, and Phyllis Young (of Women of All Red Nations). Others sent statements of support, but Minneapolis AIM was not represented (Colorado, n.d.).

In 1993, the dissident faction issued an "Edgewood Declaration," which made a case that the Minneapolis faction was trying to force an authoritarian, centralized leadership style on a national organization, while AIM has always been decentralized, with autonomous chapters led by local constituencies, in accord with Native traditions, as well as the founding ideas of AIM.

Dissidents' Tribunals

By late 1994, the split had reached a point where the Colorado faction "indicted" the Bellecourts at "tribunals" held at San Rafael, California and Rapid City, South Dakota. The opinion was written by Donald A. Grinde Jr. (Yamassee), George Martin (Tlingit), Joe D. Locust Sr. (Cherokee), and Dian Million (Athabascan).

Charges against the Bellecourts were listed as:

We, the Tribunal, find the defendant, Vernon Bellecourt, guilty of subverting the American Indian Movement (AIM), its principles and activities . . . subverting the International Indian Treaty Council, the international diplomatic arm of AIM . . . collaborating with the United States government and with other enemies of American Indian people . . . [as well as] espionage against the Miskito, Sumu, and Rama Nations, as well as the Creole and Garifuno peoples of the Nicaraguan Atlantic Coast region, misuse/misappropriating American Indian Movement funds [and] use of alcohol and drugs at AIM functions, flagrantly disregarding AIM's prohibitions against such substances at AIM functions [and] complicity in genocide through his refusal to condemn, censure, or remove Clyde Bellecourt from his alleged AIM leadership positions after Clyde Bellecourt's 1986 conviction as a drug distributor. (Final Opinion, 1994)

All of this, according to the opinion, added up to "high treason against the membership of the American Indian Movement and American Indian people in general" (Final Opinion, 1994). The finding against Clyde Bellecourt was similar, except that he also was accused of "acceptance of federal funds and funds from defense contractors" and "support for the 1990 "Act for the Protection of Indian Arts and Crafts" [that] demonstrate his inclination to empower the federal government to define who is an Indian and to stipulate the conditions that Native American spirituality can be practiced." Clyde Bellecourt was accused of "selling of drugs in the American Indian community [and committing] genocide" (Final Opinion, 1994).

The tribunal's opinion stated that although people in AIM always had accepted differences of opinion, Vernon and Clyde Bellecourt had frequently overstepped the boundaries of tolerance. Repeatedly, the tribunal said it was confronted with overwhelming evidence that the Bellecourts abused and subverted American Indian people for their own personal gain.

The tribunal also said that the Bellecourts' reliance on federal funds had distorted Minneapolis AIM's mission, as they "purport[ed] to be leaders of a liberation movement. . . . They traveled to other Indigenous nations in our hemisphere abusing our sacred pipe by using it as a tool to gain confidence among unsuspecting Indigenous people" (Final Opinion, 1994). The tribunal sentenced both Bellecourts to banishment from AIM for life.

AIM's Minneapolis council advised the Bellecourts to boycott the tribunal: "Time and time again, the memories of the original AIM neighborhood patrol and organization that was founded by Clyde Bellecourt, Dennis Banks, George Mitchell and Harold Goodsky was touched upon by community elders who helped support its efforts and build its community roots" (DeMain, 1994).

This account continued:

A small delegation of AIM members comprised of Bill Means, President of the International Indian Treaty Council, Clyde Bellecourt, AIM National president, along with Ellie Favel, who carried with her a medicine bundle and pipe from the Minneapolis ceremony, traveled to the tribunal to try to come to terms with the group. . . . They were joined by Northern California AIM director Carole Standing Elk, Southern California AIM director, Fern Mathias, AIM publicist Patti Jo King, Floyd Westerman, and IITC Information Director Yvonne Swan. A request to move the tribunal to Minnesota was apparently successful, but not before the tribunal declared the Bellecourts guilty on some of the charges. Bellecourt says the Tribunal is a smokescreen for other concerns. (DeMain, 1994)

Personalities and Ideologies

Personalities figured into the split as much as ideology. In 1994, the Bellecourts accused Churchill of being an ersatz Indian:

"The American Indian Movement doesn't need white men wannabes claiming to be Indians, claiming to be AIM directors running around representing the movement," said Bellecourt. "Who is Ward Churchill? Is he an agent, I don't know, but look at the pattern. He admits infiltrating *Soldier of Fortune* [magazine]. It is he who has been disruptive and vindictive trying to set himself up as an AIM spokesman, an AIM director and trying to take editorial control of Leonard Peltier's Defense Committee newsletter. Churchill is a man without a tribe. (DeMain, 1994)

Bellecourt charged that Churchill and Means went to Nicaragua with the help of the "Contras" during the 1980s (through Honduras) that both met with Elliot Abrams, the U.S. State Department's Assistant Secretary. For Latin American Affairs, a confidant of Oliver North, both of whom were main figures in the Iran/Contra-CIA (drugs for arms) deals that funded the Contras' arsenal.

Some Attempts to Work Together

Despite the predominance of factionalism within AIM, after 2000 some chapters did attempt to unite around specific issues. During April, 2003, several AIM chapters met at a conference entitled Support and Protection of Indian Religions and Indigenous Traditions and began a campaign against "plastic Indians" with a "Declaration of War Against Exploiters of Lakota Spirituality," to counter sales of fake Native American spiritual objects, as well anyone who used sacred ceremonies for tourism. Minneapolis AIM vowed to require proof of Native status from anyone who asserted to represent Native peoples in public.

During February, 2004, AIM sponsored a new Long Walk, to Washington D.C., from Alcatraz Island, in support of Leonard Peltier, who was still imprisoned, 28 years after the shootout at the Jumping Bull ranch for which he had been convicted in the shooting deaths of two FBI agents. In December 2008, a group of Lakota Sioux (Talon Becenti and others) visited the U.S. State Department in Washington, D.C., and handed officials a "declaration of separation from the United States," which listed treaty violations and territory illegally taken from Native peoples by the United States. The group them announced an intention to form a nation called the Republic of Lakotah.

Further Reading

"Colorado American Indian Movement." No date. http://www.coloradoaim.org/

DeMain, Paul. "AIM Supporters Convene in Minneapolis for Ceremony." 1994. http://www.coloradoaim.org/history/1994PaulDemainsupportstheBellecourts.htm

"Final Opinion and Statement of the Tribunal Panel, Autonomous Chapters of AIM vs. Vernon and Clyde Bellecourt. November 4, 1994, Rapid City, SD. http://www.coloradoaim.org/history/19941104Finalverdictissuedinrapidcity.htm

The Federal Bureau of Investigation

During the 1970s, the AIM was followed very closely by the Federal Bureau of Investigation (FBI)—so closely that the focus became nearly obsessive. The

An FBI agent takes a photo as one of the first Native Americans left Wounded Knee March 6, 1973. (AP/Wide World Photo)

Bureau's role surpassed investigation for federal prosecutors, its traditional role. The FBI charged itself with destroying AIM on the assumption that it was a domestic terrorist group. To do this, it resorted to a number of legally dubious tactics, some of which resulted in false convictions and even murder by third parties reacting to FBI intelligence. Some of these tactics, such as use of the "snitch jacket," by which rumors were spread to convince AIM members that some in their midst were government informants, were used deliberately. Steve Hendricks in *The Unquiet Grave: The FBI and the Struggle for the Soul of Indian Country* (2006) makes a case that Anna Mae Aquash was murdered from within AIM's ranks after the FBI applied the snitch jacket to her.

One Dossier: The FBI Tracks a Typical Participant at Wounded Knee

As an example of how closely the FBI tracked participants in the Wounded Knee siege, consider files compiled on Roberto F. Maestas (1938–2010), a Seattle community activist, who joined several others on a journey there in 1973. He was not a major figure in the occupation. This is but one small slice of a huge surveillance operation.

The FBI followed Roberto Maestas, Phillip Ortega, Melissa K. Johnson, Alison Bridges, and one other person whose name was deleted from agency files as they drove from Seattle to Wounded Knee, South Dakota, during early March, 1973 to support the AIM occupation there. The agents did a workup on each, finding a scattering of misdemeanor arrests for fishing rights and the occupation at Fort Lawton in Seattle. One person, whose name was deleted from other evidence (such as his service as a U.S. Army paratrooper in Vietnam) may have been Yakama fishing activist Sid Mills. This person was described as having visited "Red China" for two weeks. Another person, whose name also was deleted, was listed as an "American Indian Movement activist—potentially dangerous." Again, the use of unsupported adjectives came in handy for creating an air of illegality.

The various offices of the FBI sometimes contradicted each other. While the Minneapolis office wanted to paint Maestas as a gun-toting terrorist, an agent in Seattle reported on May 11, 1973 that the caravan (four cars) that departed Frank's Landing for Wounded Knee was carrying "only food, medicine, and clothes. . . . There was no stockpiling of arms and ammunition and no transportation of these items in quantity," excluding "their own privately owned weapons."

The memos indicated that Maestas and his group joined three other cars along the way. Soon the FBI was gathering a file for a "possible violation" of anti-riot law (ARL) statutes (Title 18, U.S. Code, Section 2101), a felony, "to travel in interstate commerce and use the facilities of interstate commerce with the intent to incite, organize, promote, encourage, participate in, and carry on a riot and to commit acts of violence in furtherance of a riot." No charge was filed.

For a year after the siege at Wounded Knee ended on May 8, 1973, the FBI expended a considerable amount of time and effort trying to link Maestas to something for which he could be prosecuted. Agents examined wire-service photos and out-takes of NBC and CBS news programs on Wounded Knee during the 71 days of the siege. During that time, the agents in the Minneapolis and Seattle offices compared notes on their various spellings of Maestas' name. Was it Robert? Mestas?

The files are full of facts that many people knew, phrased to make them sound a little bit deviant and dangerous. Agents reported that he had married Estela Ortega "in an Indian ritual ceremony . . . not considered legal." Agents conducted "frequent surveillance checks" at their residence (Estela told the author that their garbage was rifled several times). Estela Ortega also had been noted in a Houston FBI report for participating in meetings with the Young Socialist Alliance before she met Maestas. This report was carefully cross-referenced with the Seattle material.

On March 5, 1974, the Special Agent in Charge (SAC), Minneapolis office, notified the SAC in Seattle that a United Press International (UPI) photograph had been found "which depicts subject wearing a handgun (left side) and holding a rifle (left hand) as he escorts a car carrying Harlington Wood, assistant attorney general, to a checkpoint leaving Wounded Knee . . . on 3/18/73." Side arms and rifles were part of the standard uniform on both sides by that time, and FBI agents who had surrounded the encampment were toting much more than small arms. Nevertheless, the SAC in Minneapolis advised Seattle FBI on May 9, 1974, by teletype, all upper case, almost 14 months after Maestas had been photographed by the UPI:

SUBJECT SHOUILD BE CONSIDERED ARMED AND DANGEROUS. SUBJECT IS A CHICANO LEADER AND ACTIVIST IN THE SEATTLE, WASHINGTON AREA AND HAS BEEN IDENTIFIED AS CARRYING FIREARMS DURING THE AIM OCCUPATION OF WOUNDED KNEE, SOUTH DAKOTA, BETWEEN FEBRUARY 27, 1973, AND MAY 8, 1973.

The Minneapolis office then wired the Seattle office requesting an interview with Maestas. Six weeks later, on June 28, the agent reported that he had been "located in the main lobby of the Beacon Hill School. . ." Maestas, reported the agent, "demonstrated hostility and belligerence and advised that he would not be interviewed under any circumstances by the FBI."

In the end, the paper trail indicated that the FBI had nothing worth filing a criminal case, and knew it. A memo with the files stated that "prosecution has been categorically declined in this matter and Seattle Division continues to consider the matter closed" (McCreight to Maestas, 1978, 2).

The Seattle Police Department's Intelligence Unit put quite a bit of effort into Maestas. A Detective Watson researched his divorce papers, and found an affidavit from his ex-wife objecting to Maestas' links to "various movements at the University of Washington questioning the current economic situation and stability and philosophy of our country." The police report said that he had brought the ideas home and discussed them with his oldest daughter, causing her mental strain, including two suicide attempts and attempts to run away from home.

The Seattle Police files repeated, with increasing elaboration, the fiction that arms were being stored at El Centro, citing "much intelligence," but without a single shred of real evidence. The same was true of statements that arms also were being stockpiled in private homes of Chicano families on Beacon Hill, as El Centro became a magnet for "every radical group in the area." Maestas was said to have advocated overthrow of the government as he obtained $131,000 from the city for repairs to El Centro's building. "Renovation was promised," the report said, "but nothing was ever done," even as reports of extensive repairs appeared during 1973 in Seattle's two daily newspapers. (Some of these reports were written by the author of this book.)

The FBI Strikes Back

The events at Pine Ridge during the 1970s remained a subject of sharp debate for many years. Supporters of Leonard Peltier have not let the subject rest, and neither have some of the FBI agents who are part of the story. Every time Peltier supporters approach a U.S. president for clemency, or a new trial (first Bill Clinton in the 1990s, most recently, President Barack Obama), former and present-day FBI agents protest *en masse*.

Joseph H. Trimbach, who was Special Agent in Charge of the Minneapolis Division of the FBI (with jurisdiction at Pine Ridge) during the 1970s has written a book with his son John Trimbach, *American Indian Mafia: An FBI Agent's True Story About Wounded Knee, Leonard Peltier, and the American Indian Movement (AIM),* self-published by Outskirts Press in 2007.

American Indian Mafia makes a case (in the words of the book's Web site [http://www.americanindianmafia.com]) that most of the history of these events has been falsified. AIM, according to the Trimbachs, "became a criminal enterprise on the reservation." AIM, they wrote, was a "small group of radicals [who] tore a path of destruction through the Pine Ridge Reservation on their way to personal gain, fame, and fortune . . . extort[ing] funds from religious organizations, the federal government, and unsuspecting supporters, and kept much of the money for themselves."

By Trimbach's account, "AIM leaders conspired to murder their opponents, even their own members," Aquash being the best known. They assert that Dennis Banks plotted her murder. Peltier, they argue, duped many celebrities and world leaders, including Mikhail Gorbachev, Nelson Mandela, the Dalai Lama, Amnesty International, Robert Redford and many others, who argued that he is a political prisoner. Many other histories "are complicit in the cover stories, where criminals are often given a pass," according to the Trimbachs. They have, they argue, "all fallen victim to the Peltier ruse" Peltier, they assert, was "the clear perpetrator" in the killings of the two FBI agents.

The two Trimbachs argue that their work "is the long-awaited book that fills the void in an often misunderstood chapter of American history." Judge William H. Webster, former Director of the FBI and the CIA, said that the Trimbachs' "hard-hitting exposé is . . . an important contribution to our understanding of what actually happened." Lt. Col. Oliver North, best known in the United States for his role in the "Contra" war against Nicaragua during the 1980s, described the Trimbachs' work as a "myth-buster" whose "carefully compiled chronology should be read by all Americans who "seek truth behind the headlines."

So, while the shooting war between the some members of the FBI and AIM has ended, the verbal salvos still fly more than 40 years later.

Further Reading

Hendricks, Steve. *The Unquiet Grave: The FBI and the Struggle for the Soul of Indian Country*. New York: Thunder Mouth's Press, 2006.

Johansen, Bruce E. and Roberto F. Maestas. *Nuestra Familia, Nuestra Casa, Con Amor: Seattle's El Centro de la Raza*. Manuscript copy, El Centro de la Raza History Project, 2011.

Fishing Rights, Western Washington State

By 1964, the first modern civil disobedience by Native Americans was taking place on Puget Sound salmon streams, as Indian "fish-ins" dramatized Native assertion of treaties signed during the 1850s to harvest fish that state authorities had long ignored or actively contested to that time. The fishing-rights movement was maturing in the Northwest at the same time when the AIM was being formed in Minneapolis. Alcatraz Island was occupied in San Francisco Bay, Navajos were protesting coal and uranium mining, and the Iroquois were shutting down the International Bridge at Cornwall. People shuttled back and forth between the Alcatraz Island occupation and fishing protests in Western Washington during 1969, 1970, and 1971.

To the Northwest Indian nations the salmon was as central to economic life as the buffalo on the Great Plains; 80–90 percent of the traditional Puyallup diet, for example, was fish. The salmon was more than food; it was the center of a way of life. A cultural festival accompanied the first salmon caught in the yearly run. The fish was barbecued over an open fire and bits of its flesh parceled out to all. The bones were saved intact, to be carried by a torch-bearing, singing, dancing, and chanting procession back to the river, where they were placed into the water, the head pointed upstream, symbolic of the spawning fish, so the run would return in later years.

Washington became a territory of the United States on March 2, 1853, with no consent from the Indians who occupied most of the land. Isaac Stevens was appointed governor and superintendent of Indian affairs for the territory. As governor, Stevens wished to build the economic base of the territory; this required the attraction of a transcontinental railroad, which, in turn, required peace with the Indians. Stevens worked with remarkable speed; in 1854 and 1855 alone, he negotiated five treaties with 6,000 Indian people west of the Cascades. By signing the treaties, the Indians ceded to the United States 2,240,000 acres of land, an immense sacrifice for the right to fish.

In 1914, about 16 million fish were caught annually. By the 1920s annual catches had declined to an average of 6 million. In the late 1930s, following construction of several large hydroelectric dams on the Columbia River and its tributaries, the annual catch had fallen as low as 3 million, about one-sixth of what Native peoples alone had been harvesting a century earlier. By the 1970s, with more aggressive conservation measures in place, including construction of fish ladders at most major dams, the annual catch has rose to four to six million, just short of a third of the pre-contact harvest.

Militant Protection of Fishing Rights

Native American who had signed the Medicine Creek treaty, and others, were having a more difficult time harvesting enough fish to survive. By the early 1960s, state fisheries police were conducting wholesale arrests of Indians, confiscating their boats and nets. Denied justice in the state courts, the tribes pursued their claim at the federal level. During the 1960s and early 1970s, they also militantly protected their rights in the face of raids by state fisheries authorities. A nucleus of fishing-rights activists from Franks Landing, living only a few miles from the site at which the Medicine Creek Treaty had been signed, continued to fish on the basis of the treaty, which gave them the right to fish as long as the rivers run.

The week before the initial occupation of Alcatraz in November, 1964, Bob Satiacum, a Puyallup, had been arrested for exercising treaty fishing rights near Tacoma. Marlon Brando was arrested at the same time, along with John J. Yargan, a staff assistant to San Francisco's archbishop. At about the same time, the Survival of American Indians Association organized its first major protest march in Olympia, the state capita. Two thousand people attended.

The fish-ins assumed a familiar pattern:

> The game wardens—a dozen to almost fifty—would descend the banks in a stone-faced scramble toward a few [Indian] men in a canoe or skiff unloading salmon from a gillnet. Usually the [Indians] would give passive resistance— dead weight—and five officers or more would drag the men up the rugged banks toward the waiting vehicles. The dragging often got rough, with much pushing and shoving, many arms twisted way up the back, and numerous cold-cock punches. The billy clubs made their thuds. Sometimes the Indian men struck back. Sometimes Indian people on the banks threw stones and sticks at the intruders. The stench of tear gas hung in the air. (Wilkinson, 2000, 38)

Fishing-Rights Protests Escalate

The increasing intensity of fishing-rights protests during the 1960s was a matter of survival—emphasized when the fishing people banded together in a group that they named The Survival of American Indians Association. The Puyallups attracted co-pious publicity as they fished in their local river with celebrities such as Brando and comedian Dick Gregory. Other well-known people attended, such as Buffy Sainte-Marie, a popular folk singer, who was Cree, Richard White, who was becoming one of academia's best-known historians, and Elisabeth Furse, then employed by the American Friends in Seattle, who became a member of Congress from Oregon. The protests came to be called "fish-ins" a conscious reference to the black sit-ins at southern lunch counters during the civil-rights movement.

Reuben Wright Sr., a Puyallup Tribal councilman, was arrested and jailed in Pierce County. Other Puyallups and a Nisqually also were arrested. Bob Satiacum drew attention to the fishing struggle and took part in many demonstrations on the Puyallup River. Satiacum sent a letter to President Lyndon Johnson that said in part: "Bands of Indians arming. Open warfare with Washington State Department of Fish and Game certain over fishing rights guaranteed by Medicine Creek Treaty of 1854, signed by U.S. Presidents Pierce and Grant. Presidential action needed immediately to avoid bloodshed. Signed Chief Satiacum, Puyallup Indian Reservation (Johnson, 1965).

During the years of protest, Native fishermen could afford only minimal gear; fishing boats capable of using gill-nets (widely used by white commercial fishermen) were beyond their reach. The National Indian Youth Council supported Muckleshoot and other Native fishing people. In 1962, three Muckleshoots were prosecuted for gillnet fishing on the Green River. They were acquitted when Judge Hodson ruled that they were within their treaty rights. In 1963, the State sued the Muckleshoots in a case that became known as *Washington State vs. Moses*, in which a Washington State court upheld the state's right to close fishing for conservation reasons (Wilkinson, 2000).

On March 3, 1964, the National Youth Council summoned native peoples from across the United States to join fishing people in Western Washington for a rally on the grounds of the State Capitol in Olympia. In *Red Power Rising* (2011), Bradley Shreve wrote that between 1,500 and 5,000 people (depending on who was doing the counting) gathered, making the demonstration "the largest intertribal protest ever assembled" (Shreve, 2011, 130). Makahs performed traditional dances on the steps of the Capitol and at the governor's residence. A set of demands was issued to state government that amounted to allowing fishing unhindered in "usual and accustomed places" as set out in the treaties.

A Native group (and Brando) met with Governor Albert Rosellini for several hours, after which the governor spoke to the demonstrators. While Rosellini congratulated them for exercising their rights, however, he refused to back off of the state's insistence that it would set the rules. Siding with white sports-fishing groups, Rosellini characterized Indian fishing as a threat to conservation of the species, at a time when Native catch accounted for no more than 6 percent of the total (Shreve, 2011, 130–132, 136).

During 1966, four Muckleshoots were arrested for fishing by Neely Bridge. Judge Lloyd Shorett ruled against the tribe. As it resisted the Muckleshoots' rights to fish according to the federal treaties, the state was doing its best to destroy what was left of their collective identity, denying that they had existed at all. Such allegations had a political purpose: an extinct people could claim no fishing rights. By 1970, before fishing rights were restored in the Boldt ruling, a congressional delegation visiting the Muckleshoot reservation found many people living in shacks, and others whose cars had become their homes. The tribal government had no place to meet, owned a half-acre on what had been a 3,840-acre reservation, and had nearly no budget.

The confrontations by this time had become quite physical, especially on the Nisqually River adjacent to Frank's Landing, a few miles from Olympia, the state capital, and on Puyallup fishing grounds near Tacoma. Frank's landing was a small riverside settlement, what had been left after the U.S. Army in 1917 evicted the Nisquallys to build a firing range at Fort Lewis during World War II. The Frank family had refused to leave. By the 1960s, "the Landing" became a nucleus of fishing-rights activism.

On October 15, 1965, "an emotion-charged battle of paddles, sticks, and stones ensued" (American Friends, 1970, 110). Fishing rights publicity was not limited to the summoning of celebrities. Activists erected a tipi on the lawn of the city-county building in Tacoma, and sent smoke signals from the roof of Tacoma's Winthrop Hotel. At one point, an attempt to "liberate" the battleship U.S.S. *Missouri* from a dock at the Bremerton Navy Yard (west across Puget Sound from Seattle) was foiled by military police (Court Move, 1968, n.p.).

The fishing-rights battle's early "fish-ins" drew large crowds—and some rather garish newspaper headlines. "Indians Make Warlike Moves Against State" blared the *Auburn Citizen's* front page in inch-high type September 1, 1965. On May 13, 1966 between about 70 Native people and non-Indian college students marched 13 miles in support of treaty fishing rights from the Muckleshoot Community Hall, through Auburn, to District Justice Court in Federal Way. The march was coordinated by Muckleshoot fishing-rights activist Leo LeClair. Yakima, Walla Walla, Tulalip, Nisqually, Umatilla, Klallam, Arapaho, Macaw, and Cree people as well as Muckleshoots took part. The marchers carried copies of the Treaty of Point Elliott as a way of stating that federal law trumped state attempts to control Native fishing rights. A copy of the treaty was presented to Judge Robert Stead at the district court (Muckleshoot Treaty, 1966, 1).

The march was undertaken in support of four Muckleshoots (Cecil and Robert Moses, Sherman Dominick, and Larry Maurice), charged with illegal fishing in the Green River, who were scheduled to go on trial on June 29 in Judge Stead's court. Midway through the trek, marchers paused for lunch in Auburn's Lee Gover Park for lunch, and to hear speakers, some of whom included Muckleshoot Bernice

White, Nisqually Janet McCloud, and Melvin Ziontz of the American Civil Liberties Union (ACLU), which was providing legal support for the four defendants in the fishing case (Indian Treaty, 1966, 1).

The Puyallup "Fishing War"

The ground-level fishing wars peaked on September 9, 1970 during a fish-in on the Puyallup River near the urban area of Tacoma, as a multiethnic camp of about a hundred fishing-rights supporters standing vigil for an array of treaty Indians on the river was torn apart by about 300 police in riot gear who arrested about 60 people. Four shots were fired at the police, who then dispersed the crowd with a volley of their own fire and a haze of tear gas. This confrontation contributed to the filing of the federal legal case that became the Boldt ruling, as the scale of the conflict prompted federal attorneys to make it a priority.

The camp, which had been maintained all summer, was bulldozed by the state as Muckleshoot, Nisqually, Puyallup, and other fishing people were driven off the water by the state's armed fish-and-game police. Indian boats were seized and nets cut. By the time it was over, occupants of the camp had burned a railroad trestle in anger as most of them were removed in handcuffs. One activist, Alison Bridges, was dragged away by her hair as photographers recorded what became an iconic moment (Wilma, 2000).

Some of the roughly 300 people in the camp documented the arrests with video tape and provided the fishing people with food, shelter, moral support, and bail money (Mapes, 2010). All of the charges stemming from the arrests later were dropped, as judges found that drawing the state's ire by camping on a river was not a crime. A contemporary account said that "Fifty-five adults and five juveniles were arrested in an encampment that had been established one mile north of Tacoma where Highway 99 crossed the Puyallup River. Police seized firearms and knives and fishing nets, but there were no injuries. Two days later, Tacoma Police Chief Lyle Smith ordered the encampment bulldozed" (Shots Fired, 1970, A-1; Wilma, 2000). The fish-in was deemed illegal by the state after Indians fished outside of its three-day-a-week limit. The Indians said that the treaties allowed them to fish at their "usual and accustomed places" without time limits (Carson, 1970, B-10; Puyallup, 1970, A-4).

During the middle of 1971, Native fishing people learned that an agent in the State Department of Game had resigned to protest "Game Department Indian Policies and attitudes and methods of handling the fishing controversy" (Dear Sirs, 1971, 1.) The agent, who had worked in the Game Department for 12 years, said his time had been wasted, and that he had been supporting prejudice and racism. Unfortunately, for history's sake, the name of the person who had resigned had been removed from the letter.

The Case Evolves in the Courts

The fishing-rights case also was evolving in the federal courts. Before the Boldt Decision (1974) paved the way for full federal affirmation of treaty fishing rights, two other cases, known to the public as Puyallup I (1968) and Puyallup II (1973) illustrated how the law was changing. The majority opinion in both cases was written by William O. Douglas, who had been raised in Eastern Washington. In 1968, he found that the state could legally regulate off-reservation fishing if such regulation was "reasonable and necessary" to achieve "conservation" of the species. The state, of course, argued that it had been doing just that. In 1973, however, in a case regarding the state's ability to close the fishery for steelhead (which it defined as a game fish that Indians were not allowed to harvest), Douglas ruled that the state's system was not necessary for conservation.

What had happened? Douglas and other justices had read a seminal law-journal published in 1972, in which University of Washington Law Professor Ralph Johnson analyzed the Supreme Court's error in rulings on fishing rights (Johnson, 1972). In addition, Douglas' wife, Cathy, also a lawyer, had visited Frank's Landing at the behest of Hank Adams. She studied the case and became convinced that the Indians were correct.

The "Boldt Decision" (1974)

On February 12, 1974, United States District Court Judge George Boldt ruled that Indians were entitled to an opportunity to catch as many as half the fish returning to off-reservation sites which had been the "usual and accustomed places" when the treaties were signed. Boldt had put three years into the case; he used 200 pages to interpret one sentence of the treaty in an opinion which some legal scholars say is the most carefully researched, thoroughly analyzed ever handed down in an Indian fishing-rights case. The nucleus of Boldt's decision had to do with 19th-century dictionaries' definitions of "in common with." Boldt said the word meant "to be shared equally." During the next three years the Ninth Circuit Court of Appeals upheld Boldt's ruling, and the U.S. Supreme Court twice let it stand by refusing to hear an appeal by the State of Washington.

State officials and the fishermen whose interests they represented were furious at Boldt. Rumors circulated about the sanity of the 75-year-old judge. It was said that he had taken bribes of free fish and had an Indian mistress, neither of which was true. Judge Boldt was hung in effigy by angry non-Indian fishermen, who on other occasions formed "convoys" with their boats and rammed Coast Guard vessels that had been dispatched to enforce the court's orders. At least one Coast-guardsman was shot.

Among state officials during the middle and late 1970s a backlash to Indian rights formed, which would become the nucleus for a nationwide non-Indian campaign to abrogate the treaties. Washington State Attorney General (later U.S. senator) Slade Gorton called Indians "supercitizens" with "special rights," and proposed that constitutional equilibrium be reestablished not by open state violation of the treaties (Boldt had outlawed that), but by purchasing the Indians' fishing rights and abrogating the treaties on which they are based. The tribes, which had been listening to offers of money for Indian resources for a century, flatly refused Gorton's offer. To them, the selling of fishing rights would have been tantamount to termination.

Forty years after the "fishing war" reached peak intensity, participants in the confrontation reassembled on the now-quiet riverbank, with two generations of younger people born after the melee, to recall the events that led up to the legal case that produced Judge George Boldt's monumental fishing-rights ruling. Mark Bridges, a Puyallup who was 20 at the time, recalled at the reunion that vigilantes shadowed Indian fishing people even after the Boldt ruling. "It brings chills to me to think of all the things we had to fight for, and are still fighting for," he told Lynda Mapes of the *Seattle Times* during the reunion in 2010, "I've had people take shots at me while I was fishing. I've had people throw dynamite in the water next to me while I was fishing with my kids" (Mapes, 2010).

Further Reading

American Friends Service Committee. *Uncommon Controversy: Fishing Rights of the Muckleshoot, Puyallup, and Nisqually Indians.* Seattle: University of Washington Press, 1970.

Carson, Jerry. "Indians Face Court Battle over Puyallup Fishing." *Seattle Times*, September 10, 1970, B-10.

"Court Move Could End Fishing Dispute." *Tacoma News-Tribune*, March 18, 1968, n.p.

"Dear Sirs: Resignation from Washington State Game Department." July 8, 1971. Photocopy of manuscript in papers of El Centro de la Raza.

"Indian Treaty Trek Linked to Trial of 4 Muckleshoots." *Auburn Citizen*, May 18, 1966, 1.

Johnson, Ralph W. "The States Versus Indian Off-reservation Fishing: A United States Supreme Court Error," *Washington Law Review* 47, no. 2 (1972): 207–36.

Johnson, Robert. *Auburn Citizen.* September 1, 1965, Vol. 4, No. 34.

Mapes, Lynda V. "Fish-Camp Raid Etched in State History." *Seattle Times*, September 6, 2010. http://seattletimes.nwsource.com/cgi-bin/PrintStory.pl?document_id=2012827306&zsection_id=2003904401&slug=fishwar07m&date=20100906

"Muckleshoot Treaty Trek is Historic Indian Event: LeClair." *Auburn Globe–News*, May 18, 1966, 1, 11.

"Puyallup River Indian Camp Destroyed by Bulldozers." *Seattle Times*, September 11, 1970, E-7.

Shreve, Bradley. *Red Power Rising: The National Indian Youth Council and the Origins of Native Activism.* Norman: University of Oklahoma Press, 2011.

"Shots Fired, 60 Arrested in Indian-fishing Showdown." *Seattle Times*, September 9, 1970, A-1.

United States v. Washington 384 F. Supp. 312 (1974).

Wilkinson, Charles. *Messages from Frank's Landing: A Story of Salmon, Treaties, and the American Way.* Seattle: University of Washington Press, 2000.

Wilma, David. "Tacoma Police Arrest 60 Persons at a Fish-in on September 9, 1970." HistoryLink. August 25, 2000. http://historyink.org/index.cfm?DisplayPage=output.cfm&file_id=2625

Florida American Indian Movement

The Florida AIM has earned headlines by protesting local festivals that parade ersatz Indian costumes and culture. Working with traditional Seminoles, Florida AIM also has worked to reduce mercury contamination in the Everglades. It also has arranged for repatriations of more than 126 burial sites in Florida, including controversial, highly publicized conflicts at Warm Mineral Springs, Bonita Springs, Reedy Mound, and Riverview Pointe (Bradenton). Florida AIM works to prevent violations of the Indian Child Welfare Act. It has acted to combat employment discrimination, as well as against stereotypes of Native peoples by new-agers and sports mascots. Florida AIM also had collected signatures to call upon President Obama to release Leonard Peltier.

While it is based in Florida, this AIM chapter includes Indigenous peoples from all over the Western Hemisphere—North, Central, and South America "working for the civil, human, treaty and sovereign rights of Indigenous peoples as well as the recognition of, and protection of the rights of Indigenous peoples, Nations and sacred lands" (American Indian, 2007). It is allied with AIM's Grand Governing Council in Minneapolis.

AIM Florida was begun by David Goyette in 1989. After he passed away in 1996, Florida AIM set up annual awards in his memory. After several years of protests, Florida AIM took credit for "cleaning up" most of the Port Richey Chasco Fiesta:

> Due to AIM patrolling, Chasco now has a legitimate pow-wow with only a few exceptions. Due to AIM protesting, the Children's Pageant is now gone which for over 80 years depicted Native Americans as savages and less than human beings. The only festival event left that demeans Native Americans is the Chasco Krewe Float. The krewe consists of White members who dress up in beads and feathers and portray their version of Native People in a very disrespectful way. Little Black Sambo is gone! Frito Bandito is gone! Blackface is gone! Now the Chasco Krewe has to go! (Urgent, n.d.)

AIM called upon organizers of the New Port Richey Chasco Fiesta street parade to remove its Chasco Krewe Float "on the basis that it is demeaning and racist display of Native American Culture . . . [it is] offensive and sends a wrong message to the community that stereotyping and negative imagery is an acceptable behavior. . . . Studies have shown that stereotypes endanger our children's self-esteem . . . culture and spirituality used for amusement . . . leaves an indelible memory in their minds, not of pride and honor, but of shame" (Petition, 2011). The members of AIM pointed to the parade's own rules, which forbid its use to target specific groups of people. "Native Americans are political from birth, a social issue and targeted special group. Therefore, since the Chasco Krewe represents all of the above restrictions, it should not be allowed to participate in the parade," a Florida AIM petition said (Peition, 2011).

Some people, not all of them AIM members, have been arrested for trying to block the path of the annual parade, in which a number of whites dress up as ersatz "Indians" and act like fools. Daniel Callaghan (not an AIM member) "spent 30 days in jail after he blocked the path of the street parade by chaining himself to a hook he had placed in the road" (Bule, 2007).

According to an account in the St. Petersburg *Times*, "The part of the parade that really angers the protestors is the Chasco Krewe float. The float features community members wearing feathers and Indian garb. Krewe members and festival organizers have always claimed to pay tribute to American Indians and educate people about their culture" (Bule, 2009). On the contrary, said local Native people: "AIM contends desecrating Native American culture with headdresses, whooping and hollering, wearing buckskin, feathers and beads is nothing but a mockery. . . . It made Native Americans look savage and pagan" (Bule, 2009). The members of AIM compared the float's exhibit to the desecration of Christian sacraments.

Florida AIM also has protested state funding of commissions to celebrate the landing of notable Spanish conquistadors, notably Pedro Menendez de Aviles, "A brutal murderer of the indigenous of this land," during the 450th anniversary of St. Augustine (Urgent, n.d.). "We do not feel that taxpayer's money should be spent to celebrate the landing of a brutal murder of innocent people. Nor should we subsidize St. Augustine's tourist industry by providing federal monies over an eight year period," Florida AIM said on its Web page (Urgent, n.d.).

Further Reading

"American Indian Movement Florida Chapter: It's About Our Land. It's About Our People. It's about our Culture." 2007. http://www.freewebs.com/aimflorida/

Bule, Lisa. "American Indian Movement Plans to Protest Chasco Fiesta "Mockery." *St. Petersburg Times*, March 14, 2009. http://www.tampabay.com/news/business/tourism/article983881.ece

"Petition to Ban the Chasco Krewe." American Indian Movement Florida Chapter. 2011. http://www.ipetitions.com/petition/banchascoracism/

"Urgent Request for Action." American Indian Movement Florida Chapter, News. No date. http://aimflorida.webs.com/news.htm

Forbes, Jack D.

(1934–2011)
Powhatan, Lenape, et al.

Jack D. Forbes was Powhatan and Lenape (Delaware), a long-time professor of Native American Studies and anthropology at the University of California, Davis. Forbes' work helped to establish an intellectual framework for the ideology of "Red Power" that compelled action by members of the AIM and other groups that played major roles in reviving Native American cultures during the late 20th century.

Forbes, author of several books, such as *Columbus and Other Cannibals*, was an acute critic of European-centered history and culture. In books such as *The American Discovery of Europe, Apache, Navaho and Spaniard* and *Africans and Native Americans* Forbes turned his critical eye on the ways in which members of diverse cultures influence each other. He also was an important founder of Native American studies as an academic field, and as an important part of intellectual discourse in several sub-fields of history, anthropology, and law.

Many of Forbes' students (Richard Oakes, among others) went on to occupy Alcatraz Island. The 1969 Alcatraz occupation began as Forbes was building the Native American Studies program at the University of California, Davis, securing teaching positions, and developing courses for a major. Several students in the program traveled to Alcatraz, and some became leaders.

Born in Long Beach, California, Forbes was raised in the San Gabriel Valley on a half-acre farm in El Monte del Sur, as well as in Eagle Rock, and Los Angeles. He started writing on a high-school newspaper, Forbes graduated from Eagle Rock High School in 1951 and Glendale Community College in l953, then earned a bachelors degree in philosophy at the University of Southern California, in 1955, followed by a masters in 1956, and, in 1959, a PhD (in history with a minor in North American ethnology), at the same university—all by age 25, an extraordinary age.

By the early 1960s, he was among the earliest organizers of modern Native American political and cultural revival. Working to finance his college education, Forbes served on a fire crew in Lassen National Forest. He also was a truck driver with Meadow Gold Dairies.

In 1960, his career as a professor began at California State University, Northridge, where he was named to a Guggenheim Fellowship. In 1960 Forbes organized and formed the American Indian College Committee with Navajo artist Carl Gorman and others. Forbes was developing proposals for Native American Studies programs as early as 1960 at California State University—Northridge.

During 1964, Forbes assumed a professorship the University of Nevada at Reno. Three years later, he was hired as director of the research program at the Far West Laboratory for Educational Research and Development at the University of California—Berkeley. By his mid-30s, Forbes was teaching a UC-Davis, His long-time career at UC-Davis began in 1969, the same year that he was active in coordinating students' participation in the Alcatraz occupation. He also was cross-listed at UC-Davis as a professor of anthropology.

During 1968 and 1969 Forbes played an important role in organizing United Native Americans in the Bay Area; he also served as editor of *Warpath*. He also was editor of the newspapers *Tsen-Akamak* and *Attam-Akamik* at the same time.

A long-time mentor to many activist Native American students, Forbes created practical designs in higher education within the broader framework of self-determination. During the spring of 1969, Forbes prepared a proposal for an American Indian College in the University of California system. On June 30, 1969, Forbes' proposal was approved by California's state legislature. Forbes and others in 1971 founded the Deganawidah-Quetzalcoatl University, a Native-controlled institution of higher education that is now defunct. D-Q became the first off-reservation college controlled by Native Americans. In turn, D-Q laid the foundation for many other Native American tribal colleges across the United States. Forbes volunteered at D-Q for 25 years; in 2005, it lost federal funding and accreditation.

Forbes won a Fulbright Professorship during 1981–1982 at the United Kingdom's University of Warwick, during which time he also studied in the Institute of Social Anthropology and Linacre College of Oxford University and as a Visiting Professor in Literature at the University of Essex in Great Britain. He also has held the Tinbergen Chair, Erasmus University, Rotterdam. Forbes gave guest lectures in Japan, the Netherlands, Russia, Britain, Italy, Germany, France, Switzerland, Norway, Canada, Mexico, Belgium, and in other countries.

He helped to establish Native American Studies programs at dozens of universities across the United States. He received the Before Columbus Foundation: American Book Award for Lifetime Achievement (1997) and the Wordcraft Circle: Writer of the Year (Prose–Non-Fiction) Award (1999).

Inés Hernández-Avila (Nez Perce/Chicana), who followed Forbes as chair of the Native American studies department at UC-Davis, said that Forbes designed a Native American studies program with an international scope. "He was a visionary," she said. "He realized the hemisphere was indigenous. This concept is just beginning to be accepted" (Lee, 2011). "Jack was a very disciplined and conscientious scholar, always writing," said Isao Fujimoto, senior lecturer emeritus at UC-Davis, who arrived there in the late 1960s, with Forbes. Fujimoto recalled, "He was working no matter what. I remember he took his son out on a birthday treat and brought a stack of index cards with him, making notes for a class" (Lee, 2011).

Only Approved Indians, published by the University of Oklahoma Press in 1995, was Forbes' 13th book, but his first work of fiction, described as:

Stories [that] capture the remarkable breadth and variety of American Indian life. . . . Though all the main characters are of Indian descent, each is a unique combination of tribal origin, social status, age, and life-style—from native elder and college professor to lesbian barmaid and Chicano adolescent. Nevertheless, the U.S. government (and perhaps white society as a whole) narrows the definition of "Indian." In the title story, for example, two basketball teams begin fighting when one accuses the other of lacking BIA status-government recognition. When tournament officials disqualify the team that lacks "official" Indian players, the "approved" team celebrates its victory. (Only Approved, n.d.)

Forbes specialized in paradigm shifts in thinking among disciplines. According to the publisher of its second edition, *Africans and Native Americans* "explores key issues relating to the evolution of racial terminology and European colonialists' perceptions of color, analyzing the development of color classification systems and the specific evolution of key terms such as black, mulatto, and mestizo, which no longer carry their original meanings" (Africans, n.d.).

Forbes traced his intellectual roots to his family:

Growing up as a mixed-blood of part-Native American ancestry, living among relatives with unique and original opinions, exposed to very strong and independent aunts and cousins willing to break with popular conventions, and living in the midst of Mexicans of Indigenous origin in the countryside of El Monte, California, I was led thereby at any early age to explore sources about ancient America, north and south, with an openness of mind, an openness which soon brought me into conflict with books which pretended that "American" history commenced in Europe and that the Pilgrims and the Jamestown adventurers were the "first Americans". . . . All during high school and college I grappled with the Eurocentric orientation of most history texts. . . . The great challenge that we face as twenty-first century scholars is to be able to shift history away from the practice wherein each dominant group seeks to impose its own vision of the past, and instead to make the story of an entire land, a whole continent, or even the entire globe the focus of our research. (The American, n.d.)

"Jack D. Forbes believed that the Native peoples of the Americas should articulate their own histories in their own words, define who they were as individuals and as tribal members and, above all, shape and make manifest their own futures based on their own values," wrote Tanya Lee in *Indian Country Today*, shortly after he died at Sutter Davis Hospital in Davis, February 23, 2011, at age 77.

Further Reading

"Africans and Native Americans: The Language of Race and the Evolution of Red-Black Peoples." University of Illinois Press. No date. http://www.press.uillinois.edu/books/catalog/72cac6xt9780252063213.html

Forbes, Jack D. *Africans and Native Americans.* Urbana: University of Illinois Press, 1993.

Forbes, Jack D. "Alcatraz: What Its Seizure Means," in Peter Blue Cloud, ed. *Alcatraz is Not an Island.* Berkeley, CA: Wingbow Press, 1981.

Forbes, Jack D. "The American Discovery of Europe." Department of Native American Studies, University of California, Davis. No date. http://nas.ucdavis.edu/Forbes/discovery.html

Forbes, Jack D. *The American Discovery of Europe.* Urbana: University of Illinois Press, 2007.

Forbes, Jack D. *Apache, Navaho and Spaniard.* Norman: University of Oklahoma Press, 1960, 1994.

Forbes, Jack D. *Columbus and Other Cannibals.* New York: Seven Stories Press, 2008.

Forbes, Jack D. *Frontiers in American History and the Role of the Frontier Historian.* Reno, Nevada: Desert Research Institute, University of Nevada, 1966.

Forbes, Jack D. *The Indian in America's Past.* Englewood Cliffs, NJ: Prentice-Hall, 1964.

Forbes, Jack D. *Native Americans of California and Nevada.* Healdsburg, CA: Naturegraph Publishers, 1969.

Forbes, Jack D. *Native Americans and Nixon: Presidential Politics and Minority Self Determination 1969–1972.* Los Angeles: American Indian Studies Center, 1972.

Forbes, Jack D. *Only Approved Indians: Stories.* Norman: University of Oklahoma Press, 1995.

Forbes, Jack D. "Only Approved Indians: Unique Native American Stories." Department of Native American Studies, University of Californian—Davis. No date. http://nas.ucdavis.edu/Forbes/ONLY.html

Forbes, Jack D. *Red Blood: A Novel.* Penticton, BC: Theytus, 1997.

Forbes, Jack D. *Warriors of the Colorado.* Norman: University of Oklahoma Press, 1965

Forbes, Jack D. *A World Ruled by Cannibals: The Wetiko Disease of Aggression, Violence, and Imperialism.* Davis, CA: D-Q University Press, 1979.

"Jack D. Forbes (Powhatan-Renápe-Lenápe). Professor Emeritus." Department of Native American Studies, University of California—Davis. No date. http://nas.ucdavis.edu/site/people/emeritus/

Lee, Tanya. "Author and Native Studies Trailblazer Jack Forbes, 77, Passes." *Indian Country Today*, June 20, 2011. http://indiancountrytodaymedianetwork.com/2011/06/author-and-native-studies-trailblazer-jack-forbes-77-passes/

Fort Lawton Occupation (Seattle)

The occupation of Fort Lawton in Seattle was very similar to better-known earlier events at Alcatraz Island in San Francisco Bay, but the Seattle occupation produced what the Alcatraz occupation sought but failed to achieve: an enduring community center (KCTS, 2009). The Fort Lawton site, in the middle of an urban area, was a much more practical site than an island in the midst of San Francisco Bay. The island site was ideal for isolating people (thus the prison). The Daybreak Star's site was the opposite: close to the city, and easy to reach.

By 2010, the Daybreak Star Center (like El Centro) was providing services for people regardless of ethnicity, including day care and Head Start. The center's main constituency, however, is more than 85,000 Native people who have immigrated to Seattle and King Country from across the United States, 20 percent of whom live in poverty.

Nearly 100 Native Americans and their supporters laid siege to the Army's Fort Lawton in Seattle, March 10, 1970. (AP Photo/Barry Sweet)

Bernie Whitebear's Dream

Bernie Whitebear, who coordinated the takeover and construction of the Daybreak Star Center and supervised it for the rest of his life, was born during 1937 at the Colville Indian Agency in Nespelem, Eastern Washington, as a Sin Aikst (the phrase used by the Lake Indians to describe themselves). He graduated from Okanogan High School in 1955. Whitebear grew up poor at Colville. His brother Lawney Reyes said that the family "lived in tents most of the time because we couldn't afford anything else" (Parham, 2007).

After high-school graduation in 1956, Whitebear spent a frustrating year at the University of Washington, then enlisted in the U.S. Army (101st Airborne Division and Green Berets) serving from 1957 to 1959. After his Army enlistment, Whitebear bounced around short-term jobs in Tacoma. He fished on the Puyallup River and Commencement Bay with Puyallup activist Bob Satiacum, an activity that was then deemed illegal for Indians by the State of Washington's game and fishing officials, with copious harassment. During 1966, Whitebear moved to Seattle and worked for some time at the Boeing Company.

His vocation was his family; Whitebear never married. Whitebear's role as a community activist developed late in the 1960s when, in 1969, he became the first director of the Seattle Indian Health Board. Whitebear's vast sense of compassion compelled him to drive around Seattle seeking Indians who needed help, an activity described by his brother, Lawney L. Reyes, in a book, *Bernie Whitebear: An Urban Indian's Quest for Justice* (2007). The book was described by D. Anthony Tyeeme-Clark in the *American Indian Culture & Research Journal* as "a flattering vision of an extraordinary Sin Aikst man, a precious human being, someone worthy of enduring emulation and far-reaching respect" (Tyeeme-Clark, 2007, 147).

Dean Chavers recalled Whitebear: "He was a soft-spoken person, given to working with people rather than confronting them. He was always ready with a *bon mot,* a joke, a tease, or a story. Some people called him a walking anecdote" (Chavers. 2007, 580). Shortly after the occupation of Alcatraz Island, similar circumstances gave birth to an occupation of land on the former World War II-era U.S. Army base in Seattle called Fort Lawton, in Seattle's Magnolia neighborhood, which had been used as a troop trans-shipment point during World War II.

After the war the Army maintained a presence at the fort, but it had lost its purpose, so the Army scheduled it for closure. Fort Lawton, about 1,100 acres of woods, beaches, and fields about three miles northwest of downtown Seattle, was prime urban real estate. The same tactic later was used in Tacoma, where Puyallups and their allies during 1977 and 1978 occupied a government hospital that had been closed. It became an urban hub for Native Americans in the Tacoma area.

Whitebear and United Indians of All Tribes were rebuffed or lost in the bureaucratic shuffle when they first approached government agencies with plans for a community center; after an occupation, arrests, and publicity, they became recognized players. Two-and-a-half years after the first "action" at Fort Lawton, the same template was applied on Seattle's Beacon Hill as many of the same people, again a broad coalition, occupied an abandoned public school with plans to turn it into a community center. This time, Chicanos were in the lead, and the site became El Centro de la Raza, which also has endured for decades. Many of the activists in both instances already had cut their teeth confronting police power in the "fishing wars" of southern Puget Sound.

Seattle's inter-ethnic alliance lent the occupation of Fort Lawton extra support, and a special political *gravitas*. The coalition, including El Centro principal founder Roberto Maestas and many other Chicanos, assembled during the early 1970s on Lake Washington with Native peoples on Lake Washington for a show of unity with Indians fishing under terms of century-old treaties. The fishing battles also provided recruits for the occupation of Fort Lawton.

Storming the Fort

The media came calling, too, at Fort Lawton, feeding like hungry sharks on historical stereotypes, when they sensed the irony of the Indians "attacking" an Army fort, during the spring of 1970, as a half-mile-long caravan of cars lined up to blockade the base's northern and southern entrances. Indians and their allies climbed fences, hauled in tipi poles, and prepared camps. The military police evicted them, after which they returned again. Activists stormed fences and gates several times, as troops beat them back, failing, as Vera Parham (2009) wrote in *Columbia Magazine*, "to grasp the deep commitment of these protesters—men and women who had seen the deprivations of reservation life, lived the trauma of relocation, watched their families lose their lands, and suffered the racial slurs of an American public that assumed Indians had all but disappeared.".

Some days, the battle seemed a little like an open-air circus. One day. skywriter Art Bell of Bell Air Service circled the site in a small airplane, inscribing "A New Day" and "Fort Give Up. . . . Fort Surrender" (Smith, 2012, 162).

The occupiers of Fort Lawton not only included Seattle's multicultural alliance but also Native people from parts of Canada and the U.S. Great Plains, as well as California (some were veterans of the Alcatraz occupation). Thus the group's name: United Indians of All Tribes. The multicultural nature of the occupation was evident from the beginning. On March 7, 1970, the night before the first invasion of the fort, plans were made at the Filipino Community Hall. Non-Indians arrived as well: blacks, Chicanos, and whites. One was Jane Fonda. She joined the others climbing over the fence into barbed wire and tear gas. Military police dragged off the invaders and transported them to the base stockade.

One protester recalled: "We got beat up super bad and thrown into the stockades, and Bernie had his shoulder dislocated; Sid Mills, a Yakama and Vietnam war veteran, had his shoulder broken or dislocated" (Parham, 2007). Rough treatment of the occupiers by military police was covered extensively in the local newspapers, and caused many in Seattle to sympathize with the occupiers. The actress Jane Fonda was expelled from the Fort, along with 70 others who had been arrested. Once released, the invaders erected tents and tipis outside the fence. The Army erected concertina wire, dug foxholes, and zipped around the property in jeeps.

The third and final confrontation was more of a melee. "They were using tear gas . . . and jeeps were wrecked. It was horrible. They beat . . . us, hauled us away, put us in the galley . . . forbid us from even using the restroom . . . or water" (Parham, 2007). Three weeks later, the group went over the fence a third time, armed with support from more than 40 non-Indian organizations, including the Church Council of Greater Seattle. "We all went running through, ran right over the MPs one more time. . . . And, the chase [was] on again. And they [caught] us, and they beat us, and they book[ed] us. And we were expelled once again" (Parham, 2007). Believing they had made their point, the United Indians of All Tribes and their many supporters then folded their tents and began the bureaucratic slog toward a community-center site, which they eventually won.

The battle for Fort Lawton lasted long after the confrontation ended. It took several years of bureaucratic wrestling before a compromise was reached: the city of Seattle got most of the old fort for a park, as the United Indians of All Tribes received land on which to build the Daybreak Star Center. The United Indians of All Tribes negotiated a 99-year lease on 16 acres at the new Discovery Park, at $1 a year. The lease was renewable for two more 100-year terms. Construction of Daybreak Star began in 1975, with groundbreaking on September 27, 1975. A wide array of funding had been assembled from the U.S. Economic Development Administration, the City of Seattle, the United States Department of Commerce, and donations from the Makah, Colville, and Quinault tribes, the Campaign for Human Development of the Catholic Church, and the Weyerhaeuser Corp. The Center opened two years later. The Center then developed urban-Indian programs related to housing, education, and counseling, cultural awareness, and health.

Daybreak Star maintained a presence for decades, under the aegis of United Indians of All Tribes, led by Whitebear as its director, a position he held for almost 30 years, until his death in 2000, after a three-year battle with colon cancer. When Whitebear died, Washington Gov. Gary Locke, Seattle's mayor, Paul Schell, and U.S. senators Patty Murray of Washington and Daniel Inouye of Hawaii attended his funeral.

On August 2, 2000, a long procession of cars led by a police escort left the Daybreak Star Center for the Washington State Convention Center, carrying Whitebear's body to one of the largest funerals in Seattle's history. The Great Hall at the Convention Center was filled to capacity with friends, dignitaries, and the many whose lives he had touched in one way or another by the compassionate man with the silver hair—governors, senators, mayors, the great and the humble, including people from many dozens of Native nations and tribes who saw him off to the spirit world.

Recalling the Occupation 40 Years Later

Forty years after the initial occupation of Fort Lawton, nearly 300 people, including veterans of the original occupation, newcomers, and their children, were summoned to the site by the beat of a drum that had been used on March 8, 1970 as natives of many nations and their allies took a portion of the land "by right of discovery" (Mapes, 2010). Colville tribal member Randy Lewis recalled that the Fort Lawton protesters drove to the fort en masse in a long line of cars with red cloth banners streaming from their radio antennas. Gathered at the site that had been the former fort's front gate, they listened as Whitebear read a proclamation that declared the reclamation of the land. "Then all hell broke loose," Lewis said. "MPs [military police] descended on us, Jeeps were turned over, they started whaling on us, and people were thrown in jail" (Mapes, 2010).

Lewis was among the many people who pitched camp outside the gate. "We laid siege. We would not give up, and the military would not surrender. Sometimes there were 20 of us, sometimes there were 300" (Mapes, 2010). Lewis remembered that anti-Indian vigilantes sometimes attacked the camp. One night he was alone in the camp as a car filled with anti-Indian agitators drove by, throwing bottles. He threw a shovel full of hot coals from his campfire, setting the car's interior on fire. "That's the way it was back then," he said (Mapes, 2010).

An account in the Seattle *Times* said that "The action was a multicultural effort. Roberto Maestas, founder of El Centro de la Raza, remembered being helped over the fence and joining in the fray—and taking careful note. He and his supporters took over a school a few years later that became the home of El Centro. "We owe a great debt to the courage of the Indian people; they got it started," Maestas said (Mapes, 2010).

Further Reading

Chavers, Dean. *Modern American Indian Leaders: Their Lives and Their Works.* 2 vols. Lewiston, ID: Edwin Mellen Press, 2007.

KCTS-9 TV (PBS). "Bob Santos, Roberto Maestas and Larry Gossett Recall their Activism in Seattle." November 13, 2009. http://kcts9.org/video/gang-four

Mapes, Lynda V. "Native Americans Mark 40 Years Since Fort Lawton Protest." *Seattle Times*, March 9, 2010. http://seattletimes.nwsource.com/html/localnews/2011292879_lawton09m.html

Parham, Vera. "Something Worth Going up That Hill For." *Columbia Magazine* 21, no. 3 (Fall 2007): 24–32. http://columbia.washingtonhistory.org/magazine/articles/2007/0307/0307-a3.aspx.

Reyes, Lawney L. *Bernie Whitebear: An Urban Indian's Quest for Justice*. Tucson: University of Arizona Press, 2006.

Smith, Sherry L. *Hippies, Indians, & the Fight for Red Power*. New York: Oxford University Press, 2012.

Tyeeme-Clark, D. Anthony. "Review, Bernie Whitebear: An Urban Indian's Quest for Justice," *American Indian Culture & Research Journal* 31, no. 1 (2007): 145–48.

Frank, Billy, Jr.

(Born 1931)
Nisqually

Billy Frank Jr. played a major role in Native American assertion of fishing rights in Western Washington that resulted, in 1974, in the landmark federal legal case popularly called the "Boldt Decision." The decision reserved up to half the salmon catch for Native peoples who had signed treaties during the 1850s that ceded large tracts of land but retained the right to fish "in common with" citizens of Washington Territory at "usual and accustomed places." After that decision, Frank became influential in fisheries decision-making in the Northwest, and as an environmental advocate.

Battles over Fishing Rights

For many years, despite the treaties, Washington State game and fishing police arrested Indians who attempted to fish in accordance with their terms. Frank was first arrested for exercising fishing rights at age 14, in 1945, near the mouth of the Nisqually River, a few days before Christmas. He served two years in the U.S. Marines during the Korean War, then returned to the Nisqually River, and to defense of fishing rights. During the 1960s and early 1970s, Indians militantly protected their fishing rights in the face of raids by state fisheries authorities. A nucleus of fishing-rights activists from Franks Landing, living only a few miles from the site at which the Medicine Creek Treaty had been signed in 1854, continued to fish on the basis of the treaty, which gave them the right to fish as long as the rivers run.

Billy Frank Sr. (Nisqually, 1880–1980), father of Billy Frank Jr., also was active in the fishing-rights struggles. He was the original owner of Frank's Landing, a tract of land along the Nisqually River near Olympia, Washington, which became an important center of fishing-rights protests during the 1960s and early 1970s. The land was outside the bounds of the original Nisqually reservation, but, having been purchased by Frank Sr. was given trust status after his allotted land was taken as part of the Fort Lewis Army base. The bend in the river at Frank's Landing proved to be a rich fishing ground, and thus a focus of conflict between state fish and game police and Native Americans seeking to exercise their fishing rights.

By the early 1990s, Billy Frank Jr., then in his fifties, had become chairman of the Northwest Indian Fish Commission, and a leading spokesman for environmentalism in the Pacific Northwest. By 2007, he had headed this body for 22 years, "speaking for the salmon" on behalf of 19 treaty tribes. Frank has led a movement that evolved from activists claiming treaty rights to managers of resources.

Money Talks

Resistance to the Boldt decision was organized among Washington state business leaders in the Washington Water Resource Committee. Frank and other fishing-rights activists decided to boycott Seattle-First National Bank, a member of the Water Resource Committee; they discussed the idea with friends at El Centro de la Raza, a Seattle social-service agency. All agreed they had a good idea, with one flaw. They did not have enough money in the bank to make a boycott hurt. After a few weeks, however, they began to talk to other people. Frank recalled: "We got the Colvilles to pull out sixteen million [dollars]. . . . Then, the Washington State University kids started pulling their money out and the Teamsters Union, and other local people. . . . Then I flew up to Alaska to our native friends up there. . . . They passed a resolution and pulled out eighty million dollars" (Russo, 1992, 54).

By this time, the boycott had drawn notice at Sea-First.

> At that time, Mike Barry was the president of Sea-First. He called me up and he said, 'Bill, before I jump out of the seventeenth floor of the Sea-First bank, we got to have a meeting.' So, I brought in all my tribal leaders again. . . . He asked: 'What do you want us to do? He said [should] fly back to Alaska and tell the Natives to put that money back in the bank because that was only the beginning. They had another hundred fifty million that they were going to pull out. (Russo, 1992, 54)

"We know who the boss is in this country. It sure as hell isn't us," said Frank (Russo, 1992, 54). Nevertheless, the boycott was pinching the bank, the region's largest at that time, before mismanaged oil investments caused its near-bankruptcy. The Indians refused to restore their deposits unless Sea-First and other businesses called off their attack on the Boldt decision.

The Washington state offensive was one part of a nationwide backlash that emerged against treaty rights during the middle and late 1970s. This movement was fueled, as expropriation of Indian resources always have been, by non-Native economic interests. During the 1980s, the battle over who would harvest how many fish continued in western Washington, and spread to other states, such as Wisconsin.

Frank became a nationally recognized leader in the cooperative effort to restore salmon runs of the Eastern Pacific. Fisheries officials returned one of the boats they had seized from him during the "fish-ins," and Frank installed the old cedar dugout canoe in a spot of honor alongside the riverbank where his quest to fish in accordance with the treaties had begun.

Frank's efforts as activist and environmental advocate have been recognized internationally by many awards. In 1992, Frank was awarded the Albert Schweitzer Prize for humanitarianism by John Hopkins University. He also received the 2004 *Indian Country Today* Visionary Award. "You can't begin to count the times he has been beaten and thrown in jail," said Vine Deloria Jr. of Frank. "Yet, in the end, he has become a senior statesman of the State of Washington, respected and admired by people all over the state who once called for his scalp" (Harjo, 2005, 319).

Further Reading

Chavers, Dean. *Modern American Indian Leaders: Their Lives and Their Works.* 2 vols. Lewiston, NY: Edwin Mellen Press, 2007.

El Centro de la Raza 35th Anniversary. "What Kind of World Will We Leave Our Children?" October 13, 2007, Washington State Convention and Trade Center, Seattle.

Harjo, Suzan Shown. "Billy Frank, Jr., A Warrior with Wisdom and an Elder with Courage," in Jose Barreiro and Tim Johnson, eds. *America is Indian Country: Opinions and Perspectives from Indian Country Today*. Golden, CO: Fulcrum, 2005, 317–20.

Russo, Kurt, ed. *Our People, Our Land: Reflections on Common Ground.* Bellingham, WA: Lummi Tribe and Kluckhohn Center, 1992, 54–56.

G

George-Kanentiio, Douglas Mitchell

(Born 1955)
Mohawk Writer and Activist

Douglas Mitchell George-Kanentiio, a member of the Bear Clan, has been a key figure in Akwesasne Mohawk political and cultural life in the late 20th and early 21st centuries. He has participated in Mohawk land claims negotiations, was a member of the Mohawk Nation Business Committee, and a founder of the Native American Journalists Association, from which he received, in 1994, its highest kudo, the Wassaja Award for Journalism Excellence. Kanentiio was selected in 1996 to serve on the Board of Trustees for the National Museum of the American Indian. He also edited *Akwesasne Notes,* a bimonthly international journal about indigenous people worldwide, and *Indian Time*, a local newspaper at Akwesasne, which straddles the borders of Quebec, Ontario, and New York State.

George-Kanentiio also is chairman of Round Dance Productions, a nonprofit foundation formed with his wife Joanne Shenandoah, a renowned Oneida singer. This foundation preserves indigenous North American language, history, music, and art. He also is author of the books *Skywoman, Iroquois on Fire* and *Iroquois Culture and Commentary* as well as a contributor to *Treaty of Canandaigua*, *A Seat at the Table* and *Sovereignty, Colonialism and the Indigenous Nations*.

As a former Mohawk Nation delegate to the Haudenosaunee Standing Committee on Burial Rules and Regulations, Kanentiio advocated return of Iroquois sacred objects from several museums. He was a member of the Mohawk Nation Land Claims Committee for seven years and was one of the founders of the Akwesasne Communications Society which also oversaw the development of Radio CKON, the only exclusively aboriginal licensed broadcasting facility in North America.

Early Life

Kanentiio was born at Akwesasne on February 1, 1955, the fourth son and sixth child of David and Grace George. His father was a mason, a trade taught him by his father, who, in turn, carried on a family tradition reaching back many generations. The family home was located in the St. Regis Village section of Akwesasne, on the Canadian side of the reservation in the Quebec area.

The family lived across the street from the St. Regis Catholic Church, where Kanentiio helped serve mass as an altar boy. He entered the St. Regis Village School in 1961. The school was run by the Sisters of St. Anne, with religious instruction provided by a Jesuit priest, the Rev. Michael Jacobs, a Mohawk from Kahnawake. Kanentiio did well academically, scoring the highest marks in his class.

Kanentiio's mother died in 1965. Two years later, Kanentiio and 12 siblings were placed in foster homes and residential schools. He was sent to the Mohawk Institute in January 1967, remaining there until June 1968, where his experiences were unpleasant. He was placed in a foster home and entered grade 9 at the General Vanier High School, Cornwall, Ontario in September, 1968.

Life in the Mohawk Institute

George-Kanentiio recalled (2007): "Count yourself lucky if you, as a Native, never had to experience the traumas of being placed, against your will, in one of Canada's residential schools. Whatever horror tales you may have heard are true. I know because I was there. I saw the beatings, listened to the weeping of the students and saw many incidents of sexual abuse. While initially shocking to a 11-year-old from Kanatakon, I learned to suppress my outrage at seeing my friends humiliated, their spirits broken, their physical selves violated by adults who were in positions of trust and had unqualified power to do to us what they willed."

Such treatment continued well into the 1960s. In January, 1967, Doug and his brother Dean were assigned to the Mohawk Institute in Brantford, Ontario, more than 350 miles from Akwesasne (St. Regis), their family home. "We were told by the Indian Affairs social workers that the school would provide us with schooling, a warm, safe place to live and good food to eat," Doug recalled. "We should have realized the magnitude of the lie" (George-Kanentiio, 2007).

George-Kanentiio (2007) recalled that the Mohawk Institute was "for many generations [a] the source of fear for hundreds of students, confined behind its red brick exterior.". The institute comprised five large buildings: a four-floor residence hall with a dining hall, a school building, and two livestock barns. Most of the farm closed in 1967, although some crops were planted until the Institute closed two and a half years later.

George-Kanentiio (2007) said that students at the Mohawk Institute were fed burned toast with powdered milk and mush, a watery porridge "which slid through the stomach and bowels, hence the [school's popular] name 'mushhole.' This was our breakfast, an aberration of the food we had been assured would be ours in abundance. Another lie with many more to follow. The other daily meals were as bad and nutritionally corrupt. Forty years later, I feel the shadow pains of hunger whenever I think about the Institute; we were always scratching for the smallest of food morsels to fill growling stomachs."

During his days in the "mushhole," George-Kanentiio ran with an informal gang of tough, jaded young Mohawks.

We fought with the other students, mostly Crees from central Quebec. It did not matter if we lost, we needed to strike out and if a Cree was not in fist range we turned on each other. Many of the most intense brawls took place when our group turned inward and used hands, knees, teeth and feet against our own. We took the bruises and cuts then watched as the red welts rose on our hands and arms from the long, three foot heavy leather straps used with wicked force by the housefathers to punish us for, of all things, fighting. Their logic was that by beating children into submission the use of violence would be exorcised from our behavior. (George-Kanentiio, 2011)

The tough kids reflected the stark life of the school:

There were no good, nurturing words spoken at the Mushhole. We had no mentors, no adult protectors. We saw kids desperate for affection who willingly allowed themselves to be molested. We learned to position our bodies in places where the older boys could not attack. We learned quickly that the threat of violence and the resulting fear was the most effective way of controlling others.

We also realized that there was some degree of safety in a pack and as such we raised hell. We escaped a number of times, following railway tracks to the northeast, believing that in time we could walk the 500 kilometers to Akwesasne, bringing Joey and Rocky with us. Arrests by the Ontario Provincial Police and a collective strapping and denial of food was the result but we tried repeatedly, not knowing then that if we reached the reserve we would have been sent to reform schools as incorrigibles. Afterwards, many of our gang were graduated to reformatories, prisons and rehab centers.

. . . [O]ur fighting, arguing, thieving and Mohawk arrogance finally exhausted the school's administrator, a rotund ethnic German named Conrad Zimmerman, the overseer who patrolled the grounds with a massive and mean police dog. He forced us out since for our actions were being copied by the even tempered Crees while repeatedly embarrassing the school. (George-Kanentiio, 2011)

Canada later attempted to compensate students of the boarding schools with cash payments, which he said are trivial compared to the tens of millions paid to the lawyers who represented the schools' survivors, a total of $45 million as of 2007. "Each one of us, by sickening contrast, get $10,000 for the first year of our confinements and $3,000 for each year thereafter," he said (George-Kanentiio, 2007).

George-Kanentiio recalled (2007) how Joey Commanda ran away from the Mohawk Institute, walking along train tracks. George-Kanentiio wondered how much Canada would pay for the life of Commanda, an Algonquin, who was 12 years of age, after he was killed by a train near Toronto while walking along an isolated stretch of tracks, shuffling homewards hundreds of miles, "wishing his Akwesasne pals were there to show him the way." A Canadian federal government investigation of the Institute after Commanda's death led to its closure.

School and University Life

During the next five years, George-Kanentiio was placed in 15 foster homes across Ontario, Quebec, and New York, attending five different high schools before graduating from Massena (New York) High School in 1973. He had withdrawn from Grade 10 to take part in a land-reclamation action by the Mohawk people during 1970, but completed requirements the next year. In 1973, he attended the State University of New York at Oswego, which had a large Iroquois student body.

George-Kanentiio did not complete a second semester in college, and went to work at various jobs at Akwesasne before moving to Los Angeles in 1974. He then worked at the University of California at Los Angeles Medical Center and enrolled at the school in 1975, but lack of financial resources compelled him to withdraw. George-Kanentiio then lived in central California until January, 1976, returning afterward to Akwesasne and Toronto, Ontario.

In 1977, he attended the University of New Mexico before transferring to Syracuse University where he organized Native American students. George-Kanentiio played a leading role in a movement to remove the University's Indian mascot and joined with other students to advocate a Native American studies major there. He also received an internship at the Newberry Library's Native Resource Center in 1979. George-Kanentiio also took advantage of an accelerated admission program at the Antioch School of Law in Washington, D.C., in 1980, finishing four semesters, until his support was terminated as a result of his political activism.

Returning home, George-Kanentiio accepted a position as editor of *Indian Time*, a local newspaper at Akwesasne. He also served with a committee that created radio station, CKON. During the summer of 1984, Kanentiio joined Huston Smith, the author of *The Religions of Man* on an international tour of sacred sites from Rome to Israel, Istanbul, India, Thailand, China, and Korea. He also held an internship with the New York State Archives, worked at the Akwesasne Museum, and was selected as editor of the news journal *Akwesasne Notes* in 1986, a position he held for six years. George-Kanentiio continued to serve the community in many capacities, as a member of the Akwesasne Emergency Team, the Akwesasne Home for the Aged, the Akwesasne Communications Society, and in various positions with the Mohawk Nation one of which was as a land claims negotiator.

George-Kanentiio has written numerous essays and editorials about the political divisions at Akwesasne, which is governed by three Native councils and also is subject to the jurisdictions of Canada (Quebec and Ontario) and the United States (New York State). He is an advocate for the revitalization of the ancestral Mohawk government called the Mohawk Nation Council of Chiefs. He also has attempted, with others, to create an economy based on ancestral values.

Role in "The Troubles" at Akwesasne

George-Kanentiio also has been critical of the smuggling of narcotics, tobacco, firearms, and undocumented workers through the Akwesasne territory. As a result, his newspapers were banned in some businesses, his offices firebombed twice and his personal residence raked with machine-gun fire. He persisted in his opposition and received many threats against his life, but also received support from the Mohawk Nation Council and its supporters at Akwesasne.

George-Kanentiio played a direct role in the Mohawk "civil war" at Akwesasne as a newspaper editor and ultimately as a participant in a four-day gun battle in 1990 that resulted in the deaths of two Mohawk men. George-Kanentiio identified illicit casino gaming as the source of the violence at Akwesasne that began in 1986 and quickly expanded until the Mohawk reservation for a brief time became the fourth-largest Native American gambling center in North America. His articles traced the rise of gaming to the displacement of the Mohawks from their ancestral lifestyles of fishing and farming beginning after the World War II, also related to the completion of the St. Lawrence Seaway and subsequent contamination of the Akwesasne environment by industries built along that waterway.

In March 1990, the Akwesasne community split into two factions resulting in an escalation of violence and terror serious enough to warrant evacuation of the reservation on April 26. Thousands fled the community, yet there were a few isolated holdouts, one of whom was David George Jr., a brother of George-Kanentiio.

Rather than leave his brother alone against the attacks of the pro-gaming Mohawk Sovereignty Security Force (Warrior Society), George-Kanentiio picked up a firearm to protect him. With 11 other Mohawk men, George-Kanentiio then withstood four days of intense fighting (April 27–May 1) against greatly superior forces until Akwesasne was occupied by the New York State Police, Royal Canadian Mounted Police and a contingent of the Canadian Army.

George-Kanentiio was arrested by the Surete du Quebec (the provincial police) and charged with the shooting death of Harold "Junior" Edwards, one of the two victims of the gun battle. He was cleared of the killing during the preliminary hearing stage of the judicial proceedings for lack of evidence. George-Kanentiio maintained that his arrest was a political action resulting from his severe public criticisms of the U.S. and Canadian police.

International Reputation

Kanentiio also is nationally recognized as a primary source of information about Iroquoian politics and culture. His expertise has been relied upon by historians, film producers as well as television documentary directors. His articles have been published on a regular basis in the *Syracuse Herald-American*. George-Kanentiio's columns also have been published in the *Los Angeles Times, The Washington Post, Toronto Star, Rochester Democrat-Chronicle, Montreal Gazette, The London (Ontario) Free Press, Schenectady Gazette, and the Albany Times-Union.* He also has been a columnist for *News from Indian Country.*

As advisor for a television series called "How the West Was Lost," Kanentiio was extensively involved in the one-hour television documentary broadcast on the Discovery Channel in January and February 1995. The specific episode is entitled "Divided We Fall: The Iroquois and the American Revolution." From script development and review to insuring cultural accuracy as well as on-screen interviews, Kanentiio was an important part of the project.

He is also serving as a member of the board of directors for Native American Television Network. Kanentiio was selected to be a delegate to the World Parliament of Religions in Cape Town, South Africa in 1999 and again in 2004 at the Parliament of World Religions gathering in Barcelona, Spain. His experiences in Cape Town are part of the film *A Seat at the Table* released in 2004.

Kanentiio has spoken on contemporary Native American issues in such countries as Italy, Germany, Austria, Switzerland, and Luxembourg. In the United States he has lectured at the University of Connecticut, Cornell University, Syracuse University, Colgate University, and Hamilton College.

Further Reading

George-Kanentiio, Douglas M. *Iroquois on Fire: A Voice from the Mohawk Nation.* Westport, CT: Praeger, 2006.

George-Kanentiio, Douglas M. Personal communication. "Akwesasne Mohawks Expelled from the Mushhole and Other Bad Memories." November 1, 2011.

George-Kanentiio, Douglas M. "Residential School Horrors Haunt Native Americans." *Rochester [New York] Democrat-Chronicle*, December 11, 2007. http://www.democrat andchronicle.com/apps/pbcs.dll/article?AID=/20071211/OPINION02/712110317/1039/ OPINION.

Johansen, Bruce E. *Life and Death in Mohawk Country.* Golden, CO: North American Press, 1993.

Grand Governing Council

American Indian Movement

The AIM's Grand Governing Council, based in Minneapolis, supervises the faction of the AIM that asserts authority to the organization's identity, but with considerable dissension from chapters in many other cities that say they are autonomous.

The GCC zealously protects AIM trademarks, claiming (on its Web site): "SPECIAL NOTICE: The names and graphics displayed on our Website, AIMOVEMENT.ORG, our letterhead, publications and merchandise are the exclusive U.S. Patent & Trademark protected, spiritual, cultural, and intellectual property rights of the American Indian Movement. The American Indian Movement Grand Governing Council National Board of Directors is the registered owners and safe-keepers of said Marks" (GCC, 2007).

The GCC, quoting Birgil Kills Straight (Oglala Lakota), says that it is:

respected by many, hated by some, but they are never ignored . . . the catalyst for Indian Sovereignty . . . [we] intend to raise questions in the minds of all, questions that have gone to sleep in the minds of Indians and non-Indian alike. . . . From the inside AIM people are cleansing themselves; many have returned to the old traditional religions of their tribes, away from the confused notions of a society that has made them slaves of their own unguided lives. . . . AIM is first, a spiritual movement, a religious re-birth, and then the re-birth of dignity and pride in a people. (GCC, 2007)

Further Reading

American Indian Movement Council on Security and Intelligence. http://www.aimovement.org/csi/index.html.

American Indian Movement. Grand Governing Council. Official Web Site. http://www.aimovement.org/.

These links supply scanned images of declassified FBI, CIA, Justice Department, and White House documents obtained by AIM under the U.S. Freedom of Information Act.

I

International Indian Treaty Council (IITC)

The AIM established the International Indian Treaty Council in 1974 as an international arm. The IITC was led during the 1970s by Cherokee artist and author Jimmie Durham.

The IITC published a newsletter, *Treaty Council News*, which performed two functions: bringing international indigenous news to an audience of Native people and supporters in the United States and describing issues within that area to an international audience. One issue (1:2, May, 1977) described plans for the Third International Indian Treaty Conference on the Standing Rock reservation in South Dakota June 15–19, to convene a delegation to the United Nations and decide which issues to pursue. The same issue discussed plans by the federal government to colonize Native American lands for development of oil, coal, and uranium, with cooperation of several large corporations, plans for Leonard Peltier's appeals, and the need for international support of him as a political prisoner of the United States. Another issue (1:3, June, 1977) described an increase in vigilante activity against American Indians, a seizure of land by the United States on the Rosebud reservation in South Dakota, and further plans for an international Indian treaty conference the same month.

In 1979, Jimmie Durham resigned from the IITC with associate director Paul Chaat Smith in protest of AIM's ties with leaders in Cuba and other countries that were allied with the Soviet Union. The international reach of AIM, provoking internal disagreements, had become a liability. During the next decade, debate raged within AIM over whether Nicaragua's new Sandinista government was repressing the rights of Native minorities, leading to a split.

By the late 1980s, the *Treaty Council News* (8:1, June, 1988), described the fishing-rights case of David SoHappy and his relatives in Eastern Washington, a massacre of Brazilian Indians as timber companies and miners invaded their lands, abuse of human-rights workers in Guatemala, the threat of oil development to the calving grounds of caribou in northern Alaska and the Canadian Arctic, and other issues.

From September 29 through October 1, 2006, the IITC convened Tohono O'ohdam communities in southern Arizona with the AIM, the Derechos Humanos Coalition, and other groups to address these issues as part of a Border Summit of the Americas at the San Xavier District Cultural Center, Tucson, Arizona. Artist, actor, and songwriter Floyd Red Crow Westerman provided an evening concert.

The 24,000-member Tohono O'ohdam Nation (also called Papagos) has a homeland that spans the U.S.-Mexican border. Several hundred Tohono O'ohdam live on one side of the border, and must use services on the other side. At a time of heightened concern regarding border security, they find themselves at risk of deportation just to visit a doctor at the tribal hospital. They live in Mexico, but the hospital is in the United States. Many lack documents required to cross the border. This problem originated with the Gadsden Purchase (1853), when the United States bought land from Mexico south of the Gila River. For many years, the problem was largely ignored, but as immigration enforcement tightened, a visa required approval of several government agencies on both sides.

Further Reading

"Border Summit of the Americas." September 29, 2006. International Indian Treaty Council. http://www.aimovement.org/moipr/bordersummit.html

J

Janklow, William

(1939–2012)

William Janklow, attorney general and governor of South Dakota, later a member of Congress from that state, was a long-time antagonist of the AIM. Janklow at one point said that "the way to deal with AIM leaders is to put a bullet between their eyes." Janklow had campaigned for office in South Dakota on a pledge to "put the AIM leaders either in jail or under it" (Churchill and Vander Wall, 2002, 345–46). It was a key pledge because many of AIM's signature assertions, including the 1973 Wounded Knee occupation occurred in the state in which "Wild Bill" Janklow was a leading legal and political figure.

According to one political appraisal, "Janklow has been a powerful force in South Dakota politics for more than two decades. Critics have said he runs state government like a dictator, but supporters praise his successes. Janklow is proud to say he doesn't run from a fight—and he fights often. . . . He gained a reputation as hard-nosed and abrasive, but even his critics admitted he got things done" (Janklow, 2002).

Janklow was born in Chicago on September 13, 1939, but spent part of his youth, the years immediately following World War II, in Germany, where his father was one of the prosecutors of Nazis at the Nuremberg tribunals. The family moved to Flandreau, South Dakota in 1955, following the father's death, when Janklow was 16 years old. The next year he dropped out of high school and joined the U.S. marines, where he served three years. Mary Dean married Janklow, in 1960, and they had three children. Janklow then graduated from the University of South Dakota in 1964 with a Bachelor of Science degree in business administration. He also earned a law degree there in 1966.

Between 1966 and 1973, Janklow served as an attorney for legal services on the Rosebud Sioux Indian Reservation, after which he became part of the state attorney general's staff that was prosecuting AIM members on charges stemming from the Custer County Courthouse riot. During the occupation of Wounded Knee, as he was preparing to run for attorney general, Janklow was observed by AIM members wearing Army fatigues in the company of GOON squad members on the Pine Ridge reservation (William, 2002). Janklow showed up ready to do battle nearly every time members of AIM found themselves in a large-scale confrontation with police.

Former U.S. representative Bill Janklow (R-South Dakota) walks to the Moody County Courthouse, January 22, 2004, for sentencing to 100 days in prison and three years' probation on a second-degree manslaughter conviction in Flandreau, South Dakota. (AP Photo/Doug Dreyer)

Within a year, in 1974, Janklow won the state attorney general's race with 67 percent of the vote, upsetting Democrat Kermit Sande, who had hired him. Four years later, in 1978, Janklow was elected governor for the first of two four-year terms. Janklow's re-election as governor in 1982 with 71 percent of the vote was the largest margin for that office in South Dakota's history. He was elected governor twice more, in 1994 and 2002. Later, Janklow was elected to Congress. He resigned in 2004 after a conviction for manslaughter, following an automobile accident.

The Eagle Deer Case

In *The Unquiet Grave*, Steve Hendricks dissects reports of Jancita Eagle Deer's alleged rape by Janklow that kept Peter Matthiessen's *In the Spirit of Crazy Horse* off the market for nearly a decade between roughly 1983 and 1991 due to a libel lawsuit by Janklow. Janklow also sued *Newsweek* magazine over the same issue.

Peter Matthiessen's *In the Spirit of Crazy Horse* was readied for publication in the early 1980s, making a case for Peltier's innocence. The publisher, Viking, withdrew the book after Janklow threatened to sue for libel over passages in the book that linked him to the rape of Eagle Deer. Bootlegged copies of the book began to circulate, and it was published in the late 1980s after Janklow's case was dismissed by the South Dakota Supreme Court. *In the Spirit of Crazy Horse* presents, in an epilogue appended after the book had been suppressed for eight years, a case that Peltier was not the murderer of the two FBI agents. In an interview, a Native man known only as "X" confesses to the murders. In the meantime, the FBI had withheld from the public 6,000 pages of documents on the case, for reasons the agency associated with national security.

Janklow repeatedly and vigorously denied persistent reports and rumors regarding his relationship with Eagle Deer. During January of 1967, at age 15, Eagle Deer had supper with Janklow's family. In those days Janklow was well-regarded by some people on the Rosebud reservation. He helped people to the point of leaving money on his doorstep for Indians who needed to make bail after hours. While some people liked Janklow, others loathed him. For every story of an act of his kindness, another surfaced that he had been seen driving around the reservation in his underwear, swilling beer, and shooting at stray dogs. He was disbarred from the Rosebud Tribal Court in 1974, and did not appear to defend himself when summoned (Johansen and Maestas, 1979, 87).

Janklow volunteered to take Eagle Deer to a local dance, but they arrived early, before other people. Rather than leave Eagle Deer in a darkened dance hall, they took a ride in the country, during which, having stopped at a roadside gate, Janklow (according to Eagle Deer, described in Hendricks, 2006, 148–49) forced himself on her sexually, then gave her $3 not to tell anyone. She talked anyway—first to supervisors at her boarding school, then to the FBI, which declined to prosecute Janklow, citing insufficient evidence.

The rape allegation arose again during 1974 when Dennis Banks filed a complaint with the Rosebud Tribal Court. Janklow was ordered to testify, but refused. By this time he had quit doing favors for Indians, and was pledging, as a candidate for attorney general of South Dakota, to put AIM "in jail, if not under it [and] . . . to put a bullet in their heads" (Hendricks, 2006, 151). Eagle Deer and several others did testify, after which Judge Mario Gonzalez disbarred him from the Rosebud court, citing "the beastly act committed against her by Mr. Janklow" (Hendricks, 2006, 157). Gonzalez also issued a warrant for Janklow's arrest. Newspapers in South Dakota ignored the hearing and—as Hendricks points out with the wry irony that distinguishes his account—"Five days after his disbarment, two of three voters in South Dakota cast ballots for Janklow and he became the state's foremost enforcer of the law" (Hendricks, 200, 157).

Six months later, on April 4, 1975, Eagle Deer was killed by two teenagers driving a speeding Pontiac GTO as she stumbled, disoriented and disheveled, on a rural highway near Aurora, Nebraska. Hendricks devotes considerable space (pp. 194–99) to the possibility that Eagle Deer had been beaten and dumped on the highway by Douglass Durham, an FBI informant who had infiltrated AIM.

Officially, the death was reported as a traffic accident. That was not unusual. By 1975, Pine Ridge had a murder rate eight times that of Detroit, the reputed murder "capital" of the United States at the time (Johansen and Maestas, 1979 169–70). Several of those deaths involved vehicle rammings and also were reported as traffic accidents.

Janklow at 1975 Shootout

A shootout at the Jumping Bull Ranch at Pine Ridge on June 26, 1975 took the lives of two FBI agents, Ronald Williams and Jack Coler, and one Indian man, Joe Stuntz Killsright, an AIM member from Coeur d'Alene, Idaho. Leonard Peltier later was convicted of the FBI agents' killings after two other defendants (Bob Robideau and Dino Butler) were found not guilty. The FBI never investigated the death of Stuntz Killsright, who had been killed by a sniper. The scene immediately was besieged by 150 BIA police in riot gear and a number of vigilantes, along with William Janklow.

The FBI blocked the area, not allowing media access, claiming that AIM guerillas had drawn the agents into the area (they had appeared ion their own accord with a warrant for a pair of stolen cowboy boots). The reservation soon was being roamed by 400 FBI agents in combat clothing, carrying M-16s, looking for suspects, raiding homes of suspected AIM members. All of this was part of the Reservation Murders (RESMURS) investigation. In the meantime, the FBI still was complaining that it lacked manpower to investigate many other RESMURS, an acronym applied by the FBI only to the deaths of its agents, not to the scores of still unsolved Indian homicides.

Janklow sued *Newsweek* after it carried an interview criticizing him with Dennis Banks. The case was found by a District Court to be without merit. The Eight Circuit Court of Appeals affirmed the ruling. The *Newsweek* article, dated February 21, 1983, was titled "Dennis Banks's Last Stand." Janklow's claim centered on one paragraph, describing Banks's initiation of tribal charges of assault against Janklow in 1974, in connection with the allegation that he had raped Eagle Deer five years before. "The court held that *Newsweek* correctly reported the material facts of the rape allegation, that the article did not suggest the magazine believed the truth of the allegation, and that any implication that revenge motivated Janklow's prosecution of Banks was opinion and therefore non-actionable under the First Amendment." On appeal, a divided panel of Eighth Circuit Court of Appeals upheld the first two holdings but reversed the third on the ground that "the meaning that can be drawn from the *Newsweek* article—that Janklow did not commence prosecuting Banks until after Banks attempted to bring him to justice for the alleged rape of an Indian girl—is factual." *Janklow v. Newsweek, Inc.,* 759 F.2d 644, 652 (8th Cir.1985) (Janklow, 1985).

Banks evaded prosecution in South Dakota by taking sanctuary for a time in California under orders from Gov. Jerry Brown. California officials refused to extradite him to South Dakota, in part because of Janklow's anti-AIM rhetoric. Weary of life in exile, and with a change in political leadership in South Dakota, Banks returned there in 1984 to face criminal charges stemming from confrontations in South Dakota, a time when at least 65 AIM members and allies had been victims of unsolved murders on and near the Pine Ridge reservation. William, who was governor at the time, told Banks he could return to South Dakota safely.

Bad blood still was very evident, enduring over the years, when, during 2000, Janklow stepped in with all his then-formidable political might (before he killed a motorcyclist in a state of drunkenness and was forced to resign from Congress) to block requests that might have led to a pardon of Leonard Peltier by President Bill Clinton.

Janklow lost little of his bluster with time. In 2000, Gov. Janklow called a U.S. Civil Rights Commission report alleging that South Dakota discriminates against Native Americans "garbage" and "fiction" (Woster, 2000). Titled "Native Americans in South Dakota: An Erosion of Confidence in the Justice System," the report investigated a series of unsolved murders of Indians on or near nine reservations throughout the state. The bodies of six Native American men were found in Rapid Creek during two years; two others were found in a field near Pine Ridge, while one dead Indian was stuffed into a garbage can head-first in Mobridge. The report said that "On average men in Bangladesh can expect to live longer than Native American men in South Dakota . . . . Native American men living in six South Dakota counties had the shortest life expectancy in the Nation" (South Dakota, 2000). Janklow said he hadn't read the report.

On November 3, 2011, at age 72, Janklow announced that he was dying of brain cancer. He was undergoing experimental treatment at the Mayo Clinic in Minneapolis, but acknowledged that it was a long shot. He died on January 12, 2012 (Goldstein, 2012).

Further Reading

Churchill, Ward and Jim Vanderwall. *The COINTELPRO Papers: Documents from the FBI's Secret Wars Against Dissent in the United States*. Classic ed. Boston, MA: South End Press, 2002.

Goldstein, Richard. "Bill Janklow, a Four-Term Governor of South Dakota, Dies at 72." *New York Times*, January 12, 2012. http://www.nytimes.com/2012/01/13/us/bill-janklow-a-four-term-governor-of-south-dakota-dies-at-72.html

Hendricks, Steve. *The Unquiet Grave: The FBI and the Struggle for the Soul of Indian Country*. New York: Thunder's Mouth Press, 2006.

"Janklow, William J." San Francisco Chronicle/Associated Press Political Database. November, 2002. http://www.sfgate.com/cgi-bin/article.cgi?f/politics/election/2002nov/bios/hsd1rep.dtl

Matthiessen, Peter. *In The Spirit of Crazy Horse*. New York: Viking, 1991.

"South Dakota Governor Declares War on Indians." Redhawk's Lodge, Black Hills AIM. April 5, 2000. http://siouxme.com/lodge/jank2.html

United States Court of Appeals, Eighth Circuit; Sept. 12, 1985. Decided April 10, 1986 Justia US Law. http://law.justia.com/cases/federal/appellate-courts/F2/788/1300/300888

William Janklow, Appellant, v. Newsweek, Inc., Appellee 788 F.2d 1300.

"William 'Wild Bill'" Janklow: Atty General, Governor, [and] GASP, Congressman." Redhawk's Lodge. 2002. http://siouxme.com/lodge/janklow.html

Woster, Terry. "Janklow: Civil Rights Report is "Garbage.'" *Sioux Falls Argus Leader*, April 5, 2000. http://siouxme.com/lodge/civil_rights.html

K

Kunstler, William Moses

(1919–1995)

William Kunstler, the renowned radical lawyer, was the most prominent of several attorneys who helped the AIM achieve a remarkable record of victories against the U.S. government during a series of trials after the Wounded Knee occupation. Kunstler also played a leading role in the legal case of four AIM members charged with the murder of two FBI agents on the Pine Ridge reservation during June 1975. Two were found innocent, while Leonard Peltier was convicted.

In addition to defending AIM clients, Kunstler represented the Chicago Seven conspiracy trial defendants against charges of inciting riots during the 1968 Democratic National Convention during 1969 and 1970, as well as several well-known members of the Black Panther Party, when federal prosecutors indicted them. In the *New York Times,* Victor S. Navasky (1970, 217) said that. "William Kunstler is without doubt the country's most controversial and, perhaps, its best-known lawyer, period." While he was a hero to many leftists and liberals, right-wingers often said he should be disbarred.

Early Life

Kunstler was born into a Jewish family, son of a medical doctor, in New York City. He attended DeWitt Clinton High School, then matriculated at Yale University and became a member of Phi Beta Kappa, the academic honor society. He earned his legal credential at Columbia University Law School. Kunstler served in the Pacific during World War II, leaving the service as a major with a Bronze Star. Following World War II, Kunstler was admitted to the New York state bar in 1948; his first legal practice was in small-business and family law, but by the 1960s his consuming legal passion became civil rights. He also became controversial by airing radio programs on such subjects as the Alger Hiss trial.

In 1957, in his first notable civil-rights case, Kunstler defended William Worthy, a *Baltimore Afro-American* writer, who had defied a U.S. State Department ban on travel to China. The State Department offered to return Worthy's passport if he would agree not to visit any more Communist countries in the future (he had visited China on his way to Moscow, in the Soviet Union). Both Worthy and Kunstler said that the ban was unconstitutional. The case was not resolved.

After that, Kunstler worked with the American Civil Liberties Union (ACLU) to defend "Freedom Riders" in the South. He also worked to integrate libraries and public parks in Albany, Georgia. In 1962, his book *The Case for Courage* described the work of lawyers who had risked their careers for the benefit of clients engaged in controversies. His civil rights work, some of it undertaken with Martin Luther King, helped lay the legal groundwork for the Civil Rights Act of 1964. Between 1964 and 1972, he was director of the ACLU. During these years some of his more notable cases involved Angela Davis, Dr. King, Stokely Carmichael, Adam Clayton Powell, and Lenny Bruce.

The AIM Trials

Kunstler turned his attention to AIM during the occupation of Wounded Knee in the spring of 1973. He represented Russell Means during the trial that followed the occupation, where Judge Fred J. Nichol dismissed all charges and, adopting Kunstler's line of reasoning, sharply criticized federal prosecutors' ineptness. Kunstler, one of AIM's several attorneys, said: "The purpose of the trials [was] to break the spirit of the American Indian Movement by tying up its leaders and supporters in court and forcing [it] to spend huge amounts of money, time and talent to keep [its] people out of jail, instead of building an organization that can work effectively for the Indian people" (Matthiessen, 1991, 193–94).

In the AIM trials, Kunstler was combative in the courtroom, as he had been during the Chicago conspiracy trial. At the Butler–Robideau trial in Cedar Rapids, Iowa, for the murders of FBI agents Jack Coler and Ronald Williams at the Jumping Bull Ranch during June 1975, Kunstler subpoenaed several important federal-government officials about FBI counter-intelligence measures that had been used to break up AIM and the Black Panther Party.

In the murder case against Dino Butler and Robert Robideau, the government's case was damaged by weak ballistic evidence, lack of eyewitnesses, and false witnesses. At one point, during testimony of government witness Wish Draper, Butler shouted "Liar!" (Matthiessen, 1991, 297). Kunstler even led another government witness, James Harper, into confessing that he had lied many times to get what he wanted (Matthiessen, 1991, 297). The trial also featured testimony by FBI director Clarence Kelly about FBI counterintelligence (COINTELPRO) activities. Kunstler provoked Kelly into losing his temper when he raised the subject of the many AIM members and supporters who had been killed at Pine Ridge with scanty attention from the FBI, which is responsible for investigating major crimes on Indian reservations. Kelly then defended the FBI's massive response to the shooting of its agents: "If they are threatened they have a right to defend themselves" (Matthiessen, 1991, 308). Having drawn Kelly into making the defense's main point, that self-defense was a justified motive for Butler and Robideau, Kunstler excused the witness with Kelly's emphatic words ringing in the jury's ears.

Kunstler also represented Leonard Peltier in his many trials and appeals during and after the original verdict in Fargo, ND District Court that convicted him for killing the two FBI agents. It was a rare loss for Kunstler while representing AIM members, and it came at the hands of a judge, Paul Benson, whom the defense complained was uncompromisingly biased in favor of the prosecution. Tactics (such as reconstructing the government's ballistics evidence) that had worked during the Cedar Rapids trial were not allowed by Benson (Matthiessen, 1991, 574).

Peltier's case came to the attention of Amnesty International and the government of Canada, from which Peltier was extradited to face trial on the basis of the Poor Bear affidavits. Peltier's appeals were directed by several well-known legal personalities, including former U.S. Attorney General Ramsey Clark (as well as Kunstler). Peltier's third appeal for a new trial was turned down by the Eighth Circuit Court of Appeals in St. Paul, Minnesota, during 1993, for the third time, exhausting his remedies within the U.S. legal system.

Kunstler's Many Talents

Kunstler maintained an active life as an author along with his legal work. His books included *Our Pleasant Voices* (1941), *The Law of Accidents* (1954), *First Degree* (1960), *Beyond a Reasonable Doubt? The Original Trial of Caryl Chessman* (1961 and 1973), *The Case for Courage: The Stories of Ten Famous American Attorneys Who Risked Their Careers in the Cause of Justice* (1962), *And Justice For All* (1963), *The Minister and the Choir Singer: The Hall-Mills Murder Case* (1964), *Deep in My Heart* (1966), *Trials and Tribulations* (1985), *My Life as a Radical Lawyer* (1994), *Hints & Allegations: The World (In Poetry and Prose* (1994), *Politics on Trial: Five Famous Trials of the 20th Century* (2002), and *The Emerging Police State: Resisting Illegitimate Authority* (2004). Kunstler also had a secondary career as an actor. He played himself in one episode of *Law & Order* (1994), and acted as an attorney for Jim Morrison in Oliver Stone's film *The Doors,* 1991, and as a judge in *Malcolm X,* directed by Spike Lee, in 1992.

Kunstler died at age 76 in 1995 of heart failure in New York City. Sarah and Emily Kunstler, his daughters, examined his tumultuous life in *William Kunstler: Disturbing the Universe,* an hour-and-a-half documentary film released in 2009.

Further Reading

Langum David J., Sr. *William M. Kunstler: The Most Hated Lawyer in America.* New York: New York University Press, 1999.

Margolick, David. "Still Radical After All These Years". *New York Times,* July 6, 1993, B-1.

Matthiessen, Peter. *In the Spirit of Crazy Horse: The Story of Leonard Peltier.* New York: Viking, 1991.

Navasky, Victor S. "Right On! With Lawyer William Kunstler." *New York Times,* April 19, 1970, 217.

Stout, David. "William Kunstler, 76, Dies; Lawyer for Social Outcasts." *New York Times.* September 5, 1995, A-1.

L

LaDuke, Winona

(Born 1959)
Anishinabe (Ojibway) Environmental Activist and Political Figure

Ask Winona LaDuke what she does for a living, and she may say "rural economic development." That's what they called it at Harvard, where LaDuke took her undergraduate degree during the late 1970s (she also attended Antioch University). The sum of those three words is more than its parts, however. LaDuke is engaged in a reservation revolution, changing the ways that Native Americans (and many other people as well) think about how and where they get and use their energy, food, and other basics of daily life. During 2007, Winona LaDuke was inducted into the National Women's Hall of Fame in Seneca Falls, New York.

LaDuke is a passionate advocate of direct action, quoting Malcolm X, "By any means necessary." "Sometimes," LaDuke said at the University of Nebraska at Omaha November 6, 2007, "you have to put your body on the line." LaDuke, whose Anishinabe name is "Benaysayequay," meaning "Thunderbird woman," says: "I have a fervent belief that Native people should own land." Want a wind turbine on your reservation (at White Earth they have plans to go carbon neutral with five of them)? Buy the land from a non-Indian farmer or rancher and get busy. That's rural economic development, LaDuke style.

A charismatic, dynamic speaker with a long face and expressive eyes, LaDuke meets audiences one-on-one. She has written several books, lectured around the world, and twice, in 1996 and 2000, ran for vice president of the United States on the Green Party ticket with Ralph Nader. Most of her days are spent at home on the White Earth Anishinabe (also known as Chippewa or Ojibway) reservation about 200 miles northwest of Minneapolis, Minnesota. On the reservation, LaDuke leads the White Earth Land Recovery Project, started in 1989. She founded the recovery project to reclaim Anishinabe lands (originally 837,000 acres) promised by a federal treaty signed in 1867 that had been sold or stolen, often by logging companies that by 2007 was buying back real estate, installing wind and solar power, harvesting wild rice for home use and export, and feeding elders buffalo meat instead of commodity cheese (among many other things) on a $1.7 million annual budget. Anyone who can fix a reservation car, she insists, can build and install solar panels.

Green Party vice-presidential candidate Winona LaDuke, during a rally August 8, 2000, in Missoula, Montana. (AP Photo/ Chad Harder)

The White Earth Land Recovery Project has become the largest reservation-based nonprofit organization in the United States. In addition to working toward recovery of the White Earth Indian Reservation's original land, the group advocates land stewardship, language fluency, community development, and spiritual and cultural traditions (Melmer, 2007).

With a $20,000 from the first Reebok Human Rights Award, she founded the White Earth Land Recovery Project on the reservation, where she had moved during the early 1980s. The project's major goal has been regain land base in Native lands on a reservation that by 1990 was 92 percent owned by non-Indians.

LaDuke's brand of economic development relies heavily on creation of employment that produces real goods and services, keeping money at home. She disparages government programs on reservations that leave more people engaged in job training than in jobs. For example, she helped create Native Harvest, which provides food for domestic consumption and sale over the Internet. By 2007, Native Harvest's wild rice alone was bringing in $500,000 a year. "To be sovereign," she said at UNO, "you have to have an economy that is internal—grow your own food, produce your own energy."

LaDuke's Early Years

LaDuke was born in Los Angeles, daughter of Vincent LaDuke, an Indian activist during the 1950s, and Betty LaDuke, a painter and art professor. LaDuke says that her parents gave her an animating activist spirit. While studying at Harvard, she met Cherokee activist Jimmie Durham; soon she became involved in Native American environmental issues (Americans, n.d.).

By her teenaged years, LaDuke was engaged in debate at school, and, as a member of her high school's championship team in Oregon, was recruited to Harvard (she graduated in 1982), surprising nearly everyone in her community. At the age of 18, she was involved in researching the effect of uranium mining on Navajos as part of her debating activities, which led to environmental advocacy that, decades later, helped lead to a ban on such mining on the reservation. "There is no safe way to mine uranium," LaDuke said at UNO, "Most of the Navajos' uranium miners have died."

LaDuke has tirelessly lectured, written, and pressed authorities for answers on environmental issues, from the Navajo uranium mines, to Hydro-Quebec's construction sites at James Bay, to toxic waste sites on Native Alaskan and Canadian land along the Arctic Ocean. LaDuke's assertions have been confirmed by environmental scientists. As if to illustrate just how pervasive pollution of the entire Earth has become, studies of Inuit women's breast milk in the late 20th century revealed abnormally high levels of polychlorinated biphenyls (PCBs). Studies around the rim of Hudson's Bay, conducted by Dr. Eric Dewailly of Laval University in 1988, found that nursing mothers' milk contained more than six times the level of PCBs considered "safe" by the Canadian government. The fish that most Inuit eat accumulate PCBs, dioxins, mercury, and other toxic materials in the food chain.

LaDuke also publicized her findings in numerous newspaper and magazine articles, and as a founder of the Indigenous Women's Network and a board member of Greenpeace. She also initiated a national Native environmental advocacy group, Honor the Earth that raises money for economic development projects on reservations. She also was named by *Time* magazine in 1995 as one of fifty "Leaders for the Future."

The Green Party Campaign

Under ordinary circumstances, Winona LaDuke says unabashedly that she is not inclined toward electoral politics. She would rather be farming and caring for her children and grandchildren on the White Earth reservation. During the late summer of 1996, however, an extraordinary circumstance arose for LaDuke when Ralph Nader, who had been nominated to run for president by the Green Party tapped her for vice president. The Nader-LaDuke ticket received 0.6 percent of the popular vote in the November 5 general election that year. Four years later, the same ticket was influential enough in some states to be accused by liberals of diverting just enough votes from Democrat Al Gore to put Republican George W. Bush in the White House.

Accepting the 1996 nomination, LaDuke said that the United States needs "a new model of electoral politics. . . . I am interested in reframing the debate on issues of this society the distribution power and wealth, abuse of power, the rights of the natural world, the environment, and the need to consider an amendment to the U.S. Constitution in which all decisions made today would be considered in light of the impact on the seventh generation from now. Now that, I believe, is what sustainability is all about. These are vital subjects that are all too often neglected by the rhetoric of 'major party' candidates and media." President Clinton may have read LaDuke's speech, for two months later, in a proclamation observing Native American Heritage Month, he said: "It was the Iroquois who taught that in every deliberation we should consider the impact of our decisions on the next seven generations" (Johansen, 1996, 3).

The Green Party was listed on the general election ballot in 22 states, under other names in some of them, such as the Liberty, Ecology, and Community Party in Louisiana, and the Pacific Party in Oregon. The Green Party, which began organizing in 1984, by late 1996 had 29 elected officials in 10 states. The party platform focuses on increased grassroots democracy and breakup of corporate power. The platform also puts an emphasis on environmentally correct economic policy, non-violence, and social justice.

In the 1996 election, the Green Party felt slighted after The Sierra Club endorsed Bill Clinton and Al Gore as an environmentally friendly alternative to Republican candidates Bob Dole and Bill Kemp. However, a sizable number of dissidents argued that the Sierra Club should have endorsed Nader and LaDuke. The dissidents were led by former Sierra Club president David Brower. We have seen the regimes of environmental destruction move from the Great Communicator (Ronald Reagan) to the Great Capitulator (Bill Clinton) said Brower.

LaDuke agreed: "It is shameful that the Sierra Club would endorse someone of so many environmental promises and so little environmental protection", said LaDuke (1996, 38–45). She characterized President Clinton as an environmental opportunist, who said in 1992 that he would not allow any weakening of the Endangered Species Act, but who in 1994 signed legislation that froze addition of species to that list. The Sierra Club's internal conflict was reflected in the November/December, 1996 edition of its magazine, where Clinton was endorsed at the bottom of page 60, while LaDuke appeared on the cover riding a horse for a special issue on Native Americans and the Environment. She also wrote the cover story (LaDuke, 1996, 38–45).

LaDuke said her campaign brought American Indian issues into the national campaign. LaDuke also favors a constitutional amendment that would protect the air and water as common property, to be maintained free from contamination. "The rights of the people to use and enjoy air, water, and sunlight are essential to life, liberty, and the pursuit of happiness." LaDuke wrote in *Indian Country Today*, October 14, 1996.

In the waning days of the national campaign, John Nichols, an editorial writer for the Madison, Wisconsin, *Capital Times*, summarized LaDuke's contribution, saying that she "is a remarkable figure whose history of American Indian, environmental, and economic justice activism makes her uniquely qualified to participate in a national debate that desperately needs her insights. Yet, in an age of sound-bite politics, LaDuke and Nader have been largely neglected." Nichols continued: "As we move into the final stages of a campaign that has been as vapid as any in this nation's history, Winona LaDuke stands out as a lonely voice of substance" (Johansen, 1996, 4).

"Until we have an environmental, economic, and social, policy that is based on consideration of the impact on the seventh generation from now, we will be living in a society that is based on conquest, not one that is based on survival. I consider myself a patriot—not to a flag, [but] to a land," said LaDuke (Johansen, 1996, 4).

"The Good Commods"

Most of LaDuke's initiatives are more basic than national politics. She helped (with Margaret Smith, a former teacher) to build Mino-Miijim, to give wild rice and other traditional foods, including buffalo meat and hominy, to elderly people with Type 2 diabetes on the reservation. "Oh," a tribal member exclaimed "Here come the good commodities" (Kummer, 2004, 148).

LaDuke maintains that "The essence of the problem is about consumption, recognizing that a society [the United States] that consumes one third of the world's resources is unsustainable. This level of consumption requires constant intervention into other people's lands. That's what's going on" (Americans, n.d.).

On November 16, 2008, LaDuke's home on the White Earth reservation burned to the ground because of an electrical fire. LaDuke, five children, and three grandchildren escaped injury, but art, books, music, photographs, and other collectibles from LaDuke's travels around the world, as well as furniture and other possessions. Many friends banded together to replace some of the memorable pieces.

Further Reading

"Americans Who Tell the Truth: Winona LaDuke." No date. http://www.americanswho tellthetruth.org/pgs/portraits/Winona_LaDuke.html

Bowermaster, Jon. "Earth of a Nation," *Harper's Bazaar*, April, 1993.

Johansen, Bruce E. "Running for Office: LaDuke and the Green Party," *Native Americas* 18, no. 4 (Winter, 1996): 3–4.

Kummer, Corby. "Going with the Grain: True Wild Rice, for the Past Twenty Years Nearly Impossible to Find, is Slowly Being Nurtured Back to Market." *The Atlantic Monthly,* May, 2004, 145–48.

LaDuke, Winona. *All Our Relations: Native Struggles for Land and Life*. Cambridge, MA: South End Press, 1999.

LaDuke, Winona. "The Growing Strength of Native Environmentalism: Like Tributaries to a River." *Sierra*, November/December, 1996, 38–45.

LaDuke, Winona. *Last Standing Woman (History & Heritage).* Stillwater, MN: Voyageur Press, 1999.

LaDuke, Winona. *Recovering the Sacred: The Power of Naming and Claiming.* Cambridge, MA: South End Press, 2005.

LaDuke, Winona. *The Winona LaDuke Reader: A Collection of Essential Writings.* Stillwater, MN: Voyageur Press, 2002.

Melmer, David. "Winona LaDuke Inducted into National Women's Hall of Fame." *Indian Country Today,* October 15, 2007. http://www.indiancountry.com/content.cfm?id=1096415916

LaMere, Frank

(Born ca. 1954)
Winnebago (Ho-Chunk) Activist

Frank LaMere, a Winnebago (Ho-Chunk) from Eastern Nebraska, has, for many years, been AIM point man in the campaign to limit alcoholic beverage sales to Indians in the tiny border town of Whiteclay, Nebraska, near the Pine Ridge Oglala Lakota reservation, where the major business is catering to Native American drunkenness. LaMere also has served as Democratic Party chairman of the National Native American Caucus, as he urged Native people to vote, "that white man's thing" (Baker, 2004).

Attempts by AIM to shut down beer sales at Whiteclay have continued for decades, with frustrating results. In 1999, some of the major organizers at Whiteclay were the same as they had been in Gordon and Custer—AIMsters with many more lines on their faces. They listened to speeches by Russell Means, Clyde Bellecourt, and Dennis Banks, among others, protesting basic injustices, such as young white men's penchant for taking out their aggressions (sometimes with fatal results) on drunken Indians near the dusty streets of Whiteclay, population 24, where the main business is selling $3 million a year worth of beer to the people of Pine Ridge (Johansen, 1998, 5).

The sale of alcoholic beverages is illegal on the reservation; Whiteclay, 200 feet from the reservation border, is mainly comprised of four stores that sell about 4 million cans of beer per year, nearly all of them to Indians from Pine Ridge (Walker, 2007). Carson Walker (2007) of the Associated Press described a town where "Beer cans litter reservation roads and the streets of Whiteclay. People loiter outside the stores. Some try to trade tools, electronics and other things for beer." "I'm tired of my people dying. You've got 18-, 19-year-olds trading alcohol for sex," one observer told Walker. The AIM and Nebraskans for Peace called repeatedly for Nebraska to enforce its own liquor laws in Whiteclay, without success (Activists, 2003). The

Nebraska State Patrol relied that it was issuing citations, but that didn't solve the problem.

Reacting to Murders

The killing of drunken Indians by whites did not stop with protests of Wesley Bad Heart Bull's murder in the 1970s. In the late 1990s, AIM was holding rallies in the same general area—with Whiteclay a frequent backdrop—to protest a new generation of victims—two of the dead included Wilson Black Elk, 40, and Ronald Hard Heart, 39, whose bodies were found in a roadside ditch near Whiteclay.

Frustrated by the lack of official investigation into the murders, hundreds of people walked more than two miles, accompanied by a line of automobiles, traversing the two-lane blacktop to "take Whiteclay back," facing a line of a hundred Nebraska State Troopers in riot gear. Some of the Indians threw rocks at the troopers. From time to time, marchers would surge into the town. Once about 25 to 30 people trashed a grocery store, V.J.'s Market, in Whiteclay. It was said that V.J.'s owner, Vic Clarke, had treated Lakota in a demeaning manner. The store's freezer cases were destroyed and its cash registers doused with lighter fluid. Groceries were strewn through the store.

For years, Nebraska officials had been warned by LaMere and others that the situation in Whiteclay could explode. One day during the summer of 1997, LaMere, who was executive director of the Nebraska Inter-Tribal Development Corp., visited Whiteclay. He counted 32 intoxicated Indians on the town's streets at 5:15 in the morning, and 47 drunks on the streets during the afternoon, some of whom were fighting with each other. Several other Indians were passed out at the intersection of Nebraska Highway 87 with the road that leads to the reservation. A few of them were urinating on the street (Johansen, 1998, 5). Shortly after he visited Whiteclay, LaMere asked the Nebraska Liquor Control Commission to shut Whiteclay down. "I don't know what constitutes infractions of liquor laws in Whiteclay, but my good sense tells me there is something terribly wrong. . . ." LaMere told Toni Heinzl of the Omaha *World-Herald*. "What I saw . . . in Whiteclay would not be acceptable in Omaha of Lincoln," LaMere continued (Johansen, 1998, 5).

"I am ashamed to be a Nebraskan today," LaMere said on July 3, 1999, after several protesters were arrested at Whiteclay. "It was pure and simple intimidation." Gov. Mike Johanns defended the arrests for failure to obey a lawful order (Duggan, 1999). The deaths added fuel to the oft-recurring protests over beer sales at Whiteclay. The marches provoked memories of an AIM caravan to Gordon, Nebraska, 27 years earlier.

On October 4, 1999, LaMere (who was speaking with Means) told 175 people at the University of Nebraska College of Law that he had been "offended by the show of force presented by 130 Nebraska and Oglala Sioux police officers during the July 3 protest. Women, children, and old people participated in the July 3 march, only to be blocked by police clad in riot gear and armed with tear gas, with snipers on the roof. "July 3 was a dark day in the history of the state of Nebraska, for people who only wished to exercise their constitutional rights," LaMere said (Reed, 1999).

With LaMere playing a leading role, the AIM in Lincoln, the capital of Nebraska, criticized Nebraska's state government for doing nothing to stop the alcohol trafficking, despite "the wishes of the Oglala Sioux Tribal government, which has repeatedly beseeched our state officials to halt the beer sales in Whiteclay, even as the state profits. "The State of Nebraska collects a quarter of a million dollars a year in sales and liquor taxes from the sale of alcohol in Whiteclay, with not one dime being returned to the Lakota people to deal with the problems alcohol is fostering on the reservation" (A Year, 2003).

In 2003, AIM cofounder Russell Means and LaMere met with Nebraska Gov. Mike Johanns about problems in Whiteclay. Means and LaMere said they were tired of seeing native people victimized. Nothing came of it. On June 27, 2007, LaMere played a role in the erection of a blockade to interfere with transport of beer from Whiteclay to Pine Ridge erected by the Strong Heart Civil Rights Movement and Nebraskans for Peace.

Tribal police dismantled the blockade and arrested six people after only a few cars on the road from Whiteclay's beer stores to the reservation had been searched. Russell Means, Duane Martin Sr., and LaMere were arrested on charges of disorderly conduct and obstruction of justice; one man was wrestled to the ground after he refused to surrender a spear. "It looked like the violence was initiated by tribal police," said Mark Vasina of Nebraskans for Peace (Walker, 2007). About 20 tribal police broke up a blockade by roughly five people, with about 15 to 20 more (many of whom were reporters) watching.

The next day, beer sales continued.

Further Reading

"Activists Call for Enforced Laws at Whiteclay." Indianz.com., March 3, 2003. http://groups.yahoo.com/group/NatNews/message/28097

Baker, Deborah. "Dems Appeal to Indians: Get Out the Vote." Associated Press, July 28, 2004. http://www.coloradoaim.org/blog/2004/07/articles-july-28.html

Duggan, Joe. "Nine Protesters Arrested for Crossing Police Line." *Lincoln Journal-Star*, July 4, 1999. http://www.dickshovel.com/wc4.html

Johansen, Bruce E. "Whiteclay, Nebraska: The Town That Booze Built," *Native Americas* 15, no. 1 (Spring, 1998): 5.

Reed, Leslie. "Indian Activists: Arrests, Police Conduct Disturbing." *Omaha World-Herald,* October 5, 1999. http://www.omaha.com/Omaha/OWH/StoryViewer/1,3153, 230211,00.html

Walker, Carson. "Tribal Police Break up Attempted Beer Blockade." *Lincoln [Nebraska] Journal-Star,* June 27, 2007. http://journalstar.com/news/state-and-regional/govt-and-poli tics/article_f73b704d-67c6–5941–9a5b-49e70321d74a.html

"A Year of Atonement for Whiteclay. The Battle for Whiteclay Begins in Earnest." American Indian Movement, Lincoln, Nebraska, March 1, 2003. http://www.aimovement.org/calendar/whiteclay.html

Lamont, Buddy

(Died 1973)

Buddy Lamont was one of two AIM activists who were killed during the siege of Wounded Knee in 1973. The other was Frank Clearwater. Lamont, a Vietnam veteran and only son of Agnes Lamont, had lost his job with the Oglala Lakota tribe when he spoke out against Chairman Dick Wilson. The 1890 massacre at Wounded Knee was part of his family history. Agnes' mother was 12 years of age at the time, and survived the massacre. Her mother and uncle died in it (Smith and Warrior, 1996, 241).

By the end of April, 1973, Wounded Knee had become the site of full-scale firefights, as the government poured ordnance into the occupied village, lighting up the night sky with flares. Within a week, two Indians were killed, Frank Clearwater, age 47, on April 25. He had been at "The Knee" only a day, and hardly anyone knew anything about him.

Buddy Lamont was shot fatally on April 27, as thousands of rounds were poured into the village. He was shot through the heart; the stock of his rifle shattered. Power was cut off, as were telephones and running water. Food was running out. When lapses in roadblocks allowed, Agnes brought Buddy aspirin, clothes, and food. He was known as an avid and appreciative eater. She asked him to come home, but Buddy said he couldn't. Everyone was heartsick because Buddy was convivial and well-known across the reservation, where he had spent nearly his entire life. Agnes, with other Oglala women, was active in smuggling food into the besieged encampment, at considerable personal risk, until the end.

Lamont was buried on May 6. The Wilson regime had told all but family to stay away, but more than 100 people attended. Lamont's AIM colleagues gave him a hundred-gun salute (Smith and Warrior, 1996, 263). He was buried near the graves of the 1890 massacre victims. Clearwater's family also had requested burial at Pine Ridge, but Wilson denied access on grounds because he was not Oglala. Some Wilson opponents pointed out that several non-Oglala (some of them non-Indians) were buried there. "Guess we'll have to dig up all those white people," one said (Smith and Warrior, 1996, 258).

Further Reading

Smith, Paul Chaat and Robert Allen Warrior. *Like a Hurricane: The Indian Movement from Alcatraz to Wounded Knee.* New York: The New Press, 1996.

Libya, War in, and AIM

During September, 1984, Glenn Morris and Russell Means visited Libya under the aegis of Colorado AIM and the International Indian Treaty Council, the international arm of AIM. Visits were repeated in 1986, under aegis of the All African Peoples Revolutionary Party, led by Stokely Carmichael (Kwame Turé). In explicit opposition to President Ronald Reagan's travel ban the link to the regime in Libya extended to 2011, when the North Atlantic Treaty Organization used armed force to destabilize the regime of Muammar Gaddafi.

The alliance between one faction of AIM and Gaddafi's regime continued for many years, until a popular revolt deposed him. In 2011, the AIM Grand Governing Council declared that:

> We are opposed to the military aggression by the United States against a sovereign country. Bombs are indiscriminate, and we have yet to hear the atrocities that these bombs have caused on the civilian population in Libya. The United States along with partner countries, France, Italy, Germany, and Great Britain do not possess the moral high ground to act as defenders of human rights. This isn't so much about defending human rights as it is defending economic interests, and strategic interests. President Obama said in his speech on March 28th that the bombing of Libya "prevented a potential massacre." As victims of violence, U.S. aggression on our lands, chemical warfare, theft of our natural resources at the hands of the colonial U.S. government, we don't know if the U.S. has really prevented anything in Libya. . . . The real reason for bombing Libya and trying to kill its leader is to obtain its rich oil rights and revenues, and continue the operations of U.S. and European oil companies in Libya. . . . The bombing of Libya must stop. (Keshena, 2011)

Gaddafi's "crime," according to AIM, was denouncing imperialism, not killing his own people, as President Obama had maintained.

Further Reading

Colorado American Indian Movement. No date. http://www.coloradoaim.org/

Keshena, Enaemaehkiw Túpac. "American Indian Movement GGC Statement on the War in Libya." April 17, 2011. Minneapolis: Grand Governing Council, AIM. http://bermudaradical. wordpress.com/2011/04/17/american-indian-movement-ggc-statement-on-the-war-in-libya/

Littlefeather, Sacheen

(Born 1947)
Apache, Yaqui, Pueblo Actress and Activist

Sacheen Littlefeather was the stage name of a movie actress and activist who rejected an Oscar on behalf of Marlon Brando at the March 27, 1973 Academy

Awards. Littlefeather's given name is Maria Cruz, and she is of mixed ancestry (Apache, Yaqui, Pueblo, and Caucasian). Brando refused the Oscar for Best Actor Oscar in *The Godfather* in protest of the movie and television industries' stereotyping of American Indians, and to emphasize grievances associated with the ongoing occupation of Wounded Knee.

At the awards ceremony, Littlefeather said: "Marlon Brando . . . has asked me to tell you, in a very long speech which I cannot share with you presently—because of time [the producer had given her only 45 seconds]—that he . . . very regretfully cannot accept this very generous award. . . . I beg at this time that I have not intruded upon this evening and that we will, in the future . . . our hearts and our understanding will meet with love and generosity. Thank you on behalf of Marlon Brando" (*News of the Odd,* 1973). Brando (1973) said of American Indians: "We murdered them. We lied to them. We cheated them out of their lands. We starved them into signing fraudulent agreements that we called treaties which we never kept. We turned them into beggars on a continent that gave life for as long as life can remember."

A few people in the audience applauded, but many more jeered until Littlefeather walked off the stage. Later in the evening, Clint Eastwood wondered aloud whether he should present the award for Best Picture "on behalf of all the cowboys shot in John Ford westerns over the years," and Raquel Welch said, "I hope the winner doesn't have a cause," before announcing the winner of the Best Actress Oscar.

Sacheen Littlefeather tells the audience at the Academy Awards ceremony in Los Angeles, March 27, 1973, that Marlon Brando was declining his Oscar as best actor for his role in *The Godfather* to protest treatment of American Indians. (AP/ Wide World Photo)

Co-host Michael Caine criticized Brando for "Letting some poor little Indian girl take the boos," instead of "[standing] up and [doing] it himself" (*News of the Odd,* 1973).

After the ceremony, Littlefeather shared the text of Brando's statement with the press. Brando said that while he did not wish to "offend or diminish this occasion, I do not feel that I can, as a citizen of the United States, accept this or any award. . . . The motion picture community as much as anyone has been responsible for degrading the Indian" (*News of the Odd,* 1973).

Littlefeather's brief appearance on behalf of Brando as well as an appearance in *Playboy* produced a few film roles for her. Littlefeather continued her activism after the incident that made her famous, as she advocated Native Americans' work in roles suitable for them in movies. She also fought obesity, alcoholism, and diabetes, and cared for Indians with AIDS, including her brother.

Further Reading

Brando, Marlon. "The Godfather: That Unfinished Oscar Speech." *New York Times,* March 30, 1973. http://www.nytimes.com/packages/html/movies/bestpictures/godfather-ar3.html

News of the Odd. March 27, 1973. http://www.newsoftheodd.com/article1027.html

The Longest Walks (1978 and 2008)

During 1978, Dennis Banks and others in AIM conceived "The Longest Walk," which came close to tracing the route of the 1972 Trail of Broken Treaties, but on foot. Dennis Banks, who was then under sanctuary status in California against charges in South Dakota, drew up a route from Alcatraz to Washington, D.C. The Longest Walk, was intended to focus on spiritual issues and to dramatize the many forced removals of Native peoples from their homelands,. The march also raised the salience of contemporary issues, including a wave of bills in Congress to abrogate treaties.

The first of two Longest Walks began on February 11, 1978 on Alcatraz Island, and concluded 3,200 miles later on July 15, 1978, at the Washington Monument in the District of Columbia, as several thousand people of all races rallied behind a sacred pipe that had been carried the entire distance across the United States. Traditional elders then smoked tobacco that had been loaded into the pipe on Alcatraz Island. Boxer Muhammad Ali, actor Marlon Brando, Senator Ted Kennedy, and other celebrities joined the rally.

A week after the marchers arrived, the U.S. Congress passed the American Indian Religious Freedom Act. The walkers presented a manifesto at President Jimmy Carter's White House upon their arrival in July, 1978. The Congress also defeated an attempt to abrogate treaties advanced by representatives from the State of Washington who were supported by commercial and sports fishing interests angered by a federal court decision, in *United States v. Washington* (1974) that supported Indians' rights to fish under treaties negotiated during the mid-1850s. Senator Slade Gorton, who was the same state's attorney general when it lost this case, had contended that treaties made American Indians "super-citizens" with unconstitutional special rights. Proposals by Rep. Lloyd Meeds and Rep. Jack Cunningham, both of Washington, went down to defeat.

Longest Walk 2 arrived in Washington, D.C., during July of 2008, exactly three decades after the first one. It was even longer (8,200 miles), also starting at San Francisco Bay with participants from more than a hundred tribes and nations, as well as Maoris (from New Zealand), and a number of non-Indians. The two longest walks also were supported by a number of traditional elders from countries outside the United States, mostly from Japan, which Dennis Banks had visited. In a 30-page "Manifesto of Change," his walk emphasized the a need to legally protect Native sacred sites, as well as increased sovereignty, action to curtail global warming, and other forms of environmental protection. Some participants took a northern route (similar to the 1978 walk). Other traveled to the south. Both routes traversed 26 states.

M

McCloud, Janet (Yet Si Blue)

(1934–2003)
Puyallup

Janet McCloud, who was initially well-known as a fishing-rights activist in the Pacific Northwest, became a world-wide Native American advocate, "speaking to the nations of the world about the injustices committed against American Indians and actively resisting racism" (McCloud, 2003). She was "a master orator, prolific writer and political activist—a woman who helped shape state history, resurrected Indian spirituality for many and empowered the civil rights movement of native peoples worldwide" (Kamb, 2003).

Early Life

McCloud was born into the family of Chief Seath'l (Seattle) as Janet Renecker on March 30, 1934 on the Tulalip Reservation, the oldest of three girls. Raised in abject poverty, at the age of six she was panhandling on the Skid Road of the city named for her ancestor. "Mom told us how she panhandled at such a young age and that that was the reason she never passed a panhandler by without giving them something," said her son, Don McCloud Jr. (McCloud, 2003). Hers was "a world where alcohol and abuse defined her childhood . . . a hectic, rootless life . . . sometimes staying in church shelters or foster homes, other times moving to a new house because a stepfather couldn't pay the rent on the old one" (Trahant, 1999). Renecker's stepfather was an alcoholic who held few steady jobs, so few that the children often were shuttled between foster homes and churches.

Having attended public schools near Seattle, at the age of 13 Renecker was placed in a boarding school. She married and divorced at an early age, then, in the early 1950s, married Don McCloud Sr., a Puyallup Indian truck driver, electrical lineman, and fisherman. They remained married, with eight children (two boys and six girls) until he died of cancer in 1985.

The McClouds moved to Frank's Landing on the Nisqually River, where Don's stepfather, Billy Frank Sr., and his family had fished for decades, fending off the state agents. The Frank's assertion of treaty-rights extends back to at least 1937, when state agents arrested Billy Frank Sr. (Billy Frank Jr.'s father) and several other Indians for illegal fishing. "Billy Frank [senior] never ate white bread until his 60s. He lived off the land, eating salmon, roots, berries," McCloud said. "I was a city

Janet McCloud discussed fishing rights at St. Martin College in Olympia, Washington, February 18, 1966. (AP Photo/ Gary Guisinger)

kid on the river. The only salmon I ate was out of a can. I thought it was a beautiful life" (Trahant, 1999). Don picked up work where he could get it (he worked in a dog food factory for a time). Feeding the family was difficult, according to Janet, "We were so glad if we could get a fish or a deer" (Trahant, 1999).

Fishing-Rights Activism

The McClouds quickly became involved in the fishing-rights struggles along the Nisqually River that had become part of the Franks' daily life, as Native peoples in Western Washington maintained their treaty rights to fish in the face of arrests by state game agents. By 1965, Janet and several other fishing-rights advocates were going to jail on a routine basis for fishing, as the Medicine Creek Treaty of 1854 specified, in their "usual and accustomed places." The McClouds and other Native Americans set their nets at Frank's Landing along the Nisqually River and watched game wardens surround, beat, and arrest them.

During January of 1961, state game wardens burst into the McClouds's home searching for deer meat. "I just got mad," she recalled later. "I asked them, 'Do you have a search warrant?' They did. It said 'John Doe.' That was my first experience with game wardens. It made me so mad, but that's the way they treated us back then" (Trahant, 1999).

In the beginning, she said, "We were just fishing people," she said. "We didn't have any councils, we didn't have any lawyers, we didn't have any money, and we just saw ourselves as kamikazes. All we had was us, so we'd go out there and they'd beat us up, they'd mace us they'd throw us in jail, terrorize our kids and come and harass us at our homes, terrorize our kids in school . . . We were the front line" (The Great Janet McCloud, 2006).

The "fish-ins" continued until federal courts in the 1970s upheld the Indians' rights to take fish on a basis equal to sports and commercial fishermen in the area. In jail, the Indians often fasted in protest. "I didn't mind going to jail so much until Edith, my sister-in-law, said, 'And we're not eating either.' That was my first fast and we went six days without eating. They'd bring lima beans with ham, fried potatoes, and everything I loved. She could smell those good foods but wouldn't eat them. It made the fast more difficult" (Janet McCloud, 2003).

McCloud said that, at the time, she experienced a vision: "I heard a voice that sounded like Crazy Horse telling me not to be afraid. It said I wasn't alone and that I was being protected. I felt the voice so strong that all my fear and sadness went away. It's where I got my strength to face hostile audiences and all the adversity" (Janet McCloud, 2003). During the fish-ins, Janet was given the name "Yet Si Blue" (Woman Who Speaks Her Mind) signifying her advocacy of human rights.

Conflict over Fishing Intensifies

As the fishing struggle intensified, McCloud and other fishing-rights activists formed the Survival of the American Indians Association in 1964. Soon their ambit also broadened to cultural programs for Native American inmates at McNeil Island federal prison near Tacoma that became a national model as the Brotherhood of American Indians.

The McClouds, the Franks, and other fishing-rights activists began to build the case that resulted in the "Boldt Decision" of 1974 that enforced the treaties, in which U.S. District Judge George Boldt ruled in favor of 14 treaty tribes. Famous people (two examples were Marlon Brando and Dick Gregory) came to fish alongside the Indians.

One of the most violent reactions by game agents occurred on October 13, 1965, as several dozen state agents surrounded about 50 fishing Indians, most of them women and children. Within minutes after the Indians put their nets in the water, the state agents in speedboats rushed the gathering and, according to McCloud, "Things got out of hand" (Trahant, 1999), as the agents rammed the Indians' boats. On shore, Native women and children reacted to the rammings by pelting state officers with debris. The agents then reacted by beating some of them.

"Wardens were everywhere and they all seemed to be eight feet tall," McCloud wrote in the SAIA's newsletter, which she edited. "They were shoving, kicking, and pushing clubs at men, women and children. We were vastly outnumbered yet we were all trying to protect one another." Six Indians, including McCloud, were taken into custody and charged with resisting arrest, and later acquitted when films indicated that the confrontation had been provoked by the agents, not the Indians.

In the meantime, Dick Gregory was arrested for illegally fishing with the Indians, convicted and then, having been sentenced to 90 days in jail, started fasting. "Here this man is going to jail for us, living on distilled water," McCloud said. "So I collected kids off the rez and said, 'Let's go demonstrate' " (Trahant, 1999). They erected a tipi near the jail, and tourists began to gather as the state derided Gregory as a publicity hound. The state turned on sprinklers under the tipi and then arrested McCloud and her children—for what, they asked. Impeding the watering of state land? Eight days later, state troopers demolished the tipi.

McCloud as a National Leader

McCloud became a national leader after the fishing-rights issue was adjudicated. Late in the 1960s, she met Thomas Banyacya, the Hopi spiritual leader; she also came to know the Iroquois clan mother Audrey Shenandoah, who taught her Earth-centered religious beliefs. In the 1970s, she helped form the Northwest Indian Women's Circle that worked to develop leadership skills in the context of traditional values. She was active in the AIM on political issues, and worked with the Native American Rights Fund on legal issues, often using experience gained during the conflict over fishing rights. In 1985, she was instrumental in the founding of the Indigenous Women's Network. She also adamantly opposed forced sterilization of Native American women by federal Indian Health Service, after roughly 40 percent of Native women in the United States were sterilized. With Lorelie Means, Madonna Gilbert, and others McCloud also started the Women of All Red Nations (WARN).

McCloud, who farmed her family's 10 acres near Yelm, Washington, south of the Nisqually River, compared life to a garden. She told people to sow their best seeds and then care for what they produced. The McClouds taught their children to fish, put up food, and provide for anyone who came to their door in need. Traditional economy and ceremony were a path out of poverty, she believed.

Her home was characterized by McCloud as "a place to which people come for a traditional Native American ceremony, or as the first step when beginning a sojourn, or to join a tribute to the Winter Moon at the solstice. 'The elders have said this is a spiritual place. For over 30 years, we've used this land to teach our traditional ways,' McCloud said. . . . When all is going crazy . . . our people can come back to the center to find the calming effect; to reconnect with their spiritual self" (Trahant, 1999).

In 1985, McCloud hosted 300 women from many countries for five days on her 10 acres, which she calls *Sapa Dawn*, to talk about shared concerns regarding social, economic, and family problems that gave birth to the Indigenous Women's Network. "There was no motel in Yelm then," recalled McCloud. "So we put up tepees. One woman said: 'Where's the motel?' I said, 'Here's a key: tepee number one or tepee number two'" (Trahant, 1999). Dennis Banks, Russell Means, and other leaders of AIM spent time camping at Sapa Dawn, using its sweat lodge, before their occupation of Wounded Knee, South Dakota in 1973.

McCloud expressed her philosophy:

> We have to help the Indian mother . . . present the women's view. . . . We can raise the consciousness of the men and the family. We view ourselves as facilitators, not leaders, to provide a framework for our traditions and history. We provide role models for leadership . . . we are trying to take responsibility . . . Women are coming together . . . the prophesies . . . the root of the problem is genocide but how are we dealing with this? . . . The best thing to do is to organize . . . It is impossible to organize disorganized women . . . Indian women suffer from double doses of racism and sexism . . . it manifests itself in being mentally dependent . . . we know the history. (The Great Janet McCloud, 2006)

Janet McCloud Passes On

As she grew older, McCloud suffered complications from diabetes as well as high blood pressure. For two months, family and friends gathered at Sapa Dawn as her body failed. A report in the *Seattle Post-Intelligencer* said, at the time, that "Pots and pans clanked, babies cried, phones rang, doors opened and closed. Footsteps paraded across floorboards as her children, grandchildren, and great-grandchildren joined a veritable who's-who in Indian country to gather here over the past two months and accompany 'Yet-Si-Blue' on her final journey" (Kamb, 2003). McCloud's granddaughters dressed her in traditional clothing and wrapped her body in a handmade quilt.

After McCloud passed away on November 25, 2003, her family hosted an honoring in her memory on September 19 with the Puyallup Tribe that drew about 200 people. Sally, one of her daughters chuckled as she recalled: "They said we had to be tough and if we were going to be dumb, we had to be real tough. Janet's eight children stood right beside her as she fought for the fishing rights of the Natives. They remember her strength and her generosity" (Janet McCloud, 2003). She was survived by eight children, 25 grandchildren, 28 great-grandchildren, and 10 adopted children. Services were held on November 29 at the Puyallup's Chief Leschi School.

Further Reading

"The Great Janet McCloud." *Indigenous Women's Network,* March 28, 2006. http://indigenouswomen.org/Articles/The-Great-Janet-McCloud.html

"Janet McCloud. 'Yet Si Blue'." *Indian Country Today,* December 5, 2003.http://indigenouswomen.org/Our-Founding-Mothers/Janet-McCloud.html

Kamb, Lewis. "In Memory of Janet McCloud; Janet McCloud, 1934–2003: Indian Activist Put Family First." *Seattle Post-Intelligencer,* November 27, 2003. http://www.worldwidefriends.org/janetmccloud.html

Trahant, Mark. "The Center Of Everything—Native Leader Janet McCloud Finds Peace In Her Place, Her Victories, Her Family. It Has Taken Many Years To Get There." *Seattle Times* (Northwest People), July 4, 1999. http://community.seattletimes.nwsource.com/archive

Means, Russell

(1939–2012)
Oglala Lakota

One of the two best-known founders of the AIM during the 1960s and 1970s (with Dennis Banks), Russell Means parlayed his notoriety into work as an actor, author, and activist well into the 21st century.

Early Life

Means, who is Oglala Lakota, was born on November 10, 1939, in the village of Porcupine on the Pine Ridge Reservation, the eldest of four sons born to Harold and Theodora Feather Means. Both of Means's parents were educated at Indian boarding schools. Theodora Louise Feather Means, Means' mother, and Walter "Hank" Means, his father, moved their family to Vallejo, California in 1942. Walter worked as a welder in the Mare Island Naval shipyard. Means attended public schools in Vallejo and San Leandro, California.

Like many of AIM's other founders, Russell Means came to the role in his early 30s, through a varied past. Means liked stylish clothes, ran with toughs, and sold drugs. His mother Theodora for a time had him sent to a boarding school in Winnebago, Nebraska, adjacent to the Omaha reservation in Macy. (For many years, much later, Means was frequently seen at the Omaha's summer pow-wow.) The home was unstable into Russell's teenaged years, with his father's chronic alcoholism and his own petty thefts, school truancy, and drug (as well as alcohol) abuse. Means graduated from San Leandro High School in 1958.

After high school, Means moved to Los Angeles, but left the city when child-support officials came calling on behalf of a Lakota woman, Twila Smith, with whom

Lakota Sioux Russell Means leaves the District Court Building in St. Paul, Minnesota, August 1974 during the Wounded Knee trials. (AP/Wide World Photo)

he had fathered two children. Back in the San Francisco Bay area, Means joined his father in the first attempt to take over Alcatraz Island in 1964. He met a Hopi (Betty) in San Francisco, and fathered two children (Smith and Warrior, 1996, 133).

By the age of about 25, Means had taken coursework in accounting, worked as a dance instructor, and been arrested for petty theft and drunkenness, assault, and disorderly conduct. The year 1967 found him in Mission, South Dakota, on the Rosebud reservation, working on computer operations in a Community Action Project. By the summer of 1968, Means and his family had moved to Cleveland, where he took a job as director of city's American Indian Center. While there, Means set up employment and social programs, established an AIM chapter, and worked to make its main business strident opposition to the Cleveland Indians use of its American Indian Mascot, Chief Wahoo, a campaign that, by 2011, had lasted more than 40 years.

Means became an Indian activist during the early and middle 1960s. A symbolic take-over of Alcatraz Island took place in 1964 (five years before the better-known occupation during 1969) that included Means and his father. Russell later confided that his father's willingness to stand up for Indian treaty rights "made me proud to be his son, and to be a Lakota" (Means, 1995, 105). Means was in his mid-20s at the time, and had been recently fired from a security job at the San Francisco Cow Palace.

Founding the American Indian Movement

By 1969, when the longest and best-known occupation of "The Rock" took place, Means took part in the 19-month seizure. The year before, he had founded AIM with two Anishinabe (Ojibway) activists from Minnesota, Clyde Bellecourt and Dennis Banks. Means was AIM's first national director, starting in 1970. "Here was a way to be a *real* Indian, and AIM had shown it to me," declared Means. "No longer would I be content to 'work within the system.' . . . Instead, like Clyde and Dennis and the others in AIM, I would get in the white man's face until he gave me and my people our just due. With that decision, my whole existence suddenly came into focus. For the first time, I knew the purpose of my life and the path I must follow to fulfill it. At the age of thirty I became a full-time Indian" (Means, 1995, 153).

The founders of AIM developed a talent for high-profile public events that utilized popular symbols that attracted media attention. One such event took place on Thanksgiving Day of 1970, when Means and Banks led a group from AIIM that, with local Wampanoag activists in Plymouth, Massachusetts, declared a "day of mourning" for Native peoples while the rest of the United States was celebrating the 350th anniversary of the Pilgrims' arrival at Plymouth Rock. Means gave a passionate speech as he stood before a statue of Chief Massasoit, who had befriended the Pilgrims. AIM actions also often involved considerable muscle and bravado. In this case, they assumed control of a replica of the Mayflower and lathered Plymouth Rock in red paint as TV news cameras spun.

The campaigns of AIM soon expanded to include a symbolic "seizure" of the presidential carvings atop Mount Rushmore (as a 4th July "counter-celebration" in 1971) to dramatize the fact that the Black Hills are still legally owned by the Sioux (the U.S. government's land-claims payment has never been accepted). AIM raised the stakes with a caravan that crossed the United States (The Trail of Broken Treaties, 1972), ending in Washington, D.C., a week before the 1972 national elections with seizure and ransacking of the Bureau of Indian Affairs headquarters building.

Means, Banks, and others then organized the occupation of Wounded Knee, on the Pine Ridge reservation, to commemorate the massacre there in 1890, and to accentuate treaty rights by forming what they called in independent Lakota nation. As they faced off with FBI agents and Army troops, AIM seared its image into American consciousness. The occupation lasted 71 days, and made Means and Banks world famous as AIM's leaders.

After the Wounded Knee occupation ended, the federal government besieged Means and Banks with a legal assault that tied them up in court for years. Means alone endured a dozen trials on a potpourri of charges. Thirty-nine of the 40 federal charges against Means resulted in exoneration.

The FBI also infiltrated AIM with informers, through its COINTELPRO (Counter Intelligence Program), creating fear and dissension, splitting the group into factions that eroded its effectiveness as a national force, although local chapters continued to operate in many areas. COINTELPRO was a factor in the killing of Anna Mae Aquash and other AIM activists.

Means' Political and Artistic Activities

In 1974 Means ran for the Oglala Sioux tribal chairmanship against the incumbent, Dick Wilson, and lost narrowly, in a contested election that the U.S. Civil Rights Commission found was marred by widespread vote fraud. This election was part of an ongoing conflict between AIM and the Wilson government on the reservation that included the murder of at least 65 AIM activists in three years (1973–1976), many at the hands of reservation police heavily armed with weapons acquired with federal money. In 1976, Means was acquitted of the murder of Martin Montileaux in Scenic, South Dakota. In 1978, he began serving 12 months of a 48-month sentence for his role in a riot during 1974.

Over the years, after the tumult of the 1970s, Means evolved an eclectic taste in politics. He joined *Hustler* magazine publisher and pornographer Larry Flynt in a campaign for the Republican presidential nomination in 1984. Disgusted and annoyed at Flynt's tactics, however, Means withdrew his support in the midst of the campaign. Means became friends with activist Ward Churchill, who nominated him for president in the 1988 U.S. national political campaign on the Libertarian Party ticket. Means lost the nomination to former Republican congressman Ron Paul, who later returned to the Republican Party and ran for president again in the 2008 campaign. During 2001, Means also started an unsuccessful campaign for the governorship of New Mexico, but dropped out after missing a deadline to declare his candidacy. He ran again in 2002 for leadership of the Oglala Sioux tribe at Pine Ridge, winning a primary but losing the general election to incumbent John Yellow Bird Steele.

During 1981, Means and many supporters seized 880 acres within the Black Hills National Forest and named it Yellow Thunder Camp. The occupation continued for four years, as AIM took a case to court and, with Federal District Judge Robert O'Brien presiding, won a right to define the area as a sacred site. The U.S. Supreme Court reversed the decision on appeal.

In the meantime, Means traveled the world in support of various indigenous groups. He supported the Miskito Indians of Nicaragua against the Sandinistas during the 1980s, a stand that was controversial among AIM members who looked at the Sandinista regime as a political advance following the Somoza dynasty. Means was criticized for naively supporting the Reagan administration's efforts, including a trade embargo and "Contra" insurgent warfare, to topple the Sandinista regime. Means also undertook a speaking tour during 1986 that was funded by Reverend Sun Myung Moon and his Unification Church (the "Moonies").

Means' career as an actor and author has been more successful than his political aspirations. In 1992, Means played Chingachgook in *Last of the Mohicans*. He provided the voice of Chief Powhatan in Disney's *Pocahontas* (1995). He had acted in 10 other films by 2006, as well as in many guest appearances on television dramas. He published an autobiography, *Where White Men Fear to Tread,* in 1995, as well as released two music CDs and several works of art.

Means continued to be notable for his fiery rhetoric. In a speech delivered to several thousand people at the Black Hills International Survival Gathering in 1980, titled "For America to Live Europe Must Die." He criticized all European ideologies, capitalism and Marxism alike: "Capitalists, at least, can be relied upon to develop uranium as fuel only at the rate at which they can show a good profit," he said. "That's their ethic, and maybe that will buy some time. Marxists, on the other hand, can be relied upon to develop uranium fuel as rapidly as possible simply because it's the most 'efficient' production fuel available. That's their ethic, and I fail to see where it's preferable. Like I said, Marxism is right smack in the middle of the European tradition. It's the same old song" (For America, 2007).

"There is another way," Means said. "There is the traditional Lakota way and the ways of the other American Indian peoples. It is the way that knows that humans do not have the right to degrade Mother Earth, that there are forces beyond anything the European mind has conceived, that humans must be in harmony with all relations or the relations will eventually eliminate the disharmony. A lopsided emphasis on humans by humans—the European's arrogance of acting as though they were beyond the nature of all related things—can only result in a total disharmony and a readjustment which cuts arrogant humans down to size, gives them a taste of that reality beyond their grasp or control and restores the harmony" (For America, 2007).

Many years after AIM protested the murder of Raymond Yellow Thunder, Means recalled that young Lakota men were still being brutally killed in border towns.

In 1995, a white man shot an Indian in the back eleven times [in Martin, SD]. The man had to reload to keep shooting from three to four feet and they were considering charging him with manslaughter! Twenty-three years after Raymond Yellow Thunder we're protesting again in the same neighborhood. It was wintertime and snow was falling, and I looked over at my son who was holding his daughter and I said to myself: "Wait a minute. I protested in 1972 to stop this kind of frontier mentality so that my children—let alone my grandchildren—wouldn't have to go through this." I didn't join the American Indian Movement to win any popularity contests; in the seventies, attempts were made on my life and I went to prison so that this wouldn't happen again . . . but it continues in America. Everywhere Indians live there are on-going serial killings called "death by exposure [to cold weather]." (Chapman, 2001, 232)

Means married five times and divorced four times, fathering nine children. He also adopted many others. He was survived by Pearl Daniels, Means' wife since 1999.

Means died October 21, 2012 of cancer of the esophagus that had spread to his mouth, tongue, and lungs. Told his cancer was inoperable in mid0-2011, Means declined chemotherapy, and cut off his braids, a gesture of mourning He died at his ranch near Porcupine on the Pine Ridge reservation (McFadden, 2012).

Further Reading

Caldwell, Christopher. "The Antiwar, Anti-Abortion, Anti-Drug-Enforcement-Administration, Anti-Medicare Candidacy of Dr. Ron Paul." *New York Times*, July 22, 2007.

Chapman, Serle L. *We, the People: Of Earth and Elders, Vol. II*. Missoula, MT: Mountain Press Publishing Co., 2001.

"For America to Live, Europe Must Die." Speech by Russell Means at Black Hills International Survival Gathering, 1980. http://www.dickshovel.com/Banks.html

McFadden, Robert D. "Russell Means, Who Revived Warrior Image of American Indian, Dies at 72." *New York Times*, October 22, 2012. [http://www.nytimes.com/2012/10/23/us/russell-means-american-indian-activist-dies-at-72.html]

Means, Russell. *Where White Men Fear to Tread*. New York: St. Martin's Griffin, 1995.

Smith, Paul Chaat and Robert Allen Warrior. *Like a Hurricane: The Indian Movement from Alcatraz to Wounded Knee*. New York: New Press, 1996.

Mills, Sidney

(Born 1948)
Yakama

Sid Mills was one of the principal organizers of fishing-rights protests in Western Washington, most often from Franks Landing. He also was a key organizer of AIM protests nationwide, including the occupation of Alcatraz Island, the 1972 Trail of Broken Treaties, and the occupation of Wounded Knee in 1973. Back home in Washington, he continued to challenge state fisheries police even after Judge George H. Boldt's landmark fishing-rights ruling in 1974 that opened legal fisheries to many Native peoples in that area for the first time. For most of the 1970s (until the U.S. Supreme Court affirmed Boldt's ruling in 1979) state authorities refused to enforce it.

Mills was present at the occupation of Alcatraz Island. A few days after the occupation of Alcatraz began, on December 10, 1969, the *New York Times* quoted Mills as comparing the ambience of Alcatraz to reservation life: "The reservation is a prison," Mills told *Times* reporter Earl Caldwell. "They are like concentration camps. They have always been like concentration camps to Indians" (Caldwell, 1969, 43). "Alcatraz was a symbol to all Indian country that no matter where they were at or how remote of a reservation they were on, that there was something they can do to better themselves as Indian people," Mills said. "Alcatraz wasn't an island; it was an idea" (Callis, n.d.). After the occupation of Alcatraz, Mills, then 19 years old, having just returned from a tour as a U.S. Army paratrooper in Vietnam, returned to the Northwest with Hank Adams, and took up residence at Frank's Landing (Josephy, 1982, 201).

Mills protested the Vietnam War as well a violation of fishing-rights treaties by deserting from the U.S. Army at Fort Lewis (near Frank's Landing). He served six months in prison for leaving his post. "It was a matter of working for a government that was oppressing you," he said. "It didn't make any sense" (Callis, n.d.).

As he became central to fishing-rights protests, Mills married Suzette Frank, Nisqually Willie Frank Sr.'s, granddaughter. Mills was in jail for fishing that the state deemed illegal when their first child was born. During the many years that Mills and others at Franks Landing defied state authority to fish, by night, they "loaded bright, freshly cleaned Nisqually salmon into a plain white truck bound for Union Square in San Francisco, properly launched into the dark with a Frank's Landing send-off of muffled laughter and sotto voce whispers of "go get 'em!" and "You're doing the Great Spirit's work!" (Wilkinson, 2000, 42). Mills also became a bridge between the Nisquallys and his own people, the Yakamas, who also were asserting fishing rights in Eastern Washington.

Mills also took part in the occupation of Fort Lawton in Seattle during 1970, which brought about the founding of the Daybreak Star Center. This event provoked confrontations with military police. "They beat the shit out of us," Mills said. He recalled being crammed into in a holding cell with approximately a dozen other Native people who also had been arrested, including Leonard Peltier (Callis, n.d.).

Mills (a decorated veteran who had served in Vietnam and been badly wounded) joined with Hank Adams and Russell Means to lead one of two caravans in the Trail of Broken Treaties, setting out from Seattle's El Centro de la Raza in early October, 1972, just days before Chicanos and many allies had seized the vacant building as a community center. The caravan led by Means, Mills, and Adams crossed the Rocky Mountains into the northern plains, as another caravan departed San Francisco, led by Dennis Banks. These two caravans merged at Wounded Knee on the Pine Ridge reservation.

Mills's vehicle on the Trail of Broken Treaties was an old panel truck with a painted map of the caravan's route on one of its sides. The caravan stopped on reservations in Washington, Idaho, and Montana to raise gas and food money, taking on more people as well. On Columbus Day, they paused at the Crow Reservation in Montana, near the Battle of Little Bighorn's site, leaving a plaque that honored Native warriors who fought there.

Mills was among several people from the Northwest, members of the Survival of American Indians Association (SAIA) who were present at the AIM occupation of the Bureau of Indian Affairs headquarters in November, 1972 at the conclusion of the Trail of Broken Treaties. Russell Means (1996, 233), in his autobiography *Where White Men Fear to Tread,* described Mills, Hank Adams, and "a couple of other Survival of American Indian guys," "slicing up leather couches . . . Hank "got out of his chair, pulled out a pocketknife, and said, 'I've always wanted to do this.'".

Mills believed in unconditional Native sovereignty. On one occasion, he said:

> This country is destined for destruction, and there's nothing that's going to turn it back. . . . We're never, ever going to be part of this melting pot, this American society. We don't ever intend it to be. We can't be. We're different people. We're seeking our independence. We do have treaties with the United States. We do have a land base. We do have our own governments. We want to be developed without exploitation by the United States. (Simpson and Yinger, 1965, 165)

On one occasion, during July 1975 (a year after the Boldt ruling) Mills (whose age was listed as 28 in a newspaper account) and Sandy Miller, 48, a Washington State Fisheries patrolman, decided to vent their differences in an old-fashioned fist-fight. Mills was listed as executive director of SAIA at the time. The newspaper account (Fish Agent, 1975, n.p.) said the fisticuffs took place as the state was seizing 18 fishing nets that its agents alleged the Indians had strung illegally across the Nisqually River. Mills confronted Miller and challenged him to put down his nightstick and fight man-to-man. Miller accepted the challenge, and soon found himself on the ground with a bloody nose before several other fisheries agents intervened and handcuffed Mills.

Mills' Federal Bureau of Investigation file was classified by W. Mark Felt (who later was identified as Deep Throat of the Watergate case that brought down President Richard Nixon). The file revealed that Mills had been a busy anti-war activist, having served two years and four months in the Army, including a tour in Vietnam, where he was injured. Mills also was held for a time in the Fort Lewis stockade for having gone absent without leave. The FBI file noted that he had been arrested several times for fishing that the state deemed illegal, and made several presentations about fighting rights to veterans' groups, especially the GI-Civilian Alliance for Peace. He also spent more than a month in the Peoples Republic of China with a multi-ethnic delegation of about 25 people, including James Forman, leader of the International Black Workers Congress, to "build unity among the Revolutionary Third World Forces." An FBI informant noted Mills' opposition to capitalism and said he was "violence prone," and "a good talker" (Smith, 2012, 178–179).

On September 4, 1975, Mills, as director of SAIA, led demonstrations in Seattle by several Native American groups and their supporters during a visit by President Gerald Ford to the Seattle Center Exhibition Hall, demanding that the federal government "restore Native American treaty rights and stop the FBI and Army war in South Dakota," a reference to the dragnet that had closed on the area after two FBI agents and one Native man were shot to death at Pine Ridge earlier the same summer (Seattle Indians, 1975, 5).

Further Reading

Callis, Tom. "Arrested Movement: Looking Back at the American Indian Movement." *Klipsun Magazine*. No date. http://klipsun.wwu.edu/archives/w07b/story.php

"Fish Agent, Indian Fight it Out." *Tri-City Herald,* November 21, 1975, n.p.

Josephy, Alvin M. *Now That the Buffalo's Gone: A Study of Today's American Indians.* New York: Knopf, 1982.

Josephy, Alvin M., Jr. "Wounded Knee and all That: What the Indians Want. *New York Times Sunday Magazine*, March 18, 1973, 18–19, 66–83.

Means, Russell and Marvin J. Wolf. *Where White Men Fear to Tread: The Autobiography of Russell Means.* New York: St. Martin's Press, 1995.

"Seattle Indians to Demonstrate." United Press International in Ellensburg (Washington) Daily Record, September 4, 1975, 5.

Simpson, George Eaton and John Milton Yinger. *Racial and Cultural Minorities: An Analysis of Prejudice and Discrimination.* New York: Harper & Row, 1965.

Smith, Sherry L. *Hippies, Indians, & the Fight for Red Power.* New York: Oxford University Press, 2012.

Wilkinson, Charles F. *Messages from Frank's Landing: A Story of Salmon, Treaties, and the American Way.* Seattle: University of Washington Press, 2000.

Miskito Indians, Nicaragua, and the American Indian Movement

During the 1980s, the AIM split into factions over several issues. One of the most visceral was whether to support the Sandinista revolution in Nicaragua. A substantial number of people in AIM charged that the Sandinistas were forcing as many as 8,500 Miskito native people from their homes in the eastern provinces of the country. This position tended to place the supporters of the Miskitos in alliance with the "Contras" who were supported by the Reagan administration, a relationship that others in AIM found to be very uncomfortable. Some on AIM's "Grand Governing Council" in Minneapolis charged that Russell Means, Ward Churchill, and others were working with the Contras. Such activities cost AIM considerable support from left-wing non-Indians who supported the Sandinistas.

Further Reading

American Indian Movement Council on Security and Intelligence. http://www.aimove ment.org/csi/index.html

American Indian Movement. Grand Governing Council. Official Web Site. http://www. aimovement.org/0. 2007

These links supply scanned images of declassified FBI, CIA, Justice Department and White House documents obtained by AIM under the U.S. Freedom of Information Act.

Colorado American Indian Movement. No date. http://www.coloradoaim.org/

Mount Rushmore Takeovers

The Oglala Lakota (Sioux), as well as the AIM, have long maintained that the Black Hills of South Dakota (*Paha Sapa*) were taken in violation of the Ft. Laramie Treaty of 1868. Within a few years, during the early to middle 1870s, gold was discovered in the Hills, provoking a rush of non-Indian colonization. A large part of the publicity emerged from an expedition led by a young U.S. Army officer, George Armstrong Custer.

U.S. federal courts, beginning in 1980, have ruled in favor of the Oglalas, and have awarded compensation that, with interest, had surpassed $1 billion by 2010. The Oglalas have refused to accept the money, however, and maintain that at least part of the land, which the Oglala maintain is sacred, should be returned.

During the summer of 1970, beginning on August 29, United Native Americans, led by Lehman Brightman, staged a takeover of the National Monument at Mount Rushmore, with its rock carvings of four U.S. presidents, to dramatize the Native claim to the Black Hills. The protest lasted about a week. The same group had been influential in the occupation of Alcatraz Island, which was taking place in San Francisco Bay at the same time.

On July 4, 1971, the AIM, led by Russell Means and Dennis Banks, led another occupation of Mount Rushmore. Some of the protesters scaled the carvings on the mountain's face, and rumors spread that they were preparing to spill red paint over the presidents' visages (after a similar act at Plymouth Rock the previous Thanksgiving), but this never occurred. Photos of AIM members walking atop the heads of the carved presidents appeared in newspapers worldwide, however, publicizing the Lakota claim to the Black Hills.

Dennis Banks, Russell Means, and others led the AIM. The Mount Rushmore Memorial was occupied again for 10 days in 1978. On August 29, 2008, about 30 Native people staged "a small, brief, and peaceful gathering in the amphitheater at Mount Rushmore to commemorate the UNA occupation of the memorial in 1970." Quanah Parker Brightman, son of Lehman Brightman, who had played a leading role in the 1970 occupation, led a four-hour round of speeches, ceremonies, and music. Lehman Brightman was one of the speakers (Janiskee, 2008).

Over the years, the Mount Rushmore National Memorial has made attempts to incorporate Native points of view. On February 21–22, 2008, for example, elders from Native peoples in South Dakota were invited to share "their views and ideas on what information about their history, culture, and language could be presented at Mount Rushmore" (Mount Rushmore, 2008).

Further Reading

Janiskee, Bob. "Lakota Gather Peacefully at Mount Rushmore National Memorial, But Still Insist that the Black Hills Belong to Them." *National Parks Traveler*, September 4, 2008. http://www.nationalparkstraveler.com/2008/09/lakota-gather-peacefully-mount-rushmore-national-memorial-still-insist-black-hills-belong-th

"Mount Rushmore National Memorial Welcomes American Indian Elders." Black Hills News Bureau, March 12, 2008. http://nativenews.wordpress.com/2008/03/12/mount-rushmore-national-memorial-welcomes-american-indian-elders-black-hills-news-bureau/

N

National Indian Youth Council

While many histories of the "Red Power" movement trace its origins to the founding of the AIM in Minneapolis during 1968 and the occupation of Alcatraz Island in San Francisco Bay a year later, Bradley G. Shreve offers a compelling case that youth activism began during the 1950s, most notably in the Southwest. The Kiva Club (University of New Mexico), the Tribe of Many Feathers (Brigham Young University), and the Sequoyah Club of Oklahoma, among others, joined into the Regional Indian Youth Council in 1959, and the National Indian Youth Council in 1961. In contrast to AIM, which emerged from urban areas, National Indian Youth Council (NIYC) was mainly rural and reservation based.

The NIYC was composed mainly of college-educated Native students from reservations. The group was all-Native, and formed to some extent as a more militant alternative to the National Congress of American Indians (NCAI). During the late 1960s, Clyde Bellecourt of the aborning AIM sought out key NIYC members to form an alliance and seek advice. Women were the "backbone" of this group from the beginning. Viola Hatch, who served on NIYC's Board of Directors for almost four decades said that "The men knew it. They were the most militant. They were the ones who forced them [men] to get things done" (Shreve, 2011, 97). In part because many Native cultures are matriarchal or matrilineal, NIYC had a greater degree of gender equity than other student groups of the time, such as Students for a Democratic Society (SDS) and the Student Non-violent Coordinating Committee (SNCC).

The NIYC was not the first Native American student-based activist group. In 1914, young people at the University of Oklahoma formed the *Oklushe Degataga* (Cherokee, meaning "to stand together"), which later became the Sequoyah Club, after the inventor of the Cherokee alphabet. By the 1930s, this club had combined with other Native youth groups in Oklahoma in annual *Ittanaha* (Choctaw: "red man") conference. After World War II, a large number of Native American youth attended colleges and universities under the GI Bill, as the number of youth groups increased (Shreve, 2011, 43–45).

The NIYC, one of the earliest "Red Power" groups, formed after the American Indian Charter Convention held in Chicago during 1961. After two days of debate and discussion of common issues they returned to their home reservations and founded (or augmented) local groups that within two years combined into the NIYC. As the NIYC formed, its leaders (among them Herb Blatchford,

Clyde Warrior, Mary White Eagle Natani, Bernadine Eschief, Ansel Carpenter Jr., Shirley Hill Witt, Mel Thom, and others) attended several workshops and other meetings.

Adopting the tactics of the civil-rights movement, NIYC initially used demonstrations and other confrontational tactics. The NIYC, like the AIM, favored abolition of the Bureau of Indian Affairs (BIA) in favor of a national Native-controlled government with a major degree of sovereignty and local control. Clyde Warrior, most notably, modeled NIYC tactics on those of the SNCC, a major contributor to the black civil-rights movement in the U.S. South.

While the NIYC organized Native American people on a national basis, it maintained that the identity and sovereignty of individual tribes and nations were of paramount value:

> NIYC believes in tribes. We believe that one's basic identity should be with his tribe. We believe in tribalism. . . . We believe that tribalism is what has caused us to endure. Our purpose is not to create one kind of Indian, but make young Indian people moiré effective members of their tribal communities. . . . Survival of Indians as a people means the survival of Indians as a Community. A Community is the interdependence of Indian people, from which flows our religion and our sense of well-being. We affirm the tribal community as a workable and satisfying way to survive in this and other centuries. The wisdom of living this way for thousands of years has taught us this. (National Indian, 1973, 3)

While it stressed tribal identity, NIYC also saw its role as forging a "brotherhood among tribes . . . [and] a brotherhood of all Indians" (National Indian, 1973, 3).

Melvin Thom, a Paiute from Walker River, Nevada, was cofounder and early spokesman with Clyde Warrior, told federal officials in Washington, D.C., in 1967:

> We are not allowed to make those basic human choices and decisions about our personal life and about the destiny of our communities that are the mark of free, mature people. We sit of our front porches or in our yards and the world and our lives in it pass us by without our lives or aspirations having any effect. (Johnson, 1996, 2008, 33)

The NIYC was the first to use the phrase "Red Power," adapted from "black power," as members of the NIYC made fishing rights in Washington State their first major policy thrust in 1964. Fishing actions were called "fish-ins," after civil-rights movement "sit-ins." Activism was aimed at sovereignty, treaty rights, cultural preservation, and self-determination, all of which shaped indigenous development long afterward. One of NIYC's major leaders was Clyde Warrior, a full-blood Ponca who had been raised traditionally by his maternal grandparents. Warrior was a "towering intellect," a fiery orator, and a "mesmerizing" fancy dancer who also consumed "legendary amounts of tequila [and] whiskey before passing out" (pp. 58, 60). He died of liver failure at age 28 in 1968.

Bradley Shreve, chairman of the Division of Social and Behavioral Sciences at Diné College in Tsaile, Arizona, has a talent for biographical detail and the telling quote, as with Warrior, on his full-blood heritage: "The sewage of Europe does not flow through my veins" (Shreve, 2011, 60). Shreve also has a keen eye for factional differences in strategy and tactics that played havoc with the NIYC.

The acuteness of the racism described by Shreve can get quite raw. At one point around 1963, Shirley Hill Witt was driving a car with several NIYC colleagues in Michigan when their car was rammed by another on a highway. The injured Indians were picked up by an ambulance that had to go into Wisconsin because no hospitals along the route in Michigan would admit American Indians (Shreve, 2011, 111–12).

Many notable leaders emerged from the NIYC, in addition to Warrior: Hank Adams, Witt, Herbert Blatchford, Mel Thom, and Gerald Wilkinson, who led the organization from 1969 until his sudden death during 1989. In the 1980s, it took a leading role against coal gasification on the Navajo reservation, and in opposing uranium mining and milling there. Uranium mining was banned after large numbers of miners died of lung cancer. The NIYC remained active into present times, especially in legal issues, and furthering indigenous interests at the United Nations.

Further Reading

Johnson, Troy. *The Occupation of Alcatraz Island: Red Power and Self Determination.* Urbana: University of Illinois Press, 1996. 2008 ed. University of Nebraska Press.

"National Indian Youth Council Policy Statement," *Americans Before Columbus* 6, no. 3 (1973): 3.

Shreve, Bradley G. *Red Power Rising: The National Indian Youth Council and the Origins of Native Activism.* Norman: University of Oklahoma Press, 2011.

Native North American Traveling College

In 1966, having heard that that a Canadian Indian, 12-year-old Charlie Wenjack, had frozen to death on train tracks as he tried to walk home from a boarding school, Akwesasne Mohawk traditional chief Ernie Benedict decided to create a new way to deliver Native American education. Benedict believed that Native children should not be removed from their homes for education, even in remote locations. Instead, native-controlled education should travel to them with curricula that community people wanted.

The result was the Native North American Traveling College, which brought culturally relevant schooling to many Canadian reserves via caravan. Benedict's traveling college was part of a wave of new approaches to dealing with old problems among the Akwesasne Mohawks. Ray Fadden, for example, created new venues of education for Native young people when he became dissatisfied with the offerings of the Boy Scouts. His family also built its own museum as an alternative to institutional offerings. Benedict also initiated many other self-determination efforts, such as starting the St. Regis Indian Health Service on the American portion of Akwesasne.

Benedict started the Traveling College (which is now called the Native North American Traveling College and Ronathahonni Cultural Center) in 1968 to promote Native cultural revitalization across Canada and the United States. The college provided a mobile, accessible source of knowledge about Native American history and culture through curricula, visual aids, books, and artifacts, at a time when Native American studies programs were generally in their infancy. The Traveling College was rich in spirit but not in money, as Benedict carried book materials, tapes, magazines, and musical instruments in the back of a Volkswagen van, driving from one reserve (or reservation) to another. Benedict's advocacy of Native-controlled education encouraged numerous Indian survival schools at Kahnawake and Akwesasne and elsewhere. Benedict's efforts forged a network of educators, and young leaders across Canada.

When conflict over gambling exploded into violence at Akwesasne during the late 1980s and early 1990s, the Traveling College became embroiled. Its director, Barbara Barnes, was an ardent opponent of gambling, calling it "a glitter-gulch strip [with] no community controls, no government approval, no tribal regulations, and no profits to the people" (Johansen, 1993, 26). On April 23, 1990, the college's building in an old house was torched by arsonists, one of three buildings burned on the same day. The fire at the Traveling College destroyed two decades of archived print and video archives. Within a few days, phone communications were restored at the house and it resumed its role as a crisis communication center. Several other reservation houses were burned out during the same time.

Today, the Traveling College offers a travel troupe of Native singers, dancers, and speakers who respond to invitations to visit other First Nation Reserves, non-Native organizations, workshops and conferences, prisons and educational institutions. The Center publishes cultural material and posters opposing use of alcohol and illegal drugs, and also educates young Native people as cultural providers.

Further Reading

Johansen, Bruce E. *Life and Death in Mohawk Country*. Golden, CO: North American Press/Fulcrum, 1993.

Nixon, Richard M. (U. S. President)

(1913–1994)

While President Richard Nixon was right-wing on many issues, he was provoked by his Quaker faith as well as the temper of the times to provide innovative policy frameworks in Native American affairs. He was a primary advocate of "self-determination" policies that sought to encourage Native independence of the federal bureaucracy.

Nixon was, however, very much opposed to the tactics of the AIM, and was not a supporter of Native American political sovereignty. After AIM occupied (and ultimately trashed) the BIA building in Washington, D.C., during the final days of the 1972 campaign, Nixon's Justice Department indicted AIM leaders for almost 200 criminal offenses. Despite the confrontation, Nixon won the election over South Dakota Senator George McGovern, with the electoral votes of 49 states (all except Massachusetts).

Nixon had some good Native American role models. His football coach at Whittier College, for example, was a mixed-blood American Indian. Many Native people, not just AIM-style militants, did not look favorably on Nixon at the time of his first election in 1968, however. They often figured that his Republican Party would favor corporate exploitation of natural resources on reservations. Despite Nixon's shining rhetoric on social issues, exploitation of resources largely continued unchecked, as many Native people had feared. Their fears were reinforced when Walter J. Hickel, widely known as an advocate of oil company interests in Alaska, was appointed as secretary of the interior by Nixon.

Nixon Appoints Louis Bruce as Indian Commissioner

In September 1969, Nixon appointed Louis R. Bruce, a Mohawk and Sioux dairy farmer (and a registered Republican), as commissioner of Indian Affairs. Bruce's tenure at the BIA was introduced by Nixon as a sweeping change, making "progress through participation" the new "Indian policy: "[The] voice of the Indian will be heard on all questions affecting the life of the Indian. It is not this administration's policy to tell the Indian what to do, but rather to help the Indian to do what needs to be done" (Forbes, 1984, 34).

On July 8, 1970, Nixon gave a major speech on Indian policy reform that proposed to Congress a reversal of forced termination, restoration of Blue Lake to the Taos Pueblo, local control of schools by Native people, additional funding for economic development, assistance for urban Indians, as well as direct funding of Indian tribes to allow them more control over their own budgets. The proposals arrived in Congress late in the session, however, and they all were never reported out of committee.

Bruce moved to reorganize the BIA to allow more Native control of programs. He became well-known for his efforts to reconcile the positions of AIM and the Nixon administration while the militants occupied the BIA headquarters building during November 1972. This attempt at negotiation was seen as coddling of the militants by Bruce's superiors in the Interior Department. Interior Secretary Rogers Morton said, "Right now he [Bruce] couldn't even sell a hot dog in that building." Interior Department Assistant Secretary for Public Land Management Harrison Loesch said

Bruce had "blown it. He is over there in bed with them [AIM], and we don't like it from Air Force One [e.g., Nixon] on down" (Forbes, 1984, 96). Bruce was then forced to resign; he was replaced by John O. Crow, who called Bruce an "incompetent" who had "given aid to the unruly mob" (LaCourse, 1972, 5). Crow was an advocate of termination, a position that made him highly unpopular in Indian Country.

The federal government was spending more money than ever before on the "Indian problem," but most of it was being used to pad the bureaucracy and subsidize corporations. By 1972, the government was spending $2,000 a year for each reservation Indian, about 8,000 2012 dollars), but the average Indian family's total income from all sources was less than that, and not moving. Unemployment remained high (Josephy, 1973, 74). Nixon's presidency also was coincident with increasing pressure on reservation natural resources that, according to Alvin M. Josephy, had reached the dimension of a massive assault by all sorts of conglomerates: "Tribe after tribe has been split into factions as the government has encouraged and aided coal companies to strip-mine Indian land . . . [and] power companies to build monster polluting generating plants . . . and real estate and industrial-development syndicates to erect large projects among the Indian settlements for the use of non-Indians" (Josephy, 1973, 67).

Corporate Control of Natural Resources

Even during Bruce's term, very little progress was made in removing corporate control over natural resources on reservations that resulted in below-market returns and overexploitation of timber, mining, grazing land, oil, and other resources. The companies were still using the Interior Department's "trust" relationship with Indian tribes to make them "the last frontier of industrial exploitation" (Forbes, 1984, 39). Leon Cook, an Ojibwa who had been placed in charge of economic development by Bruce resigned in frustration, telling him that "You talk advocacy, but neither you nor the secretary [Rogers Morton] nor the administration has proven to me nor to Indian country that the Bureau or the federal government are in fact advocating the protection of these resources. . . . You . . . further condon [sic] the continued theft of Indian land, water, and natural resources" (NCIO News, 1971, 2).

When he used the phrase "self-determination," however, Nixon meant something entirely different from the wide-ranging political sovereignty that the AIM advocated. Nixon was, in fact, very much opposed to the kind of left-wing liberation implicit in much of the anti-Vietnam war radicalism that became so volatile while he was in office. Instead, Nixon used the concept of self-determination to support capitalist development on Indian reservations, a policy that many in AIM regarded as a new form of colonialism.

Roxanne Dunbar Ortiz, in her introduction to Jack Forbes' *Native Americans and Nixon*, quoted Forbes (1984, 9) describing Nixon's strategy as "designed to stabilize and pacify Indian protests; that is, destroy militancy in order to pave the way for exploitation of Indian resources . . . [and] to build an 'acceptable' representative group of Indians with which to negotiate, namely the National Tribal Chairman's Association . . ." Nixon's exemplary Indians were set up with federal money to "offer a chance to prove that private enterprise and minority capitalism may yet prove to be the best solution to problems of poverty" (Strickland and Gregory, 1970, 77–78). During Nixon's time as U.S. president, the number of factories on Indian reservations more than doubled, from 110 to 259. However, most of the employment went to non-Indians, as the average unemployment rate among Native Americans in the United States remained at about 40 percent between 1970 and 1974. About $100 million was spent by the federal government to enhance businesses on Indian reservations during this time (Forbes, 1984, 17). The policy, wrote Ortiz, seemed designed "to quiet the noise, not solve the problem" (Forbes, 1984, 18).

Nixon himself regarded AIM's membership as renegades; along with black, Chicano, and white activists, the Justice Department and FBI targeted AIM for infiltration and destruction under its COINTELPRO (Counter-intelligence Program) during Nixon's second term. Nixon's Justice Department (its major personnel still in place after he resigned in disgrace to avoid impeachment) hounded AIM with hundreds of indictments after the occupation of Wounded Knee in 1973. Only a few of the indictments produced convictions.

Nixon was credited by many Native people with having ended termination policies that had eradicated some reservation land bases and plunged many Indians further into poverty. Tim Giago, who originated the newspaper *Indian Country Today,* said that history should remember Nixon "for his special efforts on behalf of the Indian nations of America." Mario Gonzalez, an attorney at the time for the Oglala Sioux, said he was one of the best presidents in bringing about positive changes for Native Americans (Johnson, 1996, 219).

Further Reading

Forbes, Jack D. *Native Americans and Nixon: Presidential Politics and Minority Self-determination.* Los Angeles, CA: American Indian Culture Center, 1984.

Josephy, Alvin M, Jr. "Wounded Knee and all That: What the Indians Want." *New York Times Sunday Magazine,* March 18, 1973, 18–19, 66–83.

LaCourse, Richard. [No headline] *Wassaja* 1, no. 1(January, 1973, 16).

NICO News, 1, no. 2 (January, 1971): 2.

Strickland, Rennard and Jack Gregory. "Nixon and the Indian: Is Dick Another Buffalo Bill?" *Commonweal* 92 (September 4, 1979): 433.

O

Oakes, Richard

(1942–1972)
Mohawk

Richard Oakes was a major leader in the American Indian occupation of Alcatraz Island. A charismatic speaker, he also encountered considerable envy. His step-daughter died during the occupation, and he was shot to death shortly afterward.

Born May 22, 1942, Oakes had been an ironworker and a bartender, as well as a college student, before he became a well-known Native American militant at Alcatraz in 1969. He became the single most influential person in keeping the occupation from falling apart, at one point evicting drunks from the island by force. "The press called him the mayor of Alcatraz, but this city was like no other," wrote Smith and Warrior (1996, 35).

Edward Castillo, a fellow California Native activist, characterized Oakes as "a handsome adult, solidly built. Although he obviously was not a polished public speaker, he delivered his message with simplicity and power (Johnson et al., 1997, 121). Described as "handsome, charismatic, a talented orator and a natural leader" (Johnson et al., 1997, 28), Oakes was a resident of Akwesasne (the St. Regis Mohawk reservation) in far Upstate New York who had worked in high steel in New York City and traveled to many reservations. LaNada Boyer, a fellow leader with Oakes at Alcatraz, described him as "smart and aggressive—a handsome Mohawk who always knew what to say" (Johnson et al., 1997, 92). Oakes was mercurial. At one point he plunged into the cold bay off Alcatraz.

In California, which became Oakes' long-time home as an adult, he married Anne Marufo, a Kashia Pomo, who had five children from a previous marriage. He worked at an Indian bar in Oakland; he then began studies at San Francisco State University, where he joined several other Native students in discussing seizure of Alcatraz as a symbolic protest. He left the island, having played a major role as a spokesman for many months, in a nasty power struggle among leaders there during which his daughter was killed.

A large number of people were injured in the concrete and steel maze of the abandoned prison. The Coast Guard, having once been scorned as "the man," ended up providing ambulance service from the island to the mainland. On January 3, 1970, Yvonne Sherd, a 13-year-old stepdaughter of Richard and Anne (a Pomo from California), fell three stories down a stairwell in an empty building, never regained consciousness, and died five days later in an Oakland Public Health Service hospital of massive head injuries (Johnson et al., 1997, 93). Shortly thereafter, Oakes left the island.

Oakes and his wife Anne suspected that Yvonne had been pushed, because of resentment on the part of other occupants about his prominent role in the media, and with government negotiators. They asked the FBI and the San Francisco Coroner's Office to investigate. Neither agency was able to find clear evidence of foul play. One person on the island, Thomas Scott alleged in a video interview that Yvonne had been pushed (Johnson, 1996, 152–53).

The character of the occupation was changing. Most of the college student who had formed the early core of support had gone back to school after winter break, and a new, dissent-prone core of people was emerging, prone to "booze, boredom, and bickering" (Johnson, 1996, 154). The situation reminded some people of William Golding's novel *Lord of the Flies*, about a group of people marooned on an island who turn upon each other.

In the meantime, celebrity money continued to roll in. Black comedian Dick Gregory (who also had gone to jail in defense of fishing rights of Western Washington tribes) gave a large, but unspecified, amount. Buffy St. Marie gave $2,250, and a benefit concert was held at San Francisco's Fillmore (Johnson, 1996, 159). Rumors spread that Oakes were getting rich by siphoning donations. Lack of an organized accounting system offered no real evidence of where the money was going.

Six months after Yvonne had died, Oakes found himself in a San Francisco Indian bar, involved in an argument, during which several other Native men administered a beating, hitting him over the head several times with a pool cue. Injuries from this fight left Oakes partially paralyzed with a plastic plate in his skull (Smith and Warrior, 1996, 140).

On September 21, 1972, Oakes became embroiled in an argument with a caretaker at a YMCA camp in Mendocino County, California, north of San Francisco, over Indian youths' use of some horses without permission. The argument turned violent, the caretaker drew a gun and shot Oakes to death. He then told police that Oakes had drawn a knife on him. Police found no knife, or any other weapon on Oakes' body. The caretaker nonetheless maintained that he was acting in self-defense. He was set free on $5,000 bond. In 1973, Oakes' killer was found not guilty of voluntary manslaughter. At the trial of Oakes' killer, the principal witness for the defense said that the defendant had bragged about the slaying, saying: "It's open season on coons and Indians" (Wilkins, 2011, 100).

Further Reading

Johnson, Troy. *The Occupation of Alcatraz Island: Red Power and Self Determination.* Urbana: University of Illinois Press, 1996. 2008 ed. University of Nebraska Press.

Johnson, Troy, Joane Nagel, and Duane Champagne, eds. *American Indian Activism: Alcatraz to the Longest Walk.* Urbana: University of Illinois Press, 1997.

Smith, Paul Chaat and Robert Allen Warrior. *Like a Hurricane: The Indian Movement from Alcatraz to Wounded Knee*. New York: The New Press, 1996.

Wilkins, David E., ed. *The Hank Adams Reader: An Exemplary Native American Activist and the Unleashing of Indigenous Sovereignty*. Golden, CO: Fulcrum, 2011.

Oglala Sioux Civil Rights Organization (OSCRO)

The Oglala Sioux Civil Rights Organization (OSCRO) was nominally independent but had strong informal links to the AIM, through Russell Means. Pedro Bissonette, "a small, scrappy boxer who became the main spokesman for the traditionals" was a mainspring, along with his aunt Gladys Bissonette (Matthiessen, 1991, 66). Both were influential in seeking aid from AIM against the regime of Dick Wilson, as was Ellen Moves Camp.

The OSCRO organized shortly before the Wounded Knee siege to protest low land rentals by the Bureau of Indian Affairs at Pine Ridge. Most of the rentals were to non-Indians. The organization also protested Richard Wilson's manipulation of attempts by Oglala Sioux to impeach him. Wilson had acted to terminate his own impeachment hearing. The group also protested the presence of U.S. Marshals at Pine Ridge, asserting that the federal government had no policing jurisdiction there unless serious felonies had been committed (Matthiessen, 1991, 363–64).

In late February, 1973, OSCRO organized a march by traditional people at the BIA building in Pine Ridge Village regarding these issues. They found themselves "denied access to their own building by the well-armed marshals with their sandbag fortifications and machine guns," and realized that the political deck was stacked in favor of Wilson (Matthiessen, 1991, 64).

On February 27, about 600 traditionalists assembled at Calico Hall, a log house at the west side of Pine Ridge Village that the traditionalists used as a community meeting place. The traditional chiefs, led by Frank Fools Crow, asked the AIM for help (Matthiessen, 1991, 64). Dennis Banks and Russell Means attended the meeting. One by one, women stood up and expressed their disappointment at the fact that Pine Ridge, their home, was becoming an armed camp. They asked that "the fighting spirit return" (Matthiessen, 1991, 65).

Pedro Bissonette was the first to suggest a caravan to Wounded Knee as a "symbolic confrontation," with an en masse presence at the massacre site for a press conference to demand a congressional investigation into present-day violations of the 1868 Fort Laramie Treaty, "with special emphasis on the Wilson regime" (Churchill and Vander Wall, 1988, 141). They had planned a short-term event, not the prolonged armed confrontation with Wilson's regime and the U.S. government that would involve the first call-out of the U.S. Army on domestic soil since the Civil War. The planned press conference turned into a siege when Richard Wilson's tribal police surrounded the hamlet and sealed the dissidents inside.

As the Wounded Knee siege was ending, on April 27, 1973, Bissonette was arrested by the FBI and charged with "interfering with a federal officer in performance of his duties" (Churchill and Vander Wall, 1988, 200). The FBI then used the arrest as a pretext to pressure Bissonette to testify against AIM members who had been prominent at Wounded Knee, telling him that otherwise he would face up to 90 years in prison. He flatly refused.

On October 17, 1973, Bissonette was confronted on a street in Whiteclay, Nebraska, south of Pine Ridge, by a man that OSCRO later said was GOON Cliff Richards. They engaged in a fistfight, during which Richards was knocked to the sidewalk. Bissonette walked away. Whiteclay was off the reservation and out of the BIA police's and GOONs' jurisdiction, but a dragnet soon developed. Twenty police cars and several aircraft swept the area in search of him. An OSCRO statement said that "They hunted Pedro down like an animal and murdered him in cold blood" (Churchill and Vander Wall, 1988, 201). He died the same day.

Pine Ridge BIA Superintendent Kendall Cunningham told a different story to the Associated Press, that Bissonette had fired a gun at two Pine Ridge BIA police who were attempting to arrest him on a warrant, after which he was stopped at a roadblock and again attempted to shoot at an officer. He was then, Cunningham told the AP reporter, "shot fatally at close range" (Churchill and Vander Wall, 1988, 201). The BIA police never produced the weapon that they said Bissonette had used. Wounded Knee Legal Defense/Offense Committee attorney Mark Lane viewed the body shortly after Bissonette was shot and determined that what Cunningham had defined as "shot fatally at close range" consisted of at least seven bullet holes, evidence of a beating, and tear gas burns. The FBI closed the case as "open and shut justifiable homicide" (Churchill and Vander Wall, 1988, 203).

Further Reading

Churchill, Ward and Jim Vander Wall. *Agents of Repression: The FBI's Secret Wars Against the Black Panther Party and the American Indian Movement.* Boston: South End Press, 1988.

Matthiessen, Peter. *In the Spirit of Crazy Horse.* New York: Viking, 1991.

Ohio and North Kentucky American Indian Movement

Ohio and North Kentucky AIM, affiliated with the AIM Grand Governing Council in Minneapolis, is little more than a Web link to the GCC. Most inquiries are referred there: "AIM Support Stickers & AIM National Patches are only to be purchased from Bill Boswell and Tom Hedger in the 'Cincinnati and Northern Kentucky area'!! 'NO' one else is approved to sell this merchandise, in this area, by The AIM Grand Governing Council. You can also purchase merchandise at The AIM Store! This will insure the proceeds go to The American Indian Movement.

Any questions or comments, please contact Vernon Bellecourt or call American Indian Movement National Support Group Director—Bill Boswell, at 513-797-8944"
(The OFFICIAL, n.d.).

Further Reading

"The OFFICIAL Homepage" of AIM Support Group of Ohio & N. Kentucky. No date.
http://aimsupport.org/index2.html

P

Peltier, Leonard

(Born 1944)
Anishinabe/Ojibway. AIM Activist

An activist in the AIM during the 1973 confrontation at Wounded Knee, Leonard Peltier was caught in a shootout with FBI agents and state police at the Jumping Bull Ranch on the Pine Ridge Indian Reservation during June 26, 1975. Peltier later was convicted of killing two FBI agents, Ronald Williams and Jack Coler, during that confrontation. Peltier's initial trial, which was held in Fargo, ND Federal District Court in 1977, has since become the focus of an international protest movement aimed at obtaining a retrial. Peltier's defense characterized his conviction as a textbook example of a manufactured verdict, a major reason that Amnesty International declared Peltier a political prisoner. On October 15, 1985, the government admitted in open court that it did not have proof of who the two agents were.

Peltier is known in his native Lakota language as *Gwanth-eelass*—"He Leads the People." To the U.S. prison system, he is known as prisoner #89637–132.

Peltier's Early Life

Peltier was born on September 12, 1944, in Grand Forks, North Dakota. In 1959, he moved with his mother to Portland, Oregon, under the aegis of the U.S. government's relocation program. Peltier also worked in California as a seasonal farm worker, then left the migrant stream his way to Seattle and became a part-owner of an auto body shop. Like many migrant workers, Peltier settled out of migrant work and sought help at Seattle's El Centro de la Raza.

"We went to his shop because we heard that he helped elders get their cars fixed because in the movement we had very few cars that would work," said Ramona Bennett, cofounder of the Survival of American Indians Association, in 1964. "He was just this good Indian man who had a good reputation. Every time an elder needed help he would rescue them" (Arrested Movement, n.d.). Bennett was a character witness during Peltier's trial. "I told them he was a gentle guy. It's not in his happy nature to be killing FBI agents. He would have to be more than provoked, he would have to be under attack. It just isn't Leonard to be looking around for somebody to hurt. It's just not the kind of person he is (Callis, n.d.). By 1965, the second floor of

Former American Indian Movement activist Leonard Peltier stands in his cell doorway at Leavenworth Penitentiary in Kansas, 1992. (Taro Yamasaki/Time Life Pictures/Getty Images)

Peltier's body shop had become an unofficial half-way house for Indian ex-convicts and alcoholics who depended on his support.

Peltier spent time at Alcatraz Island during the occupation. He also took part in the occupation of Fort Lawton in Seattle's Magnolia neighborhood during 1970 on land that had been declared surplus by the U.S. Army. The United Indians of All Tribes, led by Bernie Whitebear, acquired land for the Daybreak Star Center, which still operates on a bluff over Puget Sound. Peltier also joined the fishing-rights struggle on the Nisqually and Puyallup Rivers. By the early 1970s, Peltier was actively involved with AIM at Pine Ridge, following a role in the occupation of Wounded Knee.

Shootout at the Jumping Bulls' Ranch

On June 26, 1975, two unmarked cars chased a red truck onto the Jumping Bull Ranch which was housing several families being defended by AIM. The agents opened fire on the ranch and its residents, who fired back in self-defense. Within minutes, more than 150 FBI SWAT team members, Bureau of Indian Affairs police, and Pine Ridge police had surrounded the ranch as a fierce, largely one-sided firefight erupted. Two FBI agents, Williams and Coler, were fatally wounded.

A Native American man, Joe Stuntz, aged 23, also died of a shot in the head by an unidentified government agent's sniper bullet that day. Like the murders of several dozen other Native peoples on the reservation during those tumultuous years, the FBI did not investigate Stuntz's death.

The same FBI that complained lack of manpower kept it from investigating the wave of political murders at Pine Ridge between 1973 and 1976 had enough agents to assign Coler and Williams to pursue a pair of purloined cowboy boots to the Jumping Bull Ranch on June 26, 1975—as well as hundreds of agents who mounted a nation-wide dragnet for the killers of Coler and Williams in the firefight there, for which Leonard Peltier later was convicted with questionable evidence.

In *The Unquiet Grave*, author Steve Hendricks describes the Jumping Bull firefight with uncommon acuity, in part based on his mining of FBI records under the Freedom of Information Act. He is also sensitive to the records' limitations. At Jumping Bull's, for example, the FBI reports imagined bunkers where there were root cellars and machine guns in hands that held old hunting rifles. The FBI itself was not short of firepower. (When the author of this book visited the abandoned Jumping Bull house a year later, while researching his first book, *Wasi'chu: The Continuing Indian Wars* (1979) the prairie wind whistled through hundred of bullet holes in the walls, which looked like large slabs of dirty Swiss cheese.)

Peltier's Pursuit and Prosecution

Peltier escaped the firefight, and fled to Seattle, where he hid on Bainbridge Island for six weeks before leaving for Canada (Callis, n.d.). He then crossed the U.S.-Canadian border to a Cree community in Alberta. He was arrested on February 6, 1976, and then extradited to the United States. The FBI used a false affidavit, which, upon discovery by the Canadian government some time later, provoked a diplomatic incident. Peltier was extradited anyway, after a legal challenge in Vancouver, BC.

Peltier subsequently was put on trial before an all-white jury in Fargo, North Dakota, Federal District Court in Judge Paul Benson's federal district court. Even before Peltier's trial started, the prosecution's case had begun to fall apart. Discovery proceedings produced an affidavit, signed by government witness Myrtle Poor Bear dated February 19, 1976 (before two others known to the defense, dated February 23 and March 31), which said that the woman had not been on the scene of the June 25, 1975, gun battle in which the two FBI agents had been shot to death. This information, contained in an affidavit that had not been sent to Canada by the U.S. government during Peltier's extradition hearing, contradicted the other two statements attributed to Poor Bear.

The FBI created a climate of fear during the proceedings to convince jurors that Peltier was a terrorist. The FBI contributed to the conviction of Peltier by faking evidence. Benson meanwhile denied the defense even the pretense of fair treatment. Peltier was sentenced to two life terms in prison. The conviction stood. The conviction stood even after a United States Court of Appeals, in November, 2003, condemned the fact that the government withheld evidence and intimidated witnesses.

More importantly, Poor Bear herself recanted. On April 13, out of earshot of the jury, Poor Bear told the court (having been called by the defense) that she had never seen Peltier before meeting him at the trial. Furthermore, Poor Bear said that she had not been allowed to read the three affidavits implicating Peltier in the murders that bore her name, and that FBI agents David Price and Bill Wood had threatened physical harm to herself and her children if she did not sign them. Judge Benson refused to let the jury hear Poor Bear's testimony, ruling it "irrelevant" to the case. The next day, Benson changed his mind and ruled the testimony relevant, but still would not let the jury hear it. He ruled this time that Poor Bear's testimony was prejudicial to the government's case and, if believed, could confuse the jury. According to Peltier, Poor Bear paid for her false witness with a quarter century of ostracism and "mental torture . . . from her own people" (Chapman, 2001, 243).

Prosecution testimony, which occupied the first five weeks of the trial, ranged far from events on the day of the shootings. The prosecution was allowed to bring up extraneous charges against Peltier on which he had not been tried and testimony which ran counter to the federal rules of evidence. The defense's planned two weeks of testimony was reduced to two-and-a-half days by Judge Benson, who limited defense testimony to events directly connected with the shootings themselves. Virtually every time the defense challenged the government, and before every attempt by the defense to present its case, Benson had the jury removed from the courtroom. The jury heard only parts of the defense's case.

Benson restricted rules of evidence strictly to the events of June 26, 1975. Defense attorneys were, for example, unable to mention in court the deaths of many AIM members at Pine Ridge, or discuss the not guilty verdict in the trial of Bob Robideau and Dino Butler in Cedar Rapids, Iowa federal court for the deaths of the same two agents. Peltier was convicted of killing the two FBI agents and, on June 1, 1977, Benson sentenced him to two life terms in prison.

The Impossible Sighting

The only evidence that directly linked Peltier to the killings of Coler and Williams (other than that fabricated in Poor Bear's name) came from Frederick Coward, an FBI agent, who said he had recognized Peltier from half a mile away through a seven-power rifle sight. The defense team replicated the sighting and found that the feat was impossible through such a sight at such a distance, even for a person with excellent vision. In court, defense attorneys offered to duplicate their experience for the jury, so that its members could judge for themselves the veracity of the FBI agent's statement. Judge Benson refused the request. "Finally," said Bruce Ellison, a member of the defense team "we brought in someone from a gun shop, who said that an idiot could tell you that it is impossible to recognize someone, even someone you know, from a half-mile away through a seven-power sight" (Johansen and Maestas, 1979, 114).

Three Native juveniles also testified that they had seen Peltier at the scene. Each of them also testified, under cross-examination, that their testimony had been coerced by the FBI. One of them, Mike Anderson, testified that he had been threatened with beating. Another, Wish Draper, said that he had been tied and handcuffed to a chair for three hours to elicit his statement. The third, Norman Brown, swore that he was told that if he did not cooperate he "would never walk the Earth again" (Johansen and Maestas, 1979, 115).

The prosecution, its eyewitness testimony in dispute, linked Peltier to the use of an AR-15, a semiautomatic rifle, which was not introduced as evidence because it had been blown apart during a Kansas freeway explosion on September 10, 1975. FBI agent Evan Hodge testified at the Fargo trial that the AR-15 was the weapon used to kill Agents Williams and Coler. However, the weapon tested by Agent Hodge did not match the ballistic evidence. That weapon, alleged by the government as having been used by Peltier did not kill the agents. Nonetheless, the prosecution used this weapon in court as a prop in its argument to convince the jury that Peltier shot Williams and Coler at point blank-range.

Demands for a New Trial

Following his conviction, Peltier became the object of a growing popular movement demanding a new trial. Even though the Eighth Circuit Court of Appeals in 1978 found more than 30 errors in the trial record that could have led to reversal, it permitted the verdict to stand. Further appeals over the years fared no better. Hearings on Peltier's appeal also were declined by the U.S. Supreme Court in 1978 and 1986. In the meantime, Peltier's support spread to the Soviet Union and Europe. In the Soviet Union, by 1986, an estimated 17 million people had signed petitions in his support.

In the meantime, prosecutor Lynn Crooks in 1987 said he had no idea who really had killed Coler and Williams. Any time a U.S. president came close to considering an amnesty for Peltier, the FBI and right-wing leaders closed ranks on him in vehement opposition. Parole was denied Peltier several times. President Clinton considered the case, but the political cost was too high.

Peter Matthiessen's *In the Spirit of Crazy Horse* was readied for publication in the early 1980s, making a case for Peltier's innocence. The publisher, Viking, withdrew the book after former South Dakota Governor William Janklow threatened to sue for libel over passages in the book that linked him to the rape of a young Native American woman, Jancita Eagle Deer. Bootlegged copies of the book began to circulate, and it was published in the late 1980s after Janklow's case was dismissed by the South Dakota Supreme Court. *In the Spirit of Crazy Horse* presents, in an epilogue appended after the book had been suppressed for eight years, a case that Peltier was not the murderer of the two FBI agents. In an interview, a Native man known only as "X" confesses to the murders. In the meantime, the FBI had withheld from the public 6,000 pages of documents on the case, for reasons the agency associated with national security.

During the 1980s and 1990s, as Peltier's appeals for a new trial were denied several times by U.S. federal courts, he was serving two life terms at Marion Federal Penitentiary, Illinois, and at Leavenworth Federal Penitentiary in Kansas, developing his talents as an artist, creating posters, paintings, and designs for a line of greeting cards that were sold nationwide. Peltier's case also became the focus of the feature film *Thunderheart* and a documentary, *Incident at Oglala*.

Peltier's case came to the attention of Amnesty International and the government of Canada, from which Peltier was extradited to face trial on the basis of the Poor Bear affidavits. Peltier's appeals were directed by several well-known legal personalities, including former U.S. Attorney General Ramsey Clark and attorney William Kunstler. His third appeal for a new trial was turned down by the Eighth Circuit Court of Appeals (St. Paul, Minnesota) in 1993, for the third time, exhausting his remedies within the U.S. legal system.

Even 30 to 35 years after the shootout at Jumping Bull's, the FBI was not winning any popularity polls in Indian Country. An electronic poll conducted by "Native America Calling" and *The Native American Times*, asked the question "Who do you think is the Greatest Native American?" during the late summer and early fall of 2005. Of the nearly 7,000 votes registered, the most-often named person was Leonard Peltier (Greatest Native, 2005). Bad blood still was very evident, enduring over the years, as when, during 2000, William Janklow stepped in with all his then-formidable political power (before he killed a motorcyclist in a state of drunkenness and was forced to resign from Congress) to block requests that might have led to a pardon of Peltier by President Bill Clinton.

In 2011, Peltier, at 67 years of age, remained in prison, in the U.S. Penitentiary in Lewisburg, Pennsylvania. He was held in solitary confinement June 27 through September 12, 2011 for minor infractions of prison regulations. On September 12 he was moved to the high-security U.S. Penitentiary at Coleman, Florida, far from his home among the Turtle Mountain Band of Chippewa Indians in North Dakota, making visits by family very difficult. Peltier, even at age 67, was still a marked man in the U.S. penal system.

Further Reading

American Indian Movement. "Free Peltier." No date. http://www.aimovement.org/peltier/

Banks, Dennis and Richard Erdoes. *Ojibwa Warrior: Dennis Banks and the Rise of the American Indian Movement.* Norman: University of Oklahoma Press, 2004.

Callis, Tom. "Arrested Movement: Looking Back at the American Indian Movement." *Klipsun Magazine.* No date. http://klipsun.wwu.edu/archives/w07b/story.php

Chapman, Serle L. *We, the People: Of Earth and Elders, Vol. II.* Missoula, MT: Mountain Press Publishing Co., 2001.

Churchill, Ward and Jim Vander Wall. *Agents of Repression: The FBI's Secret War Against the Black Panther Party and the American Indian Movement.* Boston: South End Press, 1990.

Greatest Native American Poll. *Native America Calling and The Native American Times,* October 15, 2005. http://terrrijean.smartwriters.com/index.2ts?page=greatestpoll

Hendricks, Steve. *The Unquiet Grave: The FBI and the Struggle for the Soul of Indian Country.* New York: Thunder's Mouth Press, 2006.

Johansen, Bruce. "Peltier and the Posse." *The Nation*, October 1, 1977, 304–07.

Johansen, Bruce E. and Roberto F. Maestas. *Wasi'chu: The Continuing Indian Wars.* New York: Monthly Review Press, 1979.

Matthiessen, Peter. *In the Spirit of Crazy Horse.* New York: Viking, 1991.

Pine Ridge Political Murders

Living at Pine Ridge and professing opposition to the Wilson regime was very hazardous to one's health during the 1970s. The murder rate at Pine Ridge between 1973 and 1976 was the highest of any jurisdiction, rural or urban, in the United States. Even if only documented politically motivated deaths were counted, the annual murder rate in the Pine Ridge reservation between Match 1, 1973, and March 1, 1976, was 170 per 100,000 population (Pine Ridge had about 15,000 permanent residents at the time). This rate is based on 66 murders in three years. For the 1970s as a whole, some observers put the number at as many as 200 (Johnson, 1996, 228–29).

By comparison, Detroit, then the reputed "murder capital" of the United States, had a rate of 20.2 in 1974. The average murder rate in the United States was 9.7 per 100,000 the same year. In a nation of 200 million people, close to the U.S. population during the early 1970s, a murder rate similar to the toll at Pine Ridge would have left about 340,000 people dead in one year (Johansen and Maestas, 1979, 83–84).

The rate of 170 deaths per 100,000 people at Pine Ridge between 1973 and 1976 includes only politically motivated murders, not deaths from other causes, such as premature deaths from malnutrition, malpractice in the reservation Indian Health Service Hospital, suicides, or alcoholism.

Between 1973 and 1976, following the occupation of Wounded Knee, the Pine Ridge reservation government led by Richard Wilson declared open season on the AIM, using a specially created armed force (Guardians of the Oglala Nation or GOONs) created with federal law-enforcement funding. At least 65 to 70 (possibly more) AIM members and supporters, were killed during these three years for political reasons. Few of the deaths were investigated by the FBI, which is charged with investigating major crimes in Indian Country by federal law. The FBI said it lacked the resources to pursue the culprits, even after Native people provided them with evidence that nearly always led to Wilson's GOONs.

From the early 1970s until his defeat for the chairman's office by Al Trimble in 1976, Wilson outfitted the "Rangers," or "flying squad," the personal police force that came to be called the GOONs, out of a $62,000 BIA appropriation (perhaps $250,000 in 2012 dollars) in 1972, expressly to combat AIM, after its occupation of the BIA Headquarters in Washington, DC. Wilson told South Dakota Senator James Abourezk:

> We organized this force to handle people like Russell Means and other radicals who were going to have what they called a victory dance at Billy Mills Hall [in Pine Ridge Village] after the destruction of the BIA office in Washington, D.C. . . . to hire a small group of people to protect our buildings, bureau office, tribal offices . . . [and so forth]. (Churchill and Vander Wall, 1988, 1936)

The local context of the Wounded Knee occupation at Pine Ridge included an intense effort to confront Wilson's policies, which often favored non-Indian ranchers, farmers, and corporations, and to try to end the violence plaguing the community. Wilson answered his detractors by stepping up the terror, examples of which were described in a chronology kept by the Wounded Knee Legal Defense-Offense Committee. One of the GOONs's favorite weapons was the automobile. Officially, such deaths could be reported as traffic accidents. Wilson had a formidable array of supporters on the reservation, many of whom criticized AIM for being urban based and insensitive to reservation residents' needs.

Following the Wounded Knee siege, the GOONs acquired fully automatic M-16 rifles and military-style communication gear courtesy of the federal government through the FBI. The federal grants that provided the arms were meant for the BIA police, but in practice the GOONs used them as well. On a reservation occupied by a paramilitary police force, the GOONs set out to exterminate AIM. Between March 1973 and March 1976, the reservation had a murder rate eight times that of Detroit, then considered the "murder capital of the United States" (Johansen and Maestas, 1979, 83). These were political murders, not the usual acts of common criminality.

One of the first fatalities was Pedro Bissonette, the major leader of the Oglala Sioux Civil Rights Organization (OSCRO), the reservation group that had sought to impeach Wilson, who died after he was shot in the chest point-blank in the chest during March 1975, after he was stopped at a police roadblock. He was left on the road and bled to death. Jeanette Bissonette, Pedro's sister-in-law, who had no role in the impeachment effort, also was shot to death. The GOONs seemed to have mistaken her for the well-known anti-Wilson activist Ellen Moves Camp.

The murders continued at a rapid pace: Jim Little of AIM was fatally beaten in September 1975; he died before an ambulance arrived an hour later from a BIA hospital; two miles away. During January 1976, Byron DeSersa, an attorney and an opponent of Wilson, was shot and then shoved into a ditch where he bled to death.

About 340 people at Pine Ridge, mainly AIM members or supporters, were victims of physical assaults (many of which resulted in property damage and injury less severe than death) during these three years. In one of many examples:

> In March 1975, the home of seventy-year-old Matthew King, an assistant to Chief Fools Crow and an uncle of Russell Means, was riddled by gunfire. Two nights later, Fools Crow's house was burned to the ground. Tribal council member Severt Young Bear's home was shot at so often that he "lost track" of the number of instances. In June, Means was shot in the back by a BIA police officer, who claimed that Means was engaging in "rowdy behavior." The following November, a BIA officer opened fire on the home of AIM supporter Chester Stone, wounding Stone, his wife, and two small children. (Churchill, 2008, 643)

In 2012, the Oglala Sioux tribe demanded a new inquiry into the "reign of terror," disputing a 12-year-old report by the FBI that most of the deaths were not criminal in nature. The number of deaths between 1973 and 1976 was put at "as many as 75" by the tribal government, of which it requested 28 be reopened, "to determine whether the cases were closed for legitimate and conclusive reasons, notwithstanding the potential criminal implication of federal agents" (Williams, 2012, A-20). The FBI refused to open the cases, reaffirming its earlier conclusion that most were a result of suicides, unintentional poisonings, or other accidents. "In many of these cases, the issue is not the lack of evidence and the attendant need for more," the tribe wrote in a letter on May 23 to Brendan V. Johnson, the United States attorney for South Dakota. "Rather, in many cases the issue is the potential impropriety of those required to investigate and prosecute these deaths" (Williams, June 15, 2012, A-20). A week later, under the glare of publicity from the *New York Times,* Johnson announced that prosecutors would reexamine the circumstances surrounding the 50 murders (Williams, June 20, 2012, A-12).

Further Reading

Churchill, Ward and Jim Vander Wall. *Agents of Repression: The FBI's Secret Wars Against the Black Panther Party and the American Indian Movement.* Boston: South End Press, 1988.

Churchill, Ward. "American Indian Movement," in Bruce E. Johansen and Barry Pritzker, eds. *Encyclopedia of American Indian History*. Santa Barbara, CA: ABC-CLIO, 2008, 638–46.

Hendricks, Steve. *The Unquiet Grave: The FBI and the Struggle for the Soul of Indian Country*. New York: Thunder's Mouth Press, 2006.

Johansen, Bruce and Roberto Maestas. *Wasi'chu: The Continuing Indian Wars*. New York: Monthly Review Press, 1979.

Williams, Timothy. "New Inquiry of 50 Deaths Tied to Tribe in S. Dakota." *New York Times,* June 20, 2012, A-12.

Williams, Timothy. "Tribe Seeks Reopening of Inquiries in '70s Deaths." *New York Times,* June 15, 2012, A-20, A-29. http://www.nytimes.com/2012/06/15/us/sioux-group-asks-officials-to-reopen-70s-cases.html

R

"Red Power" Movement

The wave of Native American activism involved much more than the AIM. The broader thrust for Native American cultural revival, land, and resource rights, involving many individuals and groups often was called "Red Power"—again, taking after "Black Power." According to Troy R. Johnson (2008, 292), "Red Power"

> was the term given to a generally post-1960 succession of highly visible, often confrontational Native American protest movements and actions that had as their goal the affirmation of American Indian identity and the reclaiming of power—political, social, and economic—over the people's lives. The movement grew out of years—centuries—of Indian poverty and political and cultural repression on reservations and, more recently, in urban environments. Characteristic of the Red Power movement were charismatic leaders, a conscious building on past resistance and social movements, the tactic of property seizure, the assertion of a pan-Indian identity, the formation of national activist organizations such as the American Indian Movement (AIM), and an agenda of self-determination for Indian people and communities.

Vine Deloria first used the term "Red Power" at a meeting of the National Congress of American Indians in 1966 (Hightower-Langston, 2006). Clyde Warrior used it in a broadcast interview a year later, when he promised that the National Indian Youth Council would lead an uprising that "would make Kenya's Mau Mau look like a Sunday school picnic" (Winfrey 1986, 238).

Precedents to "Red Power"

Native Americans faced with conquest long had been forced to act powerfully merely to survive. They had a long history, and many leaders—Tecumseh, Geronimo, Sitting Bull, and Crazy Horse were a few of many examples. George Armstrong Custer's defeat in 1876 at the Little Bighorn had long been used as a symbol of Native defiance. Native peoples had long been making common cause through groups such as the National Congress of American Indians (NCAI) as well. The modern manifestations of "Red Power" often are traced in the 1950s to members of the Iroquois Confederacy, such as Wallace "Mad Bear" Anderson who led a movement that sought to block several development projects that impinged on their lands (such as the flooding of Seneca land by the Kinzua Dam).

Outside of Iroquois country, sparks of protest fired by 1964; Alcatraz Island was occupied briefly, five years before the better-known event there in 1969. Fishing-rights protests in Western Washington State under the aegis of the Survival of American Indians Association (SAIA) intensified at about the same time.

The atmosphere for protest had been prepared in 1961 at the University of Chicago, which hosted the American Indian Chicago Conference. This conference brought together about 500 people from more than 90 Native nations and tribes who found common ground and strategies. The conference call had been put out by University of Chicago anthropology Professor Sol Tax. Participants negotiated a Declaration of Indian Purpose, a measure of growing common cause.

The Alcatraz Island occupation was heavily covered by media nation wide (and in some cases worldwide), spreading the seeds of activism to locales that had not yet experienced change. The same was true of Northwest fishing-rights protests. The momentum of protest fell on fertile ground in Minneapolis, where the AIM was organizing at the time that Alcatraz was occupied.

Alcatraz-style occupations were undertaken by Indians in several other locations where similar conditions existed: an urban area with a sizable Native population and surplus federal land that was legally available to them. The Twin Cities Naval Air Station, Ellis Island (New York City), a surplus Nike missile sites near Chicago and an abandoned Coast Guard station in Milwaukee all were occupied briefly. Old Fort Lawton was occupied in Seattle and a major Native American facility. The Daybreak Star Center was built over several years. At about the same time (November 3, 1970) several dozen Native people climbed over a barbed-wire fence at a surplus Army communications center in Davis, California, and erected a large teepee that became a cultural center. All of these efforts, according to Johnson, drew attention "to American Indian historical and contemporary grievances: unsettled land claims, conditions on reservations, recognition of cultural and social rights, tribal self-determination" (Johnson, 2008, 295).

These protests grew and assumed national character in major events such as the Trail of Broken Treaties (1972), a caravan spanning the United States, from San Francisco and Seattle to Washington, D.C., which culminated with an occupation of the BIA's headquarters in Washington, D.C., days before a national election. By this time, the AIM was the best known of several Red Power organizations.

AIM in the early 1970s planned events that captured media attention and helped many different Native American groups to make common cause. It also stoked controversy, because its tactics were too militant for some Native peoples. Other national networks, such as the "pow-wow highway" also facilitated communication between different Native Americans. Controversy brought still more attention. A national wave of interest ensued with publication of best-selling books, such as Vine Deloria Jr.'s *Custer Died for Your Sins*, and Dee Brown's *Bury My Heart at Wounded Knee*. It was at Wounded Knee, during the late winter and early spring of 1973, where all of these elements combined with a fervor previously unknown, during which roughly 250 AIM members and supporters faced off with a sizable governmental armed force.

Local occupations continued in many areas during most of the 1970s; many were temporary, but others created lasting results, such as an occupation of surplus property in Tacoma by Puyallups in 1976 that established a tribal center. Occupations also were undertaken by other minority groups on the same model. In Seattle, for example, the empty Old Beacon Hill School was seized by a Latino-led coalition during October, 1972, refurbished with community labor, and turned into El Centro de la Raza, a thriving multicultural center that has had a major impact on Seattle for more than 40 years.

Further Reading

Hightower-Langston Donna. "American Indian Women's Activism in the 1960s and 1970s." San Francisco Indymedia, March 21, 2006. http://www.indybay.org/news/2006/03/1809545.php

Johnson, Troy R. *The Occupation of Alcatraz Island: Red Power and Self Determination.* Urbana: University of Illinois Press, 1996. 2008 ed. University of Nebraska Press.

Johnson, Troy R. "Red Power," in Bruce E. Johansen and Barry Pritzker, eds. *Encyclopedia of American Indian History*. Santa Barbara, CA: ABC-CLIO, 2008, 292–97.

Josephy, Alvin M., Jr. *Red Power: The American Indians' Fight for Freedom.* New York: American Heritage Press, 1971.

Josephy, Alvin M., Jr., Joane Nagel, and Troy Johnson, eds. *Red Power: The American Indians' Fight for Freedom.* Lincoln: University of Nebraska Press, 1999.

Nagel, Joane. *American Indian Ethnic Renewal: Red Power and the Resurgence of Identity and Culture.* New York: Oxford University Press, 1996.

Shreve, Bradley. *Red Power Rising: The National Indian Youth Council and the Origins of Native Activism.* Norman: University of Oklahoma Press, 2011.

Winfrey, Robert Hill. 1986. "Civil Rights and the American Indian: Through the 1960s." PhD diss., Department of History, University of Oklahoma.

Robideau, Robert Eugene

(1946–2009)

Robert (Bob) Robideau was one of two AIM members who were found not guilty of murdering two FBI agents at Pine Ridge June 26, 1975. Leonard Peltier later was convicted of the murders.

Early Life

Born in Portland, Oregon, November 11, 1946, Robideau was the second of 12 children, in a family that had migrated from the White Earth Ojibwa reservation in Minnesota of an Anishinabe (also called Ojibwa or Chippewa), Dakota and French father and a Turtle Mountain Chippewa mother. He attended Portland's Theodore Roosevelt High School and graduated from Portland State University with a BA in cultural anthropology. Robideau also studied at the Institute of Native American Arts in Santa Fe, New Mexico.

When the AIM became active on the Pine Ridge reservation during the early 1970s, Robideau moved from Portland with several members of his family (including his cousin Leonard Peltier) to become involved in the occupation at Wounded Knee.

The Jumping Bull Shootout and the Cedar Rapids Trial

On the morning of June 26, 1975, the Butlers were camped in a tipi a half-mile south of the Jumping Bulls' house east of Pine Ridge village with several other AIM members. It was a spiritual camp, with a sweat lodge, but given recent violence that had killed several AIM members at Pine Ridge, many people had rifles. Two FBI agents, Jack R. Coler and Ronald A. Williams, drove into the compound seeking a pair of stolen cowboy boots. The members of AIM were not prepared for a shootout; the compound was filled with women and children. Harry and Cecelia Jumping Bull recently had celebrated their 50th wedding anniversary (Matthiessen, 1991, 157).

Shooting broke out, however, as more FBI agents, as well as Bureau of Indian Affairs and Pine Ridge reservation police (GOONs) arrived. When the firefight was over, Coler, Williams, and one Indian man, Joe Stuntz Killsright, lay dead. While the FBI mounted an international manhunt to find suspects in the agents' killings, Stuntz's death was never seriously investigated.

Following the shootout, most of the AIM members fled the compound, where the Jumping Bull's house had been filled with holes by incoming fire. Robideau and other AIM members were seriously injured when ammunition in a station wagon registered to Marlon Brando exploded on a highway in Kansas. Butler and Robideau were arrested and placed under $250,000 bond each, assuring that they would remain in jail until their trial. Both were found not guilty by a federal court jury in Cedar Rapids on July 13, 1975. The trial had been transferred out of Rapid City, South Dakota, after the defense argued that obtaining an unbiased jury there would have been impossible. Robideau and Butler discussed making a false confession to the crime to help Peltier (who was in Canada at the time), but decided against it (Matthiessen, 1991, 580–81).

The government's case at the Cedar Rapids trial was weak, damaged by weak ballistic evidence, lack of credible eyewitnesses, and false testimony. At one point, during testimony of government witness Wish Draper, Butler shouted "Liar!" (Matthiessen, 1991, 297). Defense Attorney William Kunstler even led another government witness James Harper, into confessing that he had lied many times to get what he wanted (Matthiessen, 1991, 297). The trial also featured testimony by FBI director Clarence Kelly about FBI counterintelligence (COINTELPRO) activities. Kunstler provoked Kelly into losing his temper when he raised the subject of the many AIM members and supporters who had been killed at Pine Ridge with scanty attention from the FBI, which is responsible for investigating major crimes on Indian reservations. Kelly then defended the FBI's massive response to the shooting of its agents: "If they are threatened they have a right to defend themselves" (Matthiessen, 1991, 308). Having drawn Kelly into making the defense's main point self-defense was a valid motive. Kunstler excused the witness with Kelly's words ringing in the jury's ears.

Robideau and Butler were found not guilty on all counts by an all-white jury. Butler and Robideau admitted having been present at Jumping Bull's the day of the shootout, and having exchanged fire with the agents—in the course of "defending our women and children" (Matthiessen, 1991, 286). The jury, in its verdict, said that Butler and Robideau had acted in self-defense, doing "only what any reasonable person would do, under the circumstances" that had been created on Pine Ridge (Churchill, 2003, 280).

Robideau's Later Life

In 1993, Robideau joined Russell Means, Ward Churchill, and others, in a dissident split from Vernon Bellecourt's AIM Grand Governing Council in the Autonomous American Indian Movement. Robideau worked intensely for the release from prison of Peltier, serving twice as National-International Director for the Leonard Peltier Defense Committee (LPDC).

Robideau later developed a talent as a painter on Native American themes. He also directed a museum dedicated to AIM's history in Barcelona, Spain. In Europe, Robideau often was critical of Indian themed sports mascots in the United States. Observing Chief Illiniwek at the University of Illinois at Urbana-Champaign, he said, "Not one university in Germany would contemplate having a rabbi as a mascot" (Robideau, 2009).

Robideau died in Barcelona at age 62, on February 17, 2009. The cause of death, according to Spanish officials, may have related to seizures stemming from shrapnel lodged in his brain after the explosion in Kansas more than three decades earlier. He was survived by wife Pilar and sons Michael and Bobby.

The Colorado AIM said of Robideau: "Bob was a great role model for AIM members everywhere. He epitomized what it was to be a member of AIM, not through posturing, not through rhetoric, but in action. He put his life on the line, and he was relentless in his defense of Indian people everywhere. He will be very deeply missed, and will always remembered" (Robert, 2009).

An inventory of work with the LPDC and the AIM, from 1973 through 1994 has been archived at the University of New Mexico, Center for Southwest Research (http://rmoa.unm.edu/docviewer.php?docId=nmu1mss557bc.xml). One online collection of Robideau's artwork is archived in Portland, Oregon's Bonnie Kahn Gallery: http://www.bonniekahngallery.com

Further Reading

"American Indian Activist Robideau Dies at 61." *Associated Press in Seattle Post-Intelligencer,* February 20, 2009. http://www.seattlepi.com/local/article/American-Indian-activist-Robideau-dies-at-61-1300590.php.

Churchill, Ward. "The Bloody Wake of Alcatraz: Repression of the American Indian Movement During the 1970s," in Ward Churchill ed. *Perversions of Justice: Indigenous Peoples and Angloamerican Law.* San Francisco: City Lights, 2003, 263–302.

"Robert Robideau—A True Defender of Indigenous Peoples Passes On." American Indian Movement of Colorado, February 18, 2009. http://colorado-aim.blogspot.com/2009/02/robert-robideau-true-warrior-passes-on.html.

Robideau, Robert. "An American Indian's View of the Cartoons." Counterpunch.org, February 10, 2006. http://www.counterpunch.org/2006/02/09/an-american-indian-s-view-of-the-cartoons/

Matthiessen, Peter. *In the Spirit of Crazy Horse.* New York: Viking, 1991.

S

Santa Barbara, California, American Indian Movement

The Santa Barbara, California chapter of the AIM calls itself "a grassroots national organization intended to restore dignity, respect and equality for Indigenous Peoples, by changing policy in local, state and national government" (Santa Barbara, n.d.). This chapter of AIM has made a priority of several issues, such as Native American mascots and imagery in Santa Barbara County, Native American families and foster care, and exploitation of Native ceremonies and artifacts.

A poster describing accomplishments by contemporary and historical Native Americans, such as astronaut, John Herrington, activist and author Vine Deloria Jr., athlete Jim Thorpe, political figure Winona LaDuke, spiritual leader Oren Lyons, and others has been distributed to local schools in Santa Barbara, such as La Colina Junior High School.

AIM Santa Barbara also has taken issue with portrayals of Native Americans that it deems insulting, such as "The Dudesons in America" on MTV "because it ridicules the culture, heritage, religion and beliefs of American Indian People of all Nations . . . [as well as] oppressive and discriminatory . . . [images] rooted in the same cloak of bigotry that has caused people to commit hate crimes against minorities for centuries" (Santa Barbara AIM, n.d.). MTV executives in 2010 refused to take the episode off the air or to apologize for it. Santa Barbara AIM then said it might sue in federal court under the civil-rights laws.

Further Reading

Santa Barbara, California, AIM. Home page. http://www.aimsb.org/

Snitch Jacket (Federal Bureau of Investigation)

The use of the snitch jacket (also called the "bad jacket") ravaged the AIM, especially when it was used along with the planting of real informants, such as Douglass Frank Durham. The FBI created rumors and other misinformation targeting some members of AIM as being its informants, when they were not. After a while, people who had known each other for years began to cast suspicions. At one point, for example, Clyde Bellecourt suspected Carter Camp of being paid off by the FBI. A violent argument ensued, after which Camp borrowed a handgun and shot Bellecourt in the stomach. Bellecourt later tried to salvage Camp's ruined reputation within AIM, but Russell Means insisted that Camp be banished from AIM. Camp left, taking much of AIM's Oklahoma chapter with him (Churchill and Vander Wall, 1988, 214–15). Perhaps the most notorious use of the "snitch jacket" technique was casting of suspicions about Anna Mae Aquash, which very likely resulted in her murder in 1976.

Further Reading

Churchill, Ward and Jim Vander Wall. *Agents of Repression: The FBI's Secret Wars Against the Black Panther Party and the American Indian Movement.* Boston: South End Press, 1988.

Hendricks, Steve. *The Unquiet Grave: The FBI and the Struggle for the Soul of Indian Country.* New York: Thunder's Mouth Press, 2006.

Sports Mascots and the American Indian Movement

One of the AIM's longest-running issues has been removing Indian-themed names from sports teams. Russell Means formed a chapter of AIM in Cleveland specifically to oppose Chief Wahoo. It still does.

Michael Haney of the National Coalition on Racism in Sports and the Media and Ken Rhyne (left) of the American Indian Movement, talk with reporters in Atlanta, October 20, 1995, during the Cleveland Indians versus Atlanta Braves World Series. (AP Photo/John Bazemore)

The mascot issue emerged during the 1960s, as the National Congress of American Indians in 1968 launched a campaign to bring an end to the use of Indian sports mascots and other media stereotypes. At about the same time, AIM's founding chapter in Minneapolis vigorously complained that calling a team "Redskins" was as insulting as "Niggers," "Spics," or "Honkies." Because of AIM, some of the first Indian stereotypes fell in the Midwest.

At the University of Nebraska at Omaha, for example, a chapter of AIM worked with students and faculty to change the school's mascot from "Indians" to "Mavericks," a beef animal with an attitude, in 1971. The change was popular on campus in part because the visual depiction of "Owumpie" (sometimes spelled "Ouampi") the "Omaha Indian" was so tacky that, by comparison, he made the Cleveland Indians' Chief Wahoo look like a real gentleman.

During the spring 1970, UNO began to recruit Native American students, some of whom objected during the school's first home football game the following fall as they watched a white student dressed as "Owumpie" run around the field in a "sacred" headdress. The mascot, described as "an angry, dark-red cartoon character with a hooked nose swinging a club and doing a war dance" (Else, 2005, 9-B) thus became an object of protest by the Native students, who joined with non-Indian allies to win support of the student government and the Faculty Senate. The next stop was the University President, Kirk Naylor Sr., who asked the opinion of the Omaha Nation's government, explaining that he thought the mascot was an honor. The real Omahas ("U'ma'has," actually) replied emphatically that they thought "Owumpie" was an insult, not an honor, so the caricature was retired during May, 1971. At UNO, an "Indian princess" also was retired as homecoming queen (Else, 2005, 9-B). Stanford University changed its Indian mascot from an Indian to a cardinal at about the same time.

Cleveland's Indians

The term "Indians" on its face, is not overtly defamatory. Sometimes the context, not the name itself, is the problem. In the case of the Cleveland's "Indians," face value is the clincher—the face, that is, of stupidly grinning, single-feathered "Chief Wahoo."

Demian Bulwa (1995) opened an essay in the University of California student newspaper following the 1995 World Series between the Atlanta Braves and the Cleveland Indians by describing a purported basketball game between the Philadelphia Amish and the New York Jews. "Do you find this tasteless and degrading?" he asked "Do you feel as ludicrous reading it as I do writing it? If the answer is 'yes' to either of these questions, then you should feel very uncomfortable about this year's World Series."

Cleveland's first professional baseball team was the Spiders, which lost 134 games in its first season. The team later was renamed "Naps." In 1914 a vote by fans gave the team the "Indians" name. A columnist at the Cleveland Plain Dealer created Chief Wahoo during the 1940s; his image first appeared on team uniforms in 1947.

In 1972, in the context of a lawsuit against the Cleveland Indians, AIM cofounder Russell Means openly critiqued the Chief Wahoo image: "That Indian looks like a damn fool, like a clown and we resent being portrayed as either savages or clowns." Means did not content himself with an attack on stereotypes, but turned to racial analogy to advance his argument against mascots. "Take the Washington Redskins . . . Redskin is a derogatory name . . . what if we called them the Washington Niggers, or Washington Rednecks, or Washington Pollacks?" (King, 2004, 195).

Until 2000, the team's official media guide said that the name was an honor for Penobscot Louis Sockalexis, who played with the Spiders during 1897, 1898, and 1899. The media guide's account did not appear until 1968, two decades after Chief Wahoo had been created, and half a century after the fans asked for the Indian team name. It also was the year that the AIM began to agitate against the Chief Wahoo imagery and the name.

Sockalexis may have been the first American Indian in the major leagues. It is unknown whether this is true, or spin-control meant to turn a slur into an affirmative-action coup. By 1999, the media guide was devoting a full to this urban legend. By this time, Chief Wahoo had become a best-selling brand, earning the team a large return on clothing and many other types of merchandise.

Sockalexis himself first suited up at Holy Cross College in Worcester, Massachusetts. during the mid-1890s. He played at Notre Dame, but was expelled for being drunk. The Spiders signed him up for $1,500, after which he hit .335 during his first season. It has been said that some fans "took to wearing Indian headdresses and screaming war whoops every time Sockalexis came to bat" (Nevard, n.d.). During July 1897, however, Sockalexis became drunk and was injured, and played very little during the rest of his career, which ended with his release in 1899. Until his death in 1913, he did manual labor in Cleveland and suffered alcoholic bouts.

The Atlanta Braves

"Braves" (like "Indians") is not a racial slur on its own. Objections from Native peoples usually arise from other acts and images. So it has been with the Atlanta Braves and their "Tomahawk Chop." This team was based in Boston for many years, and was known as the Boston Red Stockings, the Beaneaters, the Rustlers, and the Doves before it became the "Braves," and moved to Atlanta. Before it adopted the Tomahawk Chop at the behest of Ted Turner, the Atlanta Braves had Chief Noc-a-Homa, who did a stereotypical "Indian" dance outside his tepee every time the Braves hit a home run. Russell Means, a cofounder of the AIM, criticized Noc-a-Homa: "What if they called them the Atlanta Storm Troopers and every time there was a home run a man in a German military uniform came out and knocked a few Jews on the head with a baseball bat? Or Atlanta Negroes, and an old black man came out of a shack and did a soft shoe dance?" (Carley, 1972).

In October, 1995, when the Atlanta Braves arrived in Minneapolis for the World Series, they found more than 200 protestors arrayed at the stadium's gates, with placards reading (among other things), "500 Years of Oppression is Enough." Minneapolis is AIM's home town, and even the mayor had made a statement calling on the Braves to sack their Indian imagery. When the Twins management asked the police to move the demonstrators further from the Metrodome, they refused, citing the protestors' freedom of speech and assembly.

The Atlanta Braves' emphasis on Indian imagery has spawned a number of mascot wannabes, the best-known of whom is "Tomahawk Tom," a.k.a. Tom Sullivan, who previously worked as a management trainee at U-Haul. According to the *Atlanta Journal-Constitution*, Tomahawk Tom arrives at the ballpark "in an Indian headdress, a catcher's mask, and a cape" (Pomerantz, 1995). Tomahawk Tom was not officially sanctioned by the Braves, but he lead fans in Tomahawk-chop cheers, signed autographs, and passed out free baseball cards to children. Sullivan also regarded himself as an inventor of an ice-cream treat called The [Tomahawk] Chop Pop.

Mascot Parody: The "Fighting Whities"

A singular moment in the history of the mascot controversy occurred during February, 2002, when an intramural basketball team at the University of Northern Colorado composed of Native American, Latino, and European-American students collectively decided to change its name from "Native Pride" to "The Fighting Whites." The new name was a purposeful parody of North America's many Native American mascots, most notably nearby Eaton High School's Fighting Reds. It was the first time in popular memory that a multiethnic sports team had decided to adopt a European-American stereotype as a mascot. A dozen college students on an intramural basketball team suddenly found themselves playing in the stereotypical big leagues.

The team printed a few T-shirts (their uniform of choice) bearing the team's new name, and a logo: a suited, clean-cut white man with a bland smile on his face, and the slogan "Everythang's Gonna be All White." There ensued a wave of nearly instant, continent-wide publicity that stood the longstanding debate over the decency of Native sports-team mascots on its head. The Fighting Whities (as they came to be called) set thousands of virtual tongues to wagging. Everyone had an opinion on them, from the AIM to affiliates of the Ku Klux Klan. The reactions provide a flash-frozen ideoscape of racial humor in an age of political correctness.

Within weeks, the Fighting Whites had become nearly as well-known as established professional monikers such as the Washington Redskins and the Cleveland Indians. A cursory Internet search under "Fighting Whities" (on Google.com) turned up 4,700 "hits;" "Fighting Whites" provided 2,930 Web-page mentions—something of a media feeding frenzy for a mascot that had not existed three months earlier. The publicity helped to sell thousands of T-shirts and other items for a hastily endowed scholarship fund to aid Native American students. By the end of 2002, more than $100,000 had been raised for the fund (Cornelius, 2002).

As the official home page of the Fighting Whites explained, in a statement written by Ryan White (who is Mohawk), John Messner, and Charles Cuny, "We came up with the 'Fighting Whites' logo and slogan to have a little satirical fun and to deliver a simple, sincere, message about ethnic stereotyping. Since March 6, [2002], when our campus newspaper first reported on the Fighting Whites, we have been launched into the national spotlight, propelled by a national debate over stereotyping American Indians in sports symbolism" (Fighting Whites, 2002).

The Fighting Whites' parody very quickly sprang from the sports pages to the front pages. From the student newspaper, the story spread to the Greeley *Tribune*, then over the state, regional, and national Associated Press wire services. Some of the stories popped up as far away as London's *Guardian*. The "Whities" also were contacted by Fox Sports Net and NBC News, among many other electronic media. Soon, the Fighting Whites had developed at least nine T-shirt designs for sale on an Internet Site, with receipts fueled by publicity in many major daily newspapers, electronic news outlets, and such other large-audience venues as the Jay Leno Show. The effect on sales was downright salubrious. Soon the merchandise was available not only on T-shirts, but also on sweatshirts, tank tops, baseball jerseys, several styles of caps, a coffee mug, boxer shorts, and mouse pads.

On the court, the Whities confessed that they were hardly championship caliber, but soon their prowess at basketball didn't matter. Their reputation soon had very little to do with dribbling, jumping, or shooting, and more to do with the incendiary nature of the ongoing debate regarding Native American names for sports teams.

"This is our introduction to Eaton on how to live respectfully," said Russell Means, a founder of the AIM and a long-time national activist for Native American rights. "If Eaton wants to put up with this every year for their graduation, then so be it" (Nigoya, 2002). According to a report in the *Denver Post,* "Protesters marched through town—drums beating, chants rising—on their way to Eaton City Park. There were speeches of heritage and strife, racism and tolerance" (Nigoya, 2002). "They're upset, saying we ruined their graduation," Means said. "With this [mascot], they ruin every single day of our lives" (Nigoya, 2002).

Further Reading

Banks, Dennis, Laurel R. Davis, Synthia Syndnor Slowikowski, and Lawrence A. Wenner. "Tribal Names and Mascots in Sports," *Journal of Sport and Social Issues* 17 (April, 1993): 1–33.

Cornelius, Coleman. "Fightin' Whites Fund Scholarships: T-shirt Sales Reap $100,000 for Indians." *Denver Post,* December 1, 2002. http://www.denverpost.com/Stories/0,1413, 36%7E53%7E1021717%7E,00.html

" 'Fighting Whities' Make a Statement; American Indian Students Try to Raise Awareness of Stereotypes." Associated Press in *Philadelphia Daily News,* March 12, 2002. http://www.philly.com/mld/dailynews/sports/2841746.htm

Johansen, Bruce E. "Putting the Moccasin on the Other Foot: A Media History of the 'Fighting Whities,'" in C. Richard King, ed. *The Native American Mascot Controversy: A Handbook.* Lanham, MD: Scarecrow Press, 2010, 163–78.

King, C. Richard and Charles F. Springwood. *Beyond the Cheers: Race as Spectacle in College Sports.* Albany: State University of New York Press, 2001a.

King, C. Richard; and Charles F. Springwood, eds. *Team Spirits: Essays on the History and Significance of Native American Mascots.* Lincoln: University of Nebraska, 2001b.

Nigoya, D. "Mascot Foes March into Eaton; Fightin' Reds Protest Given Quiet Response." *Denver Post,* May 20, 2002. http://www.denverpost.com/framework/0,1918, 36%7E53%7E622747%7E,00.html

Sterilization of Native American Women

On the phone, during long marches, occupying federal surplus property, in court fighting for treaty rights—wherever Indian activists gathered during the "Red Power" years of the 1970s, conversation inevitably turned to the number of women who had had their tubes tied or their ovaries removed by the Indian Health Service. This was, I heard one woman joke bitterly at the time, a "fringe benefit of living in a domestic, dependent nation."

Communication spurred by activism provoked a growing number of Native American women to piece together what amounted to a national eugenic policy, translated into social reality by copious federal funding. They organized WARN (Women of All Red Nations) at Rapid City, South Dakota, as Native women from more than 30 tribes and nations met and decided, among other things, that "truth and communication are among our most valuable tools in the liberation of our lands, people, and four-legged and winged creations.

WARN and other women's organizations publicized the sterilizations, which were performed after pro-forma "consent" of the women being sterilized. The "consent" sometimes was not offered in the women's language, following threats that they would die or lose their welfare benefits if they had more children. At least two 15-year-old girls were told they were having their tonsils out before their ovaries were removed.

The enormity of government-funded sterilization has been compiled by a masters' student in history, Sally Torpy, at the University of Nebraska at Omaha. Her thesis, "Endangered Species: Native American Women's Struggle for Their Reproductive Rights and Racial Identity, 1970s–1990s," which was defended during the summer of 1998, places the sterilization campaign in the context of the "eugenics" movement.

"They took away our past with a sword and our land with a pen. Now they're trying to take away our future with a scalpel," one Native American woman told Arlene Eisen of the *London Guardian* (March 23, 1977, 8). She also said: "This total disregarded for the health and dignity of Native American women is the I.H.S. version of smallpox-infested blankets [and] the forced marches and massacres of Native peoples. Racism continues because it is so deeply entrenched—even enlightened professionals do not see Indian people as human. . . . They still think Indian people are in the way. They still want the land we have left, particularly our mineral resources . . . coal, oil, and uranium" (Johansen and Maestas, 1979, 71).

Native Americans were far from the only victims of Eugenic thinking into the 1970s. Beginning in 1929 and ending in 1978, the state of North Carolina sterilized as many as 7,600 people, "to reduce welfare costs and cleanse the gene pool" (Severson, 2011, A-13). California sterilized about 20,000 people for the same purposes. In 2012, 34 years after North Carolina's program ended, the state became the first of three-dozen states that had had such programs to put a price on the practice, deciding that each living survivor of the program should be paid $50,000. That figure was set by a state task force, subject to approval of the governor and legislature. The bill could reach $100 million for the 1,500 to 2,000 living victims, mostly minorities and people of limited income and low intelligence.

How Many Women Were Sterilized?

No one even today knows exactly how many Native American women were sterilized during the 1970s. One base for calculation is provided by the General Accounting Office, whose study covered only four of twelve IHS regions over four years (1973 through 1976). Within those limits, 3,406 Indian women were sterilized, according to the GAO (Johansen and Maestas, 1979, 71).

Another estimate was provided by Lehman Brightman, who is Lakota, and who devoted much of his life to the issue, suffering a libel suit by doctors in the process. His educated guess (without exact calculations to back it up) is that 40 percent of Native women and 10 percent of Native men were sterilized during the decade. Brightman estimates that the total number of Indian women sterilized during the decade was between 60,000 and 70,000.

By 1970, anecdotal evidence of the surge in sterilization began to accumulate, according to Torpy's detailed account. For example, welfare case workers in Apollo, Pennsylvania, had removed Norma Jean Serena's daughter Lisa, three years of age, and son, Gary, age four, from her home before she underwent a tubal ligation after the birth of her son Shawn, in 1970. One day after Shawn was removed to a foster home, Serena signed consent forms for the surgery, emotionally battered by accusations of case workers that she was an unfit mother.

Women Fight Back

Three years later, with legal assistance from the Council of Three Rivers Indian Center in Pittsburgh, Serena sued Armstrong County for return of her children from foster care. She also sued a number of area hospitals for damages related to her sterilization. A jury found that the children had been taken under false pretenses from Serena, who is of mixed Creek and Shawnee ancestry.

During trial, attorneys for Serena questioned the "evidence" on which welfare case workers had decided to take her children and recommend her sterilization. The main "problem" seemed to have been the fact that black friends of Serena visited her home, as reported by anonymous tipsters in the neighborhood who asserted fear for their own children. While one caseworker described Serena's apartment as "dirty and unkempt," and her children as "undernourished and dazed," unable to walk, speak, or hold eating utensils, a doctor who examined the children shortly afterwards found them "alert and in good health." According to Torpy's account, Serena was awarded $17,000 by a jury, and her children were ordered released to her. The Armstrong County child welfare bureaucracy stalled several months before returning the children, according to Torpy's account, and did so only after officials were confronted with a contempt-of-court citation.

Parts of Serena's case were not settled until 1979, when several doctors and a male social worker were acquitted of having violated her civil rights by taking part in her sterilization. The key issue was whether she had given consent for the operation. Serena said she could not recall having signed a consent form; the attending physician said he had explained the operation to Serena and that he was convinced she understood him. A jury agreed.

At about the same time that Serena had her run-in with caseworkers, a 26-year-old Native American woman entered the office of a Los Angeles physician in 1970 seeking a "womb transplant" because she had been having trouble getting pregnant. The doctor, who never asked her name, told the woman she had been the subject of a hysterectomy, removal of her ovaries, which cannot be reversed. The operation had been performed under false pretenses. The woman, who was engaged to be married and who had hoped to raise a family was "devastated," according to Torpy.

Last Gasp of Official Eugenics

The last vestiges of legally sanctioned eugenics played out during the 1960s, when concern about overpopulation expressed by industrial leaders in the United States (most notably by members of the Rockefeller family) became official federal policy—with massive spending to back it up—under the Nixon administration. Sterilization for the poor and minorities was officially sanctioned in 1970, just about the time students were killed at Kent and Jackson State universities as they protested expansion of the Vietnam War. Reservation populations became targets of a policy that also was being advocated nationally, especially for poor and minority women. In 1969, the American College of Obstetricians and Gynecologists also had relaxed its own restrictions on sterilizations.

In 1970, when the IHS initiated its sterilization campaign (paid 100 percent by federal funds), the Department of Health, Education, and Welfare vastly accelerated programs that paid 90 percent of the costs to sterilize non-Indian poor women, following enactment of the Family Planning Act of 1970. The rate of sterilization for women, as a whole, in the United States then jumped by 350 percent in five years, according to Torpy's research.

Before 1969, funding of sterilizations (as well as abortion) had been banned by the federal government. Between 1969 and 1974, HEW increased its family planning budget from $51 million to more than $250 million, Torpy found. HEW records reveal that between 192,000 and 548,000 women were sterilized each year between 1970 and 1977, compared to an average of 63,000 a year between 1907 and 1964, a period which included the zenith of the eugenics movement.

Torpy reports that during 1977, Dr. R. T. Ravenholt, director of the United States Agency for International Development (office for population control), said that the United States hoped to sterilize 25 percent of the world's roughly 570 million fertile women. Ravenholt linked such control measures to the " . . . normal operation of U.S. commercial interests around the world" (Johansen, 1998a). These statements were published in a news story in the *St. Louis Dispatch*.

A Captive Clientele

During this wave of sterilizations, no other medical structure had the captive clientele of the IHS, however. "Native American women represented a unique class of victims among the larger population that faced sterilization and abuses of reproductive rights," Tropy wrote in her thesis (Johansen, 1998a). "They had, and continue to have, a dependent relationship with the federal government which has put them at greater risk . . ."

Within half a decade, IHS doctors were sterilizing so many reservation women that, according to Torpy, one Native American woman was being sterilized for every seven babies born. Outside of very occasional, anecdotal reports in a few major newspapers, the mainstream media generally ignored the wave of sterilizations as it was happening. The first large audience, detailed description of the sterilizations was published not in the United States, but in Germany. Torpy tapped sources of information in small, specialized (often leftist or health related) journals of opinion that, taken together, sketch a history of the sterilization campaign. She credits Brightman and the International Indian Treaty Council and others, including Constance Redbird Pinkerton-Uri, for keeping the issue alive enough to spark the interest of Senator James Abourezk of South Dakota, which led to a General Accounting Office report and congressional oversight hearings that eventually curbed the practice.

Criticism within the Indian Health Service

By 1974, some IHS doctors who were critical of the sterilizations began investigating on their own. Pinkerton-Uri, a physician and law student who is Choctaw and Cherokee, started her own inquiry after complaints were lodged by Native patients against the Claremore, Oklahoma, IHS hospital. Taking publicity about the Serena cases and what she had found at Claremore, along with other pieces of evidence, Pinkerton-Uri began calling Senator Abourezk's office. The office also had received inquiries from Charlie McCarthy, an IHS employee in Albuquerque, regarding sterilizations of Native American women.

Torpy followed the trail of Abourezk's investigation, beginning with an intern in his office, Joan Adams, who took the initiative to investigate whether Native women were being sterilized without their consent and under duress. This preliminary investigation convinced Adams (and, later, Senator Abourezk) that further study was needed. Abourezk, using Adams' research, then called for a GAO investigation. Torpy described the findings of the GAO report, which surveyed IHS records in four of twelve Bureau of Indian Affairs regions: Albuquerque, Phoenix, Oklahoma City, and Aberdeen, South Dakota. The study covered only 46 months, between 1973 and 1976. (As of 1977, the IHS operated in 51 hospitals and 86 health centers or clinics.) Within this sample, the GAO found evidence that the IHS or its contractors had sterilized 3,406 women, 3,001 of them of child-bearing age (15–44 years).

Since the GAO study did not even begin to arrive at a total number of sterilizations, opponents of the practice looked at the data in another way, as a percentage of the women of child-bearing age in each examined area who were sterilized. In Oklahoma, using the GAO study's numbers, 1,761 of roughly 17,000 women of child-bearing age were sterilized. In Phoenix, the number was lower, 78 of 8,000; in Aberdeen, the figure was 740 of 9,000. They began to make a case that, with only 100,000 fertile Native women of child-bearing age in the United States, the sterilizations were putting a significant dent in the gene pools of many individual Native American nations. A population of 300 million (as in the United States) could support voluntary sterilization and survive, but for Native Americans it cannot be a preferred method of birth control. While other minorities might have a gene pool in Africa or Asia, Native Americans do not.

At times, the battle over sterilization became localized and quite heated. In response to Pinkerton-Uri's charges at the Claremore Hospital, physicians threatened to close the facility. In response, wrote Torpy, "an unidentified group of Native Americans pitched a tipi on the hospital lawn alongside the American Indian Movement flag" (Johansen, 1998a).

By the mid-to-late 1970s, the sterilization program was well-known on the Native movement circuit. By 1974, *Akwesasne Notes* was carrying reports describing sterilizations, and Native American women's attempts to mobilize against them. By 1977, a class action suit had been initiated by three Montana Native American women. The names of the three Northern Cheyenne women who filed the class action suit were not released publicly out of fear that they would be condemned by other Cheyennes. The class-action suit never went to court, and never directly affected anyone other than the three claimants. Attorneys for the defendants approached the women's attorneys and offered a cash settlement on condition that the case remain sealed. The women accepted the settlement.

At about the same time, Marie Sanchez, the Northern Cheyennes' chief tribal judge, conducted her own informal poll, and found that at least 30 women she contacted had been sterilized between 1973 and 1976. It was Sanchez who found two 15-year-old girls who said that they had been told they were having their tonsils out, only to emerge from a local IHS hospital without their ovaries.

Torpy's account brings what became a general pattern down to a personal level.

Another woman who had complained to a physician about migraine headaches was told that her condition was a female problem, and was advised that a hysterectomy would alleviate the problem. Her headaches continued, however, until she was diagnosed with a brain tumor.

Also during 1977, the American Indian Policy Review Commission found that the IHS lacked adequate policies, appropriations, delivery services, and oversight for provision of health services to Native Americans. Even in 1977, the rate of infant mortality on Indian reservations was three times that of the general population in the United States; the tuberculosis rate was still eight times as high. The average life span of a Native American living on a reservation was 47 years, compared with almost 71 years in the general population. The IHS seemed to be short of personnel and equipment to treat many things, but the agency always seemed to have enough doctors, nurses, equipment, and money to tie fallopian tubes and remove ovaries.

By the late 1970s, sterilizations continued at some IHS hospitals despite protests and suits. Brightman visited Claremore's IHS facility for six months during late

1978 and early 1979, collecting records for six months, and found evidence of 81 sterilizations. Brightman later related his findings as part of a speech on the U.S. Capitol steps which was recorded and played for some of Claremore's nurses, who, according to Torpy, validated that sterilizations were occurring and with greater frequency.

Sterilization in Cultural Context

Many Native women looked at the battle against sterilization as part of a broader, older, struggle to retain their families in a culturally appropriate context. The battle against sterilizations brought back memories of having children taken from their homes, beginning with the establishment of Carlisle School in 1879, to face a gauntlet of forced assimilation in a factory model of education. In 1977, roughly a third of reservation children were still attending the same system of boarding schools that had become a principal part of the assimilative model a century earlier. According to Torpy, in 1973, 33,672 Native American children lived in federal boarding schools rather than at home.

Many women also were reminded of the many Native children taken for foster care by non-Indians. In the mid-1970s, the proportion of Indian children placed in foster care in Western states (compared to the general population) ranged from 640 percent, in Idaho, to 2,000 percent, in North Dakota. This disparity was diminished (but not eliminated) by legislative measures beginning about 1980 which demanded that social workers appreciate Native ways of raising children instead of assuming that they were evidence of lack of parenting skills by Anglo-American, middle-class standards.

On many reservations today, Indian midwives or nurses advise women on whether sterilization is appropriate. The number of births to Indian women had risen to 45,871 in 1988, compared with 27,542 in 1975, according to census records cited in Torpy's thesis (Johansen, 1998a).

Further Reading

Johansen. Bruce E. "Reprise: Forced Sterilizations," *Native Americas* 15, no. 4 (Winter, 1998b): 44–47.

Johansen, Bruce E. "Sterilization of Native American Women Reviewed by Omaha Master's Student." For: José Barreiro (editor-in-chief of *Native Americas,* September, 1998a. http://www.ratical.org/ratville/sterilize.html

Johansen, Bruce E. "Stolen Wombs: Indigenous Women Most at Risk," *Native Americas* 17, no. 2 (Summer, 2000): 38–42.

Johansen, Bruce E. and Roberto F. Maestas. *Wasi'chu: The Continuing Indian Wars.* New York: Monthly Review Press, 1979.

Severson, Kim. "Payment Set for Those Sterilized in Program." *New York Times,* January 11, 2012, A-13.

Torpy, Sally. "Endangered Species: Native American Women's Struggle for their Reproductive Rights and Racial Identity: 1970s–1990s." MA thesis, History Dept., University of Nebraska at Omaha, 1998.

Stuntz, Joe Killsright

(1951–1975)

An AIM activist beginning in the early 1970s, Joe Killsright Stuntz was shot to death during a firefight that followed the killing of two FBI agents, Jack Coler and Ronald Williams, at the Jumping Bull Ranch on the Pine Ridge reservation on June 26, 1975.

Stuntz was born October 22, 1951 under the name Joseph George, a Coeur d'Alene Indian, on the Lapwai (Nez Perce) Reservation in Idaho. He was placed in a government boarding school in Indiana at the age of seven. He later was adopted by a retired, wealthy white couple whose name was Stuntz. They took him to New Mexico, where he attended art school in Santa Fe, and lived an affluent life with his parents. Stuntz married a Klallam girl named Ida Charles, and his life began to change. She knew Leonard Peltier, and was an in-law of Steve Robideau, a leader of the Peltier defense committee. The Klallams live along the northern Olympic Peninsula, where, in 1970, Stuntz was hired as a forest ranger, probably in the Olympic National Park.

The occupation of Wounded Knee made an impression on Stuntz; shortly after the occupation ended, he joined Peltier and others at Pine Ridge to attend the funeral of Pedro Bissonnette. In February, 1974, Stuntz resigned his job and moved to Pine Ridge, as part of an Indian caravan from Seattle. Ida, who joined him there with their two young children, said he had made the move to relearn "what it was like to be an Indian" (Matthiessen, 1991, 139). Stuntz took part in a Sun Dance (including traditional chest piercing) at Crow Dog's Paradise. In May, 1975, a few weeks before the shootout at Jumping Bull's, Ida returned to the Pacific Northwest with the children.

At Pine Ridge, Stuntz changed his name to "Killsright," a gift from a Pine Ridge family. He was a quiet person. Among his compatriots in AIM, Stuntz was known as "Little Joe." He told people around him that the Stuntz family was not proud of his Indian blood, but that AIM had changed that.

Killsright was shot to death about 1:30 P.M June 26, 1975. He was leading three teenagers who were armed with .22 caliber single-shot rifles as they protected women and children from a wave of FBI agents, BIA police, and GOONs with high-powered firearms. "Today," he told them, "you can be warriors" (Joe, 2011). FBI agents ordered him and others out of a small green shed near the Jumping Bulls' house with their hands raised. Instead, Killsright and his younger brother-in-law ran back into the shack and "got off a warning shot. The shot was answered by a burst from several guns at once, and in the exchange of fire that followed, a bullet struck Joe Killsright in the forehead, killing him instantly" (Matthiessen, 1991, 161–62).

The bullet in the head was the FBI's version, supported in an autopsy by W. O. Brown, the same BIA-funded coroner who, a few months later, would miss a bullet in Anna Mae Aquash's head and declare that she had died of exposure. William Delaney, South Dakota Assistant Attorney General, and National Public Radio reporter Kevin McKiernan observed " 'a burst of bullet holes in his back' when Killsright's body had been turned over, and neither mentioned any wound to the forehead. A later photo shows a bloodless hole in Joe Killsright's forehead" (Joe, 2011; Matthiessen, 1991, 197–98).

Killsright was interred on the Jumping Bull property. Eight months later, Aquash was buried next to him. The killing of Stuntz was regarded by the FBI as collateral; damage in the firefight, as the agency mounted one of the largest manhunts in its history to bring the killers of the two agents to account.

Dino Butler, Robert Robideau, and Leonard Peltier eventually were charged. The first two were acquitted on grounds of self-defense. Peltier was convicted and sentenced to two life terms in prison.

Further Reading

"Joe Killsright Stuntz—'Today You Can Be Warriors.'" Roundtree 7: Knowledge to the Social Consciousness. August 21, 2011. http://www.roundtree7.com/2011/08/joe-killsright-stuntz-today-you-can-be-warriors/

Matthiessen, Peter. *In the Spirit of Crazy Horse*. New York: Viking, 1991.

Survival of American Indians Association

Organized in 1964, the Survival of American Indians Association within a year was organizing major fishing-rights demonstrations on the Nisqually and Puyallup rivers near South Puget Sound in defense of century-old fishing rights. The increasing intensity of fishing-rights protests during the 1960s was a matter of survival—emphasized by the name of the group. Hank Adams, often SAIA's spokesman, organized the group after he was shot and nearly killed by whites while fishing on the Nisqually River. Puyallup Tribal Chair Ramona Bennett, often a spokeswoman at for the fish-ins, was shot by a vigilante, while seven months pregnant (Johnson et al., 1997, 18).

The group, cofounded by Adams, Sid Mills, Bennett, and Janet McCloud, likened the "fish-ins" to the black civil-rights struggle in southern states, calling Washington "the Mississippi of the West." [Russell Means later characterized South Dakota as "the Mississippi of the North" (Johnson 1997, 248)]. In so doing, they drew considerable support. Adams had a considerable network in black civil-rights circles; the magazine *Ebony*, a national black magazine, in February, 1967 published an extensive article on Indian civil rights that described SAIA. Celebrities, such as Jane Fonda, Marlon Brando, and Dick Gregory, also took part in the protests. At the end of December, 1975, Marlon Brando gave SAIA a 40-acre tract near Los Angeles, worth about $300,000 (Johnston, 1975, n.p.).

Small groups of Native fishing people had been challenging state authority in defense of the treaties for many years. The SAIA unified the struggle, publicized it, and brought in non-Indian support, forcing the issue, and bringing it into the legal arena until, in 1974, Judge George H. Boldt ruled in federal district court that treaty Indians were entitled to as many as half of the salmon returning to their usual and accustomed fishing areas. Even after that, in some cases until the U.S. Supreme Court affirmed Boldt's ruling in 1979, the state continued to assert enforcement power as its agents harassed Indian fishing people, seized nets, confiscated boats, and arrested several people. Only after 1979 did the state cease to harass the treaty Indians and accept them as copartners in managing fisheries. Many of SAIA's veterans had important roles in the new structure.

People in SAIA had a mixture of urban and reservation backgrounds. Under the U.S. government's relocation program, "Indians came in good faith to the city to find that there was nothing for them," said Bennett, who later became Puyallup tribal chairwoman. The program, initiated during the 1950s, was meant to dovetail with termination of reservations (Callis, n.d.).

Fishing protests began in an organized fashion a year and a half after SAIA organized, in the fall of 1965, after John Cochran, a Pierce County (Tacoma) state judge issued an injunction against Indian fishing in any way, or at any place, not approved by the state's fisheries bureaucracy. The Indians asserted that the state had no authority over federal treaties signed in 1854 and 1855. On October 7, state game wardens in a large power boat rammed a canoe occupied by Billy Frank Jr. and Al Bridges as they were tending nets on the Nisqually River. Two days later, state wardens cornered two teenaged Indians on a log jam in the same river. More Indians converged on the scene and cornered the agents, who then called for reinforcements. Soon a large group of people were engaged in a full-scale riot. "Some cars were busted up, as well as some people, according to one report" (McCloud and Casey, 1968, 30). Thurston County sheriff Clarence van Allen, who was respected by the Indians, talked everyone into desisting. The police withdrew and no one was arrested.

On October 13, 1965, SAIA held a fish-in by about 30 Indians, many of them women and children, on the Nisqually at Frank's Landing to protest the state's raids. More than 100 state wardens and other police waded into the protest as soon as the first net was set from a canoe containing six Indians, a family dog, and three newspaper reporters. Following shouts of "Get the sons of bitches," three large power boats rammed the Indians' craft (McCloud and Casey, 1968, 32). Indians on shore then turned on riot police in the underbrush along the river and "began pelting the State's agents with anything they could lay their hands on" (McCloud and Casey, 1968, 32). Eight were arrested. One young girl, Valerie Bridges, was dragged away by her hair, and other children were beaten, provoking outrage among the Indians. Evan Roberts Jr., a physician who observed the event for the American Friends Service Committee, filed a report alleging that some of the wardens had been drinking. Another observer said that the wardens "were like animals that smelled blood" (McCloud and Casey, 1968, 35).

The melee was copiously covered on radio and television, as well as in local newspapers.

On October 26, about 50 Indians held a protest march outside the Federal Courthouse in Seattle. Soon, the National Indian Youth Council joined SAIA in the protests. Marlon Brando hoisted a net, but was not arrested. Sometimes the state laid low, as in November, when Governor Dan Evans said that fish weren't running (the Indians showed off a net full of fish to show the press how much Evens knew).

Following the holidays, on January 29, 1966, Indians held a rally at Frank's Landing on a cold, rain-swept evening, meeting around a huge bonfire, which was used to light a life-sized effigy of Governor Evans. By February 6, Dick Gregory, a famous black comedian with a sharply political sense of humor, had arrived. He stayed for several weeks, and fished many times, going to jail with his wife Lillian, who was greeted at the Thurston County jail in Olympia by Indian marchers carrying flowers for her. The marchers then stopped at the Governor's mansion to protest Evans' opposition to the treaties (McCloud and Casey, 1968, 40).

Gregory was still in the area when the Muckleshoots assembled a sizable demonstration on the Green River. The Muckleshoot fish-in was the larger of the two, drawing about 300 people—fishing on the river with many more, Indian and not, onshore

Witnesses recalled:

When the large force of game wardens descended on the Green River fish-in and started to rough up a young Indian girl, the assembled Indians . . . stoned them—men, cars, and everything in sight. The wardens left the scene and made on-the-spot arrests. . . . Later four Indians who had gone fishing were arrested. (McCloud and Casey, 1968, 41)

Many other demonstrations took place until Indian fishing rights became judicially protected in the 1970s. In the meantime, the SAIA was running spot checks with fish buyers, who told them that state agents were threatening to suspend their licensers to do business if they continued to buy fish from Indians, despite the lack of any law against it. Two Indians, Danny and Alice Newton, set up a fish-buying camp on Puyallup land, but state agents put them under 24-hour surveillance and gave them traffic tickets for the smallest infractions—an inch over the center line, a mile over the speed limit, driving too slow, and so forth. In one week, the New-tons received 30 tickets (McCloud and Casey, 1968, 46). Soon they went out of business.

The SAIA also set up an "Operation Re-Education Program" to teach Native children their culture, history, and language. They also advocated a United Na-tions trusteeship for American Indians if the U.S. federal government did not ful-fill its legal obligation to protect treaties legally. This effort contributed to some of the legal actions of subsequent years, including the Boldt Decision on fishing rights.

Further Reading

Bims, Hamilton. "Indian Uprising for Civil Rights: Washington Group Hires NAACP Attorney in Red-hot Battle over Fishing Rights." *Ebony*, February, 1967, 64–65, 68, 69, 72.

Callis, Tom. "Arrested Movement: Looking Back at the American Indian Movement." *Klipsun Magazine*. No date. http://klipsun.wwu.edu/archives/w07b/story.php

Johnson, Troy, Joanne Nagel, and Duane Champagne. *American Indian Activism: Alca-traz to the Longest Walk.* Chicago: University of Illinois, 1997.

Johnston, Laurie. "Notes on People: U.S. Women Greeted by Peking Officials." *New York Times,* December 31, 1975, n.p.

McCloud, Janet and Robert Casey. "The Last Indian War." Seattle: Seattle Group Bul-letins, No. 29 and 30, 1968. Mimeographed.

T

Thanksgiving (Plymouth Rock) Protest

(1970)

The founders of the AIM developed a talent for high-profile public events that utilized popular symbols to attract media attention. The first event of this type took place on Thanksgiving Day of 1970, in Boston, when Russell Means and Dennis Banks led a group from AIM that, with local Wampanoag activists in Plymouth, Massachusetts, declared a "day of mourning" for Native peoples while the rest of the United States was celebrating the 350th anniversary of the Pilgrims' arrival at Plymouth Rock, Massachusetts.

To celebrate 350th anniversary of the Pilgrims' arrival at Plymouth Rock, the town by the same name built a replica of their ship, which they named Mayflower II. It was docked near "the rock," dated 1620. Banks and Means learned of the event and planned a surprise. It began, according to one account, "with Means leading a march through the town's streets. Singing, drumming, and carrying protest signs, the marchers stopped traffic as they walked for several miles toward Plymouth Plantation, where Banks and yet more protesters were waiting for them" (Taking Back, 2010). They confronted a group of re-enactors sitting down at a holiday feast.

The "Pilgrim Fathers" initially welcomed the Indians as an authentic historical touch. Banks then launched into a speech calling for a day of mourning. Soon, AIM had seized the Mayflower II, which tourists had been boarding for a fee. They also threw garbage at Plymouth Rock and refused orders from several police officers to desist. More police arrived as some of the AIM protesters suggested that the ship be torched. Banks calmed them. The police agreed not to arrest anyone if the protesters left the scene with minimal damage. As the confrontation broke up, however, "Means leaped onto the stone pedestal of a large statue of 17th century Wampanoag leader Massasoit . . . [and] launched into an impromptu speech. He praised the Wampanoags for generously aiding the helpless foreigners who would have otherwise starved, and he castigated White culture for its willingness to sacrifice its own people and others in the name of progress" (Taking Back, 2010).

Later that night, after crowds had dispersed, John Trudell returned with a small group of AIM people and painted Plymouth Rock bright red. The next day national media coverage put AIM on the national agenda for the first time.

Further Reading

"Taking Back Plymouth Rock." *The Public Professor,* November 23, 2010. http://www.thepublicprofessor.com/?p=931\

Thom, Mel

(1938–1984)
Navajo

Melvin Thom, a Navajo, was among a small group of Native American students who founded the National Indian Youth Council (NIYC) during the early 1960s as it evolved into a major force in the "Red Power" movement, as founders of the AIM tapped the NIYC for advice when they formed their organization in 1968. Although AIM received more media attention, NIYC was very influential in activist circles and, unlike AIM, maintains a united presence today. Most of NIYC's factionalism occurred during the 1960s, and Thom was a part of it.

Thom, who was characterized as "gregarious, honest, committed, and sincere" (Shreve, 2011, 99), was born on July 28, 1938 on the Walker River Paiute Reservation in Schurz, Nevada, among people descended from Wovoka, who had initiated the Ghost Dance movement. He graduated from Lyon County High School, and then attended Brigham Young University (BYU) in civil engineering. He was president of BYU's Indian students' club, the Tribe of Many Feathers, and also played a leadership role in the Regional Indian Youth Council (RIYC), which grew out of many collegiate groups during the late 1950s, and represented several hundred students throughout the Southwestern United States. This group then expanded its scope, especially to the fishing-rights battles of the Pacific Northwest, and became the NIYC in the early 1960s. Thom was recalled as "a brilliant organizer" and a "very creative person" (Shreve, 2011, 99). After he graduated from BYU, Thom went to work for the Federal Aviation Administration (FAA) as an assistant reservation engineer in Los Angeles.

All along, Thom took particular pride in his reservation roots, telling colleagues more than once that he had "subsisted on everything from fried jackrabbit to chow mein" (Shreve, 2011, 99). Thom often shared NIYC leadership duties with Herb Blatchford during the early years, but they had a falling out in 1965, during which Blatchford was ousted from his leadership role. It was Blatchford who, realizing that Thom was a talented organizer, had recruited him as NIYC's first president. In that role, Thom worked to expand NIYC's activities to the fishing-rights struggle in Washington State, where he and others in NIYC joined with Hank Adams and the Survival of American Indians Association (SAIA), recruiting celebrities such as Marlon Brando and initiating some of the largest demonstrations of the early "Red Power" movement, before AIM took shape in Minneapolis.

At one point, in 1967, Thom, frustrated with the slow pace of change in Indian Country, accused the National Council of American Indians (NCAI), and its president Vine Deloria Jr., of being sell-outs to the white power structure, after NCAI had passed a resolution opposing NIYC's militant protests. The conflict became personal and visceral for a time, but by 1969 and 1970, with the occupation of Alcatraz Island, Deloria, who no longer led NCAI, was calling for younger, more militant groups to cooperate with NCAI and other main-line pan-Indian organizations. In 1968, Thom led NIYC participation in Martin Luther King Jr.'s Poor Peoples' Campaign, which was seeking an "Economic Bill of Rights" to end employment discrimination and guarantee all people meaningful jobs.

Also in 1968, Thom left NIYC as the group reorganized. He moved back to his Paiute homeland, where he withdrew from activism and his health declined, as he suffered from acute arthritis sustained after an automobile accident many years earlier. On December 17, 1984, Thom took his own life. Deloria, long since recovered from the spat between NIYC and NCAI in 1967, had seen Thom a month before the suicide, and recalled that he "was huddled over and [his] hair was grey, and his face badly distorted [in pain]" (Shreve, 2011, 208).

Further Reading

Shreve, Bradley G. *Red Power Rising: The National Indian Youth Council and the Origins of Native Activism.* Norman: University of Oklahoma Press, 2011.

Trail of Broken Treaties

(1972)

During the summer of 1972, Hank Adams (a leader of "fish-ins" in Washington State) and Dennis Banks, a founder of AIM, met in Denver to plan a "Trail of Broken Treaties" caravan. Those in attendance at the initial meeting at Crow Dog's Paradise convened another meeting in Denver a month later to plan the event in detail. At the New Albany Hotel, Robert Burnette, Vernon and Clyde Bellecourt, Dennis Banks, Russell Means, George Mitchell, Reuben Snake attended. A number of other groups also sent people: the National Indian Brotherhood (Canada), the National Indian Lutheran Board, the Native American Rights Fund, the NIYC, and others. Burnette and Snake served as cochairs.

Participants in the Trail of Broken Treaties aimed to marshal thousands of protesters across the United States to march on Washington, D.C., to dramatize issues related to American Indian self-determination. Members of AIM proclaimed, with characteristic humor, that they would "retake the country from West to East like a wagon train in reverse" (Weyler 1992, 42).

At any one time, roughly 500 to 1,000 people from 20 to 30 Native tribes and nations took part (Bonney, 1977, 217). Jack Forbes, in *Native Americans and Nixon* (1984), put participation in the Trail of Broken Treaties at "2,000 Indians at one time or another" (Forbes, 1984, 91). Suzan Shown Harjo (2002) in 1992 put the size of the Trial of Broken Treaties at 800 people as it entered Washington, D.C.

Pressure on Nixon

The Trail of Broken Treaties was designed to put pressure on President Richard M. Nixon during his campaign for a second term, to correct abuses of American Indian treaties, resulting in impoverishment of many people on reservations. In 1972, for example, per capita income on the Pine Ridge Reservation was about $1,200 a year (about 5,000 in 2012 dollars), and unemployment was the worst in the United States (sometimes 80 percent). An adult living there could expect to live an average of about 45 to 50 years.

Three caravans set out from the Pacific coast in early October, merging in the Twin Cities. A spiritual leader carrying a sacred pipe led each caravan. The Pacific Northwest column, which assembled in Seattle, was coordinated by Sid Mills and Hank Adams, veterans of fishing-rights protests. A second column from San Francisco was led by veterans of the Alcatraz occupation. A smaller third caravan departed Los Angeles. By the time they reached Minneapolis, the three caravans included about 600 people.

In Minneapolis, Reuben Snake chaired four days of workshops at the state fairgrounds in St. Paul to develop a list of demands for the federal government. Out of these negotiations came the Twenty Points, drafted over two days by Hank Adams, who was sequestered in a motel room. The Twenty Points sought to revive tribal sovereignty completely. Vine Deloria Jr. called Hank Adams' Twenty Points "the best summary document of reforms put forth in this [the twentieth] century" (Johnson et al., 1997, 50).

Its numbers growing, the combined caravan of cars, trucks, and buses motored eastward through Milwaukee and Indianapolis, arriving in Washington, D.C., during late evening, November 2, with cars carrying about 1,000 people stretching four miles. Burdette had traveled ahead to arrange food and lodging, but promised help failed to materialize. The first night was spent crammed into the basement of St. Stephen and the Incarnation Church.

Exhausted and frustrated, with several hundred people laying sleeping bags toe to toe in the rat-infested basement of an old church, the Indians learned that a functionary at the BIA had directed employees there not to recognize or extend aid to the caravan's members. Such aid had been customary for Indian visitors. Not only that, but, Interior Secretary Rogers Morton refused to meet with the Indians and called them "a small, willful band of malcontents" (Josephy, 1973, 82). In a mass flash of anger at the insulting snub at the BIA, with nowhere else to go, the members of the caravan decided to march on the building at 1951 Constitution Avenue, six blocks from the White House.

Occupation of the BIA Headquarters

The next day, November 3, the group elected to stay in the Bureau of Indian Affairs (BIA) building for several hours, crowded into an auditorium, increasingly unhappy at the snail's pace of officials. When police from the General Services Administration tried to evict them at 5 P.M., the protesters refused to leave.

Suzan Shown Harjo (2002), who witnessed the BIA takeover, recalled 25 years later that:

> Once inside the building, Indians were camped all over the building, busy with security and other tasks, but mostly reading documents. Everyone talked about the thick carpeting, leather couches and chairs, running water and indoor plumbing that were more comfortable and modern than most Indian homes. . . . [M]any people in the building [were] making weapons, primarily war clubs out of chair legs and scissor blades. Beautifully carved and painted, many were museum quality in both form and function.

Harjo (1992) recalled "AIM leader Russell Means . . . was on the first floor, near the bottom steps, giving a high-volume speech with exaggerated gestures that could be seen from a distance—part Hollywood Indian sign-language and part Arthur Murray dance instructor moves (one of Means' jobs prior to joining AIM)."

Ironically, AIM had never intended to visit the BIA Headquarters building, much less occupy and pillage it. The caravan had arrived in Washington with an agenda of meetings and memorials that called for a number of other events, most of which could not be held because authorities denied permits, or people with whom they wanted to meet were not available. The Indians were infuriated after they were denied permission to enter Arlington National Cemetery to view the graves of Native war heroes, notably Ira Hayes, a Pima who was among the flag raisers at Iwo Jima during World War II.

At that point, the protesters seized the building for six days as they asserted their demands that Native sovereignty be restored and immunity be granted to all protesters. Files were seized and damage was done to the BIA building (AIM leaders asserted that federal agents had infiltrated the movement and had done most of the damage). Several hundred protesters held the BIA building for several days, demanding that Nixon respond to each of the "Twenty Points." Hank Adams, executive director of Survival of American Indians Association, was chosen by the occupiers as lead negotiator with the Nixon White House. In the meantime, Stokely Carmichael of the Student Non-Violent Coordinating Committee stopped by and gave a speech pointing out how vital the Native-rights struggle was to the national civil-rights movement (Burnette and Koster, 1974, 211).

Within a few hours, more than 1,000 Indians had massed inside the building, enough to stand down a riot squad that tried to evict them at 5 P.M., closing time. They unfurled a sign across the building's façade reading "NATIVE AMERICAN EMBASSY," and built a tipi on the front lawn. Entrances were blockaded with furniture, reports strewn in halls, and walls spray-painted. So many Molotov cocktails were assembled inside the building that tourists could small the gasoline from the street (Smith and Warrior, 1996, 157). The gas bombs were never used, but they became a potent symbol for those who stereotyped AIM as a gang of wild savages. This was not the dignified procession that Robert Burnette had planned.

Some wanted to blow up the building with their stack of Molotov cocktails, but others snuffed the fuses:

> With a theatrical flourish, [Russell] Means lit a long fuse to the Molotov cocktails and yelled, "It's a good day to die." A chorus of voices exclaimed, "Bulls**t." [several] stamped on the glowing fuse until it was not only extinguished, but also shredded.
>
> "You can't do that," Onondaga faith keeper Oren Lyons said sternly to Means. "You can't kill the people and destroy all those records. This is only a battle, not the war." (Harjo, 1992)

People standing around Means then removed the gas bomb from his hand, and handed it to Lyons, who shredded the fuse.

Sunday night, November 5, two days before the election, the Interior Department issued an ultimatum demanding that AIM vacate the building by 8 A.M. Monday. The protesters rejected it, but were not immediately evicted. Hank Adams, who had been AIM's chief negotiator throughout the occupation, telephoned the news to the government. He was asked if he could arrange to get women and children out of the building. Adams said "no"—women and children had been among those rejecting the offer. Shortly after that, the phone lines in the building went dead. Harjo later talked with John Ehrlichman, who was Nixon's chief domestic affairs advisor, recalled the president telling him: "Get those goddamn Indians out of town" (Harjo, 1992).

On Monday, a federal court ruled that the government was within its rights to remove the protesters, and a new deadline was set: 6 P.M. that day. As word of the ruling reached the occupants of the BIA building many of them were watching a fishing-rights film, *As Long as the Rivers Shall Run,* depicting the State of Washington's raids against Native people exercising their treaty fishing rights as state game wardens dragged Native women away. The combination of events provoked a last, furious trashing of the BIA building. "The earlier actions had been vandalism. This was war," wrote Smith and Warrior in *Like a Hurricane* (1996, 162).

After the final wave of vandalism, the people in the building settled back in an air of defeat, waiting for the police to club them senseless. It never happened. Instead, two days later, a surrender was negotiated and money provided to get the AIM members and supporters out of town—$66,000 in total, about 250,000 in 2011 dollars. The government pledged to form a committee to study Native complaints and address the *Twenty Points*. Technically, the government did that—a group was appointed and, one by one, it refused to implement the Twenty Points. During the same week, Richard Nixon was reelected, carrying 49 states, over George McGovern.

Departing the vandalized BIA building, AIM took 20,000 pounds—ten tons—of agency files. Vine Deloria Jr., and Hank Adams both realized that the missing files could set back work on many land rights and other legal cases, and so did their best, with varying degrees of success, to work with several people at have at least some of them returned. The FBI tracked a large number of the documents to North Carolina, "home of the occupation's rowdiest contingent, the Tuscaroras" (Smith and Warrior, 1996, 172). The agents made several arrests and reclaimed a large cache of papers. At one point (January 31, 1973), the FBI crossed wires with Adams and arrested him with a large number of BIA files a day before he was preparing to hand them over to the government.

Further Reading

Banks, Dennis and Richard Erdoes. *Ojibwa Warrior: Dennis Banks and the Rise of the American Indian Movement*. Norman: University of Oklahoma Press, 2004.

Bonney, Rachel A. "The Role of AIM Leaders in Indian Nationalism," *American Indian Quarterly* 3, no. 3 (Autumn, 1977): 209–24.

Burnette, Robert and John Koster. *The Road to Wounded Knee*. New York: Bantam, 1974.

Deloria, Vine, Jr. *Behind the Trail of Broken Treaties: An Indian Declaration of Independence*. Austin: University of Texas Press, 1985.

Forbes, Jack D. *Native Americans and Nixon: Presidential Politics and Minority Self-determination*. Los Angeles, CA: American Indian Culture Center, 1984.

Harjo, Suzan Shown. "Trail of Broken Treaties: A 30th Anniversary Memory." *Indian Country Today,* November 6, 2002. http://indiancountrytodaymedianetwork.com/2002/11/trail-of-broken-treaties-a-30th-anniversary-memory/

Johnson, Troy, Joane Nagel, and Duane Champagne, eds. *American Indian Activism: Alcatraz to the Longest Walk*. Urbana: University of Illinois Press, 1997.

Josephy, Alvin M., Jr. "Wounded Knee and all that: What the Indians Want." *New York Times Sunday Magazine,* March 18, 1973, 18–19, 66–83.

Means, Russell and Marvin J. Wolf. *Where White Men Fear to Tread: The Autobiography of Russell Means*. New York: St. Martin's Griffin, 1995.

Smith, Paul Chaat and Robert Allen Warrior. *Like a Hurricane: The Indian Movement from Alcatraz to Wounded Knee*. New York: The New Press, 1996.

Trail of Broken Treaties: BIA, I'm Not Your Indian Anymore. Rooseveltown, NY: Akwe-sasne Notes, 1973.

Weyler, Rex. *Blood of the Land.* Philadelphia: New Society Publishers, 1992.

Trail of Self-Determination

(1976)

Four years after the AIM's Trail of Broken Treaties lit up the United States' politi-cal landscape on election eve, the Trail of Self-Determination attempted another publicity coup, and was mainly ignored by Washington, D.C.'s political establish-ment. After Wounded Knee's occupation, three years of terror at Pine Ridge, and the shootings of two FBI agents and one Native American man, also at Pine Ridge, the non-Indian media and public were showing signs of AIM fatigue.

In 1976, the United States was observing the bicentennial of its Declaration of Independence, and the Trail of Self-Determination assembled as a counterpoint to the official celebrations. As in 1972, a caravan traveled from several points in western urban areas (leaving early in February) and united (this time in Lawrence, Kansas) to discuss its demands. After that, the caravan rode to Washington, D.C., arriving on July 4, the bicentennial Independence Day, where officials refused to hear them, or study their detailed plans. Forty-seven demonstrators were arrested at the BIA headquarters that had been occupied and ransacked in 1972.

Like most of AIM's cross-country caravans and walks, the Trail of Self-Determination had a manifesto assembled by the group, coordinated by Hank Adams, to remake the face of the U.S. government's relationship with Native nations and tribes. The manifesto listed 10 points of negotiation, all unfinished business from centuries of colonialism. Some of the 1976 manifesto was borrowed from the "Twenty Points" of the Trail of Broken Treaties four years earlier, but it also showed an evolution in thinking.

The document was assembled at a workshop in Lawrence, Kansas, May 13–17, 1976, attended by several hundred Native people from a wide variety of Native communities taking part in the caravan, regarded by them as an outline for Indian "true self-government . . . an agenda for the next Congress and administration of the United States government—an agenda that must be accepted and acted upon, if the basic obligations of a government to a people are not to be forever denied" (Trail, 1976, frontispiece).

PART I: (Provisional Government) An Office of Sovereign Indian Relations and Community Reconstruction.

PART II: Construction of Local and Regional Governments to find National Leaders.

POINT III: Native American-United States Treaty Relations: Commitments-Violations.

POINT IV: Resubmission of Unratified Treaties to the Senate.

POINT V: Land Reform and Restoration of a Minimum 110-million Acre Native Land Base.

POINT VI: Restoration of Constitutional Treaty-making Authority and the Establishment of [a] Treaty Commission to Make New Treaties.

POINT VII: Jurisdiction for Violent Offences against Native Americans; Jurisdiction over Non-Indians (Public Law 280).

POINT VIII: Native American Rehabilitation and Release Program from State and Federal Prisons and Establishment of an Indian Grand Jury.

POINT IX: Protection of Indian Religious Freedom and "New Education Programs" (De-urbanization Program).

PART X: 1/Diagrams; 2/Map; 3/Position Paper. (Trail, 1976, frontispiece)

The proposal was issued on July 4, 1976, and called itself "a birthday message to the government of the United States of America. . . . That can enable you to begin your third century by recovering the great Iroquois principles embodied in your own Constitution" (Trail, 1976, 1–2).

The opening statement, formulated at Haskell Institute on May 18, 1976 by "The Sovereign Women's Bicentennial Message," reads as an indictment. Part of it said:

> As you remove our trees and minerals, as you harvest our fish, divert our water supplies, move your white communities upon our lands, gather the foods provided for us by the Great Spirit, and run your cattle onto our properties, you establish your unbroken record as the tenth generation of parasites. You cannot claim these conditions as being the responsibility of your ancestors. You cannot claim no shame or no guilt. As long as the materials of your homes belong to us, and you heat your homes with our fuel, and use power derived from our beautiful rivers and streams to keep your lights and entertainment centers working, drive cars manufactured from materials ripped from our Mother Earth, and feed yourselves the foods from our land, beaches and streams, all in violation of 372 Treaties signed by your government, you as elected representatives share, and continue the guilt of this nation's pathetic history. (Trail, 1976, 2)
>
> We have lived in fear of the injustice of your judicial system, in fear of your removal of our beautiful children, in fear of the lies forced into the heads of our children by your educational system, ion fear of your police attacks against our young men, in fear of the isolation and starvation of your cities,

and in fear of a future of poverty and unemployment on our reservations. (Trail, 1976, 2–3)

The document's introduction pointed to energy exploitation of Native lands, including coal and uranium mining as a perversion of the Interior Department's trust responsibility to Native peoples, even as the Twenty Points advanced by the Trail of Broken Treaties had been met "with a show of naked force and endless court prosecutions in a hopeless attempt to sweep the 'Indian Problem' out of the public focus" (Trail, 1976, 1).

This manifesto set out a set of very basic changes in the way the United States conducted its relations with Native peoples, in keeping with the theme of self-determination. To begin, it proposed replacement of the Indian Affairs bureaucracy with a Native-run National Indian Council of 25 or fewer members within the executive branch of the federal government. Administration would be handled through an Office of Sovereign Relations and Community Reconstruction.

As the name of the newly proposed office suggested, the emphasis here was on sovereignty ("Native people are talking about their sovereignty, and not just self-government or program operation," p. 5). The proposal meant to remake the ways in which Native people conducted their lives "starting at the family-unit level and leading to a National Indian Council" (p. 5).

Under this plan, "elders, traditional leaders, clans, societies, headsmen, or whatever [other] method each sovereign nation deems" would meet and decide how to best govern Indian Country along traditional lines (p. 5). Representatives would then be sent to a regional and national council. The proposal cited the Haudenosaunee (Iroquois) Confederacy as an example.

The proposal—very detailed and legalistic, running to several thousand words—envisioned a system that would totally recast Native Americans' relationship with non-Indian United States and its government. Among other things, it provided that

— The provisions of treaty protection be extended to members of many hundreds of Native bands and tribes with whom agreements had never been negotiated, or whose treaties had not been ratified by the U.S. Senate.

— Ways be found to address conflicts over lands, resources, and rights outside a system of litigation that provided for endless appeals and steep legal fees. The proposal estimated that Indians had paid attorneys more than $72 million between 1962 and 1975 (p. 6).

— Termination acts against the Menominee, Klamath, and other Native peoples be repealed. (This was accomplished during following years.)

— Indian transportation, commerce, and trade remain outside state jurisdiction.

— Jurisdiction over major crimes against Indians, on or off reservations, remain solely a federal matter, not subject to state laws or limits, requiring repeal of partial state jurisdiction under Public Law 280.

— Native religious freedom be protected by law. (This was accomplished by federal law after this proposal was made.)

— The land claims of Mexican-Americans (Chicanos) be respected in accordance with the Treaty of Guadalupe-Hidalgo, negotiated in 1848 at the conclusion of the Mexican-American War.

Further Reading

"Trail of Self-Determination Proposal." July 4, 1976. Mimeographed. In archives of El Centro de la Raza, Seattle. Retrieved August 17, 2011.

Trudell, John

(Born 1946)
Santee Sioux

One of the founders and principal activists of the AIM, John Trudell by the early 21st century was well known nationally and internationally as a musician and a poet of uncommon political acuity. He was the subject of filmmaker Heather Rae's documentary film *John Trudell,* released in 2006. "He has one of the most engaging minds I have ever known," said Wilma Mankiller, former principal chief of the Oklahoma Cherokees. The actor Kris Kristofferson said that Trudell "is a crazy lone wolf, poet, prophet, preacher, warrior full of pain and fun and laughter and love. . . . He is a reality check" (Chapman, 2001, 264).

Trudell was born to a Santee Sioux father and Mexican Indian mother in Omaha, Nebraska, in 1946. Trudell's grandfather on his mother's side had fought with Pancho Villa. Trudell spent much of his childhood on the Santee Sioux reservation in northern Nebraska. He dropped out of high school shortly before he joined the U.S. Navy to escape oppressive surroundings. Trudell served two tours in or near Vietnam during the war, between 1965 and 1969. He met his first wife, Fenicia "Lou" Ordonez, while stationed in Long Beach, California.

During the occupation of Alcatraz Island, Trudell became a major spokesman. He was a member of the elected governing council for a time, and hosted a half-hour radio show, "Radio Free Alcatraz," five days a week on KPFA-FM in Berkeley, beginning during December, 1969. Trudell missed many of the show dates, however, because of complications related to the occupation. "Calm, articulate, and quietly intense . . . he became the island's public face," wrote Smith and Warrior

John Trudell talks to members of the media after a band of Indians occupied a remote former Nike site near Richmond, California, June 14, 1971. (AP Photo/Richard Drew)

(1996, 71). The shows also were carried on WBAI-FM in New York City and KPFK-FM in Los Angeles.

By the late 1960s, Trudell became an early activist in AIM. He served as its national chairman between 1973 and 1979 and took part in the Trail of Broken Treaties and its occupation of the BIA Washington, D.C., headquarters in 1972, as well as the confrontation at Wounded Knee (1973). Beginning in 1976, he coordinated AIM's work on behalf of AIM member Leonard Peltier. Between 1969 and 1979, the FBI compiled a 17,000-page dossier on Trudell, finding him very intelligent and, therefore, very dangerous (Rae, 2005).

"Our cultural identity is getting stronger," said Trudell, "And I think that is the biggest accomplishment that came out of that period of political activism. It rekindled the spirit of Native people at large. It re-lit that fire" (Chapman, 2001, 272).

A House Fire Kills Trudell's Family

During AIM's early days, John met his second wife, Tina Trudell, in 1971. She was an activist in her own right, well-known for her high political profile regarding sovereignty issues on the Duck Lake reservation in Nevada. During February, 1979, Tina, who was pregnant, was trapped and incinerated in a burning home with three children (ages one, three, and five) and Tina's mother. The BIA issued a report asserting that the fire was caused by a faulty fireplace trap.

A private investigator hired by Trudell concluded that the house's chimney trap had been plugged, making a fire from that source unlikely. Some witnesses said they saw a line of fire on the roof of the house that may have resulted from a firebomb. Speculation was widespread that the house had been set aflame in retribution for the Trudells' political activities. John said any assumption that the fire was set solely to get back at him "minimizes who she [Tina] was" (Rae, 2005). However, the fire occurred within hours after Trudell had burned a United States flag on the steps of the FBI headquarters in Washington, D.C., to protest treatment of Peltier.

Speaking of his development as a writer, Trudell said: "Putting my love in boxes reconnected me with the Earth." Six months after the fire, he began to write poetry to cope with his grief—"a gift," he said, from Tina. Trudell also became active in the antinuclear movement as well as other environmental issues after many Navajo uranium miners died of radiation-induced lung cancer. For indigenous peoples, he said, dying from uranium poisoning or alcoholism was just as effective a form of genocide as the use of bullets by an invading army.

A Trenchant Critic

Trudell is known as trenchant critic of the established order. "Don't trust anyone who isn't angry. We cannot change the economic system until the people control the land," he said during Rae's film. "Civilization is not civilizing—it is brutalizing. Is it God's will to rape the land?" The words that lead Trudell's home page on the Internet are "I'm just a human being trying to make it in a world that is very rapidly losing its understanding of being human." Indian treaties, said Trudell, "are agreements between your ancestors and my ancestors [and] the supreme law of the land. If you do not obey the treaties, you have no spiritual connection to the land" (Rae, 2005).

Trudell continued to be active in AIM throughout his life and was one of the key organizers of a protest march that forced the cancellation of Denver's Columbus Day Parade in 1992, the 500th anniversary of Columbus' first voyage to the Americas.

Asked whether Native Americans should observe Columbus Day, he paused, then said that would be "like asking the American People to observe Osama bin Laden Day. Columbus was a terrorist to us" (Rae, 2005).

In 1982, Trudell began recording poetry with traditional Native music. In 1983, his debut album *Tribal Voice* was released on his Peace Company label. Trudell joined with Kiowa guitarist Jesse Ed Davis to record three albums during the 1980s:

the first, *AKA Graffiti Man* (1986), was called the best album of that year by Bob Dylan. The music on *AKA Graffiti Man* mixes the spoken word, rock-and-roll, and Northern Plains musical traditions. Trudell's CD *Bone Days* (2002) was produced by actress Angelina Jolie on Daemon Records, at a time when he led a band called Bad Dogs. *Madness & The Moremes* (2007) encapsulated his music career. By 2007 he had produced about a dozen recordings and three books of poetry.

Trudell also has acted in several motion pictures. He appeared in the documentary film *Incident at Oglala* (1992) and performed the role of Jimmy Looks Twice in the feature film *Thunderheart* (1992). Both films examine the incidents surrounding the trial of Peltier. He also played a role in *Smoke Signals* (1998), which is based on a Sherman Alexie novel. In another role, Trudell played Coyote in Hallmark's made-for-television-movie *Dreamkeeper* (2003).

Further Reading

Chapman, Serle L. *We, the People: Of Earth and Elders, Vol. II.* Missoula, MT: Mountain Press Publishing Co., 2001.

Igliori, Paola, Stickman: *John Trudell.* New York: Inanout Press, 1994.

John Trudell Home Page. http://www.johntrudell.com/bio.html

Rae, Heather, director. "Trudell." (DVD), 2005.

Smith, Paul Chaat and Robert Allen Warrior. *Like a Hurricane: The Indian Movement from Alcatraz to Wounded Knee.* New York: The New Press, 1996.

Trudell, John. *Lines from a Mined Mind: The Words of John Trudell.* Golden, CO: Fulcrum, 2008.

Trudell, John. *This Ain't El Salvador.* West Chester, PA: Learning Alliance, 1996.

U

United Nations Declaration on the Rights of Indigenous Peoples

With background work by the AIM's International Indian Treaty Council, the United Nations General Assembly on September 13, 2007, adopted a Declaration on the Rights of Indigenous Peoples. A total of 144 member states voted in favor, 4 against, and 11 abstained. The four negative votes were the United States, Canada, Australia, and New Zealand, largely because the declaration criticized their colonial policies. The Declaration advocated self-determination, return of traditional lands and territories, revival of traditional languages and customs, and return of sacred sites and natural resources.

The declaration outlined the rights of an estimated 370 million indigenous peoples around the world. It also declared discrimination against them illegal. After more than 20 years of debate, the Declaration was not binding, but it did:

> set out the individual and collective rights of indigenous peoples, as well as their rights to culture, identity, language, employment, health, education and other issues. The Declaration emphasizes the rights of indigenous peoples to maintain and strengthen their own institutions, cultures and traditions, and to pursue their development in keeping with their own needs and aspirations. It also prohibits discrimination against indigenous peoples and promotes their full and effective participation in all matters that concern them, and their right to remain distinct and to pursue their own visions of economic and social development. (United Nations, 2007)

General Assembly President Sheikha Haya said that "the importance of this document for indigenous peoples and, more broadly, for the human rights agenda, cannot be underestimated. By adopting the Declaration, we are also taking another major step forward towards the promotion and protection of human rights and fundamental freedoms for all." She warned, however, that "even with this progress, indigenous peoples still face marginalization, extreme poverty and other human rights violations. They are often dragged into conflicts and land disputes that threaten their way of life and very survival; and, suffer from a lack of access to health care and education" (United Nations, 2007).

Further Reading

"United Nations Adopts Declaration Rights of Indigenous Peoples." UN News Centre, September 13, 2007. http://www.un.org/apps/news/story.asp?NewsID=23794

Uranium and Navajos

The mining of uranium became a major political issue during the 1970s, as many men who had mined it beginning in the 1940s began to die of lung cancer. Activists in the Coalition for Navajo Liberation (CNL) sought to have uranium mining and milling outlawed on the reservation as soon as its human toll became evident, a position that eventually prevailed in the Navajos' government after a quarter-century of debate and industry lobbying. Esther Keeswood, a member of the CNL from Shiprock, New Mexico, a reservation city near tailings piles, said in 1978 that the CNL had documented the deaths of at least 50 residents (including several uranium miners) from lung cancer and related diseases. The number of deaths increased steadily after that.

The first uranium was mined on Navajo land during the late 1940s; the Indians dug the ore that started the United States' stockpile of nuclear weapons. For 30 years after the first atomic explosions in New Mexico, uranium was mined much like any other mineral. More than 99 percent of the product of the mines was waste, cast aside as tailings near mine sites after the uranium had been extracted. One of the mesa-like waste piles grew to be a mile long and 70-feet high. On windy days, dust from the tailings blew into local communities, filling the air and settling on the water supplies. The Atomic Energy Commission assured worried local residents that the dust was harmless.

The Kerr-McGee Company, the first corporation to mine uranium on Navajo Nation lands (beginning in 1948) found the reservation location extremely lucrative. There were no taxes at the time, no health, safety, or pollution regulations, and few other jobs for the many Navajos recently home from service in World War II. Labor was cheap. The first uranium miners in the area, almost all of them Navajos, remember being sent into shallow tunnels within minutes after blasting.

They loaded the radioactive ore into wheelbarrows and emerged from the mines spitting black mucus from the dust, and coughing so hard it gave many of them headaches. Such mining practices exposed the Navajos who worked for Kerr-McGee to between 100 and 1,000 times the limit later considered safe for exposure to radon gas. Officials for the Public Health Service (PHS) have estimated these levels of exposure; no one was monitoring the Navajo miners' health in the late 1940s. Many of the men did not even speak English. The Navajo language contains no indigenous word for "radioactivity."

Thirty years after mining began, an increasing number of deaths from lung cancer made evident the fact that Kerr-McGee had regarded miners' lives as cheaply as their labor. As Navajo miners continued to die, children who played in water that had flowed over or through abandoned mines and tailing piles came home with burning sores.

A 1976 Environmental Protection Agency report found radioactive contamination of drinking water on the Navajo reservation in the Grants, New Mexico, area, near a uranium mining and milling facility. Doris Bunting of Citizens Against Nuclear Threats, a predominantly white group that joined with CNL and the National Indian Youth Council to oppose uranium mining, supplied data indicating that radium-bearing sediments had spread into the Colorado River basin, from which water is drawn for much of the Southwest. Through the opposition to uranium mining in the area, among Indians and non-Indians alike, runs a deep concern for the long-term poisoning of land, air, and water by low-level radiation. It has produced demands from Indian and white groups for a moratorium on all uranium mining, exploration, and milling until the issues of untreated radioactive tailings and other waste-disposal problems are faced and solved.

The United States' Biggest Uranium Spill

The biggest expulsion of radioactive material in the United States occurred on July 16, 1979, at 5 A.M. on the Navajo Nation, shortly after President Carter had proposed plans to use more nuclear power and fossil fuels. On that morning, more than 1,100 tons of uranium mining wastes—tailings—gushed through a packed-mud dam near Church Rock, New Mexico. With the tailings, 100 million gallons of radioactive water gushed through the dam before the crack was repaired.

By 8 A.M., radioactivity was monitored in Gallup, New Mexico, nearly 50 miles away. The contaminated river, the Rio Puerco, showed 7,000 times the safe standard of radioactivity for drinking water below the broken dam shortly after the breach was repaired, according to the Nuclear Regulatory Commission. The few newspaper stories about the spill outside of the immediate area noted that the area was "sparsely populated" and that the spill "poses no immediate health hazard." After the Rio Puerco spill, several Navajos said that calves and lambs were being born without limbs, or with other severe birth defects. Other livestock developed sores, became ill, and died after drinking from the river.

Death in the Mines

The enormous spill of nuclear waste into the Rio Puerco was but one incident in a distinctly nuclear way of life in Navajoland. The nuclear-mining legacy of 30 years blows through the outlying districts of Shiprock, New Mexico, the Navajos' largest city, on windy days. The hot, dry winds shave radioactive dust from the tops and sides of large tailings piles around the city. One of them is 70-feet high and a mile long. Until the mid-1970s, the Atomic Energy Commission assured the Navajos of Shiprock that the tailings were harmless.

Lung cancer results from inhalation of radon gas, a byproduct of uranium's decay into radium. Miners who worked for Kerr-McGee during the 1940s were exposed to between 100 and 1,000 times the dosage of radon now considered safe by the federal government. Harris Charley, who worked in the mines for 15 years, told a U.S. Senate hearing in 1979, "We were treated like dogs. There was no ventilation in the mines." Pearl Nakai, daughter of a deceased miner, told the same hearing that "No one ever told us about the dangers of uranium" (Grinde and Johansen, 1995, 214). The Senate hearings were convened by Sen. Pete Domenici, New Mexico Republican, who was an early supporter of compensation for disabled uranium miners, and for the families of the deceased.

The 1979 Senate hearings were part of a proposal to compensate the miners for what investigators called deliberate negligence. Radioactivity in uranium mines was linked to lung cancer by tests in Europe by 1930. Scientific evidence linking radon gas to radioactive illness existed after 1949, but measures to ventilate the Navajo mines were never taken, as the government pressured Kerr-McGee and other producers to increase the amount of uranium they were mining. The PHS recommended ventilation in 1952, but the Atomic Energy Commission said it bore no responsibility for the mines, despite the fact that it bought more than three million pounds of uranium from them in 1954 alone. The PHS monitored the health of more than 4,000 miners between 1954 and 1960 without telling them of the threat to their health.

Bills that would compensate the miners were introduced, discussed, and died in Congress for a dozen years. By 1990, the death toll among former miners had risen to 450, and was still rising. Relatives of the dead recalled how the miners had eaten their lunches in the mines, washing them down with radioactive water, never having been told that it was dangerous.

Compensation was finally approved after more than a decade of congressional debate. Next, the federal bureaucracy stood in the way. By the early 1990s, about 1,100 Navajo miners or members of their families had applied for compensation related to uranium exposure. The bureaucracy had approved 328 cases, denied 121, and withheld action on 663.

Cleanup Planned at Spill Site, After Three Decades

After almost three decades of appeals from the Navajo Nation, the U.S. Environmental Protection Agency in September, 2011, approved plans to clean up the Northeast Church Rock Mine, near Gallup, New Mexico, the largest abandoned uranium mine on Navajo territory. The mine was used between 1967 and 1982 by United Nuclear Corporation, which left behind roughly 1.4 million tons of uranium and radium-contaminated soil near a 125-acre United Nuclear Corporation uranium mill site. This mill and mine was the site of the United States' largest release of radioactive waste.

On July 16, 1979, after a dam that had been restraining mounds of water-logged tailings failed, flooding spilled the Puerco River in New Mexico downstream to Chambers, Arizona. According to the Navajo Nation, the spill, "combined with more than 20 years of discharges of untreated and poorly treated uranium mine water, has contributed to long-term contamination of the Puerco River in New Mexico and Arizona" (Cleanup, 2011).

The site has long been designated a Superfund site by the EPA, co-managed by the Nuclear Regulatory Commission. The site is near the border of the Navajo Nation, on trust territory, but the mill site is privately owned. A small number of people live near the site, down-wind and down-stream of mining tailings waste piles. The people in the area graze cattle, sheep, and horses.

The clean-up was expected to require several years, and, according to an Environment News Service report "will place the contaminated soil in a lined, capped facility employing the most stringent standards in the country. When complete, the cleanup will allow unrestricted surface use of the mine site for grazing and housing, according to the EPA" (Cleanup, 2011). People in the area have been at risk "from inhaling radium-contaminated dust particles and radon gas or utilizing contaminated rainwater and runoff that has pooled in the ponds. There is an elevated risk associated with livestock that may graze and water on the site." Radium exposure at high levels over several years, according to the EPA, over a long period of time "can result in anemia, cataracts, and cancer, especially bone cancer, and death" (Cleanup, 2011).

"This is an important milestone in the effort to address the toxic legacy of historic uranium mining on the Navajo Nation," said Jared Blumenfeld, administrator for the Pacific Southwest Region. "This plan is the result of several years of collaboration between EPA, the Navajo Nation, and the Red Water Pond Road community living near the mine." "On behalf of the Navajo Nation, I appreciate the efforts of the U.S. EPA and Navajo EPA, and the cooperation from the state of New Mexico to clean up contaminated Navajo trust lands," said Ben Shelly, president of the Navajo Nation (Cleanup, 2011). The spill, in addition to many miners' deaths, has been a major reason that the Navajo Nation has banned uranium mining and milling.

By 2012, as a five-year cleanup program by the U.S. federal government was about to expire, Navajo lands were still contaminated by several hundred highly radioactive uranium mine sites.

During the summer of 2010, a Navajo cattle rancher, Larry Gordy, found one such site in his grazing land near Cameron, Arizona, 60 miles east of the Grand Canyon, and called the EPA, which found a radioactivity level that, in two days, would expose a human being (or a sheep) to levels of toxicity considered unsafe for a year. Such exposure can lead to malignant tumors and other serious health problems, according to Lee Greer, a biologist at La Sierra University in Riverside, California (MacMillan, 2012).

"If this level of radioactivity were found in a middle-class suburb, the response would be immediate and aggressive," said Doug Brugge, a public health professor at Tufts University medical school and an expert on uranium. "The site is remote, but there are obviously people spending time on it. Don't they deserve some concern?" "The government can't afford it; that's a big reason why it hasn't stepped in and done more," said Bob Darr, a spokesman for the Department of Energy. "The contamination problem is vast" (MacMillan, 2012). Cleaning all the mines would probably cost hundreds of millions of dollars, said Clancy Tenley, a senior EPA official who oversees its "uranium legacy program."

Most of the mining companies that abandoned sites on Navajo land have gone out of business. General Electric, however, has been billed $44 million for its role in the Northeast Church Rock Mine, near Gallup, New Mexico. The EPA itself has spent $60 million. Chevron paid an undisclosed amount to clean up the Mariano Lake Mine in New Mexico (MacMillan, 2012).

Further Reading

Brugge, Doug and Timothy Benally. *The Navajo People and Uranium Mining.* Albuquerque: University of New Mexico Press, 2006.

"Cleanup Planned for Largest Abandoned Uranium Mine on the Navajo Nation. "Environment News Service, September 29, 2011. http://www.ens-newswire.com/ens/sep2011/2011–09–29–092.html

Eichstaedt, Peter. *If You Poison Us: Uranium and American Indians.* Santa Fe, New Mexico: Red Crane Books, 1995.

Grinde, Donald A., Jr. and Bruce E. Johansen. *Ecocide of Native America: Environmental Destruction of Indian Lands and Peoples.* Santa Fe, Clear Light, 1995.

MacMillan, Leslie. "Uranium Mines Dot Navajo Land, Neglected and Still Perilous." *New York Times*, March 31, 2012. http://www.nytimes.com/2012/04/01/us/uranium-mines-dot-navajo-land-neglected-and-still-perilous.html

Pasternak, Judy. *Yellow Dirt: An American Story of a Poisoned Lands and a People Betrayed.* New York: Free Press, 2010.

V

Virginia Chapter, American Indian Movement

The Virginia Chapter of the AIM, with Rabiah Yazzie (a Seminole), Mike Wicks, Thomas Lewis, Kathy Morning Star, Ellery Pennock in the lead, has made Indian-themed mascots its major issue for several years, as "an issue that goes in hand strongly with education, is encouraging and embracing diversity. This must be implemented correctly in order for all people to truly learn. Understanding is the key, and knowing that perpetuating myths, stereotypes and misinformation about any race results in negating and denigrating a people" (AIM Virginia, n.d.).

AIM Virginia personalizes the issue:

> Imagine being a young American Indian person attending a school that uses an Indian as its mascot. You are American Indian, the football team is playing against another school. You go to the game and upon arrival to the opposing teams school, there are effigies of Indians hanging in the trees, some burnt, some with signs saying "kill the Indians . . . beat the Indians". Not a healthy environment for a young person to grow up in. It is also detrimental to youth of all cultural backgrounds . . . lending to the thought that it is acceptable to use racial stereotyping in this day and time. It perpetuates racism and in the learning years of school sets the precedence that it is acceptable to use racist figures, slogans, and names. This is not what the youth of today should be learning in their formative years. (AIM Virginia, n.d.)

This chapter said that use of other ethnic groups in such a manner would not be tolerated.

Virginia AIM, which is allied with the AIM Grand Governing Council, has been active in campaigns that debase Native American culture, such as school mascots and fake ceremonies. The Virginia AIM chapter mounted a campaign to alert everyone, Native and not, to avoid fakery of history and culture:

Do Not. . . .

Do Not go to Non-Indian run Pow Wows

Do Not buy Indian items from Non-Indian vendors

Do Not buy jewelry from the Orient that markets itself as Indian

Do Not Pay to pray

Do Not buy AIM memberships—there is no such thing, it is a matter of commitment, not money

Do Not agree with racism of any kind—Racism is Racism

Do Not mix religions; it is a conflict, you can't do both

Do Not pay for Sweats, Sundances, and Vision Quests. These items are not for sale. (Virginia Chapter, n.d.)

Virginia AIM also compiled a list of 75 schools in Virginia that use Native American Racial Mascots: Braves (9), Chiefs (3), Indians (51), Squaws (1), and Warriors (12). Some of the schools with Indian-themed mascots also have Indian-themed names, but these are not deemed racially offensive. These include many of the schools in Powhatan County.

"We are a race of people, not objects. We need the support and help of educators to let all people know this is not honoring us, it is demeaning and offensive to us," Virginia AIM said. However, the group was disappointed by the lack of action on this issue following a meeting with members of the Virginia Council on Indians, which is sanctioned by the state's government. "We were in hopes that the issue would be taken seriously and work would begin towards eliminating mascots in the schools," the statement said. "We want to work with the Council on this issue to bring it closer to fruition and are all ready to do this. We are in hopes that the letters and faxes supporting the removal of Indian mascots that are being sent to all schools in the state of Virginia will aid in the discontinuance of Indian mascots. We also want to see the removal of the huge statue of the brave at Braves Stadium in Richmond Virginia" (Position Statement, n.d.).

Further Reading

"AIM Virginia Chapter." "Position Statement of Virginia AIM and the American Indian Cultural Resource Center on the Mascot Issue." No date. http://www.aics.org/aimva/aimva.html

"Position Statement of Virginia AIM and the American Cultural Resource Center on the Mascot Issue." No date. http://www.aics.org/aimva/aimva.html

Virginia Chapter. American Indian Movement. No date. http://www.aics.org/aimva/aimva.html#donot

W

Walk for Justice

(1994)

Beginning February 11, 1994, at Alcatraz Island, and ending July 15 at Washington D.C.'s Lincoln Memorial, 28 Native American activists led by Dennis Banks walked across the United States in defense of Leonard Peltier, as well as "to draw attention to issues ranging from treaty rights and grave desecration to nuclear waste dumping, land-use disputes, fishing rights, and sports team mascots" (Native, 1994). The issues were outlined in a 26-page manifesto prepared for Congress.

While the 28 walkers from 21 Native tribes and nations completed the entire, 3,800-mile journey, several thousand people took part along the way. Some were from Japan, Australia, Denmark, France, Germany, Britain, as well as from across the United States.

At the Lincoln Memorial, they demanded that President Bill Clinton free Peltier via executive clemency, who was serving two life sentences for the murders of FBI agents Jack Coler and Ronald Williams during a shootout at the Jumping Bull ranch on the Pine Ridge Oglala Sioux reservation on July 25, 1975.

Sage was burned and a traditional pipe was smoked on the steps of the Lincoln Memorial. "We knew from the beginning that we would have a hard time and that the many nations of people would help us along the way," said Banks. "What we were not prepared for was the great amount of support shown to us. Overwhelming" (Native, 1994).

An Associated Press report said that "Several tribal elders wore red T-shirts reading 'Free Peltier.' Others donned colorful, traditional clothing, beating drums and singing Friday as temperatures rose into the 90s. Large black, red and yellow banners read, 'Respect Mother Earth' and 'The Black Hills Are Not For Sale'" (Native, 1994).

Clinton did not heed the demand, as FBI Director Louis J. Freeh issued a statement opposing clemency, saying, "Peltier's guilt has been firmly established" (Native, 1994).

Further Reading

"Native American Activists Finish Cross-Country 'Walk for Justice.'" *Associated Press in Los Angeles Times,* July 16, 1994. http://articles.latimes.com/1994–07–16/news/mn-16156_1_native-american-activists

Ward Valley (California) Nuclear Waste Protest

A village of tents and tipis grew in the desert 22 miles west of Needles, California, during the last half of February, 1998, as several hundred Native American and non-Indian environmentalists put their bodies on the line in an attempt to stop construction of a dump for low-level nuclear waste on land they regard as sacred, with the AIM providing security.

By the third week of February, roughly 250 people were camped at "ground zero" of Ward Valley, 80 acres of federally owned land designated for the waste site. The encampment prevented soil testing necessary for planning of the dump, which had been proposed to receive waste from hospitals, nuclear plants, and other industries that cannot dispose radioactive materials in other landfills.

By February 19, occupants of the encampment had defied two sets of federal orders to leave the site, and had blocked roads leading to it. A 15-day order that had been issued in late January expired on February 14. A new, five-day eviction order issued that day expired on February 19, with protesters still eyeball-to-eyeball with a circle of Bureau of Land Management (BLM) vehicles that had surrounded their camp. Protesters said that the BLM and other federal agents had been rumbling around the camp in large land rovers and flying over it in small aircraft and helicopters at odd hours of the night in an attempt to intimidate the campers and deprive them of sleep. Religious ceremonies continued in the camp amid the glare of headlamps and the drone of aircraft overhead. Some of the protesters had chained themselves together. After complaints (and arrival of news-media reporters) the vehicles were withdrawn from the perimeter of the camp.

Steve Lopez, a Fort Mojave native spokesman, said that the Ward Valley is central to the creation stories of many Native American peoples in the area, as well as the habitat of endangered tortoise species. "Taking away the land is taking away part of ourselves. They used to use bullets to kill our people off. Now it's radioactive waste," Lopez said (Johansen, 1998, 7). Ward Valley also is sacred to many Native peoples in the area because of its proximity to Spirit Mountain, the birthplace of their ancestors.

The protesters included a number of elders affiliated with five Colorado River basin tribes (Fort Mojave, Chemehuevi, Cocopah, Quechan, and Colorado River Indians), who refused to move, along with the rest of the protesters. Instead, people in the encampment sent out appeals for supplies and more visitors, asking, according to a Colorado AIM posting on the Internet, "for the physical presence of anyone willing to travel to Ward Valley and participate in the protection of this sacred land and the people defending it" (Johansen, 1998, 7). Donations of food, water, blankets, batteries, and rain gear were requested. Wally Antone of the Colorado River Native Nations Alliance said, "Our ceremonies will continue here and our elders will not move. You will have to drag us out, and I say those words with honor" (Johansen, 1998, 7).

On February 18, as the BLM's second deadline was set to expire, leaders of the camp invited five BLM officials to their central fire for a religious ceremony, after which the officials were told that the protesters would not move. Andy Mader of Arizona AIM said via Internet that all the cellular phones in the camp were malfunctioning. Some suspected that the government had shut them down. Meanwhile, supporters of the protest outside the camp had received phone calls indicating that several other AIM chapters were sending people to Ward Valley.

Tom Goldtooth of the Indigenous Environmental Network reported from the camp via Internet that the protest had become so vigorous not only because the land is regarded as sacred by Native peoples, but also because many southern California and Arizona urban areas rely on the Colorado River for water that could be polluted by the proposed waste dump. The same water is used to irrigate crops in both the United States and Mexico.

A position paper circulated by Save Ward Valley, an environmental coalition, stated that the proposed dump lies above a major aquifer, 18 miles from the Colorado River. Furthermore, the report asserted that all six of the presently active nuclear waste dumps in the United States are leaking. U.S. Ecology, the contractor selected for the Ward Valley site, presently operates four of those six dumps, the position paper said.

The coalition also asserted that all the waste buried at such sites is not low level. As much as 90 percent of the radioactivity proposed for burial would come from nuclear power plants, including cesium, strontium, and plutonium, the statement said.

Speaking on behalf of the coalition, Tom Goldtooth, who coordinated protests by non-Native supporters, evaluated the protest, which eventually caused plans for the dump to be shelved:

> Incorporating the importance of your traditional ways and the use of the sacred Fire as the foundation for guidance and resistance as we fight for environmental justice and Native rights has proven successful at Ward Valley. I applaud the many non-natives from the peace movement to the anti-nuclear movement and the global human family that raised the consciousness of the world that the sacred tortoise and the ecology of a desert environment must not be sacrificed anymore by the whims of the nuclear waste industry. I witnessed the coming together of the non-Native supporters and the Colorado River tribal communities and Tribal Nations in an historical moment where everyone agreed to fight together with one mind and one spirit to defend the sacredness of the Mother Earth and to defend the sovereignty of the Fort Mojave Tribal Nation. (Goldtooth, 2001)

Further Reading

Goldtooth, Tom. National Director, Indigenous Environmental Network. Indigenous Environmental Network Statement to Nora Helton, Chairwoman, Fort Mojave Indian Tribe,

Other Lower Colorado River Indian Tribal Leaders, Tribal Community Members, Elders and Non-Native Groups and Individuals, in Reference to the Ward Valley Victory Gathering to Celebrate the Defeat of a Proposed Nuclear Waste Dump, Ward Valley, California. February 16, 2001. http://www.ienearth.org/ward_valley2.html

Johansen, Bruce. "Ward Valley: A 'Win' for Native Elders," *Native Americas* 15, no. 2 (Summer, 1998): 7–8.

Warrior, Clyde M.

(1939–1968)
Ponca. Civil-rights Activist

An important thinker, fiery orator, and activist in the "Red Power" movement, Clyde Merton Warrior blazed an intellectual trail through Indian Country in the 1960s before his sudden death of liver failure at the age of 28 brought on by acute alcoholism that he could not escape. He was, according to a friend, full of "thunder and lightning and tears" (Cobb, n.d.). Warrior has been compared to Malcolm X, as a powerful leader who died at a very young age.

Warrior's Early Life

Warrior was born to Gloria Collins in Ponca City, Oklahoma, on August 31, 1939, and grew up with Ponca traditions taught him by his grandparents Bill and Metha Collins. As a boy, he became known for his ability to memorize and perform Ponca dances and music; by age 15 he was a well-known fancy dancer. During the summer of 1961, Warrior worked with the Student Non-violent Coordinating Committee on voter education (Hightower, 2006). Earlier, he called the Bureau of Indian Affairs (BIA) a white colonialist institution (Day, 1971, 513).

Warrior always had a great love of Native American tradition. In addition to dancing, he learned the Ponca language from his grandparents, and memorized songs and ceremonies. He was an acute student of Native history, especially personalities of people who had been devoted to Native Liberation. When the National Indian Youth Council (NIYC), which he helped to found, proposed scholarships, Warrior proposed that they be named after Geronimo, "in honor of a true Indian patriot" (Shreve, 2011, 16). To Warrior, the future would be built on a foundation of tradition.

Warrior attended the Chicago Conference in 1961, a workshop involving about 600 Native American leaders from across the United States, representing 67 tribes and nations that afterward were credited with incubating much of the activism that sparked the self-determination movement of the 1960s and 1970s. Attendees at the conference drew up a Declaration of Indian Purpose that they sent to President John F. Kennedy. Even as he worked with left-liberal groups such as SNCC, he professed admiration of Republican Barry Goldwater in the 1964 U.S. presidential campaign (Shreve, 2011, 158).

A year after the Chicago Conference, Warrior was elected as president of the Southwest Regional Indian Youth Council at Cameron Junior College, Lawton, Oklahoma. In 1962, he was named the group's outstanding student. Working at Cameron, the University of Oklahoma and at Northeastern State College, Tahlequah, Oklahoma, in 1966 he earned a bachelor's degree in education.

Warrior was a prime mover among young activists who were disappointed that older leaders were not moving quickly enough. He minced no words. "It was sickening to see American Indians get up and just tell obvious lies about how well the federal government was treating them, what fantastic and magnificent things the federal government was doing for us," he later recalled (Cobb, n.d.).

A Key Leader of the National Indian Youth Council

After the Chicago Conference, in August 1961, Warrior and several other young activists founded the NIYC in Gallup, New Mexico, with the expressed purpose of "attaining a greater future" for Native people (Clyde Merton Warrior, n.d.). The NIYC's program formed a basis for decades of development of sovereignty, what years later came to be called "nation-building." He repeatedly asked Indian audiences: "How long will you tolerate this?"

The NIYC was composed mainly of college-educated Native students from reservations who came together at the American Indian Charter Convention held in Chicago during 1961. Melvin Thom, a Paiute from Walker River, Nevada, was cofounder and early spokesman with Warrior, who told federal officials in Washington, D.C., in 1967:

> We are not allowed to make those basic human choices and decisions about our personal life and about the destiny of our communities that are the mark of free, mature people. We sit on our front porches or in our yards and the world and our lives in it pass us by without our lives or aspirations having any effect. (Johnson, 1996, 2008, 33)

Between 1962 and his death in 1968, Warrior was a key leader of NIYC. At the same time, he worked with the Denver Commission on Human Relations, where he was coeditor of *Indian Voices*, the commission's journal. He advised the National Congress of American Indians, and worked with the Rev. Martin Luther King's Poor People's Campaign, including the 1963 march on Washington during which King gave his "I Have a Dream" speech. Warrior also presented provocative speeches at the University of South Dakota and Oberlin College, among other colleges and universities. Warrior married Della Hopper, an Oto, in 1965. They had two daughters.

Warrior became known as a speaker who gave voice to a sense of anger that others shared but dared not express. A remembrance of him by the Ponca Nation outlined the sharp edge of his rhetoric:

In essays such as "Don't Take 'No' for An Answer," "Which One Are You?," "Time for Indian Action," "How Should an Indian Act?," and "Poverty, Community, Power," he talked about taking pride in Indianness, demanded respect for traditions, and condemned the dominant society for dehumanizing and alienating tribal people. He threw his support behind the fish-ins in the Pacific Northwest, testified before Congress, cajoled the Commissioner of Indian Affairs, criticized established tribal leaders, and protested outside the White House. In word and deed and spirit, Clyde Warrior inspired the nationalist movement that would be known as Red Power. (Cobb, n.d.)

In 1966, NIYC leaders were watching when SNCC leader Stokely Carmichael shouted the words "black power" at a rally in Greenwood, Mississippi. "A month later," wrote Bradley Shreve in his history of NIYC, "at a Fourth of July parade in Oklahoma City, Clyde Warrior painted 'Red Power!' on one side of his car and 'Custer Died for Your Sins' on the other" (Warrior, 2011, 159). Warrior and Mel Thom created havoc at that event by crashing the parade lineup in that car.

His Speeches Spared No One

Warrior's speeches spared no one, with their "vitriolic denunciations of the BIA, middle-class American culture, and those Indians he variously labeled "slobs," "jokers," "redskin white-nosers," "ultra-pseudo-Indians," and "Uncle Tomahawks" (Cobb, 2003; Warrior, 1964, 2). He railed at a system that he called "a horrendous combination of colonialism, segregation, and discrimination" but never gave up hope that he and other activists could change it for the better (Cobb, 2003; Warrior, 1964, 2). He spoke of an imminent Indian rebellion that would make the Watts riots in Los Angeles look "like a Sunday School picnic" (Cobb, 2003).

Just as his career was reaching an early stage of maturity, Warrior died suddenly in Enid, Oklahoma of cirrhosis of the liver early in July, 1968. A friend, Mel Thom, a Walker River Paiute, said of him: "Our leader is gone, but the spirit of such a leader is never gone. We can still hear him teasing, laughing, cussing, singing, and talking as few men could. We will always hear him. His words made Indian people feel good… . In his short life he brought us a long way ahead in our struggle for human equality" (Cobb, n.d.).

Further Reading
Cobb, Daniel. "Clyde Merton Warrior." Ponca Nation. No date. http://www.ponca.com/warrior_memorial/warrior_memorial.html

Cobb, Daniel M. "QUESTION: To What Extent Do Scholars Have a Responsibility to the Indigenous Communities They Study and How Can They Fulfill this Responsibility? Telling Stories." HNet: Humanities and Social Sciences On-line. April 16, 2003. http://h-net.

msu.edu/cgi-bin/logbrowse.pl?trx=vx&list=H-AmIndian&month=0304&week=c&msg=
HCsIvR1zFFV/%2BqdO3DWGLA&user=&pw=

Cornell, Stephen E. *The Return of the Native: American Indian Political Resurgence.* New York: Oxford University Press, 1988.

Day, Robert. "The Emergence of Activism as Social Movement," in Alvin Josephy, ed. *Red Power: The American Indians' Fight for Freedom.* New York: American Heritage Press, 1971.

Hightower-Langston Donna. "American Indian Women's Activism in the 1960s and 1970s." *Indymedia,* March 21, 2006. http://www.indybay.org/news/2006/03/1809545.php

Johnson, Troy. *The Occupation of Alcatraz Island: Red Power and Self Determination.* Urbana: University of Illinois Press, 1996. 2008 ed.

Shreve, Bradley G. *Red Power Rising: The National Indian Youth Council and the Origins of Native Activism.* Norman: University of Oklahoma Press, 2011.

Smith, Paul Chaat and Robert Allen Warrior. *Like a Hurricane: The Indian Movement from Alcatraz to Wounded Knee.* New York: The New Press, 1996.

Warrior, Clyde. "On Current Indian Affairs," *Americans Before Columbus* 2, no. 2 (May, 1964): 2.

Warrior, Clyde. "We Are Not Free," in Alvin M. Josephy Jr., Joane Nagel, and Troy Johnson, eds. *Red Power: The American Indians' Fight for Freedom*, 2nd ed. Lincoln: University of Nebraska Press, 1999, 16–21.

Warrior, Clyde. "Which One Are You? The Five Types of Young Indians," in Stan Steiner, ed. *The New Indians.* New York: Harper & Row, 1968.

Wilkinson Charles F. *Blood Struggle: The Rise of Modern Indian Nations.* New York: W.W. Norton, 2005.

Westerman, Floyd Red Crow

(1936–2007)
Sisseton-Wahpeton Sioux. Musician and Activist

An influential Native singer and actor, Floyd Red Crow Westerman was known to large audiences for his role as the wise old sachem Ten Bears in *Dances With Wolves* (1990). He played a shaman who was consulted by Jim Morrison in Oliver Stone's *The Doors* (1991) and had a role in "Clearcut" (1992). His television credits included Uncle Ray on *Walker, Texas Ranger*, One Who Waits, on *Northern Exposure* and several appearances as Albert Hosteen on the *X-Files*. He also played George Little Fox on *Dharma & Greg* (Floyd Red Crow Westerman, 2007).

Before (and during) his career as an actor for mass audiences, Westerman was known in Native America as a folksinger and activist. His recordings included: *Custer Died for Your Sins* (based on his close friend Vine Deloria Jr.'s book of the same title), *Indian Country,* and *The Land is Your Mother.*

Floyd Red Crow Westerman at the premiere of the film Hidalgo at Hollywood's El Capitan Theatre, March 1, 2004. (Getty/Albert L. Ortega)

Westerman was a participant and performer at the first annual Native American Music Awards (popularly known as "Nammys") in 1996, performing with Joanne Shenandoah in a tribute for a Nammy Hall of Fame Inductee, the late Buddy Red Bow. Westerman also was named recipient of the Nammy Living Legend Award (2002). He received the Nammys' Best Country Recording for "A Tribute to Johnny Cash" in the 2006 Nammy awards. Cash was known throughout Indian Country for his support of Native-rights issues, evidenced as early as 1963 by release of an album, *Bitter Tears: Ballads of the American Indian,* with its sarcastic needling of George Armstrong Custer, its salute to treaty rights in *As Long As the Grass Shall Grow,* and the haunting *Ballad of Ira Hayes.*

Music was Westerman's first love. Born on the Sisseton-Wahpeton Dakota Sioux reservation in South Dakota, he was sent to boarding school. He left home at a young age with an old guitar and a suitcase, traveling across the United States, playing country music standards, as well as his own songs. Many of these songs were drawn from Native-rights controversies based on battles for the land, Native identity and sovereignty, as well as protection of the environment. He graduated from Northern State College in South Dakota, then moved to Denver where he performed in piano bars.

Westerman's first recording contract, signed in 1969, produced his first album, *Custer Died for Your Sins.* In 1970, his second collection of recorded songs reflected the same themes. Westerman was very popular outside the United States, where he performed at least 60 times (Actor's Goal, 2007).

The AIM became a major activity for Westerman shortly after its formation in 1968. He also acted as a spokesman for the International Indian Treaty Council, traveling around the world and appearing before the United Nations to advocate improved social and economic conditions for indigenous peoples. In 1982, these themes and environmental issues were the main focus of his third collection of recorded songs, *This Land Is Your Mother.* During his musical career, Westerman played with several well-known musicians, including Willie Nelson, Kris Kristofferson, Buffy St. Marie, Joni Mitchell, Jackson Browne, Harry Belafonte (to protest nuclear power), and Sting (to protest destruction of rain forests).

He has received many other awards, including a Congressional Certificate of Special Recognition, the Award for Generosity from the Americans for Indian Opportunity, Cultural Ambassador by the International Treaty Council, a Lifetime Achievement Award from the City of Los Angeles, and the Integrity Award from the Multicultural Motion Picture Association (Floyd Red Crow Westerman, 2007).

Westerman passed on to the spirit world on December 13, 2007, at Cedars Sinai Hospital in Los Angeles, following complications from leukemia. Mohawk journalist Doug George-Kanentiio remembered him this way: "Floyd . . . was not egotistical or full of rage. He went through the emotional and physical traumas of the notorious boarding school system yet whenever I met him he was given to laughter and ready for a good story. He was, in many ways, like his great friend Vine Deloria: aware of the absurdities of life but enjoying his time here. He was a strong presence on and off the stage and played a really hard guitar" (George, 2007).

Further Reading

"Actor's Goal: Indian Rights." *New York Times* in *Omaha World-Herald,* December 30, 2007, 8-A.

"Floyd Red Crow Westerman Journeys on to the Spirit World." Native American Music Awards, December 13, 2007. www.nativeamericanmusicawards.com

George-Kanentiio, Doug, Personal communication, December 18, 2007.

Whitebear, Bernie

(1937–2000)
Sin Aikst (Colville, Lake Indians)

Bernie Whitebear, a long-time Native American community activist, was part of a unique pan-ethnic consensus in the Seattle area that produced strong support for fishing rights, as well as the Daybreak Star Center, one of the country's most notable urban Indian centers. Whitebear was the major leader in founding the Daybreak Star Center, then served as its long-term director. "No one helped more Indians in need in the last century than Bernie Whitebear," said Vine Deloria Jr. (Reyes, 2006, back cover). Dean Chavers recalled Whitebear: "He was a soft-spoken person, given to working with people rather than confronting them. He was always ready with a *bon mot*, a joke, a tease, or a story. Some people called him a walking anecdote" (Chavers, 2007, 580).

Whitebear's vast sense of compassion led him to drive around Seattle seeking out Indians who needed help, an activity described by his brother, Lawney L. Reyes, in a book, *Bernie Whitebear: An Urban Indian's Quest for Justice* (2007). The book was described by D. Anthony Tyeeme-Clark in the *American Indian Culture & Research Journal* as "a flattering vision of an extraordinary Sin Aikst man, a precious human being, someone worthy of enduring emulation and far-reaching respect" (Tyeeme-Clark, 2007, 147).

Whitebear was part of the "Gang of Four," (also called "the Four Amigos") a unique group of pan-ethnic leaders in the Seattle area who united in a way that has been rare in American politics. A group of long-time friends who played important roles in various ethnic groups, Whitebear, with Latino leader Roberto Maestas, founder in 1972 and long-time director of El Centro de la Raza, Bob Santos, a Filipino and Asian community leader, and Larry Gossett, who for many years has exercised an important political role in the Black community, from student activist at the University of Washington to King County councilman.

Together, the Four Amigos lent support to each others' causes, such as Indian fishing rights, support for farm-worker rights, and a successful effort to rename [Rufus] King Country after Martin Luther King Jr. All four understood that ethnic identity and issues were not mutually exclusive. Maestas, for example, is partly Pueblo Indian, from New Mexico, and Whitebear (an adopted name; he was born as Bernard Reyes) was partially Latino.

Whitebear's Early Life

Whitebear was born in 1937 at the Colville Indian Agency in Nespelem, Eastern Washington, as a Sin Aikst (the phrase used by the Lake Indians to describe themselves) He graduated from Okanogan High School in 1955. After graduation, during 1956, he spent a frustrating year at the University of Washington, then dropped out. Whitebear bounced around short-term jobs in Tacoma.

During the summer of 1956, Whitebear met Bob Satiacum, a Puyallup fisherman and early activist who exercised his treaty fishing rights in local rivers and Tacoma's Commencement Bay, meanwhile enduring taunts from hundreds of white fishing people. Fishing was at best a part-time avocation, so a year later Whitebear decided to make a major change in his life. He joined the U.S. Army, became a paratrooper with the 101st Airborne, and a Green Beret. Returning to Seattle in 1959, he went to work at the Boeing Company in Seattle as an aircraft installer.

Whitebear found that he had a natural stage presence. With several other Boeing workers he staged *Annie Get Your Gun,* playing Sitting Bull. In one scene, he toted Annie across the state. This worked well as long as Whitebear, who was a short man, carried a diminutive Annie. In one staging, however, the actress playing Annie was larger than Whitebear, so "when Bernard struggled to carry her across the stage floor . . . . the audience broke into uncontrollable laughter" (Reyes, 2006, 89).

Later, Whitebear assembled an Indian dance group with the Koleda Dance Ensemble, a Balkan group, and toured Greece and Turkey, then Britain and France.

At the same time, Whitebear was looking for ways to organize volunteer doctors and dentists to provide services to Native people, which led to the Seattle Indian Health Board, of which he became executive director in 1968. He also sought to raise Indians' public profile in Seattle by staging pow-wows, some of which were quite large, big enough to assemble in the Seattle Center's Arena, a basketball and trade-show venue. Whitebear also became friends with Puyallup, Nisqually, and Muckleshoot fishing-rights activists on Puget Sound as the "fishing wars" intensified in the 1960s.

Occupation of Fort Lawton

Whitebear had cultivated a dream for many years, that Seattle-area Indians would build a community center to replace a small, dark, space in downtown Seattle. When he and other activists learned that the U.S. Army was about to declare as surplus Fort Lawton, northwest of downtown, near Seattle's Queen Anne neighborhood, they jumped at the chance, using the occupation of Alcatraz Island as a model. Indians and supporters arrived from all over the United States to bolster the occupation during 1970. While the occupation of Alcatraz did not produce any long-lasting results, the Fort Lawton action eventually produced the Daybreak Star Center, with a sweeping view of Puget Sound. Whitebear, a leader of the occupation as head of United Indians of All Tribes, became executive director of Daybreak Star, and held the position for almost 30 years.

Seattle's inter-ethnic alliances gave the occupation of Fort Lawton extra support, and a special "edge." The media came calling, too, when they sensed the irony of the Indians "attacking" an Army fort. The base remained active even after plans to declare it surplus were being considered. In the spring of 1970, a half-mile-long caravan of cars lined up to blockade at the base's north and south entrances. Indians and their allies climbed fences, hauled in tipi poles, and prepared to stay. Military police evicted them, after which they returned. The confrontation lasted seven years before a compromise was reached: the city of Seattle received most of the old fort for a park, but the United Indians of All Tribes received land on which to build Daybreak Star, which was begun in 1975 and opened two years later.

The occupation of the fort was very much a pan-Indian movement affair, reinforced by the name of the group that coordinated it—United Indians of All Tribes—which became a foundation once the occupation ended and the bureaucratic battle was joined to acquire land and raise money necessary for a cultural center. Seattle increasingly had become home to Native people from a wide variety of tribes and nations. Twenty acres was granted in 1971, and the 20,000 square foot Daybreak Star Center opened with 3,000 people in attendance May 13, 1977.

The name and the building's design were inspired by words of the Lakota holy man Black Elk:

> Then as I stood there two men were coming from the east head-first like arrows flying and in between them rose the Daybreak Star. They came and gave an herb to me and said "with this on earth you shall undertake anything and do it. " It was the daybreak star herb, the herb of understanding, and they told me to drop it on the earth. I saw it falling far and when it struck the earth it rooted and grew and flowered four blossoms on one stem, a black, a white, a scarlet, and a yellow. And the rays from there streamed upward to the heavens so that all creatures saw it, and in no place was there darkness. (Reyes, 2006, 113)

The *Seattle Post-Intelligencer* described the center as a work of art, inside and out. The major inside corridors featured work by major Native artists from across the continent, acquired with $80,000 that Whitebear had raised while a member of the Seattle Arts Commission. The center soon became the site of events ranging from weddings to dinner theaters, salmon feasts, inter-tribal meetings, and pow-wows. The center also distributed day-to-day social and health services for people who needed them, with an emphasis that people of all ethnicities were welcome—the four sacred colors that Black Elk had described. With 120 people on staff by 1985, programs included child development, an art gallery, and referrals to employment, education, foster care, medical and dental care, as well as many others.

Even as he was wheeling and dealing with Seattle's movers and shakers, Whitebear sat in police squad cars at night to make sure Indians on the streets were being treated fairly. At one police hearing, he said: "Remember: it isn't that Indians can't handle alcohol; they simply can't handle this life" (Reyes, 2006, 116). He also counseled young Indian inmates in penitentiaries around Washington State.

Whitebear passed over in July 16, 2000, after a three-year battle with colon cancer. Washington Gov. Gary Locke, Seattle's mayor, Paul Schell, and U.S. senators Patty Murray of Washington and Daniel Inouye of Hawaii attended his funeral. On August 2, 2000, a long procession of cars led by a police escort left the Daybreak Star Center for the Washington State Convention Center, carrying Whitebear's body to one of the largest funerals in Seattle's history. The Great Hall at the Seattle Convention Center was filled to capacity with friends, dignitaries, and the many whose lives he had touched in one way or another by the compassionate man with the silver hair—governors, senators, mayors, the great and the humble, including people from many dozens of Native nations and tribes who saw him off to the spirit world.

Further Reading

Chavers, Dean. *Modern American Indian Leaders: Their Lives and Their Works.* 2 vols. Lewiston, ID: Edwin Mellen Press, 2007.

Reyes, Lawney L. *Bernie Whitebear: An Urban Indian's Quest for Justice.* Tucson: University of Arizona Press, 2006.

Tyeeme-Clark, D. Anthony. "Review, *Bernie Whitebear: An Urban Indian's Quest for Justice,*" *American Indian Culture & Research Journal* 31, no. 1 (2007): 145–48.

Whiteclay, Nebraska, and the American Indian Movement

The AIM has maintained a long-standing campaign to limit alcoholic beverage sales to Indians in the tiny border town of Whiteclay, Nebraska, south of the Pine Ridge Oglala Lakota reservation, population 12, where only major business in town is catering to Native American drunkenness. From four metal shacks along Whiteclay's main road, 13,000 cans of beer and malt liquor sell on an average day (an annual sale of more than 5 million cans for more than roughly $4 million), nearly all of it to Oglala Sioux from the Pine Ridge Indian Reservation, which banned alcohol sales during the 1970s (Johansen, 1998, 5).

The favored drink is Hurricane High Gravity Lager, a malt liquor that is 8.1 percent alcohol, two-thirds the strength of most wines. Aside from its four alcohol outlets, Whiteclay's has two small grocery stores and an auto-body shop. The sheriff's office of Sheridan County is responsible for patrolling Whiteclay, but it has only five officers who operate out of a small office 19 miles away. The Pine Ridge police have 38 officers, but no jurisdiction in the town. Tom Poor Bear, an Oglala Lakota activist who organized against alcohol sales at Whiteclay, said: "Oglalas spend millions of dollars in Whiteclay and there isn't even a bathroom we are allowed to use there. Whiteclay is one of the dirtiest little places in Nebraska . . . and we are tired of Whiteclay laughing at us all the way to their banks with our money" (Chapman, 2001, 190).

Whiteclay was sited on what was once Oglala Lakota land; many Oglalas have advocated (without legal success) that the reservation border be moved a few hundred yards south to put the alcohol peddlers out of business. Claims of Lakota control to the ground on which Whiteclay sits are based on surveys taken for the Fort Laramie Treaty of 1868, which place Whiteclay within reservation borders. Documents related to the Dawes (Allotment) Act, notably legislation passed by Congress in 1889 to break up what was then called "The Great Sioux Nation" also support this assertion. An executive order issued in 1882 by President Chester Arthur created

American Indians drinking on a street in Whiteclay, Nebraska, just before an American Indian Movement protest march June 7, 2003. (AP Photo/William Lauer)

a 50-square-mile "buffer zone" (which includes the site of Whiteclay) south of the Pine Ridge reservation expressly to curtail the liquor trade. This order was rescinded on January 25, 1904, by President Theodore Roosevelt with the rationale that non-Indians needed the land.

Indians' Murders Protested in 1999

On June 26, 1999—123 years and one day after their ancestors had removed George Armstrong Custer's scalp—Lakotas gathered in Whiteclay to demand details describing how Wilson "Wally" Black Elk, 40, and Ronald Hard Heart, 39, had died. Their partially decomposed bodies had been found June 8. Many people at Pine Ridge believe that the way in which Black Elk and Hard Heart died was similar to how two other Lakota, Wesley Bad Heart Bull, and Raymond Yellow Thunder, were killed during AIM's early days—beatings to death by white toughs having what they regarded as a sporting time with inebriated Oglala Lakotas.

A month and more after the killings of Black Elk and Hard Heart, the men's reservation relatives knew little or nothing, officially, of how they had died. Law enforcement officials in Nebraska and FBI agents talked vaguely of "foul play" and "following leads," while anger spread at Pine Ridge. Pine Ridge tribal police chief Stan Star Comes Out told the Omaha *World-Herald* that the remains of the two men had been wounded and bloody. He also said the two men had been bludgeoned to death. The bodies were found on the Pine Ridge (South Dakota) side of the line, but many Lakota believe the men were murdered in Nebraska, closer to Whiteclay, after which their bodies were dragged across the border.

Lakota community responses to the deaths of Yellow Thunder and Bad Heart Bull provided a provocation (one of many) for the AIM occupation of Wounded Knee the next year. Yellow Thunder was kidnapped and beaten to death during the middle of February, 1972, in Gorton, Nebraska (about 25 miles southeast of Whiteclay, and 13 miles south of Pine Ridge) by several white toughs. Four young men were charged with manslaughter (not murder), and two of them convicted. By March, Gordon was the scene of rallies of more than 1,000 Lakota and allies demanding justice for Yellow Thunder. Two brothers who were convicted of manslaughter served 10 months (of a two-year sentence) and two years (of a six-year sentence), respectively. Shortly after the murder of Yellow Thunder in 1972, Wesley Bad Heart Bull was stabbed to death by a young white man near Custer, South Dakota (in the Black Hills southwest of Rapid City). The assailant was charged with second-degree manslaughter, provoking demonstrations, some of which turned violent, at the courthouse in Custer, organized by AIM.

In 1999, some of the major organizers were the same as they had been in Gordon and Custer—AIMsters with many more lines on their faces. They listened to speeches by Russell Means, Clyde Bellecourt, and Dennis Banks, among others, protesting basic injustices, such as young white men's penchant for taking out their aggressions (sometimes with fatal results) on drunken Indians near the dusty streets of Whiteclay.

For years, Nebraska officials had been warned by activist Frank LaMere and others that the situation in Whiteclay could explode. One day during the summer of 1997, LaMere, a Winnebago who was executive director of the Nebraska Inter-Tribal Development Corp., visited Whiteclay. He counted 32 intoxicated Indians on the town's streets at 5:15 in the morning, and 47 drunks on the streets during the afternoon, some of whom were fighting with each other. Several other Indians were passed out at the intersection of Nebraska Highway 87 with the road that leads to the reservation. A few of them were urinating on the street (Johansen, 1998, 5).

Shortly after he visited Whiteclay, LaMere asked the Nebraska Liquor Control Commission to shut Whiteclay down. "I don't know what constitutes infractions of liquor laws in Whiteclay, but my good sense tells me there is something terribly wrong . . ." LaMere told Toni Heinzl of the Omaha *World-Herald*. "What I saw . . . in Whiteclay would not be acceptable in Omaha of Lincoln," LaMere continued (Johansen, 1998, 5).

The Pine Ridge reservation in 1996 had an alcoholism-related death rate of 61.9 per 100,000 people, twice the average for Native American reservations, and nine times the national average of 7.1. The liver-disease death rate at Pine Ridge (Shannon County) at 211.3 per 100,000 (caused mainly by alcoholism) is 13 times that of the United States (Fuller, 2012, 51). On the two-mile highway between Pine Ridge village and Whiteclay, tribal police issue at least 1,000 driving-while-intoxicated citations per year. Despite the police presence, residents who live along the road are constantly pestered by drunks. Several family dogs have been shot to death along the road as well.

Protest Marches in Whiteclay

In reaction to the murders of Hard Heart and Black Elk, a "Rally for Justice"—250 people walking accompanied by about 150 automobiles—traversed the two-lane blacktop to "take Whiteclay back" on June 26. As the larger rally was breaking up in Whiteclay, about 25 to 30 people trashed a grocery store, V. J.'s Market, in Whiteclay. It was said that V. J.'s owner, Vic Clarke, had treated Lakota in a demeaning manner. The store's freezer cases were destroyed and its cash registers doused with lighter fluid. Groceries were strewn through the store.

On Saturday, July 3, 1999, about 100 sheriff's deputies and state patrol officers, many of them in riot gear, barricaded Whiteclay's business district. Ironically, the Nebraska State Patrol had met one of the protesters' demands: for Friday and Saturday at least, the beer stores of Whiteclay were closed, on one of their busiest weekends of the year. During Friday afternoon, caravans of cars from Pine Ridge circled Whiteclay and its barricades in an air of ghostly quiet, using several back roads.

Aside from a few rocks thrown and nine brief arrests (including Russell Means), the July 3 march came and went without notable physical contact between the Lakota Sioux and the hundred SWAT-suited police officers barricading Whiteclay. Many participants in the march stressed the spiritual nature of their actions. Marchers stopped four times to pray (and to give elderly marchers some rest) during the hour and a half it took the group of several hundred people to move from Pine Ridge to Whiteclay on a hot and unusually humid day.

As they approached Whiteclay, marchers debated whether to cross a line of yellow plastic tape that police had strung across the road into the village. Most urged restraint, but Russell Means urged the group on. One man who was riding a pinto pony tried to crash the line, but was stopped by police. Means and the eight others who were arrested also stepped over the line, briefly, as they were cited for failure to obey a lawful order, to establish a basis for a later court case (the activists contended that their arrests were illegal). They were released an hour later. Other marchers threw mud at the helmeted troopers. A few spit on them, and cursed. One protester plastered a bumper sticker reading "YOU ARE ON INDIAN LAND" across one officer's helmet.

As the dust settled in Whiteclay following the second rally, the beer stores opened briefly Monday morning, but closed once again after Clyde Bellecourt told Stuart Kozel, owner of the Jumping Eagle Inn, that opening his store would provoke another confrontation with AIM.

On Saturday, July 10, a smaller rally was held, followed by another march and motorcade from Pine Ridge to Whiteclay. Roughly 100 people on foot and in cars sang and drummed as they paraded up and down Whiteclay streets, unimpeded by police this time. AIM members posted "eviction notices" on the four beer stores, then withdrew to tipis and tents erected on the site where the bodies of Black Elk and Hard Heart had been found June 8. The people in the camp pledged to maintain it (along with weekly demonstrations in Whiteclay) until the border town goes "dry."

In the meantime, LaMere, one of nine people who had been arrested at the initial rally, appealed again to the Nebraska Liquor Control Commission to shut down Whiteclay's beer businesses permanently. Once again, the board did not act; within days the activists were gone and most of the Indians remaining on the streets of Whiteclay were, once again, falling down drunk.

The Oglala Sioux File Suit

By 2012, AIM demands to stop Whiteclay's alcohol sales had become the gist of an Oglala Sioux tribal lawsuit. The tribe hired Tom White, an Omaha attorney, and authorized him to sue the town's alcohol merchants as well as their suppliers. By that time, annual sales were 5 million cans (Duggan, 2012, 1-A). The lawsuit named Whiteclay's four beer stores, four distributors in Western Nebraska, and several large, name-brand brewers. The Oglala Sioux Tribe also filed an amended complaint in Lincoln, Nebraska U.S. District Court seeking an injunction that would limit beer sales in Whiteclay "to an amount that can reasonably be consumed" in a village of fewer than 12 people with no public drinking establishments (Duggan, February 23, 20–12, 6-B).

White, announcing the lawsuit February 9 at a press conference on the steps of the State Capitol in Lincoln, asserted that the beer sales are illegal because nearly all of it is consumed on the Pine Ridge reservation, where alcoholic beverages are banned. "They are helping people violate the law," White said. "This lawsuit is about holding them responsible and stopping the devastation of an entire people and culture" (Duggan, 2012, 1-A).

The lawsuit demands $500 million in monetary damages. Pine Ridge tribal president John Yellow Bird Steele, said that 90 percent of criminal cases in the reservation court system and an equal proportion of illnesses there were caused or aggravated by alcohol. "We believe we can't get ahead, or function, without Whiteclay being addressed," he said (Williams, 2012). Pine Ridge tribal police made 20,000 alcohol-related arrests during 2011. Twenty-five percent of babies at Pine Ridge are born with fetal alcohol syndrome or fetal alcohol spectrum disorder (Williams, 2012). White said that 85 percent of families at Pine Ridge are affected by alcoholism. One-fourth of babies there suffer from symptoms of fetal-alcohol disorders. According to an account by Timothy Williams in the *New York Times,*

> After the lawsuit was filed, Whiteclay's two-lane road, Highway 87, bustled with traffic driving to and from the beer stores. Dozens of people in various states of inebriation wandered along the road. Other men and women were passed out in front of abandoned buildings. A [recording of] Hank Williams Jr's [song], "I'd Rather Be Gone," was among the detritus along the road, as well as empty liquor bottles, a copy of "Tabernacle Hymns No. 3," soiled clothing and a dead puppy. (Williams, 2012)

Victor Clarke, who has lived in Whiteclay 19 years and owns Arrowhead Foods (which does not sell alcohol) said that residents of nearby towns want Whiteclay's problems contained there. "People don't want Whiteclay to go away," he said. "The state of Nebraska doesn't want Whiteclay to go away because it allows problems to be isolated in this one little place. You hear people in the towns around here, saying, 'We don't want these guys in our town'" (Williams, 2012).

Seeking to stem beer sales at Whiteclay through the Nebraska Legislature, opponents of Whiteclay's commerce sought to enact an "Alcohol Impact Zone," only to find that industry lobbyists had beat them to the punch. Such zones, which have been implemented in several cities where alcohol is a severe problem, limit store hours, and prohibit sale of single beers and high-alcohol content brands. Whiteclay stores are generally open from 8 A.M. to 11 P.M. The bill stalled in the General Affairs Committee as its sponsors learned that seven of eight members had received $21,000 in campaign contributions during the previous five years from Anheuser Busch, brewers of Hurricane High Gravity, the malt liquor of choice at Whiteclay. Nebraska's Republican governor, Dave Heineman, also had received $40,000 from the company since 2002 (Williams, 2012, A-14, A-18). State Senator Tyson Larson, a member of the General Affairs Committee who has received contributions from Anheuser Busch believes firmly that alcohol consumption (even addictive drunkenness) is a personal choice that the state has no business regulating (Williams, 2012, A-18).

The beer companies agreed with Larson. On April 27, 2012, they filed a motion to dismiss the case, arguing that a ruling restricting beer sales at Whiteclay would force them to discriminate against residents of Pine Ridge. As the beer distributors defended the right of Lakotas to buy their products at Whiteclay on freedom-of-speech grounds, AIM activist Frank LaMere, a member of the Winnebago Tribe of Nebraska, said the state of Nebraska had "blood on their hands." Any action short of shutting down Whiteclay "and crippling the enterprise that peddles alcoholism among the Lakota people is unacceptable," he said. LaMere continued:

> The death toll exacted on the Lakota people by Anheuser Busch and its partners continues to rise, and the sooner the Sheridan County hell-hole can be leveled, the better off Nebraska will be. County, state and liquor industry officials have long known of the lawlessness and illegal activities that go on there, but they have been allowed to run from their responsibilities as public trustees by reducing the sad reality to a discussion about personal responsibility and market demand. (LaMere, 2012)

The Oglala Lakotas' $500 million suit against Whiteclay's beer dealers and distributors was dismissed in a federal court in Nebraska during the first week of October, 2012. After the dismissal, the Pine Ridge tribal government discussed another way to hobble the beer sales at Whiteclay, legalizing alcohol consumption on the reservation. That might reduce traffic accidents caused by drunken drivers in the Whiteclay area, and allow the tribe to tax alcohol sales on the reservation (Williams, October 5, 2012, A-15).

Further Reading

"Beer Companies Seek Dismissal of Oglala Sioux Tribe's Lawsuit." *Associated Press in Omaha World-Herald*, May 1, 2012, 2-B.

Chapman, Serle L. *We, the People: Of Earth and Elders, Vol. II*. Missoula, MT: Mountain Press Publishing Co., 2001.

Duggan, Joe. "Amid Lawsuit, Tribe Seeks Limit on Beer Sales in Town." *Omaha World-Herald,* February 23, 2012, 6-B.

Duggan, Joe. "Tribe Goes to Source in Lawsuit over Alcohol Sales: The Oglala Sioux Target the Whiteclay, Neb. Supply Chain from Stores to Brewers." *Omaha World-Herald,* February 10, 2012, 1-A, 2-A.

Fuller, Alexandra. "In the Shadow of Wounded Knee." *National Geographic*, August, 2012, 30–67.

Johansen, Bruce E. "Whiteclay, Nebraska: The Town That Booze Built," *Native Americas* 15, no. 1 (Spring, 1998): 5.

LaMere, Frank. "Blood on Their Hands." *New York Times*, May 16, 2012. http://www.nytimes.com/roomfordebate/2012/05/16/how-to-address-alcoholism-on-indian-reservations/nebraska-and-anheuser-busch-caused-the-disaster-at-pine-ridge-and-whiteclay

Williams, Timothy. "At Tribe's Door, a Hub of Beer and Heartache." *New York Times,* March 6, 2012. http://www.nytimes.com/2012/03/06/us/next-to-tribe-with-alcohol-ban-a-hub-of-beer.html

Williams, Timothy. "Indian Beer Bill Stalls; Industry Money Flows." *New York Times,* April 12, 2012, A-14, A-18.

Williams, Timothy. "Tribe Considers Lifting Alcohol Ban in South Dakota." *New York Times*, October 5, 2012, A-15.

White Roots of Peace

Pollution of the Akwesasne Mohawk community's air, land, and water provoked Mohawks to leave home and seek work across the United States and Canada, mainly after World War II. Many worked in the military and urban construction trades, among the legendary "Mohawks in High Steel." The traditional farming and hunting economy no longer supported a growing population. In so doing, Akwesasne people, mostly men, became acquainted with the rising clamor for recognition of civil and human rights by Native and other disenfranchised peoples. They became leaders in national forums, of which *Akwesasne Notes* was one. The North American Indian Traveling College and White Roots of Peace also spring from the same roots.

The White Roots of Peace which soon traveled across the United States as a mobile consciousness-raising group, had its origins in the Akwesasne Counselor Organization, founded by Scots-Irish activist Ray Fadden, who was married into (and adopted by) the Akwesasne Mohawks. Fadden started the group during the mid-1930s, as it "traveled far and wide inculcating Indian pride among Mohawk youth . . . hoping to influence a group of young Mohawk . . . to take up leadership roles in the Mohawk Longhouse" (Johnson et al., 1996, 16–17). During the "Red Power" era, the White Roots of Peace became a mobile teaching group composed of musicians, dancers, speakers, artists, and writers from dozens of Native nations across North America operating under the wing of the Mohawk Nation.

Jerry Gambill, who also was the first editor of *Akwesasne Notes* (a non-Indian who also worked in the Canadian Department of Indian Affairs) worked with Ernest Benedict and others to build the White Roots of Peace into a traveling troupe that visited Native peoples, urban and rural, in both Canada and the United States, sharing Iroquois culture, most notably the Great Binding Law (also called the Great Law of Peace).

The White Roots carried Native-produced publications such as *Akwesasne Notes* across the United States and Canada, and stocked other magazines and newspapers, as well as books related to Native American cultural revival. The group often bypassed mainstream media and took their message directly to urban Indian centers, Indian reservations, prisons, and schools, as they taught people to organize on the community level, with a philosophy rooted in Indian sovereignty and indigenous law. The White Roots carried posters, books, and other activist artwork, and provided entertainment by traditional dancers and singers. The group often took its educational mission to colleges and universities.

The White Roots of Peace also visited the site of major events in the Red Power movement, such as the occupation of Alcatraz in 1969, the BIA occupation in 1972, and the siege of Wounded Knee in 1973. Connections were made with Mohawks far and wide; Richard Oakes, an ironworker who was 26 years of age at Alcatraz, was from Akwesasne. He played a major role in the occupation at Alcatraz.

Further Reading

George-Kanentiio, Doug. "*Akwesasne Notes*: How the Mohawk Nation Created a Newspaper and Shaped Contemporary Native America." Manuscript copy provided to author, September 15, 2011.

Johnson, Troy, Joane Nagel, and Duane Champaign, eds. *American Indian Activism: Alcatraz to the Longest Walk*. Urbana: University of Illinois Press, 1996.

Wilson, Richard

(1936–1990)
Oglala Lakota

Richard Wilson, a diehard opponent of the AIM, was the single most powerful political leader on the Pine Ridge reservation during the occupation of Wounded Knee in 1973, and three years afterward during which the reservation was enveloped in violent factional conflict.

Wilson was the first Oglala Lakota tribal chairperson to serve two consecutive terms. He worked as a self-employed plumber, owner of a gas station, and on other short-term projects after his defeat by Al Trimble for the tribal chairmanship in 1976. Wilson also held the traditional role of pipe carrier. He was known for feeding anyone who came to his door, and he had a major role in beginning a Lakota community college on the reservation, as well as a number of other tribal enterprises. Wilson died of a heart attack in 1990, as he was preparing to run for a third term as tribal chairman.

Steve Hendricks (2006, 47), in *The Unquiet Grave: The FBI and the Struggle for the Soul of Indian Country* (2006), sketched Wilson:

> He favored dark glasses and a habiliment of High Plains haute: two parts polyester, one part snakeskin. His hair was martially buzzed, his head was of medicine ball proportion, and the blood vessels of his cheeks suggested he was not afraid of a good tipple. His body was less brick than well-filled bag.

Alvin M. Josephy Jr. described Wilson as "a short, corpulent man who drank heavily, indulged in threats and bullying, and walked around in dark glasses that made him look like a caricature of a rural sheriff," a man who became tribal chairman in 1974 as he was "charged with buying hundreds of votes with drinks and payoffs, using money which bootleggers and other whites allegedly gave him for promises of favors and contracts on the reservation" (Josephy, 1982, 243). Once in office, Wilson used federal money to hire his own personal police force, the GOONs (Guardians of the Oglala Nation), described by Josephy as "composed largely of unemployed toughs and Wilson's drinking companions and relatives . . . [who] roughed up and threatened anyone they disliked or who they thought was opposed to Wilson" (1982, 244). The GOONs did more than rough people up. They killed them.

Dissent at Pine Ridge

By early in 1973, dissident was boiling over on the Pine Ridge reservation, just as traditional people there asked AIM for help against Wilson, who was accused by full-bloods in outlying districts of favoring mixed bloods (most notably members of his family) for employment with the tribe on a reservation where the government was nearly the only source of steady work. Nepotism was nothing new at Pine Ridge, but what Wilson had introduced was a personal police force—Guardians of the Oglala Nation—GOONs to its adversaries—who physically intimidated anyone who exercised his or her first-amendment rights in ways that Wilson found disagreeable.

When AIM began to make itself obvious on Pine Ridge at the invitation of Wilson's opponents, tensions increased. At one point, early in 1973, Russell Means was "welcomed" home with a beating by two GOONs. Soon, Means was campaigning against Wilson for political office, calling him a liar, a drunk, dictator, drunk, embezzler, and other things. Wilson called Means an outsider, a Communist, and a young long-hair worthy of having his braids trimmed.

Early in 1973, February 11, following AIM's activities at the BIA headquarters in Washington, D.C., and at the Custer, South Dakota riot, about 75 U.S. Marshals of its elite rapid response team, the Special Operations Group (SOG), who were trained as a domestic version of the U.S. Army's Green Berets, took up positions in tiny Pine Ridge Village. Dissidents called their outpost "Camp Wilson." People drove to town from miles away to see a machine-gun nest that they had installed (Smith and Warrior, 1996, 196).

One result of the escalating conflict between Wilson and Oglala Lakota traditionalists allied with AIM was the 71-day occupation of Wounded Knee in 1973. The struggle between AIM and Wilson also took place in the realm of tribal electoral politics. When Wilson sought reelection in 1974, Russell Means, an Oglala who had helped found AIM, challenged him. In the primary Wilson trailed Means, 667 votes to 511. Wilson won the final election over Means by fewer than 200 votes in balloting that the U.S. Commission on Civil Rights later found was permeated with fraud. The Civil Rights Commission recommended a new election, which was not held; Wilson answered his detractors by stepping up the terror, examples of which were described in a chronology kept by the Wounded Knee Legal Defense-Offense Committee. One of the GOON's favorite weapons was the automobile; officially, such deaths could be reported as "traffic accidents."

Wilson sometimes supervised GOON beatings personally. During February 1975, traditionalists at Pine Ridge invited a team of attorneys and legal workers to Pine Ridge to gather evidence against Wilson. After a day of work, they returned to the small

Cessna aircraft they were using to find it riddled with bullets. Forced to drive to Rapid City, the attorneys and aides were stopped at a roadblock of several cars filled with GOONs at the western edge of Pine Ridge. About 30 men, Wilson included, emerged from the cars, tore open the convertible's roof, and grabbed the lawyers and aides as Wilson shouted "Stomp 'em!" The lawyers and legal aides were beaten and told they would be killed if they returned to the reservation. This account was documented by the Wounded Knee Defense-Offense Committee, and described by syndicated columnist Jack Anderson in several hundred newspapers during May 1975. Roger Finzel, an attorney from Sioux Falls, South Dakota and Eda Gordon, a legal worker, supported the account with a polygraph test (Johansen and Maestas, 1979, 88).

Wilson also had a formidable array of supporters on the reservation, many of whom criticized AIM for being urban-based and insensitive to reservation residents' needs. Mona Wilson, one of Wilson's daughters, who was 17 years of age in 1973, recalled that he cried in his mother's arms at the time. Speaking about the events two decades later, Wilson's wife, Yvonne, and two daughters recalled him as a kind and compassionate father who had the interests of his people at heart. They said that Wilson supported AIM when it protested the 1972 murder of Raymond Yellow Thunder in the reservation border town of Gordon, Nebraska. Only later, as events culminated in the weeks-long siege of Wounded Knee, did Wilson and AIM leaders become deadly enemies.

Further Reading

Hendricks, Steve. *The Unquiet Grave: The FBI and the Struggle for the Soul of Indian Country.* New York: Thunder's Mouth Press, 2006.

Johansen, Bruce E. "Peltier and the Posse." *The Nation*, October 1, 1977, 304–07.

Johansen, Bruce E. and Roberto F. Maestas. *Wasi'chu: The Continuing Indian Wars.* New York: Monthly Review Press, 1979.

Josephy, Alvin M., Jr. *Now That the Buffalo's Gone: A Study of Today's American Indians.* New York: Knopf, 1982.

LaMay, Konnie. "20 Years of Anguish." *Indian Country Today,* February 25, 1993. n.p.

Matthiessen, Peter. *In the Spirit of Crazy Horse.* New York: Viking, 1991.

Smith, Paul Chaat and Robert Allen Warrior. *Like a Hurricane: The Indian Movement from Alcatraz to Wounded Knee.* New York: The New Press, 1996.

U.S. Commission on Civil Rights. "Report of Investigation: Oglala Sioux Tribe, General Election, 1974." October, mimeographed. Washington, D.C.: Civil Rights Commission.

Women of All Red Nations (WARN)

Women within the AIM formed their own organizations to combat sexism. In 1974, Lorilei DeCora Means, a Minneconjou Lakota, Madonna Thunderhawk, and Phyllis Young, both Hunkpapa Lakota, established Women of All Red Nations

(WARN). The women said that they, and their children, bore special burdens of inadequate health care, poor nutrition, government sterilization policies, domestic violence, unemployment, poverty, and drug abuse on reservations and in urban Indian communities. After Wounded Knee, with most of AIM's men charged with a seemingly endless rounds of criminal prosecutions, women had to maintain the movement's organization was well as home life (Josephy et al., 1999, 52).

Women and Tradition

The women of WARN organized within a rich context of Native American matriarchal and matrilineal tradition. While patriarchal societies do exist in Native America, they are rare. The majority recognize an important role of women in the life of society as a whole, as well as within the home. Unlike Anglo-American cultures, Native American tradition does not subordinate the role of the home to the world of work that pays money. As transmitters of culture through generations, women have an immensely important role in most indigenous cultures. They also play a crucial role in politics. The Haudenosaunee (Iroquois), for example, have a women's council based on its clans, which selects leaders for a more visible Grand Council that is composed of men. A favorite Iroquois women's aphorism is: "It's Okay that the men go out ahead—so that we can tell them where to go." If men take actions contrary to Iroquois law while serving on the council, the women have a right to impeach, and replace, them (Mann, 2000, 178–79).

Women, especially elders, have been prominent in modern-day Native social and political movements. Emma Yazzie, who was 70 years of age during the 1970s, became an important Navajo leader against coal strip mining as her herds of sheep were devastated by mining pollution (Johansen and Maestas, 1979, 143–44).

Yazzie took visitors to the bottom of coal strip mines near her hogan to watch draglines at work, telling them: "Don't go alone. They'll turn you away. They're afraid of me!" (Johansen and Maestas, 1979, 145). Yazzie had been known to show her disgust at the mining by unearthing surveyors' sticks and dumping them on supervisors' desks. Yazzie found herself between coal strip mines and the Four Corners coal-fired electrical plant, which puts out a polluting plume so large that NASA astronauts observed it from Earth orbit. Her sheep had, by 1976, become small, skinny, and sickly, with gray wool. The Four Corners plant exports power to Los Angeles, Phoenix, Las Vegas, Nevada, and other cities in the region. Yazzie's Hogan had no electricity.

Elder women such as Janet McCloud and Ramona Bennett played important roles in assertions of fishing rights in Western Washington during the 1960s and 1970s. An elder Nisqually woman described how she protected young men who were fishing against arrest by state game agents:

> One of the boys went down to the river to fish, and his mother went up on the bank. And she said: "This boy is nineteen years old and we've been fighting

on this river for as many years as he's been alive. And no one is going to pound my son around, no one is going to arrest him. No one is going to arrest my son, or I am going to shoot them." And she had a rifle. (Katz, 1977, 147)

Women such as Ellen Moves Camp and Gladys Bissonette assumed leadership in organization of the Oglala Sioux Civil Rights Organization (OSCRO) and the work of the AIM at Pine Ridge during the early 1970s, including the 71-day occupation by AIM of Wounded Knee in 1973.

Sexism and Feminist Philosophy

Ironically, one of the women's largest problems within AIM, at least initially, was the young men's insufficient knowledge of Native matriarchal and matrilineal traditions. Many of them had been raised in cities, with a sense of ghetto macho. They had to be educated out of it, and, as the years passed and they studied traditions, this changed.

The organization of WARN, on the model of a traditional woman's society, was part of that process. Other women's societies were formed as well; Janet McCloud's Northwest Indian Women's Circle, started in 1981, was an example, as was the Indigenous Women's Network founded by Winona LaDuke (White Earth Chippewa) and Ingrid Wasinawatok-El Issa (Oneida). Wasinawatok-El Issa was very active in AIM and in the International Indian Treaty Council as well.

Phyllis Young, a WARN cofounder, explained: "Our organization of an Indian woman's organization is not a criticism or division from our men. In fact, it's the exact opposite. Only in this way can we organize ourselves as Indian women to meet our responsibilities, to be fully supportive of the men, to work in tandem with them as partners" (Jaimes and Halsey, 1992, 329).

Many Native American women found themselves differing from white feminists who argued that the main problem was male supremacy. "To this, I have to say, with all due respect, *bullshit,*" said Janet McCloud. "Our problems are what they've been for the last several hundred years: white supremacism and colonialism. And that's a supremacism and colonialism of which white feminists are still very much a part" (Jaimes and Halsey, 1992, 332).

Of the 65 or more Native people killed for political reasons on the Pine Ridge reservation between 1973 and 1976, at least 21 were women and two were children (Jaimes and Halsey, 1992, 328). Madonna Thunderhawk, a cofounder of WARN, and a Hunkpapa Lakota AIM member, said: that "Indian women have had to be strong because of what this colonialist system has done to our men . . . alcohol, suicides, car wrecks ….And after Wounded Knee, while all that persecution of the men was going on, we women had to keep things going" (Jaimes and Halsey, 1992, 328).

Lorilei DeCora Means said, as WARN was being organized:

We are *American Indian* women, in that order. We are oppressed, first and foremost, as American Indians, as peoples colonized by the United States of

America, not as women. As Indians, we can never forget that. Our survival—the survival of every one of us—man, woman, and child—depends on it. Decolonization is the agenda, the whole agenda, and until it is accomplished it is the only agenda that counts for American Indians." (Jaimes and Halsey, 1992, 314)

Use of BIA Secret Files

Following AIM's occupation of the BIA head office in Washington, D.C., at the conclusion of the Trail of Broken Treaties during November of 1972, WARN seized secret files recording the involuntary sterilization of Native American women in large numbers during the 1960s and 1970s. The sterilizations—more than 3,400 at three Indian Health Service hospitals alone—were the last official part of a eugenics movement that had been more popular in the United States during the 1920s and 1930s, when several states passed laws restricting reproduction of people officials regarded as socially dysfunctional and unproductive. These laws fell out of favor after the Nazis took them to even more extreme lengths during the 1930s and 1940s in Germany and its conquered territories. The BIA was one place where the policies had survived. Native American women reacted with rage.

In a study released during 1974, WARN said that as many as 42 percent of Native women in the reproductive age range had been sterilized (Jaimes and Halsey, 1992, 326). As a result of political organizing spurred by this rage, the Indian Health Service was transferred from the BIA to the Department of Health and Human Services in 1978, as sterilizations stopped. This campaign was regarded as a survival issue affecting future generations, along with, according to Paula Gunn Allen,

> Alcoholism and drug abuse (our own and that of our husbands, lovers, parents, children) poverty, rape, incest, battering by Indian (and non-Indian) men . . . high infant mortality due to substandard medical care, nutrition, and health information, poor educational opportunities, or education that takes us away from our traditions, language, traditions, and communities, suicide, homicide... lack of economic opportunities, sub-standard housing, sometimes violent and often virulent racist attitudes. (Jaimes and Halsey, 1992, 326–27)

Further Reading

Jaimes, M. Annette and Tersea Halsey. "American Indian Women: At the Center of Indigenous Resistance in Contemporary North America," in M.A. Jaimes, ed. *The State of Native North America: Genocide, Colonization, and Resistance*. Boston: South End Press, 1992, 311–44.

Johansen, Bruce E. and Roberto F. Maestas. *Wasi'chu: The Continuing Indian Wars.* New York: Monthly Review Press, 1979.

Josephy, Alvin M., Jr., Joane Nagel, and Troy Johnson, eds. *Red Power: The American Indians' Fight for Freedom.* Lincoln: University of Nebraska Press, 1999.

Katz, Jane B. *I Am the Fire of Time: The Voices of Native American Women.* New York: E.P. Dutton, 1977.

Mann, Barbara Alice *Iroquoian Women: The Gantowisas.* New York: Peter Lang Publishing, 2000.

Matthiessen, Peter. *In the Spirit of Crazy Horse.* New York: Viking, 1991, 417.

Wounded Knee Occupation

(1973)

The 71-day occupation of Wounded Knee began on February 28, 1973. On March 11, 1973, AIM members declared their independence as the Oglala Sioux Nation, defining its boundaries according to the Treaty of Fort Laramie, 1868. After much gunfire and negotiation, AIM's occupation of Wounded Knee ended on May 7, 1973.

Harlington Wood, of the U.S. Attorney General's office, is escorted by American Indian Movement (AIM) supporters to a conference with AIM leaders in Wounded Knee, South Dakota, 1973, during occupation by American Indians. (AP/Wide World Photo)

"Wounded Knee" had become a household word in the United States about 1970 in large part because of a book by historian Dee Brown, *Bury My Heart at Wounded Knee: An Indian History of the American West*, a best-seller for much of the Alcatraz occupation. The seizure of Wounded Knee by Native American activists had a profound impact on non-Indians, as news of the conflict was spread worldwide through the media. The occupation had a major effect on American culture. At the 1973 Academy Awards, held as Wounded Knee was being occupied, Marlon Brando refused to accept an Oscar to protest the treatment of American Indians.

Local issues at Pine Ridge laid the basis for the national attention given AIM as it occupied the small village of Wounded Knee early in 1973. Many traditional people on the Pine Ridge Reservation had rallied around AIM. Some people detested the brutality of the tribal police while others wanted help in settling fractionalized heirship problems that inhibited ranching and agriculture on the reservation.

At one point, federal officials considered an armed attack on the camp, but the plan was ultimately discarded. Dennis Banks and Russell Means, AIM's best-known leaders, stated that they would hold out until the Senate Foreign Relations Committee had reviewed all broken treaties and the corruption of the BIA had been exposed to the world. Roughly 300 people took part, on the average, at any one time, although several hundred more slipped in and out, past police barricades or through the surrounding pastures and woodlands. By one count, Native peoples from about 180 bands, tribes, and nations took part in the occupation (Bonney, 1977, 217).

Pedro Bissionette, the main leader of the Oglala Sioux Civil Rights Organization (OSCRO) was the first to suggest a caravan to Wounded Knee as a "symbolic confrontation," with an en masse presence at the massacre site for a press conference to demand a congressional investigation into present-day violations of the 1868 Fort Laramie Treaty, "with special emphasis on the Wilson regime" (Churchill and Vander Wall, 1988, 141). The primary aim was a short-term event, not the prolonged armed confrontation with Wilson's regime and the U.S. government that would involve the first call-out of the U.S. Army on domestic soil since the Civil War.

Wounded Knee, 1890: Historical Contest

Memories of the Wounded Knee massacre were still raw at Pine Ridge in 1973. The site was (and today remains) freighted with memories. Members of AIM thus chose the site for important historical reasons. Wounded Knee was the historical site of what the U.S. Army still maintains was a "battle," in late December of 1890. In a possible attempt to justify the events at Wounded Knee, the Army awarded almost 20 Medals of Honor to participants in the engagement. It remains the record for the highest number of Medal of Honor winners for any single engagement in U.S. history. It actually was a massacre, in which the Indians were slaughtered.

Many of the Indians sought refuge in a nearby ravine which turned out to be a trap as, according to Hugh Reilly, an associate professor at the University of

Nebraska at Omaha who has written extensively about the area's history. Hotch-kiss guns on the ridge sprayed bullets across the camp, taking deadly aim at people hiding in the ravine. At least 170 Indians died (some of whom were tracked down and shot miles from the scene of the original altercation). Most of them were women and children. Among the attacking troops, 25 were killed and 39 were wounded. Because much of the fire was delivered from a roughly circular position around the Indian camp, most of the soldiers who died were killed or wounded by their compatriots.

This was a time when newspapers routinely pumped up their circulations with ribald reporting, a practice in which a newspaper editor in Aberdeen, South Dakota, L. Frank Baum (who later would author the *Oz* books) called for extermination of Indians at the time of the massacre. Two decades earlier, in 1870, Mark Twain had written that exterminating destitute Indians in Nevada and Utah would be "a good, fair, desirable candidate for extermination if ever there was one" (Twain, 1992, 444).

The sober reporting of the *Omaha World-Herald* stood in stark contrast to the Indian-baiting of the Omaha *Bee*. An indication of the *Bee's* literary ambiance was provided by a poem it published in 1873, which was unearthed by Reilly. The poem was titled "Hunt Them Down." The poem, which called for extermination in the rawest of language, had several verses, including the following two:

> Hunt the murderous Modoc down,
> Bid, the paltering cease.
> Martyred Canby's blood demands,
> Righteous vengeance at our hands.
> Aye, nor Canby's blood alone.
> Death these fiends have broadcast sown.
> Let them pay each gory crown.
> Hunt them down!
>
> Hunt the savage murderers down.
> Red of hand and black of heart.
> Lies and treachery all their art.
> Cowards, robbers, pawns, and scum,
> Of the desert whence they come.
> All the human that they bear,
> Seems the outward shape they wear.
> Reeking with unnumbered crimes,
> Faithless unbred a thousand times. (Reilly, 1997, 46)

In 1973, a sense of raw racism was palpable. As the hamlet of Wounded Knee was seized, Russell Means found, at a small museum, a 19th-century ledger of receipts for beef. The cavalry captain in charge had invented names for the Indians who were provided with beef, such as "Shits in His Food, She Comes Nine Times, F—ks His Daughter, and Maggott Dick, to recall a few" (Hendricks, 2006, 63).

A News Conference Becomes a Siege

Accounts of the initial takeover of Wounded Knee differ. Instead of an aborted news conference, Smith and Warrior wrote (1996, 200–10) that after Pine Ridge traditional chiefs gave AIM the go-ahead to take over the hamlet, a caravan of 54 cars formed and drove defiantly through Pine Ridge Village,

> rolled through the winter night; old people and kids and tough guys and aunts and uncles. Red flags fluttered from some cars' antennas. When they drove through Pine Ridge [village], startled [U.S.] marshals and GOONs drew their guns, expecting a confrontation. But instead of stopping, the caravan drove straight through town, horns blowing. (Smith and Warrior, 1996, 201)

AIM leaders and about 200 Indian supporters continued en route to Porcupine, South Dakota, February 27, 1973, where they encountered Dick Wilson, with GOONs waiting for them. The caravan then drove to Wounded Knee, with its small museum, trading post, two churches, and gas station.

A lead car containing Dennis Banks and Chief Fools Crow stopped to pay homage at the grave site of the Native people who were killed in the 1890 massacre. Spiritual leaders Pete Catches and Leonard Crow Dog stopped as well, as a number of other cars continued to Wounded Knee's small commercial district, and staged what they later called a "lightning raid," seizing the gas station, museum, church, and trading post. When Banks arrived, he gave a command not to touch anything,

> But it was too late . . others [had] stormed the store, stripping it bare in moments, seizing guns, ammunition, food, and clothing. Frenzied Oglalas took pleasure in ransacking the place . . . Pedro Bissionette . . . put on a headdress from the museum and jumped on a display case, waving a handgun until he crashed through the glass top. (Smith and Warrior, 1996, 202)

At about that time, the occupiers began to realize that they were being sealed in by a well-armed circle of U.S. marshals, GOONs, BIA police, and others. The old guns they had with them (or had seized from the store) were hardly even capable of reaching the positions of the armed force surrounding them. Nevertheless, they declared the place a liberated zone and demanded U.S. Senate hearings on violations of the Fort Laramie Treaty of 1868.

The Defense Department supplied helicopters and Phantom jets, 130,000 rounds of M-16 ammunition,17 armored personnel carriers, more than 24,000 flares, 4,000 rounds of M-1 ammunition, 24,000 flares, 12 M-79 grenade launchers, 600 cases of C-S gas, 100 rounds of M-40 high explosive rounds (Johnson, 2008, 304). Much of the ordnance came from stockpiles that also supplied U.S. forces in Vietnam. The siege resembled a battle in other ways. Many of the AIM members were veterans of the Vietnam War, well-versed in the digging of trenches and handling of large caliber weapons, patrols, and roadblocks.

Providing food for a community of several hundred people under siege was a challenge. Some food was smuggled through police lines, but fresh meat was acquired on the hoof. Writing in his memoir, *Ojibwe Warrior* (2004), Banks noted that occupants of Wounded Knee rustled cattle from local ranches. Most of the AIM leaders were urban people, however, who had to learn quickly how to process meat on the hoof. Crow Dog's Paradise, 80 miles east of Wounded Knee, became a major point for the gathering of food and other supplies that were smuggled into the besieged hamlet through the blockade. Most of the smuggling was done at night, on foot, with backpacks, along winding trails in the rolling hills.

The composition of the group inside the hamlet surprised many observers. In addition to the young, urban Indians of AIM, Vine Deloria Jr. wrote that "a strong contingent of Sioux traditional people were at Wounded Knee. Revered medicine men and several well-known holy men were taking part in the occupation. Representatives of the Iroquois League were at Wounded Knee," some of the same peacemakers who had literally defused the confrontation at the BIA the previous November. "The more that Indian people saw of the Wounded Knee protest, the more seriously they began to take it," Deloria wrote (1974, 75).

The people of Pine Ridge, several of whom had relatives inside the hamlet, took the occupation seriously. In early March, impatient spokesmen for the federal government issued an ultimatum: the protestors would walk out with their hands up, or police and troops would end the confrontation by force. The message went through Pine Ridge like a jolt of electricity as several hundred Indian people, remembering the trigger-happy Seventh Calvary at the 1890 Wounded Knee Massacre, got into their cars and encircled the federal forces, reservation police, and GOONs from the outside. The confrontation was covered on national television, and sympathetic telegrams and telephone calls poured into the White House. The deadline was canceled (Deloria, 1974, 75–76).

Instead, on March 11, Russell Means announced on national television that the people inside Wounded Knee had declared themselves independent, as the Oglala Sioux Nation, under the Fort Laramie Treaty of 1868. The confrontation endured almost two more months, as the besieging forces poured munitions into the defiant hamlet. Frank Clearwater was fatally shot as he slept on a cot. Lawrence Lamont, a Pine Ridge Lakota, was a fatally shot on April 26. In addition to the two Indian men shot to death, a U.S. Marshal, Lloyd Grimm, was paralyzed in the legs from the waist down. After the two deaths, both sides, worried that the violence had gotten out of hand, and agreed to a ceasefire, which was violated several times. By early May, however, exhaustion set in, and the occupiers surrendered. As at Alcatraz in 1969, and at the BIA in 1972, the world had become more aware of problems facing American Indians, but little else had changed.

Further Reading

Banks, Dennis and Richard Erdoes. *Ojibwa Warrior: Dennis Banks and the Rise of the American Indian Movement.* Norman: University of Oklahoma Press, 2004.

Bonney, Rachel A. "The Role of AIM Leaders in Indian Nationalism," *American Indian Quarterly* 3, no. 3 (Autumn, 1977): 209–24.

Churchill, Ward and Jim Vander Wall. *Agents of Repression: The FBI's Secret War Against the Black Panther Party and the American Indian Movement.* Boston: South End Press, 1990.

Deloria, Vine, Jr. *Behind the Trail of Broken Treaties.* Austin: University of Texas Press, 1985.

Hendricks, Steve. *The Unquiet Grave: The FBI and the Struggle for the Soul of Indian Country.* New York: Thunder's Mouth Press, 2006.

Johansen, Bruce E. and Roberto F. Maestas. *Wasi'chu: The Continuing Indian Wars.* New York: Monthly Review Press, 1979.

Johnson, Troy. *American Indian Activism: Alcatraz to the Longest Walk.* Urbana: University of Illinois Press, 1997.

Johnson, Troy R. "Occupation of Wounded Knee," in Bruce E. Johansen and Barry Pritzker, eds. *Encyclopedia of American Indian History.* Santa Barbara, CA: ABC-CLIO, 2008, 303–05.

Josephy, Alvin, Jr. *Red Power: The American Indians' Fight for Freedom* New York: McGraw-Hill, 1971.

Matthiessen, Peter. *In the Spirit of Crazy Horse.* New York: Viking, 1991.

Reilly, Hugh. *Treatment of Native Americans by the Frontier Press 1868–1891, an Omaha, Nebraska Study.* Master's thesis, University of Nebraska at Omaha, 1997.

Twain, Mark. *Mark Twain: Collected Tales, Sketches, Speeches & Essays, 1852–1890.* Vol. I. New York: The Library of America, 1992.

Wounded Knee Trials

Following the occupation of Wounded Knee, AIM members Dennis Banks and Russell Means were charged by the U.S. Justice Department with three counts of assault on federal officers, one charge each of conspiracy and one each of larceny. Facing five charges each, Banks and Means could have been sentenced to as many as 85 years in prison. For several months in 1974, the defense and prosecution presented their cases in a St. Paul, Minnesota federal court.

On September 16, Judge Fred J. Nichol dismissed all the charges. The judge said that the FBI's agents had lied repeatedly during the trial while under oath and had often furnished defense attorneys with altered documents. The prosecution also had placed an informer in the defense, an illegal act. Judge Nichol said that R. D. Hurd,

American Indian Movement leader Dennis Banks and his attorneys prepared for his trial January 8, 1974, following the 71-day siege of Wounded Knee, South Dakota. (AP/Wide World Photo)

the federal prosecutor, had deliberately deceived the court with sloppy case work. In his statement dismissing all charges, Judge Nichol noted that the waters of justice had been "polluted" by governmental misconduct. "It's hard for me to believe that the FBI, which I have revered for so long, has stooped so low," said Judge Nichol (Churchill and Vander Wall, 1988, 294). To the chagrin of the judge and jurors, the Justice Department responded by presenting Hurd with an award for "superior performance" during the trial.

After 562 arrests and 185 federal indictments related to the Wounded Knee occupation, the government obtained only 15 convictions. At a rate of 7.7 percent, that conviction rate was one-tenth the average for criminal trials in the Eighth Circuit, in which the cases were tried (Hendricks, 2006, 141). Even those few convictions were for minor offenses, such as trespassing and interfering with delivery of the mail. For example, according to one analyst, "Spiritual leader Leonard Crow Dog, Oklahoma AIM leader Carter Camp, and Stan Holder, who headed security at Wounded Knee, were convicted of interfering with a group of marshals who had attempted to enter the AIM perimeter disguised as postal inspectors. Ultimately, federal prosecutors obtained only fifteen guilty verdicts, none for substantial offenses" (Churchill, 2008, 642). Attorneys Beverly Axelrod, Ken Tilson, and others, working through the Wounded Knee Legal Defense/Offense Committee (WKLDOC) repeatedly won cases against squadrons of Justice Department attorneys.

Kafka 101

The government kept AIM busy for years. The legal campaign was not meant to obtain convictions as much as it was pursued to dismember AIM by tying activists into legal knots. After the occupation of Wounded Knee ended on May 7, 1973, the federal government buried AIM with indictments. By February 1974, Dennis Banks and Russell Means had been charged with everything that prosecutors could find in the federal criminal code: kidnapping, car theft, criminal conspiracy, and assaulting federal officers. AIM found itself tied up in a seemingly endless round of indictments, arrests, hearings, and so forth. They could do nothing else, and whatever funds AIM could raise was gobbled up in legal defense.

Russell Means was hounded for years on several charges that were mainly specious: "He was even tried for murder in 1976, despite the fact that his alleged victim stated repeatedly before he died that Means was not one of the assailants" (Churchill, 2008, 642). Means was convicted of a felony that resulted from a minor brawl in a courtroom after Means, exhausted by the seemingly endless legal song and dance, refused to stand up when the judge entered court in 1974 during Sarah Bad Heart Bull's trial.

During November 1975, Dennis Banks and his wife Kamook were charged under federal and firearms explosives laws with Russell Redner Kenny Loud Hawk. The charges were dismissed for lack of evidence the next year. In 1980, the government filed much the same indictment against the same people; charges were dismissed in 1983 because the government was working so slowly that it violated the constitutional right to a speedy trial. All in all, Russell Means alone was charged with 37 felonies and three misdemeanors (Johnson et al., 1997, 250).

During 1986, government prosecutors convinced the U.S. Supreme Court to reinstate the charges; six months after that the case was dismissed a third time. The Justice Department seemed to be taking a course in Kafka 101, from his novel *The Trial,* in which defendants became ensnared in endless rounds of prosecution for its own sake. The government was not finished. Charges were filed a fourth time in 1988, after which Banks, who had become very tired of the whole legal circus, agreed to plead guilty pro forma if charges were dropped against everyone else.

In the meantime, Richard "Mohawk" Billings and Paul "Skyhorse" Durant of Los Angeles AIM were charged with murder (and torture) of a local taxi driver. Local police actually had arrested other people nearly immediately after the murder, but the FBI intervened and convinced the prosecutors to allow the local suspects to turn states evidence against the AIM members. When the case came to court the lack of evidence provoked an acquittal of both the men. A primary witness confessed to the murder. Once again, the government was doing little except harassing members of AIM. Skyhorse and Mohawk also had been held in jail for almost four years on suspicion of the murder.

William Kunstler, one of AIM's several attorneys, said: "The purpose of the trials [was] to break the spirit of the American Indian Movement by tying up its leaders and supporters in court and forcing [it] to spend huge amounts of money, time and talent to keep [its] people out of jail, instead of building an organization that can work effectively for the Indian people" (Matthiessen, 1991, 193–94).

Further Reading

Churchill, Ward. "American Indian Movement," in Bruce E. Johansen and Barry Pritz-ker, eds. *Encyclopedia of American Indian History*. Santa Barbara, CA: ABC-CLIO, 2008, 638–46.

Hendricks, Steve. *The Unquiet Grave: The FBI and the Struggle for the Soul of Indian Country*. New York: Thunder's Mouth Press, 2006.

Matthiessen, Peter. *In the Spirit of Crazy Horse: The Story of Leonard Peltier*, 2nd ed. New York: Viking, 1991.

Y

Yellow Thunder, Raymond

(ca. 1920–1972)

On February 20, 1972, when police found Raymond Yellow Thunder's body slumped over the steering wheel of a pickup truck in a Gordon, Nebraska used-car lot, he had been dead for several days of a cerebral hemorrhage. Gordon is a border town nearly adjacent to the Pine Ridge reservation where Native people might cash a check, buy hardware, or see a movie, none of which they could do at home. The people of Gordon depended on these visits, but the discovery of a dead Indian's body initially raised few eyebrows.

Yellow Thunder, a Lakota, had been a good man, a 51-year-old cowboy from the traditional Oglala village of Porcupine. He had lived in and near Gordon for several years and worked on many local ranches. He regularly returned to Porcupine on weekends to see children; he was a good cook and a willing babysitter, and usually he brought groceries with him (Smith and Warrior, 1996, 113). When he missed a weekend visit, Yellow Thunder's relatives became worried, and contacted police. The relatives also searched Gordon's windswept, frozen streets looking for him. When the body was found, Yellow Thunder had been dead for days of exposure and head injuries. Such attacks on Indian people by white racists were not uncommon on the Pine Ridge Reservation. The police largely ignored the situation, and white judges refused to try whites for crimes against Indians. Following Yellow Thunder's death, AIM was called upon to bring national attention to the cruel nature of the murder (Johnson, 2008, 303).

An account of Yellow Thunder's last days began to emerge: four whites, brothers Melvin and Leslie Hare, Bernard Ludder, and Robert Bayless seized Yellow Thunder outside of a bar, forced him to drink alcohol, then partially stripped and beat him. They then loaded Yellow Thunder into the back of a pickup truck and drove around town, to a dance at American Legion Hall No. 34, where they called him a "drunken Indian." Bleeding and disoriented, the four whites forced Yellow Thunder to dance. The whites then forced Yellow Thunder out the door into a cold Nebraska winter night, where he wandered for a while, and then died (Johnson, 2008, 303).

Yellow Thunder's relatives were angry, but Indians had been angry in Gordon before. Yellow Thunder's relatives appealed first to all of the usual law-enforcement agencies—the Bureau of Indian Affairs, the FBI, and the local police. Receiving no responses, they finally asked the AIM for help.

Russell Means, one of the primary founders of AIM, also was from Porcupine. His mother, Theodora, had lived there. An Oglala named Young Bear drove to Minneapolis to ask for AIM's help. A few days later, a caravan from AIM, numbering in the hundreds of people, arrived at Billy Mills Hall in Pine Ridge Village for a rally. Within a week, more than 1,400 Native people from about 80 tribes had besieged Gordon, demanding justice. Means said they had arrived to "put Gordon on the map," and "if justice isn't immediately forthcoming, we will take Gordon off the map" (Johnson et al., 1997, 246).

The members of AIM also arranged with the Oglala Lakota tribe to move more than $1 million in bank deposits out of Gordon's banks (Smith and Warrior, 1996, 116). The Justice Department promised an investigation, as Sheridan County Attorney Michael Smith charged the men who had beaten Yellow Thunder with manslaughter (not murder) and false imprisonment, releasing them on $6,250 bail each. He called what had happened a "cruel practical joke" carried out by "pranksters." Many Native people were incensed by the light charge and low bail.

Further Reading

Johnson, Troy R. "Occupation of Wounded Knee," in Bruce E. Johansen and Barry Pritzker, eds. *Encyclopedia of American Indian History*. Santa Barbara, CA: ABC-CLIO, 2008, 303–05.

Smith, Paul Chaat and Robert Allen Warrior. *Like a Hurricane: The Indian Movement from Alcatraz to Wounded Knee*. New York: The New Press, 1996.

Yellow Thunder Camp

In 1981, Russell Means led an AIM contingent into the Black Hills to found Camp Yellow Thunder, named for the Lakota man who had been murdered, on an 880-acre site to demonstrate the sacred nature of the Black Hills. The encampment lasted until 1985. By that time, the members of the camp had obtained a federal court ruling that defended their occupancy of the camp, as well as the right of the Lakota (by treaty) to treat the entire Black Hills (instead of small sites within the area) as sacred (*U.S. v. Means*, 1985). This decision later was overturned by the U.S. Supreme Court (Lyng, 1988).

Twenty cars departed Porcupine, on the Pine Ridge reservation on April 4, 1981, carrying stoves, tipi poles, sacred pipes, food, and cold-weather camping gear, bound for the Black Hills, to establish Yellow Thunder Camp, 12 miles southwest of Rapid City, on federal land. The idea was conceived by Russell Means and other AIM members as a way to begin a Native reclamation of the *Paha Sapa*, "Hills that are Black," based on a guarantee in the 1868 Fort Laramie Treaty that the Hills are theirs for "undisturbed use." The occupation also was legally rooted in the American Indian

A marcher supporting the Dakota–American Indian Movement's Yellow Thunder Camp raises his fist on October 1, 1982 in Rapid City, South Dakota. (AP/Wide World Photo)

Freedom of Religion Act (1978), and a federal law passed in 1987 that allowed free use of wilderness sites for schools and churches.

The camp was established as light snow fell, at the base of steep red cliffs, on a site with clean running water. A claim was filed with the U.S. Forest Service for 800 acres around the camp. A large number of FBI agents later appeared at the edge of the camp, but did not move to evict its people. The occupation enjoyed widespread press coverage that also deterred a possibly bloody intervention (Josephy et al., 1999, 214–15).

Historical Significance of the Black Hills *(Paha Sapa)*

Black Elk, a Lakota (Sioux) medicine man, was 11 years old during the summer of 1874 when, by his account (published in *Black Elk Speaks* by John Neihardt), an expedition under Gen. George Armstrong Custer invaded the *Paha Sapa* (hills that are black), the holy land of the Lakota. The Black Hills had been guaranteed to the Lakota "in perpetuity" by the Fort Laramie Treaty of 1868.

Custer's expedition was on a geological mission, not a military one. His "army" included not only troops, but also surveyors and assayers, as well as a brass band. Custer was looking for gold. He found it, wiring to the outside world that the hills contained the yellow metal that makes white men crazy (Black Elk's words) from the grassroots down. In Custer's wake, several thousand gold seekers poured into the sacred Black Hills, ignoring the Fort Laramie treaty.

In the words of Black Elk, the Lakota and Cheyenne painted their faces black— went to war—to regain the Black Hills. The result was Custer's Last Stand, one of the best-remembered debacles in U.S. military history during which an overconfident Custer led his march-weary men and horses into a Lakota and Cheyenne encampment that was twice the size his scouts had estimated.

The Black Hills never were legally ceded by treaty. The Lakota have never accepted the United States' offer of $17.5 million. On April 12, 2010, the Black Hills land claim settlement fund, with accrued interest, passed $1 billion. Mount Rushmore still stands on Lakota land, surrounded by gaudy tourist traps, including glittering new gambling establishments.

According to the 1868 Fort Laramie Treaty, three-quarters of the adult members of the signatory tribes must accept any settlement.

Uranium in the Black Hills

In January 1977, another group of government employees followed General Custer's footsteps into the Black Hills, and emerged from their geological errand bearing news of uranium-bearing Precambrian rock formations near Nemo, southwest of Rapid City. The news ignited another rush for claims, which again ignored the question of Lakota title. Between February 15 and April 15, 1977, more than 1,200 location certificates were filed in the area, many of them by large companies such as Johns-Manville, American Copper & Nickel, and Homestake Mining. Homestake had grown rich on the Custer strike, earning profits which later helped to buy William Randolph Hearst a newspaper empire.

Other large companies joined the uranium rush elsewhere in the Black Hills. The Tennessee Valley Authority, looking to fuel the 17 nuclear power plants for which it had licenses, acquired leases on 65,000 Black Hills acres and on 35,000 more acres just west of the Wyoming border. Two mining methods were being considered: strip mining and underground mining in which a chemical solution would be injected into the ground to dissolve the uranium before a radium-rich slush is drawn to the surface. Because the Black Hills are a watershed for much of western South Dakota, Native people, as well as local ranchers and farmers objected because such solution mining could pollute the underground water on which ranchers and farmers rely.

During the 1970s, AIM leaders raised questions about resource exploitation. If AIM leaders were not tied up on criminal prosecutions, they could be pressing treaty claims to land which contains rich stores of fossil fuel and mineral wealth. As Leonard Peltier (who was convicted of killing two FBI agents at Pine Ridge in 1975) wrote from prison,

> We may have been happy with the land that was originally reserved for us. But continually over the years, more and more of our land has been stolen from us by the Canadian and American governments. In the late 19th century, land was stolen for economic reasons . . . We were left with what was believed to be worthless land. Still, we managed to live and defied [the] wish to exterminate us. Today, what was once called worthless land suddenly becomes valuable as the technology of white society advances. [That society] would now like to push us off our reservations because beneath the barren land lie valuable mineral resources. (Johansen and Maestas, 1979, 120)

Further Reading

Johansen, Bruce E. and Roberto Maestas. *Wasi'chu: The Continuing Indian Wars*. New York: Monthly Review Press, 1979.

Josephy, Alvin M., Jr., Joane Nagel, and Troy Johnson, eds. *Red Power: The American Indians' Fight for Freedom*. Lincoln: University of Nebraska Press, 1999.

Lazarus, Edward. *Black Hills, White Justice: The Sioux Nation v. the United States: 1775 to the Present*. New York: Harper-Collins, 1991.

Lyng v. Northwest Indian Cemetery Protection Association 485 U.S. 459 (1988).

Neihardt, John G. *Black Elk Speaks*. New York: William Morrow & Co., 1932.

United States vs. Means, et al., Civ. No. 81-5131, U.S. District Court for the District of South Dakota, December 9, 1985.

Primary Sources

1. Marlon Brando Declines an Oscar

On March 27, 1973, during the occupation of Wounded Knee, Marlon Brando declined an Academy Award from the Screen Actors' Guild (an "Oscar") as Best Actor for his role in *The Godfather,* as a protest against treatment of American Indians. The following statement, only the first part of which was read at the ceremony, explains why he did it.

Hello. My name is Sacheen Littlefeather. I am an Apache and I am the president of the National Native American Affirmative Image Committee. I'm representing Marlon Brando this evening and he has asked me to tell you, in a very long speech which I cannot share with you presently—because of time—but I will be glad to share with the press afterward, that he must very regretfully cannot accept this very generous award. And the reason for this being is the treatment of American Indians today by the film industry and on television in movie re-runs, and also the recent happenings at Wounded Knee. I beg at this time that I have not intruded upon this evening and that we will, in the future, our hearts and our understanding will meet with love and generosity. Thank you on behalf of Marlon Brando.

For 200 years we have said to the Indian people who are fighting for their land, their life, their families and their right to be free: "Lay down your arms, my friends, and then we will remain together. Only if you lay down your arms, my friends, can we then talk of peace and come to an agreement which will be good for you."

When they laid down their arms, we murdered them. We lied to them. We cheated them out of their lands. We starved them into signing fraudulent agreements that we called treaties which we never kept. We turned them into beggars on a continent that gave life for as long as life can remember. And by any interpretation of history, however twisted, we did not do right. We were not lawful nor were we just in what we did. For them, we do not have to restore these people, we do not have to live up to some agreements, because it is given to us by virtue of our power to attack the rights of others, to take their property, to take their lives when they are trying to defend their land and liberty, and to make their virtues a crime and our own vices virtues.

But there is one thing which is beyond the reach of this perversity and that is the tremendous verdict of history. And history will surely judge us. But do we care? What kind of moral schizophrenia is it that allows us to shout at the top of our national voice for all the world to hear that we live up to our commitment when every page of history and when all the thirsty, starving, humiliating days and nights of the last 100 years in the lives of the American Indian contradict that voice?

It would seem that the respect for principle and the love of one's neighbor have become dysfunctional in this country of ours, and that all we have done, all that we have succeeded in accomplishing with our power is simply annihilating the hopes of the newborn countries in this world, as well as friends and enemies alike, that we're not humane, and that we do not live up to our agreements.

Perhaps at this moment you are saying to yourself what the hell has all this got to do with the Academy Awards? Why is this woman standing up here, ruining our evening, invading our lives with things that don't concern us, and that we don't care about? Wasting our time and money and intruding in our homes.

I think the answer to those unspoken questions is that the motion picture community has been as responsible as any for degrading the Indian and making a mockery of his character, describing him as savage, hostile and evil. It's hard enough for children to grow up in this world. When Indian children watch television, and they watch films, and when they see their race depicted as they are in films, their minds become injured in ways we can never know.

Recently there have been a few faltering steps to correct this situation, but too faltering and too few, so I, as a member in this profession, do not feel that I can as a citizen of the United States accept an award here tonight. I think awards in this country at this time are inappropriate to be received or given until the condition of the American Indian is drastically altered. If we are not our brother's keeper, at least let us not be his executioner.

I would have been here tonight to speak to you directly, but I felt that perhaps I could be of better use if I went to Wounded Knee to help forestall in whatever way I can the establishment of a peace which would be dishonorable as long as the rivers shall run and the grass shall grow.

I would hope that those who are listening would not look upon this as a rude intrusion, but as an earnest effort to focus attention on an issue that might very well determine whether or not this country has the right to say from this point forward we believe in the inalienable rights of all people to remain free and independent on lands that have supported their life beyond living memory.

Thank you for your kindness and your courtesy to Miss Littlefeather. Thank you and good night.

From Sacheen Littlefeather

I was a young woman in my mid-twenties when I delivered that message and that prayer to an international television audience at the 45th Academy Awards presentation in 1973. That evening was an ending and a beginning . . . an ending to my career in the film industry and a beginning of what I hope is the healing process to the thread of institutionalized racism with which the fabric of our society was woven. Because of the mention of Wounded Knee I came to the attention of the FBI who arranged to have me "white-listed" in Hollywood so that I never worked in the film industry again.

Source: Available at American Indian Movement. Letters. http://www.aimovement.org/moipr/letters.html

2. Declaration of Indian Purpose

Beginning with the founding of the National Congress of American Indians in 1944, Native Americans established national organizations to demand a greater voice in determining their own destiny. In 1961, some 700 Indians from 64 tribes met in Chicago to attack termination and formulate an Indian political agenda and a shared declaration of principles. This *"Declaration of Indian Purpose"* was given to John F. Kennedy by the National Congress of American Indians in 1961. Extracts appear below.

. . . We, the Indian People, must be governed by principles in a democratic manner with a right to choose our way of life. Since our Indian culture is threatened by presumption of being absorbed by the American society, we believe we have the responsibility of preserving our precious heritage. . . .

We believe in the inherent right of all people to retain spiritual and cultural values, and that the free exercise of these values is necessary to the normal development of any people. . . .

We believe that the history and development of America show that the Indian has been subjected to duress, undue influence, unwarranted pressures, and policies which have produced uncertainty, frustration, and despair. . . .

What we ask of America is not charity, not paternalism, even when benevolent. We ask only that the nature of our situation be recognized and made the basis of policy and action.

Source: American Indian Chicago Conference, University of Chicago, June 13–20, 1961, 5–6. Available at Digital History. "Native American Voices." No date. http://www.digitalhistory.uh.edu/disp_textbook.cfm?smtID=3&psid=727

3. The Alcatraz Proclamation

The takeover of Alcatraz Island was made with a proclamation stating reasons for the occupation, with ample parody.

THE ALCATRAZ PROCLAMATION: to the Great White Father and his People (1969 takeover of Alcatraz) Fellow citizens, we are asking you to join with us in our attempt to better the lives of all Indian people.

We are on Alcatraz Island to make known to the world that we have a right to use our land for our own benefit.

In a proclamation of November 20, 1969, we told the government of the United States that we are here to create a meaningful use for our Great Spirit's Land.

We, the native Americans, reclaim the land known as Alcatraz Island in the name of all American Indians by right of discovery.

We wish to be fair and honorable in our dealings with the Caucasian inhabitants of this land, and hereby offer the following treaty:

We will purchase said Alcatraz Island for twenty-four dollars in glass beads and red cloth, a precedent set by the white man's purchase of a similar island about 300 years ago. We know that $24 in trade goods for these 16 acres is more than was paid when Manhattan Island was sold, but we know that land values have risen over the years. Our offer of $1.24 per acre is greater than the $0.47 per acre the white men are now paying the California Indians for their lands.

We will give to the inhabitants of this island a portion of the land for their own to be held in trust . . . by the Bureau of Caucasian Affairs . . . in perpetuity—for as long as the sun shall rise and the rivers go down to the sea. We will further guide the inhabitants in the proper way of living. We will offer them our religion, our education, our life-ways in order to help them achieve our level of civilization and thus raise them and all their white brothers up from their savage and unhappy state. We offer this treaty in good faith and wish to be fair and honorable in our dealings with all white men.

We feel that this so-called Alcatraz Island is more than suitable for an Indian reservation, as determined by the white man's own standards. By this, we mean that this place resembles most Indian reservations in that:

1. It is isolated from modern facilities, and without adequate means of transportation.

2. It has no fresh running water.

3. It has inadequate sanitation facilities.

4. There are no oil or mineral rights.

5. There is no industry and so unemployment is very great.

6. There are no health-care facilities.

7. The soil is rocky and non-productive, and the land does not support game.

8. There are no educational facilities.

9. The population has always exceeded the land base.

10. The population has always been held as prisoners and kept dependent upon others.

Further, it would be fitting and symbolic that ships from all over the world, entering the Golden Gate, would first see Indian land, and thus be reminded of the true history of this nation. This tiny island would be a symbol of the great lands once ruled by free and noble Indians.

What use will we make of this land?

Since the San Francisco Indian Center burned down, there is no place for Indians to assemble and carry on tribal life here in the white man's city. Therefore, we plan to develop on this island several Indian institutions:

1. A Center for Native American Studies will be developed which will educate them to the skills and knowledge relevant to improve the lives and spirits of all Indian peoples. Attached to this center will be travelling universities, managed by Indians, which will go to the Indian Reservations, learning those necessary and relevant materials now about.

2. An American Indian Spiritual Center, which will practice our ancient tribal religious and sacred healing ceremonies. Our cultural arts will be featured and our young people trained in music, dance, and healing rituals.

3. An Indian Center of Ecology, which will train and support our young people in scientific research and practice to restore our lands and waters to their pure and natural state. We will work to de-pollute the air and waters of the Bay Area. We will seek to restore fish and animal life to the area and to revitalize sea-life which has been threatened by the white man's way. We will set up facilities to desalt sea water for human benefit.

4. A Great Indian Training School will be developed to teach our people how to make a living in the world, improve our standard of living, and to end hunger and unemployment among all our people. This training school will include a center for Indian arts and crafts, and an Indian restaurant serving native foods, which will restore Indian culinary arts. This center will display Indian arts and offer Indian foods to the public, so that all may know of the beauty and spirit of the traditional Indian ways.

Some of the present buildings will be taken over to develop an American Indian Museum which will depict our native food and other cultural contributions we have given to the world. Another part of the museum will present some of the things the white man has given to the Indians in return for the land and life he took: disease, alcohol, poverty, and cultural decimation (as symbolized by old tin cans, barbed wire, rubber tires, plastic containers, etc.). Part of the museum will remain a dungeon to symbolize both those Indian captives who were incarcerated for challenging white authority and those who were imprisoned on reservations. The museum will show the noble and tragic events of Indian history, including the broken treaties, the documentary of the Trail of Tears, the Massacre of Wounded Knee, as well as the victory over Yellow-Hair Custer and his army.

In the name of all Indians, therefore, we reclaim this island for our Indian nations, for all these reasons. We feel this claim is just and proper, and that this land should rightfully be granted to us for as long as the rivers run and the sun shall shine.

We hold the rock!

————signature————

"Whenever the white man treats the Indian as they treat each other then we shall have no more wars. We shall be all alike—brothers of one father and mother, with one sky above us and one country around us and one government for all."

Source: "The Alcatraz Proclamation." 1969. http://www.yvwiiusdinvnohii.net/history/AlcatrazProclamation1969.htm

4. The Bureau of Caucasian Affairs

Parody is used to show non-Indians how Indians' lives are controlled by government agencies.

The Bureau of Caucasian Affairs, Department of the United Native Americans (U.N.A.) are proud to announce that it has bought the state of California from the whites and is throwing it open to Indian settlement. U.N.A. bought California from three winos found wandering in San Francisco. U.N.A. determined that the winos were the spokesmen for the white people of California. These winos promptly signed the treaty, which was written in Sioux, and sold California for three cases of wine, one bottle of gin, and four cases of beer.

Lehman L. Brightman, the Commissioner of Caucasian Affairs, has announced the following new policies: The Indians hereby give the whites four reservations of ten acres each at the following locations: Death Valley, The Utah Salt Flats, The Badlands of South Dakota, and the Yukon in Alaska.

These reservations shall belong to the whites "for as long as the sun shines or the grass grows" (or until the Indians want it back). All land on the reservations, of course, will be held in trust for the whites by the Bureau of Caucasian Affairs, and any white who wants to use his land in any way must secure permission from Commissioner Brightman. Of course, whites will be allowed to sell handicrafts at stands by the highway.

Each white will be provided annually with one blanket, one pair of tennis shoes, an ample supply of Spam, several bricks of commodity cheese, and a copy of *The Bible.* You also may be able to serve as a B.C.A. reservation superintendent. Applicants must have less than one year of education, must not speak English, must have an authoritarian personality, proof of dishonesty, and a certificate of incompetence. No whites need apply.

Commissioner Brightman also announced the founding of four boarding schools, to which white youngsters will be sent at the age of six (6). "We want to take those kids far away from the backward culture of their parents," he said. The schools will be located on Alcatraz Island; the Florida Everglades; Point Barrow, Alaska; and Hong Kong. All courses will be taught in Indian languages, and there will be demerits for anyone caught speaking English. All students arriving at the school will immediately be given I.Q. tests to determine their understanding of Indian languages and hunting skills.

Hospitals will be established for the reservations as follows: Whites at Death Valley may go to the Bangor, Maine Hospital; those at the Utah Salt Flats may go to Juneau, Alaska Hospital; those at the Yukon may go to the Miami Beach Hospital; and those at the Badlands may go to the Hospital in Honolulu, Hawaii. Each hospital will have a staff of two part-time doctors and a part-time chiropractor who have all passed first-aid tests. And each hospital will be equipped with a scalpel, a jack knife, a saw, a modern tourniquet, and a large bottle of aspirin.

In honor of the whites, many cities, states, counties, and products will be given traditional white names. A famous Indian movie director has even announced that in his upcoming film, "Custer's Last Stand" he will use real white actors to play the parts of soldiers, speaking authentic English—although, of course, the part of Custer will be played by noted Indian actor Wes Studi.

Certain barbaric white customs will, of course, not be allowed. Whites will not be allowed to practice their heathen religions, and will be required to attend Indian ceremonies. Missionaries will be sent from each tribe to attend Indian ceremonies. Missionaries will be sent from each tribe to convert the whites on the reservations. White churches will be turned into amusement parks or museums and golf courses. The churches themselves will be demolished and the bricks and ornaments sold as souvenirs and curiosities. Anglos' bones will be disinterred from cemeteries and housed in museums. Skeletal remains of Anglos will be put on display and their skulls will be studied, measured, scrutinized, and analyzed so that Indian people can determine just what is wrong with White people. White cemetery land will be distributed among people wishing to build roller-skating rinks and convenience stores.

There will be two separate but distinct legal and judicial systems; one for Indians and one for whites. Indians will hold all the judicial seats, legislative seats, and will staff all police and fire departments. Whites can become police officers and fire fighters on their designated reservations, but may act only in minor roles. Legal and judicial authority comes directly from the Bureau of Caucasian Affairs. Several holidays will be developed to honor White people's contributions to society. To further honor them, corporations and schools will be encouraged to develop pageants, festivals, sporting events, and for-profit items that can carry the images, and names of the white people. Educational books (history, archeology, astronomy, medicine, music, literature, art, etc.) will reflect the many contributions of white people on pages 1, 2, and part of page 3 of every book. The rest of the pages will focus strictly on Indian history and contributions.

Source: "The Bureau of Caucasian Affairs." http://www.pantherslodge.com/una.html and several other sites.

5. Reservations for Whites

Another example of putting the moccasin on the other foot is a tongue-in-cheek proposal of reservations for European-Americans. This parody satirizes the Anglo-American practice of signing treaties with Native Americans with no leadership positions who had been appointed as "chiefs" for the occasion, then loaded with alcohol, presented with documents that they couldn't read, giving Indians useless land in places no non-Indian would want (until, of course, uranium or oil was found under the tumbleweeds). This jest may have been composed by Lehman L. Brightman, California Native professor and long-time activist who is named in the piece as "Commissioner of Caucasian Affairs." This account also parodies boarding schools, the seizure of Native American remains for scientific study, and the use of Native burial grounds for profane purposes.

The 500-year lease of Turtle Island is now up. If you are not of Aboriginal descent, leave. If by some chance you have some affinity for this land, you may stay, but you are subject to the Whiteman Act.

SECTION 1. All whites must carry cards identifying that they are white.

SECTION 2. All whites must live on reservations. This is to protect the White culture from any influence of Indian culture. These reservations will be set out, but the ruling Indians and all Whites must move to one immediately regardless of ability to travel.

Note: Property will be held in trust for the whites because they do not know how to use the land. Thus, the Indian government has full control of housing and resources on the reservation.

SECTION 3. No whites are allowed to leave the Reservation for longer than six months or else he or she will no longer be classified as white. They will be thrown off the reservation, away from home, family and friends. Irregardless of whether the white person in question has gone to fight in the U.S. armed forces, has found work off the reservation or has gone to a university, the person will lose his or her white status.

SECTION 4. All reservations will be forced to elect a Chief. If the Department of White Affairs does not like the elected Chief and Council it reserves the right to replace them without appeal.

SECTION 5. Christian ceremonies are now banned. Since it is known that whites have bad knees, and that Christianity has a savage kneeling ritual, all Christians must be converted to Native Spirituality.

SECTION 6. No white is allowed to consume alcohol on or off the reservation because all whites are alcoholics.

SECTION 7. All reservations will have a white agent who will decide everything from who will be chief to who can have a child.

SECTION 8. If at any time the ruling Indian government needs land, it reserves the right to take the land from the reservation.

Source: "Reservations for Whites." Andre Cramblit [andrekar@ncidc.org] Via Digest for IndigenousNewsNetwork@topica.com, issue 114, June 19, 2003.

6. President Nixon's Special Message on Indian Affairs, July 8, 1970

A new direction of Indian policy which aimed at Indian self-determination was set forth by President Richard Nixon in a special message to Congress in July 1970. Nixon condemned forced termination and proposed recommendations for specific action. His introduction and conclusion are printed here.

To the Congress of the United States:
The first Americans—the Indians—are the most deprived and most isolated minority group in our nation. On virtually very scale of measurement—employment, income, education, health—the condition of the Indian people ranks at the bottom.

This condition is the heritage of centuries of injustice. From the time of their first contact with European settlers, the American Indians have been oppressed and brutalized, deprived of their ancestral lands and denied the opportunity to control their own destiny. Even the Federal programs which are intended to meet their needs have frequently proved to be ineffective and demeaning.

But the story of the Indian in America is something more than the record of the white man's frequent aggression, broken agreements, intermittent remorse and prolonged failure. It is a record also of endurance, of survival, of adaptation and creativity in the face of overwhelming obstacles. It is a record of enormous contributions to this country—to its art and culture, to its strength and spirit, to its sense of history and its sense of purpose.

It is long past time that the Indian policies of the Federal government began to recognize and build upon the capacities and insights of the Indian people. Both as a matter of justice and as a matter of enlightened social policy, we must begin to act on the basis of what the Indians themselves have long been telling us. The time has come to break decisively with the past and to create the conditions for a new era in which the Indian future is determined by Indian acts and Indian decisions.

Self-Determination Without Termination

The first and most basic question that must be answered with respect to Indian policy concerns the history and legal relationship between the Federal government and Indian communities. In the past, this relationship has oscillated between two equally harsh and unacceptable extremes.

On the other hand, it has—at various times during previous Administrations—been the stated policy objective of both the Executive and Legislative branches of the Federal government eventually to terminate the trusteeship relationship between the Federal government and the Indian people. As recently as August of 1953, in House Concurrent Resolution 108, the Congress declared that termination was the long-range goal of its Indian policies. This would mean that Indian tribes would eventually lose any special standing they had under Federal law: the tax exempt status of their lands would be discontinued; Federal responsibility for their economic and social well-being would be repudiated; and the tribes themselves would be effectively dismantled. Tribal property would be divided among individual members who would then be assimilated into the society at large.

This policy of forced termination is wrong, in my judgment, for a number of reasons. First, the premises on which it rests are wrong. Termination implies that the Federal government has taken on a trusteeship responsibility for Indian communities as an act of generosity toward a disadvantaged people and that it can therefore discontinue this responsibility on a unilateral basis whenever it sees fit. But the unique status of Indian tribes does not rest on any premise such as this. The special relationship between Indians and the Federal government is the result instead of solemn obligations which have been entered into by the United States Government. Down through the years through written treaties and through formal and informal agreements, our government has made specific commitments to the Indian people. For their part, the Indians have often surrendered claims to vast tracts of land and have accepted life on government reservations. In exchange, the government has agreed to provide community services such as health, education and public safety, services which would presumably allow Indian communities to enjoy a standard of living comparable to that of other Americans.

This goal, of course, has never been achieved. But the special relationship between the Indian tribes and the Federal government which arises from these agreements continues to carry immense moral and legal force. To terminate this relationship would be no more appropriate than to terminate the citizenship rights of any other American.

The second reason for rejecting forced termination is that the practical results have been clearly harmful in the few instances in which termination actually has been tried. The removal of Federal trusteeship responsibility has produced considerable disorientation among the affected Indians and has left them unable to relate to a myriad of Federal, State and local assistance efforts. Their economic and social condition has often been worse after termination than it was before.

The third argument I would make against forced termination concerns the effect it has had upon the overwhelming majority of tribes which still enjoy a special relationship with the Federal government. The very threat that this relationship may someday be ended has created a great deal of apprehension among Indian groups and this apprehension, in turn, has had a blighting effect on tribal progress. Any step that might result in greater social, economic or political autonomy is regarded with suspicion by many Indians who fear that it will only bring them closer to the day when the Federal government will disavow its responsibility and cut them adrift.

In short, the fear of one extreme policy, forced termination, has often worked to produce the opposite extreme: excessive dependence on the Federal government. In many cases this dependence is so great that the Indian community is almost entirely run by outsiders who are responsible and responsive to Federal officials in Washington, D.C., rather than to the communities they are supposed to be serving. This is the second of the two harsh approaches which have long plagued our Indian policies. Of the Department of Interior/s programs directly serving Indians, for example, only 1.5 percent are presently under Indian control. Only 2.4 percent of Indian health programs are run by Indians. The result is a burgeoning Federal bureaucracy, programs which are far less effective than they ought to be, and an erosion of Indian initiative and morale.

I believe that both of these policy extremes are wrong. Federal termination errs in one direction, Federal paternalism errs in the other. Only by clearly rejecting both of these extremes can we achieve a policy which truly serves the best interests of the Indian people. Self-determination among the Indian people can and must be encouraged without the threat of eventual termination. In my view, in fact, that is the only way that self-determination can effectively be fostered.

This, then, must be the goal of any new national policy toward the Indian people to strengthen the Indian's sense of autonomy without threatening this sense of community. We must assure the Indian that he can assume control of his own life without being separated involuntary from the tribal group. And we must make it clear that Indians can become independent of Federal control without being cut off from Federal concern and Federal support. My specific recommendations to the Congress are designed to carry out this policy. . . .

The recommendations of this administration represent an historic step forward in Indian policy. We are proposing to break sharply with past approaches to Indian problems. In place of a long series of piece-meal reforms, we suggest a new and coherent strategy. In place of policies which simply call for more spending, we suggest policies which call for wiser spending. In place of policies which oscillate between the deadly extremes of forced termination and constant paternalism, we suggest a policy in which the Federal government and the Indian community play complementary roles.

But most importantly, we have turned from the question of *whether* the Federal government has a responsibility to Indians to the question of *how* that responsibility can best be furthered. We have concluded that the Indians will get better programs and that public monies will be more effectively expended if the people who are most affected by these programs are responsible for operating them.

The Indians of America need Federal assistance—this much has long been clear. What has not always been clear, however, is that the Federal government needs Indian energies and Indian leadership if its assistance is to be effective in improving the conditions of Indian life. It is a new and balanced relationship between the Unites States government and the first Americans that is at the heart of our approach to Indian problems. And that is why we now approach these problems with new confidence that they will successfully be overcome.

Source: Public Papers of the Presidents of the United States: Richard Nixon, 1970, pp. 564–67, 576.

7. Fort Laramie Treaty—1868
Treaty with the Sioux—Brulé, Oglala, Miniconjou, Yanktonai, Hunkpapa, Blackfeet, Cuthead, Two Kettle, Sans Arcs, and Santee—and Arapaho

Along with the fishing-rights treaties in Washington State (Medicine Creek, Point Elliott, and others), the Fort Laramie Treaty of 1868 has been the most often cited by

Red Power advocates. It was negotiated after the Civil War, a time when the U.S. Army was weak on the Plains, and contains some remarkable concessions. It set aside a large area, which came to be called "The Great Sioux Nation," that included not only the Black Hills, but also parts of what became North and South Dakota, Wyoming, and Nebraska. After 15 articles spelling out what the Indians will get (such things as a suit of wool clothing) Articles 16 provides that: "The United States hereby agrees and stipulates that the country north of the North Platte River and east of the summits of the Big Horn Mountains shall be held and considered to be unceded Indian territory, and also stipulates and agrees that no white person or persons shall be permitted to settle upon or occupy any portion of the same." In subsequent years, this land base was whittled to the present-day reservations.

15 Stat., 635.
Ratified, Feb. 16, 1869
Proclaimed, Feb. 24, 1869

Articles of a treaty made and concluded by and between Lieutenant-General William T. Sherman, General William S. Harney, General Alfred H. Terry, General C. C. Augur, J. B. Henderson, Nathaniel G. Taylor, John B. Sanborn, and Samuel F. Tappan, duly appointed commissioners on the part of the United States, and the different bands of the Sioux Nation of Indians, by their chiefs and head-men, whose names are hereto subscribed, they being duly authorized to act in the premises.

ARTICLE 1. From this day forward all war between the parties to this agreement shall forever cease. The Government of the United States desires peace, and its honor is hereby pledged to keep it. The Indians desire peace, and they now pledge their honor to maintain it.

If bad men among the whites, or among other people subject to the authority of the United States, shall commit any wrong upon the person or property of the Indians, the United States will, upon proof made to the agent and forwarded to the Commissioner of Indian Affairs at Washington City, proceed at once to cause the offender to be arrested and punished according to the laws of the United States, and also re-imburse the injured person for the loss sustained.

If bad men among the Indians shall commit a wrong or depredation upon the person or property of any one, white, black, or Indian, subject to the authority of the United States, and at peace therewith, the Indians herein named solemnly agree that they will, upon proof made to their agent and notice by him, deliver up the wrong-doer to the United States, to be tried and punished according to its laws; and in case they wilfully [sic] refuse so to do, the person injured shall be re-imbursed for his loss from the annuities or other moneys due or to become due to them under this or other treaties made with the United States. And the President, on advising with the Commissioner of Indian Affairs, shall prescribe such rules and regulations for ascertaining damages under the provisions of this article as in his judgment may be proper. But no one sustaining loss while violating the provisions of this treaty or the laws of the United States shall be re-imbursed therefor [*sic*].

ARTICLE 2. The United States agrees that the following district of country, to wit, viz: commencing on the east bank of the Missouri River where the forty-sixth parallel of north latitude crosses the same, thence along low-water mark down said east bank to a point opposite where the northern line of the State of Nebraska strikes the river, thence west across said river, and along the northern line of Nebraska to the one hundred and fourth degree of longitude west from Greenwich, thence north on said meridian to a point where the forty-sixth parallel of north latitude intercepts the same, thence due east along said parallel to the place of beginning; and in addition thereto, all existing reservations on the east bank of said river shall be, and the same is, set apart for the absolute and undisturbed use and occupation of the Indians herein named, and for such other friendly tribes or individual Indians as from time to time they may be willing, with the consent of the United States, to admit amongst them; and the United States now solemnly agrees that no persons except those herein designated and authorized so to do, and except such officers, agents, and employes [*sic*]of the Government as may be authorized to enter upon Indian reservations in discharge of duties enjoined by law, shall ever be permitted to pass over, settle upon, or reside in the territory described in this article, or in such territory as may be added to this reservation for the use of said Indians, and henceforth they will and do hereby relinquish all claims or right in and to any portion of the United States or Territories, except such as is embraced within the limits aforesaid, and except as hereinafter provided.

ARTICLE 3. If it should appear from actual survey or other satisfactory examination of said tract of land that it contains less than one hundred and sixty acres of tillable land for each person who, at the time, may be authorized to reside on it under the provisions of this treaty, and a very considerable number of such persons shall be disposed to commence cultivating the soil as farmers, the United States agrees to set apart, for the use of said Indians, as herein provided, such additional quantity of arable land, adjoining to said reservation, or as near to the same as it can be obtained, as may be required to provide the necessary amount.

ARTICLE 4. The United States agrees, at its own proper expense, to construct at some place on the Missouri River, near the center of said reservation, where timber and water may be convenient, the following buildings, to wit: a warehouse, a storeroom for the use of the agent in storing goods belonging to the Indians, to cost not less than twenty-five hundred dollars; an agency-building for the residence of the agent, to cost not exceeding three thousand dollars; a residence for the physician, to cost not more than three thousand dollars; and five other buildings, for a carpenter, farmer, blacksmith, miller, and engineer, each to cost not exceeding two thousand dollars; also a schoolhouse or mission-building, so soon as a sufficient number of children can be induced by the agent to attend school, which shall not cost exceeding five thousand dollars.

The United States agrees further to cause to be erected on said reservation, near the other buildings herein authorized, a good steam circular-saw mill, with a grist-mill and shingle-machine attached to the same, to cost not exceeding eight thousand dollars.

ARTICLE 5. The United States agrees that the agent for said Indians shall in the future make his home at the agency-building; that he shall reside among them, and keep an office open at all times for the purpose of prompt and diligent inquiry into such matters of complaint by and against the Indians as may be presented for investigation under the provisions of their treaty stipulations, as also for the faithful discharge of other duties enjoined on him by law. In all cases of depredation on person or property he shall cause the evidence to be taken in writing and forwarded, together with his findings, to the Commissioner of Indian Affairs, whose decision, subject to the revision of the Secretary of the Interior, shall be binding on the parties to this treaty.

ARTICLE 6. If any individual belonging to said tribes of Indians, or legally incorporated with them, being the head of a family, shall desire to commence farming, he shall have the privilege to select, in the presence and with the assistance of the agent then in charge, a tract of land within said reservation, not exceeding three hundred and twenty acres in extent, which tract, when so selected, certified, and recorded in the "land-book," as herein directed, shall cease to be held in common, but the same may be occupied and held in the exclusive possession of the person selecting it, and of his family, so long as he or they may continue to cultivate it.

Any person over eighteen years of age, not being the head of a family, may in like manner select and cause to be certified to him or her, for purposes of cultivation, a quantity of land not exceeding eighty acres in extent, and thereupon be entitled to the exclusive possession of the same as above directed.

For each tract of land so selected a certificate, containing a description thereof and the name of the person selecting it, with a certificate endorsed thereon that the same has been recorded, shall be delivered to the party entitled to it, by the agent, after the same shall have been recorded by him in a book to be kept in his office, subject to inspection, which said book shall be known as the "Sioux Land-Book."

The President may, at any time, order a survey of the reservation, and, when so surveyed, Congress shall provide for protecting the rights of said settlers in their improvements, and may fix the character of the title held by each. The United States may pass such laws on the subject of alienation and descent of property between the Indians and their descendants as may be thought proper. And it is further stipulated that any male Indians, over eighteen years of age, of any band or tribe that is or shall hereafter become a party to this treaty, who now is or who shall hereafter become a resident or occupant of any reservation or Territory not included in the tract of country designated and described in this treaty for the permanent home of the Indians, which is not mineral land, nor reserved by the United States for special purposes other than Indian occupation, and who shall have made improvements thereon of the value of two hundred dollars or more, and continuously occupied the same as a homestead for the term of three years, shall be entitled to receive from the United States a patent for one hundred and sixty acres of land including his said improvements, the same to be in the form of the legal subdivisions of the surveys of the public lands. Upon application in writing, sustained by the proof of two disinterested witnesses, made to the register of the local land-office when the land sought to be entered is within a land district, and when the tract sought to be entered is not in any land district, then upon said application and proof being made to the Commissioner of the General Land-Office, and the right of such Indian or Indians to enter such tract or tracts of land shall accrue and be perfect from the date of his first improvements thereon, and shall continue as long as he continues his residence and improvements, and no longer'. And any Indian or Indians receiving a patent for land under the foregoing provisions, shall thereby and from thenceforth become and be a citizen of the United States, and be entitled to all the privileges and immunities of such citizens, and shall, at the same time, retain all his rights to benefits accruing to Indians under this treaty.

ARTICLE 7. In order to insure the civilization of the Indians entering into this treaty, the necessity of education is admitted, especially of such of them as are or may be settled on said agricultural reservations, and they therefore pledge themselves to compel their children, male and female, between the ages of six and sixteen years, to attend school; and it is hereby made the duty of the agent for said Indians to see that this stipulation is strictly complied with; and the United States agrees that for every thirty children between said ages who can be induced or compelled to attend school, a house shall be provided and a teacher competent to teach the elementary branches of an English education shall be furnished, who will reside among said Indians, and faithfully discharge his or her duties as a teacher. The provisions of this article to continue for not less than twenty years.

ARTICLE 8. When the head of a family or lodge shall have selected lands and received his certificate as above directed, and the agent shall be satisfied that he intends in good faith to commence cultivating the soil for a living, he shall be entitled to receive seeds and agricultural implements for the first year, not exceeding in value one hundred dollars, and for each succeeding year he shall continue to farm, for a period of three years more, he shall be entitled to receive seeds and implements as aforesaid, not exceeding in value twenty-five dollars.

And it is further stipulated that such persons as commence farming shall receive instruction from the farmer herein provided for, and whenever more than one hundred persons shall enter upon the cultivation of the soil, a second blacksmith shall be provided, with such iron, steel, and other material as may be needed.

ARTICLE 9. At any time after ten years from the making of this treaty, the United States shall have the privilege of withdrawing the physician, farmer, blacksmith, carpenter, engineer, and miller herein provided for, but in case of such withdrawal, an additional sum thereafter of ten thousand dollars per annum shall be devoted to the education of said Indians, and the Commissioner of Indian Affairs shall, upon careful inquiry into their condition, make such rules and regulations for the expenditure of said sum as will best promote the educational and moral improvement of said tribes.

ARTICLE 10. In lieu of all sums of money or other annuities provided to be paid to the Indians herein named, under any treaty or treaties heretofore made, the United States agrees to deliver at the agency-house on the reservation herein named, on or before the first day of August of each year, for thirty years, the following articles, to wit:

For each male person over fourteen years of age, a suit of good substantial woolen clothing, consisting of coat, pantaloons, flannel shirt, hat, and a pair of home-made socks.

For each female over twelve years of age, a flannel skirt, or the goods necessary to make it, a pair of woolen hose, twelve yards of calico, and twelve yards of cotton domestics.

For the boys and girls under the ages named, such flannel and cotton goods as may be needed to make each a suit as aforesaid, together with a pair of woolen hose for each.

And in order that the Commissioner of Indian Affairs may be able to estimate properly for the articles herein named, it shall be the duty of the agent each year to forward to him a full and exact census of the Indians, on which the estimate from year to year can be based.

And in addition to the clothing herein named, the sum of ten dollars for each person entitled to the beneficial effects of this treaty shall be annually appropriated for a period of thirty years, while such persons roam and hunt, and twenty dollars for, each person who engages in farming, to be used by the Secretary of the Interior in the purchase of such articles as from time to time the condition and necessities of the Indians may indicate to be proper. And if within the thirty years, at any time, it shall appear that the amount of money needed for clothing under this article can be appropriated to better uses for the Indians named herein, Congress may, by law, change the appropriation to other purposes; but in no event shall the amount of this appropriation be withdrawn or discontinued for the period named. And the President shall annually detail an officer of the Army to be present and attest the delivery of all the goods herein named to the Indians, and he shall inspect and report on the quantity and quality of the goods and the manner of their delivery. And it is hereby expressly stipulated that each Indian over the age of four years, who shall have removed to and settled permanently upon said reservation and complied with the stipulations of this treaty, shall be entitled to receive from the United States, for the period of four years after he shall have settled upon said reservation, one pound of meat and one pound of flour per day, provided the Indians cannot furnish their own subsistence at an earlier date. And it is further stipulated that the United States will furnish and deliver to each lodge of Indians or family of persons legally incorporated with them, who shall remove to the reservation herein described and commence farming, one good American cow, and one good well-broken pair of American oxen within sixty days after such lodge or family shall have so settled upon said reservation.

ARTICLE 11. In consideration of the advantages and benefits conferred by this treaty, and the many pledges of friendship by the United States, the tribes who are parties to this agreement hereby stipulate that they will relinquish all right to occupy permanently the territory outside their reservation as herein defined, but yet reserve the right to hunt on any lands north of North Platte, and on the Republican Fork of the Smoky Hill River, so long as the buffalo may range thereon in such numbers as to justify the chase. And they, the said Indians, further expressly agree:

1st. That they will withdraw all opposition to the construction of the railroads now being built on the plains.

2d. That they will permit the peaceful construction of any railroad not passing over their reservation as herein defined.

3d. That they will not attack any persons at home, or travelling, nor molest or disturb any wagon-trains, coaches, mules, or cattle belonging to the people of the United States, or to persons friendly therewith.

4th. They will never capture, or carry off from the settlements, white women or children.

5th. They will never kill or scalp white men, nor attempt to do them harm.

6th. They withdraw all pretence of opposition to the construction of the railroad now being built along the Platte River and westward to the Pacific Ocean, and they will not in future object to the construction of railroads, wagon-roads, mail-stations, or other works of utility or necessity, which may be ordered or permitted by the laws of the United States. But should such roads or other works be constructed on the lands of their reservation, the Government will pay the tribe whatever amount of damage may be assessed by three disinterested commissioners to be appointed by the President for that purpose, one of said commissioners to be a chief or head-man of the tribe.

7th. They agree to withdraw all opposition to the military posts or roads now established south of the North Platte River, or that may be established, not in violation of treaties heretofore made or hereafter to be made with any of the Indian tribes.

ARTICLE 12. No treaty for the cession of any portion or part of the reservation herein described which may be held in common shall be of any validity or force as against the said Indians, unless executed and signed by at least three-fourths of all the adult male Indians, occupying or interested in the same; and no cession by the tribe shall be understood or construed in such manner as to deprive, without his consent, any individual member of the tribe of his rights to any tract of land selected by him, as provided in article 6 of this treaty.

ARTICLE 13. The United States hereby agrees to furnish annually to the Indians the physician, teachers, carpenter, miller, engineer, farmer, and blacksmiths as herein contemplated, and that such appropriations shall be made from time to time, on the estimates of the Secretary of the Interior, as will be sufficient to employ such persons.

ARTICLE 14. It is agreed that the sum of five hundred dollars annually, for three years from date, shall be expended in presents to the ten persons of said tribe who in the judgment of the agent may grow the most valuable crops for the respective year.

ARTICLE 15. The Indians herein named agree that when the agency-house or other buildings shall be constructed on the reservation named, they will regard said reservation their permanent home, and they will make no permanent settlement elsewhere; but they shall have the right, subject to the conditions and modifications of this treaty, to hunt, as stipulated in Article 11 hereof.

ARTICLE 16. The United States hereby agrees and stipulates that the country north of the North Platte River and east of the summits of the Big Horn Mountains shall be held and considered to be unceded Indian territory, and also stipulates and agrees that no white person or persons shall be permitted to settle upon or occupy any portion of the same; or without the consent of the Indians first had and obtained, to pass through the same; and it is further agreed by the United States that within ninety days after the conclusion of peace with all the bands of the Sioux Nation, the military posts now established in the territory in this article named shall be abandoned, and that the road leading to them and by them to the settlements in the Territory of Montana shall be closed.

ARTICLE 17. It is hereby expressly understood and agreed by and between the respective parties to this treaty that the execution of this treaty and its ratification by the United States Senate shall have the effect, and shall be construed as abrogating and annulling all treaties and agreements heretofore entered into between the respective parties hereto, so far as such treaties and agreements obligate the United States to furnish and provide money, clothing, or other articles of property to such Indians and bands of Indians as become parties to this treaty, but no further.

In testimony of all which, we, the said commissioners, and we, the chiefs and headmen of the Brulé' band of the Sioux nation, have hereunto set our hands and seals at Fort Laramie, Dakota Territory, this twenty-ninth day of April, in the year one thousand eight hundred and sixty-eight.

[followed by signatures and seals]

Source: National Archives and Records Administration, General Records of the United States Government, Record Group 11. ARC Identifier 299803.

8. U.S. Supreme Court Ruling, Black Hills

United States courts have held the expropriation of the Black Hills, in South Dakota, to be illegal. Proposed compensation for the taking by 2011, with interest, had passed $1 billion. The Oglala refuse to accept the payment. The Supreme Court ruling is excerpted here.

U.S. Supreme Court
UNITED STATES v. SIOUX NATION OF INDIANS, 448 U.S. 371 (1980)
448 U.S. 371
UNITED STATES v. SIOUX NATION OF INDIANS ET AL.
CERTIORARI TO THE UNITED STATES COURT OF CLAIMS.
No. 79–639.
Argued March 24, 1980.
Decided June 30, 1980.

Under the Fort Laramie Treaty of 1868, the United States pledged that the Great Sioux Reservation, including the Black Hills, would be "set apart for the absolute and undisturbed use and occupation" of the Sioux Nation (Sioux), and that no treaty for the cession of any part of the reservation would be valid as against the Sioux unless executed and signed by at least three-fourths of the adult male Sioux population. The treaty also reserved the Sioux' right to hunt in certain unceded territories.

Subsequently, in 1876, an "agreement" presented to the Sioux by a special Commission but signed by only 10% of the adult male Sioux population, provided that the Sioux would relinquish their rights to the Black Hills and to hunt in the unceded territories, in exchange for subsistence rations for as long as they would be needed. In 1877, Congress passed an Act (1877 Act) implementing this "agreement" and thus, in effect, abrogated the Fort Laramie Treaty.

Throughout the ensuing years, the Sioux regarded the 1877 Act as a breach of that treaty, but Congress did not enact any mechanism by which they could litigate their claims against the United States until 1920, when a special jurisdictional Act was passed. Pursuant to this Act, the Sioux brought suit in the Court of Claims, alleging that the Government had taken the Black Hills without just compensation, in violation of the Fifth Amendment. In 1942, this claim was dismissed by the Court of Claims, which held that it was not authorized by the 1920 Act to question whether the compensation afforded the Sioux in the 1877 Act was an adequate price for the Black Hills and that the Sioux' claim was a moral one not protected by the Just Compensation Clause.

Thereafter, upon enactment of the Indian Claims Commission Act in 1946, the Sioux resubmitted their claim to the Indian Claims Commission, which held that the 1877 Act effected a taking for which the Sioux were entitled to just compensation and that the 1942 Court of Claims decision did not bar the taking claim under *res judicata*. On appeal, the Court of Claims, affirming the Commission's holding that a want of fair and honorable dealings on the Government's part was evidenced, ultimately held that the Sioux were entitled to an award of at least $17.5 million, without interest, as damages under the Indian Claims Commission Act, [448 U.S. 371, 372] for the lands surrendered and for gold taken by trespassing prospectors prior to passage of the 1877 Act.

But the court further held that the merits of the Sioux' taking claim had been reached in its 1942 decision and that therefore such claim was barred by *res judicata*. The court noted that only if the acquisition of the Black Hills amounted to an unconstitutional taking would the Sioux be entitled to interest. Thereafter, in 1978, Congress passed an Act (1978 Act) providing for *de novo* review by the Court of Claims of the merits of the Indian Claims Commission's holding that the 1877 Act effected a taking of the Black Hills, without regard to *res judicata*, and authorizing the Court of Claims to take new evidence in the case. Pursuant to this Act, the Court of Claims affirmed the Commission's holding. In so affirming, the court, in order to decide whether the 1877 Act had effected a taking or whether it had been a noncompensable act of congressional guardianship over tribal property, applied the test of whether Congress had made a good-faith effort to give the Sioux the full value of their land. Under this test, the court characterized the 1877 Act as a taking in exercise of Congress' power of eminent domain over Indian property. Accordingly, the court held that the Sioux were entitled to an award of interest on the principal sum of $17.1 million (the fair market value of the Black Hills as of 1877), dating from 1877.

Held:

1. Congress' enactment of the 1978 Act, as constituting a mere waiver of the *res judicata* effect of a prior judicial decision rejecting the validity of a legal claim against the United States, did not violate the doctrine of the separation of powers either on the ground that Congress impermissibly disturbed the finality of a judicial decree by rendering the Court of Claims' earlier judgments in the case mere advisory opinions, or on the ground that Congress overstepped its bounds by granting the Court of Claims jurisdiction to decide the merits of the Black Hills claim, while prescribing a rule for decision that left that court no adjudicatory function to perform. *Cherokee Nation v. United States*, 270 U.S. 476. Congress, under its broad constitutional power to define and "to pay the Debts . . . of the United States," may recognize its obligation to pay a moral debt not only by direct appropriation, but also by waiving an otherwise valid defense to a legal claim against the United States. When the Sioux returned to the Court of Claims following passage of the 1978 Act, they were in pursuit of judicial enforcement

of a new legal right. Congress in no way attempted to prescribe the outcome of the Court of Claims' new review of the merits. *United States v. Klein,* 13 Wall. 128, distinguished. Pp. 390–407. [448 U.S. 371, 373]

2. The Court of Claims' legal analysis and factual findings fully support its conclusion that the 1877 Act did not effect a "mere change in the form of investment of Indian tribal property," but, rather, effected a taking of tribal property which had been set aside by the Fort Laramie Treaty for the Sioux' exclusive occupation, which taking implied an obligation on the Government's part to make just compensation to the Sioux. That obligation, including an award of interest, must now be paid. The principles that it "must [be] presume[d] that Congress acted in perfect good faith in the dealings with the Indians of which complaint is made, and that [it] exercised its best judgment in the premises," *Lone Wolf v. Hitchcock,* 187 U.S. 553, 568 , are inapplicable in this case. The question whether a particular congressional measure was appropriate for protecting and advancing a tribe's interests, and therefore not subject to the Just Compensation Clause, is factual in nature, and the answer must be based on a consideration of all the evidence presented. While a reviewing court is not to second-guess a legislative judgment that a particular measure would serve the tribe's best interests, the court is required, in considering whether the measure was taken in pursuance of Congress' power to manage and control tribal lands for the Indians' welfare, to engage in a thorough and impartial examination of the historical record. A presumption of congressional good faith cannot serve to advance such an inquiry.

220 Ct. Cl. 442, 601 F.2d 1157, affirmed.

BLACKMUN, J., delivered the opinion of the Court, in which BURGER, C.J., and BRENNAN, STEWART, MARSHALL, POWELL, and STEVENS, J.J., joined, and in Parts III and V of which WHITE, J., joined. WHITE, J., filed an opinion concurring in part and concurring in the judgment, post, p. 424. REHNQUIST, J., filed a dissenting opinion, post, p. 424.

Deputy Solicitor General Claiborne argued the cause for the United States. With him on the briefs were Solicitor General McCree, Assistant Attorney General Moorman, William Alsup, Dirk D. Snel, and Martin W. Matzen.

Arthur Lazarus, Jr., argued the cause for respondents. With him on the brief were Marvin J. Sonosky, Reid P. Chambers, Harry R. Sachse, and William Howard Payne. *

[Footnote *] Steven M. Tullberg and Robert T. Coulter filed a brief for the Indian Law Resource Center as amicus curiae. [448 U.S. 371, 374]

MR. JUSTICE BLACKMUN delivered the opinion of the Court.

This case concerns the Black Hills of South Dakota, the Great Sioux Reservation, and a colorful, and in many respects tragic, chapter in the history of the Nation's

West. Although the comes down to a claim of interest since 1877 on an award of over $17 million, it is necessary, in order to understand the controversy, to review at some length the chronology of the case and its factual setting.

I

For over a century now the Sioux Nation has claimed that the United States unlawfully abrogated the Fort Laramie Treaty of April 29, 1868, 15 Stat. 635, in Art. II of which the United States pledged that the Great Sioux Reservation, including the Black Hills, would be "set apart for the absolute and undisturbed use and occupation of the Indians herein named." Id., at 636. The Fort Laramie Treaty was concluded at the culmination of the Powder River War of 1866–1867, a series of military engagements in which the Sioux tribes, led by their great chief, Red Cloud, fought to protect the integrity of earlier-recognized treaty lands from the incursion of white settlers.

The Fort Laramie Treaty included several agreements central to the issues presented in this case. First, it established the Great Sioux Reservation, a tract of land bounded on the east by the Missouri River, on the south by the northern border of the State of Nebraska, on the north by the forty-sixth parallel of north latitude, and on the west by the one [448 U.S. 371, 375] hundred and fourth meridian of west longitude, in addition to certain reservations already existing east of the Missouri. The United States "solemnly agree[d]" that no unauthorized persons "shall ever be permitted to pass over, settle upon, or reside in [this] territory." Ibid.

Second, the United States permitted members of the Sioux tribes to select lands within the reservation for cultivation. Id., at 637. In order to assist the Sioux in becoming civilized farmers, the Government promised to provide them with the necessary services and materials, and with subsistence rations for four years. Id., at 639.

Third, in exchange for the benefits conferred by the treaty, the Sioux agreed to relinquish their rights under the Treaty of September 17, 1851, to occupy territories outside the reservation, while reserving their "right to hunt on any lands north of North Platte, and on the Republican Fork of the Smoky Hill river, so long as the buffalo may range thereon in such numbers as to justify the chase." Ibid. The Indians also expressly agreed to withdraw all opposition to the building [448 U.S. 371, 376] of railroads that did not pass over their reservation lands, not to engage in attacks on settlers, and to withdraw their opposition to the military posts and roads that had been established south of the North Platte River.

Fourth, Art. XII of the treaty provided:

"No treaty for the cession of any portion or part of the reservation herein described which may be held in common shall be of any validity or force as against the said Indians, unless executed and signed by at least three fourths of all the adult male Indians, occupying or interested in the same." Ibid. 4

. . ..

The aforementioned findings fully support the Court of Claims' conclusion that the 1877 Act appropriated the Black Hills "in circumstances which involved an implied undertaking by [the United States] to make just compensation to the tribe." 32 *United States v. Creek Nation,* 295 U.S., at 111. [448 U.S. 371, 422] We make only two additional observations about this case. First, dating at least from the decision in *Cherokee Nation v. Southern Kansas R. Co.,* 135 U.S. 641, 657 (1890), this Court has recognized that Indian lands, to which a tribe holds recognized title, "are held subject to the authority of the general government to take them for such objects as are germane to the execution of the powers granted to it; provided only, that they are not taken without just compensation being made to the owner." In the same decision the Court emphasized that the owner of such lands "is entitled to reasonable, certain and adequate provision for obtaining compensation before his occupancy is disturbed." Id., at 659. The Court of Claims gave effect to this principle when it held that the Government's uncertain and indefinite obligation to provide the Sioux with rations until they became self-sufficient did not constitute adequate consideration for the Black Hills.

Second, it seems readily apparent to us that the obligation to provide rations to the Sioux was undertaken in order to ensure them a means of surviving their transition from the nomadic life of the hunt to the agrarian lifestyle Congress had chosen for them. Those who have studied the Government's reservation policy during this period of our Nation's history agree. See n. 11, supra. It is important to recognize [448 U.S. 371, 423] that the 1877 Act, in addition to removing the Black Hills from the Great Sioux Reservation, also ceded the Sioux' hunting rights in a vast tract of land extending beyond the boundaries of that reservation. See n. 14, supra. Under such circumstances, it is reasonable to conclude that Congress' undertaking of an obligation to provide rations for the Sioux was a quid pro quo for depriving them of their chosen way of life, and was not intended to compensate them for the taking of the Black Hills.

In sum, we conclude that the legal analysis and factual findings of the Court of Claims fully support its conclusion that the terms of the 1877 Act did not effect "a mere change in the form of investment of Indian tribal property." *Lone Wolf v. Hitchcock,* [187 U.S., at 568 [448 U.S. 371, 424]. Rather, the 1877 Act effected a taking of tribal property, property which had been set aside for the exclusive occupation of the Sioux by the Fort Laramie Treaty of 1868. That taking implied an obligation on the part of the Government to make just compensation to the Sioux Nation, and that obligation, including an award of interest, must now, at last, be paid.

The judgment of the Court of Claims is affirmed.

It is so ordered.

Source: *United States v. Sioux Nation,* 448 US 371 (1980).

Selected Bibliography

Primary Resources and Key Web Sites

Alcatraz and American Indian Activism: A Photographic History of the 1969–1971 Occupation of Alcatraz Island by Indians of All Tribes, Inc. http://www.csulb.edu/~gcampus/libarts/am-indian/alcatraz/index.html

"Alcatraz is Not an Island: Timeline of Indian Activism." Public Broadcasting System. 2002. http://www.pbs.org/itvs/alcatrazisnotanisland/timeline.html

American Indian Movement: The home pages for AIM, headquartered in the Twin Cities. http://www.dickshovel.com/AIMIntro.html Also: [http://www.aimovement.org/. Accessed January 4, 2007].

National Indian Youth Council Web page http://www.niyc-alb.org/history.htm

Wounded Knee Legal Defense/Offense Committee Records. Minnesota Historical Society, Minneapolis. 143 boxes.

References

"ABC: Americans Before Columbus." *OCLC On-line Union Catalogue.* Dublin, OH: OCLC, 1998.

"Activists Call for Enforced Laws at Whiteclay." *Indianz.com,* March 3, 2003. http://groups.yahoo.com/group/NatNews/message/28097

"Actor's Goal: Indian Rights." *New York Times* in *Omaha World-Herald,* December 30, 2007, 8-A.

"Africans and Native Americans: The Language of Race and the Evolution of Red-Black Peoples." University of Illinois Press. No date. http://www.press.uillinois.edu/books/catalog/72cac6xt9780252063213.html

"AIM Fire: The American Indian Movement Targets the Rocky." *Denver Westword,* December 15, 2005, n.p.

"AIM Virginia Chapter. Position Statement of Virginia AIM and the American Indian Cultural Resource Center on the Mascot Issue." No date. http://www.aics.org/aimva/aimva.html

American Friends Service Committee. *Uncommon Controversy: Fishing Rights of the Muckleshoot, Puyallup, and Nisqually Indians.* Seattle: University of Washington Press, 1970.

"American Indian Activist Robideau Dies at 61." *Associated Press* in *Seattle Post-Intelligencer,* February 20, 2009, n.p.

"American Indian Movement Arizona Chapter Addresses the Desecration of Sacred Ceremonies." Statement of American Indian Movement, Arizona Chapter, February 2, 1998. http://www.dickshovel.com/dese.html

American Indian Movement Council on Security and Intelligence. http://www.aimove ment.org/csi/index.html. These links supply scanned images of declassified FBI, CIA, Justice Department and White House documents obtained by AIM under the U.S. Freedom of Information Act.

"American Indian Movement Florida Chapter: It's about Our Land. It's about Our People. It's about our Culture." 2007. http://www.freewebs.com/aimflorida/

American Indian Movement. Free Peltier. No date. http://www.aimovement.org/peltier/

American Indian Movement. Grand Governing Council. Official Web Site. http://www.aimovement.org/0. 2007

"Americans Who Tell the Truth: Winona LaDuke." No date. http://www.americanswho tellthetruth.org/pgs/portraits/Winona_LaDuke.html

Anderson, Robert, et al. *Voices from Wounded Knee.* Rooseveltown, NY: Akwesasne Notes, 1974.

Anderson, Wallace (Mad Bear). "The Lost Brother: An Iroquois Prophecy of Serpents," in Shirley Hill Witt and Stan Steiner, eds. *The Way: An Anthology of American Indian Literature.* New York: Vintage, 1972, 243–47.

Annual Report for 1995: Muckleshoot Tribal Council. Auburn, WA: Muckleshoot Indian Tribe, 1995.

Appleford, Rob. "Jimmie Durham and the Carpentry of Ambivalence," *Social Text* 28, no. 4 (2010): 91–111.

Baker, Deborah. "Dems Appeal to Indians: Get Out the Vote." *Associated Press,* July 28, 2004. http://www.coloradoaim.org/blog/2004/07/articles-july-28.html

Ball, Milnar. "Constitution, Court, Indian Tribes." *American Bar Foundation Research Journal* 1 (1987): 1–140.

Ballentine, Betty and Ian. *The Native Americans Today.* Atlanta: Turner Publishing, 1993.

Banks, Dennis, Laurel R. Davis, Synthia Syndnor Slowikowski, and Lawrence A. Wenner. "Tribal Names and Mascots in Sports." *Journal of Sport and Social Issues* 17 (April, 1993): 1–33.

Banks, Dennis and Richard Erdoes. *Ojibwa Warrior: Dennis Banks and the Rise of the American Indian Movement.* Norman: University of Oklahoma Press, 2004.

Barsh, Russel L. *The Washington Fishing Rights Controversy: An Economic Critique.* Seattle: University of Washington School of Business Administration, 1977.

Bates, Tom. "The Government's Secret War on the Indian." *Oregon Times,* February–March 1976, 14.

Baylor, Timothy. 1994. *Modern Warriors: Mobilization and Decline of the American Indian Movement (AIM), 1968–1979.* PhD diss., Department of History, University of North Carolina at Chapel Hill.

"Beer Companies Seek Dismissal of Oglala Sioux Tribe's Lawsuit." *Associated Press* in *Omaha World-Herald,* May 1, 2012, 2-B.

Bims, Hamilton. "Indian Uprising for Civil Rights: Washington Group Hires NAACP Attorney in Red-hot Battle over Fishing Rights." *Ebony,* February, 1967, 64–65, 68, 69, 72.

"Biography: Hank Adams." *Answers.com.* 2006. http://www.answers.com/topic/hank-adams

Bloom, Alexander and Wini Brienes. *Takin' it to the Streets.* New York: Oxford University Press, 1995.

Blue Cloud, Peter. *Alcatraz Is Not an Island.* Berkeley, CA: Wingbow Press, 1972.

Bonney, Rachel A. "The Role of AIM Leaders in Indian Nationalism." *American Indian Quarterly* 3, no. 3 (Autumn, 1977): 209–224.

Brack, Fred. "Fishing Rights: Who is Entitled to Northwest Salmon?" *Seattle Post-Intelligencer Northwest Magazine*, January 16, 1977, 8–10.

Brand, Johanna. *The Life and Death of Anna Mae Aquash.* Toronto: Lorimer, 1978.

Brando, Marlon. "The Godfather: That Unfinished Oscar Speech." *New York Times*, March 30, 1973. http://www.nytimes.com/packages/html/movies/bestpictures/godfather-ar3.html

Brennan, Charlie. "Churchill Finds Fans at Calif. Fest; C.U. Professor Gives Keynote address at Anarchist Book Fair." *Rocky Mountain News*, March 28, 2005, 4-A.

Brennan, Charlie. "Tribe Clarifies Stance on Prof.; Milder Statement Explains Churchill's 'Associate' Label" *Rocky Mountain News*, May 21, 2005, 16-A.

Brown, Dee. 1970. *Bury My Heart at Wounded Knee: An Indian History of the American West.* New York: Bantam, 1970.

Brugge, Doug and Timothy Benally. *The Navajo People and Uranium Mining.* Albuquerque: University of New Mexico Press, 2006.

Bule, Lisa. "American Indian Movement Plans to Protest Chasco Fiesta Mockery." *St. Petersburg Times,* March 14, 2009. http://www.tampabay.com/news/business/tourism/article983881.ece

"The Bureau of Caucasian Affairs." The Bureau of Caucasian Affairs. http://www.pantherslodge.com/una.html

Burnett, Sara. "C.U. Panel: Fire Prof; Churchill Should be Cut Loose, Say Six of Nine Who Cast Secret Ballots." *Rocky Mountain News*, June 14, 2006. http://www.rockymountainnews.com/drmn/education/article/0,1299,DRMN_957_4773332,00.html

Burnette, Robert and Richard Erdoes. *The Tortured Americans.* Englewood Cliffs, New Jersey: Prentice-Hall, 1971.

Burnette, Robert and John Koster. 1974. *The Road to Wounded Knee.* New York: Bantam, 1974.

Caldwell, Christopher. "The Antiwar, Anti-Abortion, Anti-Drug-Enforcement-Administration, Anti-Medicare Candidacy of Dr. Ron Paul." *New York Times Magazine*, July 22, 2007.

Caldwell, Earl. "Determined Indians Watch and Wait on 'the Rock.'" *New York Times,* December 10, 1969, 37, 43.

Callis, Tom. "Arrested Movement: Looking Back at the American Indian Movement." *Klipsun Magazine.* No date. http://klipsun.wwu.edu/archives/w07b/story.php

Canning, Susan. "Jimmie Durham," *The New Art Examiner* 23, no. 2 (1995): 31–35.

Carroll, Vincent. "On Point: Vine Deloria's Other Side." *Rocky Mountain News*, November 18, 2005. http://www.rockymountainnews.com/drmn/columnist/0,1299,DRMN_23972_106,00.html#bio

Carson, Jerry. "Indians Face Court Battle Over Puyallup Fishing." *Seattle Times*, September 10, 1970, B-10.

Castillo, Edward. "A Reminiscence of the Alcatraz Occupation." *American Indian Culture and Research Journal* 18, no. 4 (1994): 111–22.

Cassirer, Ernest. *An Essay on Man*. New Haven, CT: Yale University Press, 1944.

Central Indiana AIM Support Group. Mission Statement. No date. http://www.oocities.org/capitolhill/7153/

El Centro de la Raza 35th Anniversary. "What Kind of World Will We Leave Our Children?" October 13, 2007, Washington State Convention and Trade Center, Seattle.

Champagne, Duane, ed. *The Native North American Almanac: A Reference Work on Native North Americans in the United States and Canada*. Detroit, MI: Gale Research, 1994.

Champagne, Duane, ed. *Chronology of Native North American History: From Pre-Columbian Times to the Present*. Detroit, MI: Gale Research, 1994.

Chapman, Serle L. *We, the People: Of Earth and Elders, Vol. II*. Missoula, MT: Mountain Press Publishing Co., 2001.

Chavers, Dean. *Modern American Indian Leaders: Their Lives and Their Works*. 2 vols. Lewiston, ID: Edwin Mellen Press, 2007.

Chrisman, Gabriel. "The Fish-in Protests at Franks Landing." Seattle Civil Rights and Labor History Project. 2006. http://depts.washington.edu/civilr/fish-ins.htm

Churchill, Ward. "American Indian Movement." In Bruce E. Johansen and Barry Pritzker, eds. *Encyclopedia of American Indian History*. Santa Barbara, CA: ABC-CLIO, 2008, 638–46.

Churchill, Ward. "The Bloody Wake of Alcatraz: Repression of the American Indian Movement During the 1970s," in Ward Churchill, ed. *Perversions of Justice: Indigenous Peoples and Anglo-American Law*. San Francisco: City Lights, 2003, 263–302.

Churchill, Ward. "Death Squads in the United States: Confessions of a Government Terrorist." In *From a Native Son: Selected Essays in Indigenism, 1985–1995*. Boston, MA: South End Press, 1996, 231–70.

Churchill, Ward. "Some People Push Back: On the Justice of Roosting Chickens." 2001. No Date. http://www.kersplebedeb.com/mystuff/s11/churchill.html

Churchill, Ward. *Struggles for the Land*. Monroe, ME: Common Courage Press, 1993.

Churchill, Ward and Jim Vander Wall. *Agents of Repression: The FBI's Secret War Against the Black Panther Party and the American Indian Movement*. Boston, MA: South End Press, 1990.

Churchill, Ward and Jim Vander Wall. *Agents of Repression: The FBI's Secret Wars Against the Black Panther Party and the American Indian Movement*. Boston, MA: South End Press, 2002.

Churchill, Ward and Jim Vander Wall. *The Cointelpro Papers*. Boston, MA: South End Press, 1990.

"Cleanup Planned for Largest Abandoned Uranium Mine on the Navajo Nation." *Environment News Service*, September 29, 2011. http://www.ens-newswire.com/ens/sep2011/2011–09–29–092.html

Cleveland [Ohio] American Indian Movement. No date. http://www.clevelandaim.us/

Cobb, Daniel M. "Clyde Merton Warrior." Ponca Nation. No date. http://www.ponca.com/warrior_memorial/warrior_memorial.html

Cobb, Daniel M. "QUESTION: To What Extent Do Scholars Have a Responsibility to the Indigenous Communities They Study and How Can They Fulfill this Responsibility? Telling Stories." HNet: Humanities and Social Sciences On-line. April 16, 2003. http://h-net.msu.edu/cgi-bin/logbrowse.pl?trx=vx&list=H-AmIndian&month=0304&week=c&msg=HCsIvR1zFFV/%2BqdO3DWGLA&user=&pw=

Cobb, Daniel M. and Loretta Fowler. *Beyond Red Power: American Indian Politics and Activism Since 1900*. Santa Fe, NM: School of Advanced Research, 2007.

Cohen, Fay G. *The Indian Patrol in Minneapolis: Social Control and Social Changes in an Urban Context*. PhD dissertation, University of Minnesota, 1973.

Cohen, Fay G. *Treaties on Trial: The Continuing Controversy over Northwest Indian Fishing Rights*. Seattle: University of Washington Press, 1986.

Colorado American Indian Movement. No date. http://www.coloradoaim.org/

Cook, Joan. "Louis R. Bruce, Ex-Commissioner Of Indian Affairs, is Dead at 83." *New York Times*, May 24, 1989. http://www.nytimes.com/1989/05/24/obituaries/louis-r-bruce-ex-commissioner-of-indian-affairs-is-dead-at-83.html

Cornelius, Coleman. "Fightin' Whites Fund Scholarships: T-shirt Sales Reap $100,000 for Indians." *Denver Post*, December 1, 2002. http://www.denverpost.com/Stories/0,1413,36%7E53%7E1021717%7E,00.html

Cornell, Stephen. *The Return of the Native; American Indian Political Resurgence*. New York: Oxford University Press, 1988.

Costo, Rupert. "Alcatraz." *The Indian Historian* 3, no. 9 (1970), n.p.

"Court Move Could End Fishing Dispute." *Tacoma News-Tribune*, March 18, 1968, n.p.

Curtin, Dave, Howard Pankratz, and Arthur Kane. "Questions Stoke Ward Churchill's Firebrand Past." *Denver Post*, February 13, 2005, A-1.

Dahl, Corey. "Indian Activist and Popular Author Dies; Vine Deloria Jr. was a Retired C.U. [Colorado University] Professor." *Boulder (Colorado) Daily Camera*, November 15, 2005. http://www.dailycamera.com/bdc/obituaries/article/0,1713,BDC_2437_4239604,00.html

Dao, James. "In California, Indian Tribes with Casino Money Cast Off Members." *New York Times*, December 13, 2011, A-1, A-22.

Deloria, Vine, Jr. "Alcatraz, Activism, and Accommodation." *American Indian Culture & Research Journal* 18 (1994): 25–32.

Deloria, Vine, Jr. *American Indian Policy in the Twentieth Century*. Norman: University of Oklahoma Press, 1985.

Deloria, Vine, Jr. *Behind the Trail of Broken Treaties*. New York: Delacorte Press, 1974.

Deloria, Vine, Jr. *Behind the Trail of Broken Treaties: An Indian Declaration of Independence*. Austin: University of Texas Press, 1985.

Deloria, Vine, Jr. *Behind the Trail of Broken Treaties*. Austin: University of Texas Press, 1990.

Deloria, Vine, Jr. "Commentary: Research, Redskins, and Reality," *American Indian Quarterly* 15, no. 4 (Fall, 1991): 457–68.

Deloria, Vine, Jr. *Custer Died for Your Sins: An Indian Manifesto*. [1969] Norman: University of Oklahoma Press, 1988.

Deloria, Vine, Jr. *God is Red*. New York: Laurel, Dell, 1983.

Deloria, Vine, Jr. *God is Red: A Native View of Religion*. 2nd ed. Golden, CO: North American Press/Fulcrum, 1992.

Deloria, Vine, Jr. *The Indian Affair*. New York: Friendship Press, 1974.

Deloria, Vine, Jr. "Indigenous Peoples' Literature." No date. http://www.indians.org/welker/vine.htm

Deloria, Vine, Jr. *The Metaphysics of Modern Existence*. San Francisco: Harper & Row, 1979.

Deloria, Vine, Jr. "The Most Important Indian." *Race Relations Reporter* 5, no. 21 (November, 1974): 26–28.

Deloria, Vine, Jr. *The Nations Within*. New York: Pantheon, 1984.

Deloria, Vine, Jr. *Red Earth, White Lies: Native Americans and the Myth of Scientific Fact*. New York: Scribner, 1995.

Deloria, Vine, Jr. *We Talk, You Listen: New Tribes, New Turf*. New York: Macmillan, 1970.

Deloria, Vine, Jr. and Clifford Lytle. *American Indians: American Justice*. Austin: University of Texas Press, 1984.

Dell, Dillingham Brint. "Indian Women and IHS Sterilization Practices," *American Indian Journal* 3 (January, 1977): 1.

DeLuca, Richard. "We Hold the Rock—The Indian Attempt to Reclaim Alcatraz Island." *California History: The Magazine of the California Historical Society* 62 (Spring, 1983): 2–24.

DeMain, Paul. "AIM Supporters Convene in Minneapolis for Ceremony." Colorado AIM, 1994. http://www.coloradoaim.org/history/1994PaulDemainsupportstheBellecourts.htm

Dewing, Rolland, ed. *The FBI Files on the American Indian Movement and Wounded Knee*. (Microfilm) Frederick, MD: University Publications of America, 1986.

Dewing, Rolland. *Wounded Knee: The Meaning and Significance of the Second Incident*. New York: Irvington Publishers, 1985.

Downs, Alan C. "Aquash, Anna Mae Pictou," in Bruce E. Johansen and Barry M. Pritzker, eds. *Encyclopedia of American Indian History*, Santa Barbara, CA: ABC-CLIO, 2007, 651–53.

Duggan, Joe. "Amid Lawsuit, Tribe Seeks Limit on Beer Sales in Town." *Omaha World-Herald*, February 23, 2012, 6-B.

Duggan, Joe. "Nine Protesters Arrested for Crossing Police Line." *Lincoln Journal-Star,* July 4, 1999. http://www.dickshovel.com/wc4.html

Duggan, Joe. "Tribe Goes to Source in Lawsuit over Alcohol Sales: The Oglala Sioux Target the Whiteclay, Neb. Supply Chain from Stores to Brewers." *Omaha World-Herald*, February 10, 2012, 1-A, 2-A.

Dunsmore, Roger. "Vine Deloria, Jr.," in Andrew Wiget, ed. *Handbook of Native American Literature*. New York: Garland Publishing, 1996, 411–15.

Durham, Jimmie. In Jean Fisher, ed. *A Certain Lack of Coherence: Writings on Art and Cultural Politics*, London: Kala Press, 1993.

Durham, Jimmie. "American Indian Culture: Traditionalism and Spiritualism in a Revolutionary Struggle," in Jean Fisher, ed. *A Certain Lack of Coherence: Writings on Art and Cultural Politics*. London: Kala Press, 1993. http://historymatters.gmu.edu/d/6904

Durham, Jimmie. "Attending to Words and Bones: An Interview with Jean Fisher," *Art and Design* 10, no. 7–8(1995): 47–55.

Durham, Jimmie. *Columbus Day*. Albuquerque, New Mexico: West End Press, 1983.

Durham, Jimmie. "Geronimo!" in Lucy R. Lippard, ed. *Partial Recall: Photos of Native North Americans*. New York: The New Press, 1992, 55–58.

Durham, Jimmie. "Jimmie Durham: Interviewed by Mark Gisbourne," *Art Monthly* 173 (February, 1994): 7–11.

Durham, Jimmie. *Jimmie Durham: My Book, the East London Coelacanth*. London: ICA Book Works, 1993.

Durham, Jimmie. *The Second Particle Wave Theory*. Sunderland, UK: University of Sunderland, 2005.

Durham, Jimmie. "Various Element of Cowboy Life'" and "Cherokee-US Relations," *The American West*. Compton Verney, Warwickshire: Compton Verney. 2005, 9–22; 51–59.

Eichstaedt, Peter. *If You Poison Us: Uranium and American Indians*. Santa Fe, New Mexico: Red Crane Books, 1995.

Etlinger, Charles. "Indian Scholar Blows Holes in Theories: Deloria Says Lazy Scientists Adjust Facts to Fit Ideas." *Idaho Statesman*, February 28, 1998, 1-B.

"'Fighting Whites' Make a Statement; American Indian Students Try to Raise Awareness of Stereotypes." *Associated Press* in *Philadelphia Daily News*, March 12, 2002. http://www.philly.com/mld/dailynews/sports/2841746.htm

"Final Opinion and Statement of the Tribunal Panel, Autonomous Chapters of AIM vs. Vernon and Clyde Bellecourt." November 4, 1994, Rapid City, SD. http://www.coloradoaim.org/history/19941104Finalverdictissuedinrapidcity.htm

"Fish Agent, Indian Fight it Out." *Tri-City Herald*, November 21, 1975, n.p.

Fixico, Donald. *Termination and Relocation: Federal Indian Policy, 1945–1960.* Albuquerque: University of Mexico Press, 1986.

"Floyd Red Crow Westerman Journeys On To the Spirit World." Native American Music Awards, December 13, 2007. www.nativeamericanmusicawards.com

"For America to Live, Europe Must Die." Speech by Russell Means at Black Hills International Survival Gathering, 1980. http://www.dickshovel.com/Banks.html

Forbes, Jack D. "The American Discovery of Europe." Department of Native American Studies, University of California—Davis. No date. http://nas.ucdavis.edu/Forbes/discovery.html

Forbes, Jack D. *Africans and Native Americans*. Urbana: University of Illinois Press, 1993.

Forbes, Jack D. "Alcatraz: What Its Seizure Means," in Peter Blue Cloud, ed. *Alcatraz Is Not An Island*. Berkeley, CA: Wingbow Press, 1981.

Forbes, Jack D. *The American Discovery of Europe*. Urbana: University of Illinois Press, 2007.

Forbes, Jack D. *Apache, Navaho and Spaniard*. Norman: University of Oklahoma Press, 1960, 1994.

Forbes, Jack D. *Columbus and Other Cannibals*. New York: Seven Stories Press, 2008.

Forbes, Jack D. *Frontiers in American History and the Role of the Frontier Historian*. Reno: Desert Research Institute, University of Nevada, 1966.

Forbes, Jack D. *The Indian in America's Past*. Englewood Cliffs, NJ: Prentice-Hall, 1964.

Forbes, Jack D. *Native Americans of California and Nevada*. Healdsburg, CA: Naturegraph Publishers 1969.

Forbes, Jack D. *Native Americans and Nixon: Presidential Politics and Minority Self Determination 1969–1972*. Los Angeles: American Indian Studies Center, University of California, 1972, 1981.

Forbes, Jack D. *Only Approved Indians: Stories*. Norman: University of Oklahoma Press, 1995.

Forbes, Jack D. "Only Approved Indians: Unique Native American Stories." University of Californian—Davis, Department of Native American Studies. No date. http://nas.ucdavis.edu/Forbes/ONLY.html

Forbes, Jack D. *Red Blood: A Novel*. Penticton, BC: Theytus, 1997.

Forbes, Jack D. *Warriors of the Colorado*. Norman: University of Oklahoma Press, 1965.

Forbes, Jack D. *A World Ruled by Cannibals: The Wetiko Disease of Aggression, Violence, and Imperialism*. Davis, CA: D-Q University Press, 1979.

Fortunate Eagle, Adam. *Alcatraz! Alcatraz! The Indian Occupation of 1969–1971*. Berkeley, CA: Heyday Books, 1992.

Frosch, Dan. "Professor's Dismissal Upheld by Colorado Supreme Court." *New York Times*, September 11, 2012.

Fuller, Alexandra. "In the Shadow of Wounded Knee." *National Geographic*, August, 2012, 30–67.

Gates, Paul W., ed. *The Rape of Indian Lands*. New York: Arno Press, 1979.

George-Kanentiio, Doug. "*Akwesasne Notes*: How the Mohawk Nation Created a Newspaper and Shaped Contemporary Native America." Manuscript copy provided to author by email, September 15, 2011.

George-Kanentiio, Doug. "Deloria as I Knew Him," *Indian Time* 23, no. 46 (November 17, 2005): 2–3.

Getches, David H., Charles F. Wilkinson, and Robert A. Williams, Jr. *Cases and Materials on Federal Indian Law*, 4th ed. American Casebook Series. St. Paul, MN: West, 1998.

Goldstein, Richard. "Bill Janklow, a Four-Term Governor of South Dakota, Dies at 72." *New York Times*, January 12, 2012. http://www.nytimes.com/2012/01/13/us/bill-janklow-a-four-term-governor-of-south-dakota-dies-at-72.html

Goldtooth, Tom. National Director, Indigenous Environmental Network. Indigenous Environmental Network Statement to Nora Helton, Chairwoman, Fort Mojave Indian Tribe, Other Lower Colorado River Indian Tribal Leaders, Tribal Community Members, Elders and Non-Native Groups and Individuals, in Reference to the Ward Valley Victory Gathering to Celebrate the Defeat of a Proposed Nuclear Waste Dump, Ward Valley, California. February 16, 2001. http://www.ienearth.org/ward_valley2.html

Gordon-McCutchan, R. C. *The Taos Indians and the Battle for Blue Lake.* Santa Fe, New Mexico: Red Crane Books, 1991.

Graves, Theodore D. "The Personal Adjustment of Navajo Indian Migrants to Denver, Colorado," *American Anthropologist* 72, no. 1 (1970): 35–54.

"Greatest Native American Poll." *Native America Calling and The Native American Times.* October 15, 2005. http://terrrijean.smartwriters.com/index.2ts?page=greatestpoll

"The Great Janet McCloud." Indigenous Women's Network. March 28, 2006. http://indigenouswomen.org/Articles/The-Great-Janet-McCloud.html

Grinde, Donald A., Jr. and Bruce E. Johansen. *Ecocide of Native America: Environmental Destruction of Indian Lands and Peoples.* Santa Fe, New Mexico: Clear Light, 1995.

Grossman, Mark. *The ABC-CLIO Companion to the Native American Rights Movement.* Santa Barbara, CA: ABC-CLIO, 1996.

Hank Adams Papers, 1958–1978. Princeton University. Seeley G. Mudd Manuscript Library. Archived 2008. mudd@princeton.edu; http://www.princeton.edu/~mudd

Harjo, Suzan Shown. "Billy Frank, Jr., a Warrior with Wisdom and an Elder with Courage," in Jose Barreiro and Tim Johnson, eds. *America is Indian Country: Opinions and Perspectives from Indian Country Today.* Golden, CO: Fulcrum, 2005, 317–20.

Harjo, Suzan Shown. "Harjo: Why Native Identity Matters: A Cautionary Tale." *Indian Country Today*, February 10, 2008. http://www.indiancountry.com/content.cfm?id=1096410335

Harjo, Suzan Shown. "Trail of Broken Treaties: A 30th Anniversary Memory." *Indian Country Today*, November 6, 2002. http://indiancountrytodaymedianetwork.com/2002/11/trail-of-broken-treaties-a-30th-anniversary-memory/

Harlan, Bill. "Lakota Group Secedes from U.S." *Rapid City Journal*, December 21, 2007. http://www.rapidcityjournal.com/articles/2007/12/21/news/local/doc476a99630633e335271152.txt.

Harvey, Byron. *Thoughts from Alcatraz.* Phoenix, AZ: Arequipa Press, 1970.

Hendricks, Steve. *The Unquiet Grave: The FBI and the Struggle for the Soul of Indian Country.* New York: Thunder's Mouth Press, 2006.

Hertzberg, Hazel W. *The Search for an American Indian Identity: Modern Pan-Indian Movements*. Syracuse: Syracuse University Press, 1971.

Hightower-Langston, Donna. "American Indian Women's Activism in the 1960s and 1970s." *Indymedia*, March 21, 2006. http://www.indybay.org/news/2006/03/1809545.php

Huck, Susan L.M. *Renegades: The Second Battle of Wounded Knee*. Belmont, MA: American Opinion, 1973.

Hughes, J. Donald. *American Indian Ecology*. El Paso: University of Texas Press, 1983.

Igliori, Paola. *Stickman: John Trudell*. New York: Inanout Press, 1994.

"In Honor of Vine Deloria, Jr. (1933–2005)." Statement by Colorado American Indian Movement, November 14, 2005.

"In Memoriam: Vine Deloria, Jr." *Indian Country Today*, November 17, 2005. http://www.indiancountry.com/content.cfm?id=1096411939

"*Indian Country Today*: Hank Adams, the Lifelong Activist." Northwest Indian Fisheries Commission. March 1, 2006. http://www.nwifc.org/2006/01/hank-adams-wins-indian-country-todays-american-indian-visionary-award/

"Indian Treaty Trek Linked to Trial of 4 Muckleshoots." *Auburn Citizen*, May 18, 1966, 1.

"Jack D. Forbes (Powhatan-Renápe-Lenápe). Professor Emeritus." University of California—Davis. Department of Native American Studies. No date. http://nas.ucdavis.edu/site/people/emeritus/

Jaimes, M. Annette, ed. *The State of Native America: Genocide, Colonization and Resistance*. Boston, MA: South End Press, 1992.

Jaimes, M. Annette and Tersea Halsey. "American Indian Women: At the Center of Indigenous Resistance in Contemporary North America," in M.A. Jaimes, ed. *The State of Native North America: Genocide, Colonization, and Resistance*. Boston, MA: South End Press, 1992, 311–44.

"Janet McCloud. 'Yet Si Blue.'" *Indian Country Today*, December 5, 2003. http://indigenouswomen.org/Our-Founding-Mothers/Janet-McCloud.html

Johansen, Bruce E. "The Black Hills Uranium Rush." *The Nation*, April 19, 1979, 393–96.

Johansen, Bruce E., ed. *The Encyclopedia of Native American Legal Tradition*. Westport, CT: Greenwood Press, 1997.

Johansen, Bruce E. *Life and Death in Mohawk Country*. Golden, CO: North American Press/Fulcrum, 1993.

Johansen, Bruce E. *The Native Peoples of North America: A History*. Westport, CT: Praeger, 2005.

Johansen, Bruce E. "The New York Oneidas: A Case Study in the Mismatch of Cultural Tradition and Economic Development," *American Indian Culture & Research Journal* 26, no. 3 (2002): 25–46.

Johansen, Bruce E. "Peltier and the Posse." *The Nation*, October 1, 1977, 304–07.

Johansen, Bruce E. "Putting the Moccasin on the Other Foot: A Media History of the 'Fighting Whities,' " in C. Richard King, ed. *The Native American Mascot Controversy: A Handbook*. Lanham, MD: Scarecrow Press, 2010, 163–78.

Johansen. Bruce E. "Reprise: Forced Sterilizations." *Native Americas* 15, no. 4 (Winter, 1998): 44–47.

Johansen, Bruce E. "The Reservation Offensive." *The Nation*, February 25, 1978, 204–07.

Johansen, Bruce E. "Running for Office: LaDuke and the Green Party." *Native Americas* 18, no. 4 (Winter, 1996): 3–4.

Johansen, Bruce E. *Silenced! Academic Freedom, Scientific Inquiry, and the First Amendment Under Siege in America*. Westport, CT: Praeger, 2007.

Johansen, Bruce E. "Sterilization of Native American Women Reviewed by Omaha Master's Student." *Native Americas*, September, 1998. http://www.ratical.org/ratville/sterilize.html

Johansen, Bruce E. "Stolen Wombs: Indigenous Women Most at Risk," *Native Americas* 17, no. 2 (Summer, 2000): 38–42.

Johansen, Bruce. "Ward Valley: A 'Win' for Native Elders," *Native Americas* 15, no. 2 (Summer, 1998): 7–8.

Johansen, Bruce E. "Whiteclay, Nebraska: The Town That Booze Built," *Native Americas* 15, no. 1 (Spring, 1998): 5.

Johansen, Bruce E. "Will Clinton Pardon Him? Leonard Peltier's Continuing Bid for Freedom," *Native Americas* 14, no. 3 (Fall, 1997): 54–57.

Johansen, Bruce E. and Donald A. Grinde, Jr. *The Encyclopedia of Native American Biography*. New York: Henry Holt, 1997.

Johansen, Bruce E. and Roberto F. Maestas. *Wasi'chu: The Continuing Indian Wars*. New York: Monthly Review Press, 1979.

John Trudell Home Page. No date. http://www.johntrudell.com/bio.html

Johnson, Kirk. "University of Colorado Chancellor Advises Firing Author of Sept. 11 Essay." *New York Times*, June 27, 2006. http://www.nytimes.com/2006/06/27/education/27churchill.html

Johnson, Kirk. "University President Resigns at Colorado Amid Turmoil." *New York Times*, March 8, 2005. http://www.nytimes.com/2005/03/08/national/08colorado.html

Johnson, Kirk. "Vine Deloria Jr., 'Champion of Indian Rights, Dies at 72.'" *New York Times*, November 15, 2005. http://www.nytimes.com/2005/11/15/national/15deloria.html

Johnson, Ralph W. "The States Versus Indian Off-reservation Fishing: A United States Supreme Court Error." *Washington Law Review* 47, no. 2 (1972): 207–36.

Johnson, Troy R. *Alcatraz Is Not An Island*. Documentary Film. San Francisco: Diamond Island Productions, 1999.

Johnson, Troy R. *The American Indian Occupation of Alcatraz Island: Red Power and Self-Determination*. Lincoln: University of Nebraska Press, 2008.

Johnson, Troy R. "Occupation of Alcatraz Island," in Bruce E. Johansen and Barry Pritzker, eds. *Encyclopedia of American Indian History*. Santa Barbara, CA: ABC-CLIO, 2008, 287–92.

Johnson, Troy R. "Red Power," in Bruce E. Johansen and Barry Pritzker, eds. *Encyclopedia of American Indian History*. Santa Barbara, CA: ABC-CLIO, 2008, 292–97.

Johnson, Troy R. "The Roots of Contemporary Native American Activism," in Albert Hurtado and Peter Iverson, eds. *Major Problems in American Indian History*. Boston, MA: Houghton-Mifflin, 2001.

Johnson, Troy R. and Joane Nagel, eds. "Alcatraz Revisited: The 25th Anniversary of the Occupation." *American Indian Culture & Research Journal* 18, no. 4 (special edition). Los Angeles, CA: American Indian Studies Center, 1994.

Johnson, Troy R., Joane Nagel, and Duane Champaign, eds. *American Indian Activism: Alcatraz to the Longest Walk*. Urbana: University of Illinois Press, 1996.

Johnson, Troy R., Joane Nagel, and Duane Champagne. *American Indian Activism: Alcatraz to the Longest Walk*. Urbana: University of Illinois Press, 1997.

Johnston, Laurie. "Notes on People: U.S. Women Greeted by Peking Officials." *New York Times*, December 31, 1975, n.p.

Josephy, Alvin M., Jr. *The American Indian Fight for Freedom*. New Haven, CT: Yale University Press, 1978.

Josephy, Alvin M., Jr. *Now That the Buffalo's Gone: A Study of Today's American Indians*. New York: Knopf, 1982.

Josephy, Alvin M., Jr. *Red Power: The American Indians' Fight for Freedom*. New York: American Heritage Press, 1971.

Josephy, Alvin M., Jr. "Wounded Knee and All That: What the Indians Want." *New York Times Sunday Magazine*, March 18, 1973, 18–19, 66–83.

Josephy, Alvin M., Jr., Joane Nagel, and Troy Johnson, eds. *Red Power: The American Indians' Fight for Freedom*. Lincoln: University of Nebraska Press, 1999.

Kamb, Lewis. "In Memory of Janet McCloud; Janet McCloud, 1934–2003: Indian Activist Put Family First." *Seattle Post-Intelligencer*, November 27, 2003. http://www.worldwidefriends.org/janetmccloud.html

Katz, Jane B. *I Am the Fire of Time: The Voices of Native American Women*. New York: E.P. Dutton, 1977.

KCTS-9 TV (PBS) "Bob Santos, Roberto Maestas and Larry Gossett Recall Their Activism in Seattle." November 13, 2009. http://kcts9.org/video/gang-four

Kemnitzer, Luis. "Personal Memories of Alcatraz, 1969," *American Indian Culture and Research Journal* 18, no. 4 (1994): 103–09.

Keshena, Enaemaehkiw Túpac. "American Indian Movement Grand Governing Council Statement on the War in Libya." April 17, 2011. AIM Grand Governing Council. March 30, 2011. http://www.aimovement.org/moipr/WarInLibya.html

Kilborn, Peter. "Pine Ridge, a Different Kind of Poverty." *New York Times* in *Omaha World-Herald*, September 30, 1992, 9.

King, C. Richard and Charles F. Springwood. *Beyond the Cheers: Race as Spectacle in College Sports*. Albany: State University of New York Press. 2001.

King, C. Richard and Charles F. Springwood, eds. *Team Spirits: Essays on the History and Significance of Native American Mascots*. Lincoln: University of Nebraska, 2001.

Kinzer, Stephen. "U.S. Indians Enlist in the Miskito Cause." *New York Times*, November 10, 1985, 1.

Kubal, Timothy. *Cultural Movements and Collective Memory: Christopher Columbus and the Rewriting of the National Origin Myth*. New York: Palgrave Macmillan, 2008.

Kummer, Corby. "Going with the Grain: True Wild Rice, for the Past Twenty Years Nearly Impossible to Find, is Slowly Being Nurtured Back to Market." *Atlantic Monthly*, May, 2004, 145–48.

LaDuke, Winona. *All Our Relations: Native Struggles for Land and Life*. Boston, MA: South End Press, 1999.

LaDuke, Winona. "The Growing Strength of Native Environmentalism: Like Tributaries to a River." *Sierra*, November/December, 1996, 38–45.

LaDuke, Winona. *Last Standing Woman (History & Heritage)*. Stillwater, MN: Voyageur Press, 1999.

LaDuke, Winona. *Recovering the Sacred: The Power of Naming and Claiming*. Cambridge, MA: South End Press, 2005.

LaDuke, Winona. *The Winona LaDuke Reader: A Collection of Essential Writings*. Stillwater, MN: Voyageur Press, 2002.

LaMay, Konnie. "20 Years of Anguish." *Indian Country Today*, February 25, 1993, n.p.

LaMere, Frank. "Blood on Their Hands." *New York Times*, May 16, 2012. http://www.nytimes.com/roomfordebate/2012/05/16/how-to-address-alcoholism-on-indian-reservations/nebraska-and-anheuser-busch-caused-the-disaster-at-pine-ridge-and-whiteclay

Langum David J., Sr. *William M. Kunstler: The Most Hated Lawyer in America*. New York: New York University Press, 1999.

Lazarus, Edward. *Black Hills, White Justice: The Sioux Nation v. the United States: 1775 to the Present*. New York: HarperCollins, 1991.

Lee, Tanya. "Author and Native Studies Trailblazer Jack Forbes, 77, Passes." *Indian Country Today*, June 20, 2011. http://indiancountrytodaymedianetwork.com/2011/06/author-and-native-studies-trailblazer-jack-forbes-77-passes/

Lippard, Lucy. "Jimmie Durham: Postmodernist Savage," *Art in America* 81, no. 2, February, 1993, 62–69.

Lovely, Lori. "Birthday Rally Seeks Freedom for Leonard Peltier." *NUVO: Indy's Alternative Voice*, September 16, 2011. http://www.nuvo.net/NewsBlog/archives/2011/09/16/slideshow-leonard-peltier-birthday-rally

Lovely, Lori. "Effort to Start a New Indiana AIM Chapter." *NUVO: Indy's Alternative Voice*. No date. http://www.nuvo.net/indianapolis/effort-to-start-a-new-indiana-aim-chapter/Content?oid=2351505

Lovely, Lori. "Land of the (Disrespected) Indians." *NUVO: Indy's Alternative Voice*. September 21, 2011. http://www.nuvo.net/indianapolis/land-of-the-disrespected-indians/Content?oid=2351498

Lyng v. Northwest Indian Cemetery Protection Association 485 U.S. 459 (1988).

Lyons, Oren, John Mohawk, Vine Deloria, Jr., Laurence Hauptman, Howard Berman, Donald A. Grinde, Jr., Curtis Berkey, and Robert Venables. *Exiled in the Land of the Free: Democracy, Indian Nations, and the Constitution*. Santa Fe, New Mexico: Clear Light Publishers, 1992.

MacMillan, Leslie. "Uranium Mines Dot Navajo Land, Neglected and Still Perilous." *New York Times*, March 31, 2012. http://www.nytimes.com/2012/04/01/us/uranium-mines-dot-navajo-land-neglected-and-still-perilous.html

Mann, Barbara Alice. *Iroquoian Women: The Gantowisas*. New York: Peter Lang Publishing, 2000.

Mapes, Lynda V. "Fish-camp Raid Etched in State History." *Seattle Times*, September 6, 2010. http://seattletimes.nwsource.com/cgi-bin/PrintStory.pl?document_id=2012827306&zsection_id=2003904401&slug=fishwar07m&date=20100906

Mapes, Lynda V. "Native Americans Mark 40 Years Since Fort Lawton Protest." *Seattle Times*, March 9, 2010. http://seattletimes.nwsource.com/html/localnews/2011292879_lawton09m.html

"Marlon Brando—Blood Brother to the Redman." American Indian Movement of Colorado. July, 2, 2004. http://www.coloradoaim.org/blog/2004/07/marlon-brando-blood-brother-to-redman.html

Margolick, David. "Still Radical After All These Years." *New York Times*, July 6, 1993, B-1.

Matthiessen, Peter. *In the Spirit of Crazy Horse*. New York: Viking, 1991.

McCloud, Janet and Robert Casey. "The Last Indian War." Seattle: Seattle Group Bulletins, No. 29 and 30, 1968. Mimeographed.

McFadden, Robert D. "Russell Means, Who Revived Warrior Image of American Indian, Dies at 72." *New York Times*, October 22, 2012. http://www.nytimes.com/2012/10/23/us/russell-means-american-indian-activist-dies-at-72.html

Means, Russell and Marvin J. Wolf. *Where White Men Fear to Tread: The Autobiography of Russell Means*. New York: St. Martin's Press, 1995.

Melmer, David. "Winona LaDuke Inducted into National Women's Hall of Fame." *Indian Country Today*, October 15, 2007. http://www.indiancountry.com/content.cfm?id=1096415916

Messerschmidt, James W. *The Trial of Leonard Peltier*. Boston, MA: South End Press, 1983, 8.

Meyer, John M., ed. *American Indians and U.S. Politics*. Westport, CT: Greenwood Press, 2002.

Miller, Bruce J. "The Press, the Boldt Decision, and Indian-White Relations," *American Indian Culture & Research Journal* 17, no. 2 (1993): 75–98.

Minnesota Historical Society. "American Indian Movement (AIM)." History Topics. No date. http://www.mnhs.org/library/tips/history_topics/93aim.html

Mosedale, Mike. "Bury My Heart." City Pages (Minneapolis), February 16, 2000. http://www.citypages.com/2000–02–16/news/bury-my-heart/

"Muckleshoot Treaty Trek is Historic Indian Event: LeClair." *Auburn Globe-News*, May 18, 1966, 1, 11.

Mulvey, Laura, et al. *Jimmie Durham*. London: Phaidon, 1995.

Nabakov, Peter. *Native American Testimony: A Chronicle of Indian-White Relations from Prophecy to the Present, 1492–1992*. New York: Viking Press, 1991.

Nagel, Joane. *American Indian Ethnic Renewal*. New York: Oxford University Press, 1997.

Nagel, Joane. *American Indian Ethnic Renewal: Red Power and the Resurgence of Identity and Culture*. New York: Oxford University Press, 1996.

"National Indian Youth Council Policy Statement." *Americans Before Columbus* 6, no. 3 (1973): 3.

"Native American Activists Finish Cross-Country 'Walk for Justice.'" *Associated Press* in *Los Angeles Times*, July 16, 1994. http://articles.latimes.com/1994–07–16/news/mn-16156_1_native-american-activists

Navasky, Victor S. "Right On! With Lawyer William Kunstler." *New York Times,* April 19, 1970, 217.

Neihardt, John G. *Black Elk Speaks*. New York: William Morrow & Co., 1932.

Nevard, David. "Wahooism in the USA." *A Red Socks Journal*. No date. http://www.ultranet.com/~kuras/bhxi3d.htm

News of the Odd. March 27, 1973. http://www.newsoftheodd.com/article1027.html

Nigoya, D. "Mascot Foes March into Eaton; Fightin' Reds Protest Given Quiet Response." *Denver Post*, May 20, 2002. http://www.denverpost.com/framework/0,1918,36%7E53%7E622747%7E,00.html

"The OFFICIAL Homepage" of AIM Support Group of Ohio & N. Kentucky. No date. http://aimsupport.org/index2.html

Parham, Vera. "Something Worth Going up That Hill For." *Columbia Magazine* 21, no. 3 (Fall 2007): 24–32. http://columbia.washingtonhistory.org/magazine/articles/2007/0307/0307-a3.aspx.

Pasternak, Judy. *Yellow Dirt: An American Story of a Poisoned Lands and a People Betrayed*. New York: Free Press, 2010.

Peltier, Leonard. *Prison Writings: My Life is My Sun Dance*. New York: St. Martin's Press, 1999.

"Penthouse Interview: Vernon Bellecourt. He is the Symbol of the Most Militant Indian Group Since Geronimo." *Penthouse International Magazine for Men*, July, 1973, 59–64, 122, 131–32.

"Petition to Ban the Chasco Krewe." American Indian Movement Florida Chapter. 2011. http://www.ipetitions.com/petition/banchascoracism/

"Position Statement of Virginia AIM and the American Cultural Resource Center on the Mascot Issue." No date. http://www.aics.org/aimva/aimva.html

"Press Release: Navajo Film & Media Campaign Win Clean Up of Uranium." The Return of Navajo Boy. http://navajoboy.com/29661/press-release-navajo-film-media-campaign-win-clean-up-of-uranium/

"Professor Lehman L. Brightman—President of United Native Americans on KAOS." March 4, 2011. http://ravenredbone.wordpress.com/2011/03/04/professor-lehman-l-brightman-president-of-united-native-americans-on-kaos/

"Puyallup River Indian Camp Destroyed by Bulldozers." *Seattle Times*, September 11, 1970, E-7.

Rave, Jodi. "Reporter's Notebook: Controversial C.U. Professor Stretches Truth." *Billings Gazette*, February 6, 2005. http://www.billingsgazette.com/index.php?display=rednews/2005/02/06/build/nation/67-reporters-notebook.inc

Reed, Leslie. "Indian Activists: Arrests, Police Conduct Disturbing." *Omaha World-Herald*, October 5, 1999. http://www.omaha.com/Omaha/OWH/StoryViewer/1,3153,230211,00.html

Reilly, Hugh. "Treatment of Native Americans by the Frontier Press 1868–1891, an Omaha, Nebraska Study." Master's thesis, University of Nebraska at Omaha, 1997.

Reyes, Lawney L. *Bernie Whitebear: An Urban Indian's Quest for Justice*. Tucson: University of Arizona Press, 2006.

Revolutionary Activities within the United States: the American Indian Movement: Report of the Subcommittee to Investigate the Administration of the Internal Security Act and Other Internal Security Laws. Committee on the Judiciary, United States Senate, Ninety-fourth Congress, second session. September, 1976.

"Robert Robideau—a True Defender of Indigenous Peoples Passes On." American Indian Movement of Colorado. February 18, 2009. http://colorado-aim.blogspot.com/2009/02/robert-robideau-true-warrior-passes-on.html

Robideau, Robert. "An American Indian's View of the Cartoons," Countercurrents.org, February 10, 2006.

Russo, Kurt, ed. *Our People, Our Land: Reflections on Common Ground*. Bellingham, WA: Lummi Tribe and Kluckhohn Center, 1992, 54–56.

Ryser, Rudolph C. (principal investigator). *Indian Self-Government Process Evaluation Project, Preliminary Findings*. Olympia, WA: Center for World Indigenous Studies, 1995.

Sanchez, John and Stuckey, E. Mary. "The Rhetoric of American Indian Activism in the 1960s and 1970s," *Communication Quarterly* (2000): 120–36.

Santa Barbara, California, AIM. Home page. http://www.aimsb.org/

Sayer, John William. *Ghost Dancing the Law: The Wounded Knee Trials*. Cambridge, MA: Harvard University Press, 1997.

Sayer, John William. "Social Movements in the Courtroom: The Wounded Knee Trials, 1973–1975." PhD thesis, University of Minnesota, 1991.

Schaaf, Gregory. "Banks, Dennis," in Bruce E. Johansen and Barry M. Pritzker, eds. *Encyclopedia of American Indian History*. Santa Barbara: ABC-CLIO, 2007, 656–57.

"Seattle Indians to Demonstrate." *United Press International in Ellensburg (Washington) Daily Record*, September 4, 1975, 5.

Senese, Guy. *Self-Determination and the Social Education of Native Americans*. Westport, CT: Praeger, 1991.

Severson, Kim. "Payment Set for Those Sterilized in Program." *New York Times*, January 11, 2012, A-13.

Shreve, Bradley. *Red Power Rising: The National Indian Youth Council and the Origins of Native Activism*. Norman: University of Oklahoma Press, 2011.

Shiff, Richard. "The Necessity of Jimmie Durham's Jokes," *Art Journal* 51, no. 3 (1992): 74–80.

"Shots Fired, 60 Arrested in Indian-fishing Showdown." *Seattle Times*, September 9, 1970, A-1.

Simpson, George Eaton and John Milton Yinger. *Racial and Cultural Minorities: An Analysis of Prejudice and Discrimination*. New York: Harper & Row, 1965.

Smith, Paul Chaat and Robert Allen Warrior. *Like a Hurricane: The American Indian Movement from Alcatraz to Wounded Knee*. New York: New Press, 1996.

Smith, Sherry L. *Hippies, Indians, & the Fight for Red Power*. New York: Oxford University Press, 2012.

"Some Border Compassion, Please. Local Issues: American Indian Movement Arizona Chapter." No date. http://www.oocities.org/aim_arizona_chapter/localissues.html

"South Dakota Governor Declares War on Indians." Redhawk's Lodge, Black Hills AIM, April 5, 2000. http://siouxme.com/lodge/jank2.html

"'S-Peak:' American Indian Movement Arizona Chapter. SQUAW—Facts on the Eradication of the 'S' Word." No date. http://www.oocities.org/aim_arizona_chapter/S-Peak.html

Steiner, Stan. *The New Indians*. New York: Harper & Row, 1968.

Stern, Kenneth S. *Loud Hawk: The United States Versus the American Indian Movement*. Norman: University of Oklahoma Press, 1994.

Stout, David. "William Kunstler, 76, Dies; Lawyer for Social Outcasts." *New York Times*, September 5, 1995, A-1.

Strickland, Rennard and Jack Gregory. "Nixon and the Indian: Is Dick Another Buffalo Bill?" *Commonweal* 92 (September 4, 1979): 433.

Talbot, Steve. "Free Alcatraz: The Culture of Native American Liberation," *Journal of Ethnic Studies* 6, no. 3 (Fall, 1978): 80–89.

Tizon, Alex. "The Boldt Decision: 25 Years—The Fish Tale That Changed History." *Seattle Times*, February 7, 1999. http://community.seattletimes.nwsource.com/archive/?date=19990207&slug=2943039

Torpy, Sally. "Endangered Species: Native American Women's Struggle for their Reproductive Rights and Racial Identity: 1970s–1990s." MA thesis, History, University of Nebraska at Omaha, 1998.

Trahant, Mark. "The Center of Everything—Native Leader Janet McCloud Finds Peace in Her Place, Her Victories, Her Family. It Has Taken Many Years To Get There." *Seattle Times* (Northwest People) July 4, 1999. http://community.seattletimes.nwsource.com/archive

Trahant, Mark. "Honoring an American Indian Visionary." *Seattle Post-Intelligencer*, March 5, 2006. http://www.seattlepi.com/opinion/261658_trahant05.html

Trail of Broken Treaties: BIA, I'm Not Your Indian Anymore. Rooseveltown, NY: Akwesasne Notes, 1973.

Trudell, John. *This Ain't El Salvador*. West Chester, PA: Learning Alliance, 1996.

Trudell, John. *Lines from a Mined Mind: The Words of John Trudell*. Golden, CO: Fulcrum, 2008. *Tulee v. Washington* 315 U.S. 681 (1942).

Twain, Mark. *Mark Twain: Collected Tales, Sketches, Speeches & Essays, 1852–1890*. Vol. I. New York: The Library of America, 1992.

Tyeeme-Clark, D. Anthony. "Review, Bernie Whitebear: an Urban Indian's Quest for Justice (2006)," *American Indian Culture & Research Journal* 31, no. 1 (2007): 145–48.

"United Nations Adopts Declaration Rights of Indigenous Peoples." UN News Center, September 13, 2007. http://www.un.org/apps/news/story.asp?NewsID=23794

U.S. Commission on Civil Rights. "Fishing in Western Washington—a Treaty Right, a Clash of Cultures." In *Indian Tribes, a Continuing Quest for Survival: a Report of the United States Commission on Civil Rights*. Washington: U.S. Government Printing Office, 1981, 61–100.

U.S. Commission on Civil Rights. "Report of Investigation: Oglala Sioux Tribe, General Election, 1974," mimeograph. Washington, DC: Civil Rights Commission, October 1974.

United States Congress. Senate Committee on the Judiciary. Subcommittee to Investigate the Administration of the Internal Security Act and Other Internal Security.

United States vs. Means, et al., Civ. No. 81–5131, U.S. District Court for the District of South Dakota, December 9, 1985.

United States v. Washington: 384 F. Supp. 312 (1974).

United States v. Winans 198 U.S. 371 (1905).

"Urgent Request for Action." American Indian Movement Florida Chapter, News. No date. http://aimflorida.webs.com/news.htm

"Vintage Classics. Marlon Brando Tribute: Civil Rights." No date. http://levitchcrocetti.proboards.com/index.cgi?board=marlonbrando&action=display&thread=1050

Virginia Chapter. American Indian Movement. No date. http://www.aics.org/aimva/aimva.html#donot

Walker, Carson. "Man is Arrested in Activist's Death." Associated Press in Indigenous-NewsNetwork@topica.com, April 2, 2003.

Walker, Carson. "Tribal Police Break up Attempted Beer Blockade." *Lincoln [Nebraska] Journal-Star*, June 27, 2007. http://journalstar.com/news/state-and-regional/govt-and-politics/article_f73b704d-67c6–5941–9a5b-49e70321d74a.html.

"War and Consequences: the American Indian Movement vs. the National Park Service at Fort Laramie, Part II." *National Parks Traveler*, April, 2011. http://www.nationalparkstraveler.com/2011/04/war-and-consequences-american-indian-movement-vs-national-park-service-fort-laramie-part-ii7992

Ward v. Race Horse 163 U.S. 504(1896).

Warrior, Clyde. "On Current Indian Affairs," *Americans Before Columbus* 2, no. 2 (May, 1964): 2.

Warrior, Clyde. "We Are Not Free," in Alvin M. Josephy Jr., Joane Nagel, and Troy Johnson, eds. *Red Power: The American Indians' Fight for Freedom*, 2nd ed. Lincoln: University of Nebraska Press, 1999, 16–21.

Warrior, Clyde. "Which One Are You? The Five Types of Young Indians," in Stan Steiner, ed. *The New Indians*. New York: Harper & Row, 1968.

Washburn, Wilcomb E. *Red Man's Land/White Man's Law: A Study of the Past and Present State of the American Indian*. New York: Scribner's, 1971.

Weir, David and Lowell Bergman. "The Killing of Anna Mae Aquash." *Rolling Stone*, April 7, 1977, 51–55.

Weisman, Joel. "About That 'Ambush' at Wounded Knee." *Columbia Journalism Review*, September/October 1975, n.p.

"Welcome to the American Indian Movement, Arizona Chapter. What is the American Indian Movement?" No date. http://www.oocities.org/aim_arizona_chapter/

Wesson, Marianne. *Report of the Investigative Committee of the Standing Committee on Research Misconduct at the University of Colorado at Boulder concerning Allegations of Research Misconduct against Professor Ward Churchill*. May 9, 2006. www.colorado.edu/news/reports/churchill/churchillreport051606.html

Weyler, Rex. *Blood of the Land: The U.S. Government and Corporate War Against the American Indian Movement*, 2nd ed. Philadelphia, PA: New Society Publishers, 1992.

Whitten, Les. "Tribute to Hank Adams." *Indian Country Today*, January 12, 2006. http://www.highbeam.com/doc/1P1–118940793.html

Williams, Timothy. "At Tribe's Door, a Hub of Beer and Heartache." *New York Times*, March 6, 2012. http://www.nytimes.com/2012/03/06/us/next-to-tribe-with-alcohol-ban-a-hub-of-beer.html

Williams, Timothy. "Indian Beer Bill Stalls; Industry Money Flows." *New York Times*, April 12, 2012, A-14, A-18.

Wilitz, Teresa. "An Anniversary Celebration: Native American Author Exults in Gadfly Role at Newberry Conference." *Chicago Tribune*, September 15, 1997, 1 (Tempo).

Wilkins, David. "Native Visionary Spoke for All Disadvantaged Americans." *Indian Country Today*, December 1, 2005. http://www.indiancountry.com/content.cfm?id=1096412026

Wilkins, David E., ed. *The Hank Adams Reader: An Exemplary Native American Activist and the Unleashing of Indigenous Sovereignty*. Golden, CO: Fulcrum, 2011.

Wilkinson, Charles F. *Blood Struggle: The Rise of Modern Indian Nations*. New York: W.W. Norton, 2005.

Wilkinson, Charles F. *Messages from Frank's Landing: A Story of Salmon, Treaties, and the American Way*. Seattle: University of Washington Press, 2000.

William, Janklow. *Appellant, v. Newsweek, Inc., Appellee* 788 F.2d 1300. United States Court of Appeals, Eighth Circuit; September 12, 1985. Decided April 10, 1986 Justia U.S. Law. http://law.justia.com/cases/federal/appellate-courts/F2/788/1300/300888

"William J. Janklow." *San Francisco Chronicle*/Associated Press Political Database. November, 2002. http://www.sfgate.com/cgi-bin/article.cgi?f=/politics/election/2002nov/bios/hsd1rep.dtl

Williams, Matt. "Renowned Native American Scholar Dies." *Colorado Daily*, November 14, 2005. http://www.coloradodaily.com/articles/2005/11/14/news/c_u_and_boulder/news2.txt

Williams, Timothy. "New Inquiry of 50 Deaths Tied to Tribe in S. Dakota." *New York Times*, June 20, 2012, A-12.

Williams, Timothy. "Tribe Considers Lifting Alcohol Ban in South Dakota." *New York Times*, October 5, 2012, A-15.

Williams, Timothy. "Tribe Seeks Reopening of Inquiries in '70s Deaths." *New York Times*, June 15, 2012, A-20, A-29. http://www.nytimes.com/2012/06/15/us/sioux-group-asks-officials-to-reopen-70s-cases.html

"William 'Wild Bill'" Janklow: Atty General, Governor, [and] GASP, Congressman." Redhawk's Lodge. 2002. http://siouxme.com/lodge/janklow.html

Wilma, David. "Tacoma Police Arrest 60 Persons at a Fish-in on September 9, 1970." *HistoryLink*, August 25, 2000. http://historyink.org/index.cfm?DisplayPage=output.cfm&file_id=2625

Wilson, Edmund. *Apologies to the Iroquois: With a Study of the Mohawks in High Steel*, by Joseph Mitchell. New York: Farrar, Straus and Cudahy, 1959.

Winfrey, Robert Hill. "Civil Rights and the American Indian: Through the 1960s." PhD diss., Department of History, University of Oklahoma, Norman, OK, 1986.

Wittstock, Laura Waterman and Elaine J. Salinas. "A Brief History of the American Indian Movement." No date. http://www.aimovement.org/ggc/history.html

"Wounded Knee, 1890–1973." St. Paul, MN: Wounded Knee Legal Defense/Offense Committee, 1973.

Woster, Terry. "Janklow: Civil Rights Report is "Garbage." *Sioux Falls Argus-Leader*, April 5, 2000. [http://siouxme.com/lodge/civil_rights.html]

"A Year of Atonement for Whiteclay. The Battle for Whiteclay Begins in Earnest." American Indian Movement, Lincoln, Nebraska, March 1, 2003. http://www.aimovement.org/calendar/whiteclay.html

Ziegelman, Karen. 1985. Generational Politics and American Indian Youth Movements of the 1960s and 1970s. Master's thesis, University of Arizona. http://www.indybay.org/newsitems/2006/03/21/18095451.php

Index

Bold page numbers refer to the main entries.

About the Author

BRUCE E. JOHANSEN is Jacob J. Isaacson University Research Professor in Communication and Native American Studies at University of Nebraska at Omaha, having worked there since 1982, meanwhile producing 37 books, mainly in Native American studies and on environmental subjects. These include *The Encyclopedia of Global Warming Science and Technology* (two vols., Greenwood, 2009), *Global Warming in the 21st century* (three vols., Praeger, 2006), co-editor (with Barry M. Pritzker) of the four-volume *Encyclopedia of American Indian History* (ABC-CLIO, 2007), and the forthcoming *Encyclopedia of American Indian Culture* (Greenwood, 2016).